New Directions in Australian Studies

New Directions in Australian Studies

Papers of the Inaugural Conference of
The Asian Association for the Study of Australia (AASA)
'Creative Configurations'
Kerala, India (1997)

edited by

Cynthia vanden Driesen
&
Adrian Mitchell

PRESTIGE

Published by
PRESTIGE BOOKS
3/28, East Patel Nagar
New Delhi 110 008

2000

ISBN: 81-7551-084-6

Composed by Vivek Mathur, Delhi 110 006 Ph. 3981867
Printed by Chaman Offset Printers, New Delhi 110 002

Contents

NEW TRENDS—ABORIGINAL ISSUES

MIGRATION AND MULTI-CULTURAL AUSTRALIA

FEMALE EXPERIENCE AND EMPOWERMENT

AUSTRALIA-ASIA CONNECTIONS

INDIAN RESPONSES TO AUSTRALIAN WRITING

EUROPEAN PERSPECTIVES

Acknowledgements

We thank all the contributors to this volume for their co-operation and patience. the referees, to whom papers were submitted, for their valuable suggestions, and indeed all the participants in the conference who contributed to the success of this inaugural venture. Indian participation was, naturally, preponderant but there were also participants from Sri Lanka and Singapore who chaired sessions presented papers and contributed positively in a variety of ways. The great efforts of Professor K. Radha, the Indian convenor of the conference, and the co-operation of the Vice-Chancellor and Syndicate members of the University of Kerala must be specially acknowledged.

Our warmest thanks are due to the Australia-India Council for its financing of this publication and the generous assistance which made this inaugural conference possible on the scale on which it was held. Edith Cowan University's support through its Arts Faculty and the Office of the (then) Dean of Overseas Programmes, Professor Steve Hunter, is also gratefully acknowledged. We must also record our appreciation of the assistance of the Literature Fund of the Australia Council which enabled a number of Australian writers to attend the conference. This made possible a writers' Colloquium between the visitors and local writers which was a unique feature of this conference (see Appendix).

With the actual work of publication, Dr. R.K. Dhawan and Dr. Suman Bala have rendered sterling assistance. For their efficient secretarial support we thank Ms. Rosemary Seneviratne and Ms. Margaret Marshall. A special thank-you to Ms. Jane Quinsee of ECU's School of Language and Literature whose cheerful and generous assistance was always available.

Introduction

Cynthia vanden Driesen

This collection of papers from the inaugural conference of AASA requires a brief historical sketch to place it in perspective. AASA (the Asian Association for the Study of Australia) was formed in 1995. It was intended to loosely 'complete' the group of international associations that have been formed to focus on Australian Studies—EASA (The European Association for the Study of Australia) and BASA (The British Association for the Study of Australia) were others. A unique feature of the new Association was the involvement of Australian office-bearers along with Asian office-holders.

Events moved swiftly with the establishment of the Australian Studies Centre at the University of Kerala under the directorship of Professor K. Radha[1]. Her determined efforts, combined with those of other AASA committee members and the generous sponsorship of organizers (acknowledged elsewhere in this volume) enabled the staging of this inaugural conference with a degree of ceremony and fanfare hardly perhaps to be expected of so new an association. While memories of other events—walking on Kovalam Beach, the culture show, the writers' colloquium, the varied 'private' visits to the temple, to Cochin—will now be relegated to photographs and memories, this book encapsulates the intellectual experiences, the debates and issues focussed on at the conference. The conference theme of 'creative configurations, the expanding Australian experience' enforced consideration of the broadening of intellectual horizons over a range of disciplines. Though literature was an important focus, education, women's studies and literary theory provided areas across which the theme was pursued.

For several of the Asian academics the expansion into new spaces of growth seemed most often represented by a shift of focus from those Australian literary figures who seemed to have absorbed critical attention in India for decades (A.D. Hope, Patrick White, Judith Wright) to embrace new figures like Peter Carey, Elizabeth Jolley, Thomas Keneally. The other interesting development is the Asian focus on cross-cultural influences, so K. Radha traces the Hindu doctrine of transmigration in Rodney Hall's poem, Ravichandra comments on A.D. Hope's inspiration drawn from the picture of the temple dancer. Raghu's article traces a little-known but intriguing interchange between an Australian critic and a well-known Indian poet writing in English.

Perhaps the best point at which to begin to survey this charting of new directions in the Australian ethos is to chronicle the observations of the theorists. Bill Ashcroft's paper directly addresses the conference theme in his speculations that these kinds of interactions between post-colonised cultures could open avenues for creative departures from the cultural hegemony that the ex-coloniser power continues to exercise long after its military departure through the sheer power of its linguistic dominance since English remains as the primary discourse through which the cultural values of Europe-England are fetishised. Post-colonial contact should enable perceptions of shared strategies, the development of a theoretical language and a grasp of the transformative potential of literary and cultural discourse. The dialogue with Asian culture should prove particularly intriguing since white Australian culture is inevitably positioned in that ambivalent space occupied by the settler colonies where the dominant white culture is inevitably complicitous with the erstwhile colonizing power—the only reason it is there in the first place.

David Carter also sees this latest phase of Australian culture as distinctive. He observes a progression from a phase of British hegemony to one of American dominance and thence (borrowing a phrase from Meaghan Morris) to "positive unoriginality" as popular culture has become increasingly influential particularly after the 1960s. For David McKie, new knowledges 'out there' require the re-alignment of traditional boundaries between disciplines. Sharyn Pearce's paper shows how new strategies can supplement new knowledges. Children's literature usually marginalised as an avenue for investigation, offers a relatively untapped terrain for exploration of myths of national identity.

With the mined position occupied by the Aborigines in the Australian context, it is hardly unusual that many papers focussed on Aboriginal issues. Debjani Ganguly's paper takes up the doubly marginalised figure of the Aboriginal woman writer. She explores the controversy (triggered by comments from Mudrooroo) that with the work of these writers being focussed mainly on individual women's struggles they are not adequately 'communal' and therefore less politically significant. The two papers by Colin and Susan Kenworthy show the changing pedagogic strategies designed to focus contemporary students' attention on issues pertaining to racism. Moving from examining how the 1905 W.A. Aborigines Act while apparently aimed at improving the lot of the Aborigines actually disempowered them through excessive regulation of every aspect of their lives, Susan moves on to outline strategies for teaching secondary school students how to develop resistant readings of contemporary racist texts. Colin Kenworthy's paper outlines a number of teaching strategies for teaching post-colonial reading practices in schools, so that students realize the ways in which writing from a European perspective hides or distorts Aboriginal experience. These papers record the courageous acknowledgement of past mistakes and a taking up of the challenge of reconciliation which represents one of the key issues which faces contemporary Australia. In another conference, held in Perth, W.A. (also referred to by Alison Broinowski in her keynote speech at this conference), one speaker expressed the view that Australia's regional image problem was intimately connected to her treatment of her Aboriginal inhabitants[2]. The Kenworthy papers give a practical insight into some of the ways new creative configurations are shaping ways of (possibly) healing old wounds. Whatever other interesting insights provided by Lucy Frost's paper, it does project a realisation that in today's Australia an Aboriginal heritage, at least for the creative artist, could be a positive inheritance.

Along with the exploration of Aboriginal issues, perhaps it is in the expansion of critical attention bestowed on the work of writers from multicultural backgrounds, that more creative configurations become discernible. Laurie Clancy's commentary on the work of Adib Khan and Yasmine Gooneratne, is taken further by Carmel Kelly's exploration of the gendered terrain of women's writing in the field. Kateryna Longley articulates the intriguing idea that study of immigrant family histories could make a significant contribution of Australian understanding of the term 'multi-culturalism' and indeed Australia's sense of itself as a nation. Since these disasporan histories reach out in various directions to homelands spread out across the globe as well as give different accounts of history and home in Australia, they interrogate the validity of the simpler linear historical accounts which have hitherto shaped understanding of the Australian past. While the Kenworthy papers show how changes in intellectual (and political) attitudes in the sphere of Aboriginal issues impinge (or should impinge) in a highly practical way on classroom strategies, Basil Jayatilaka's paper outlines the challenges for teachers of music encountering students from different cultural backgrounds, pointing out that music teaching in Australia has had up to now a monocultural, eurocentric direction. In today's multicultural classrooms, teachers need to take count of perceptual differences and different learning processes that students from different ethnic backgrounds bring to bear in learning music.

Looking back to the 1890s definition of 'Australianness' the omission of the female underlines the importance of women's issues in contemporary Australia. It is interesting that an Indian male critic should have chosen to explore facets of Australian female achievement in poetry. Glen Phillips' paper on Prichard emphasizes her pioneering contributions in the novel. The unique advantages of multi-disciplinary conferences are highlighted when key areas of interest such as women's issues can be highlighted over a range of disciplines and the articulation of female experience in literature compared with awareness of changed attitudes in the realities of the actual social context and the continued struggle for modes of expression that signal advances for the female. Sue-Ellen Murray's paper traces changing attitudes to woman's most uniquely female experience in her body. Her concern is to replace the recorded public knowledge about menstruation in Australia mostly gleaned from medical textbooks and shrouded by a veil of secrecy by more women-centred understandings reflective of women's own experiences. At the base of this study is a challenge to the attitude that regards science and medicine as the arbiters of knowledge and an insistence that ways of knowing must include women's feelings and experiences. Lekkie Hopkins explores modes of female empowerment and ways of defining power in terms unique to these experiences.

Australia's relationship to Asia, the pros and cons of what is sometimes referred to as the 'Asianisation' of Australia, is surely one of the key issues facing the country. Politicians, diplomats, businessmen, educationists alike recognise that Australia has a distinctive role in the region. Creative writers have made their own contribution to the debate. Dennis Haskell's discussion of Bruce Dawe's poetry explores Dawe's castigation of Australian indifference to Asia and along with this his critique of some Asian mores as reflected in events in Timor, Tibet and elsewhere. To pass over the work of Australian novelists who have been preoccupied with this relationship to Asia (Koch, Drewe, D'Alpuget) would have been a regrettable omission in a conference such as this. Adrian Mitchell's paper on Christopher Koch fills this gap to some extent and offers some interesting speculation on the unique nature of the Australian hero. As distinct from the classical hero, he is incomplete in many ways, his heroic space is characterized by an absence of centrality or involvement. In Koch's novel *Highways to a War* it is climaxed by an actual disappearance into the 'other', as Mike Langford steps across the border into Cambodia.

Following on these glimpses into the Australian consciousness of Asia, it is appropriate to close this survey of the conference contribution with a comment on papers which present an European perspective on Australia. There could be something of a sense of contradiction in reading Isabel Santaollalla's contribution alongside of Livio Dobrez's paper. They present together, a juxtapositioning of the old with the new. The newer perception seems to be almost a non-perception and this is surprising considering the length of time Dobrez shows that the Antipodes has been an entity known (albeit as an exotic element) to the European consciousness. Whatever the relative lack of knowledge of Australia amongst the (admittedly limited) sample of the Spanish population surveyed by Santaollalla, Dobrez's wide-ranging paper shows the historic links between Australia and Europe and traces the progressive expansion in European consciousness of the Antipodes. Part of the new configurations triggered further by such cross-cultural dialogues as that generated by this conference will assuredly mean expansions of experience not only for Australia but for her neighbours the world over.

Australia-India Connections—Some Reflections

Adrian Mitchell

India has from the beginning been a residual presence in Australian cultural history; but a few years ago, when the Raj was all the rage in film and TV and print, at the time of *The Jewel in the Crown* and *Gandhi* and the M.M. Kaye books, public interest picked up considerably in Australia as in the rest of the world. *Merchant Ivory* and *A Passage to India* sustained that interest: the novels of Ruth Prawer Jhabvala appeared at eye level on the shelves of bookshops and soon after, in the new acquisitions displays in public libraries. (For the Australian audience the name was resonant enough, never mind how resistant to her Indian critics had been). It would be easy to write these off as 'media events' if that is the phrase. But in Australia at least they were not so much creating as revealing an interest in India that has been there all along.

It is true that publicity hype engenders a fashion just for a season—a season that can be measured exactly by the appearance and disappearance of the display units in bookshops. Yet in this country the fascination with India goes on, especially in the bits and pieces of the old Empire. Eighteenth and nineteenth-century British culture accommodates the rich fact of India, and we in turn absorb our—what?—intimations by that route, if not directly. For example, it's probably only in recent generations that Clive of India has dropped out of the schools' general history syllabus. We learned about India as much as anything through the percolation of Imperial military history both formally and in terms of its values, through our junior education. We read our fathers' school-prize copies of

G.A. Henty and others—do you remember *The Tiger of Mysore*, *With Clive in India* and *Through the Sikh War*? As we read those mid-century romances too, *King of the Khyber Pass* and so on, all those useful books about how to hunt a tiger (and learning that discreet word "spoor", though as I understand it, there was something puzzling—why would Jim Corbett and the like want to pick it up?) and in more recent times M.M. Kaye and Paul Scott. And there are the other fashions, and evidence of fashions too—in the 1960s the flower children, having emptied their minds over something euphemistically called buddha sticks, looked to India to supply spiritual guidance—transcendental meditation and the guru. Followed, in terms of fashion, by warehouses full of cheap clothing, brassware and so on. I'm not sure whether what we see at Paddy's market are the last remnants of that fashion, or whether the stocks are continually replenished but there's no shortage of supply. And we benefited by India's linguistic export too, picking up all those useful words like *pyjamas, nabob, godown* (though when you look carefully at the origins of all this Kiplingesque word-list, you find that India has been trading on to us value-added goods. But *bungalow* was the authentic article.)

These are all universal features; or at least to that part of the universe coloured faded cherryplum. The fact is, however, that India has a rather special significance for Australia, and always has had. But as far as I know a proper account of that connection has still to be written.

It begins of course with the First Settlement, with the transport ships heading off to India when once the convicts had been offloaded; and soon after that the foundling colony was sending off to India for grain, both to feed the colony and for grain seed. By the 1890s there was a small informal immigration programme under way—which is to say politely that India was supplying cheap labour to private individuals. Indians were working as builders' labourers in Albany as early as 1835-6. A number of British who had been in India settled in Australia and brought the household retinue with them. And there was also the fashionable element in this—do you remember the little personal servant Teapot in Hal Porter's *The Tilted Cross*? (His grandfather's passion for India, recounted in *The Watcher on the Cast-iron Balcony*, is testimony to a different fashion in a different era.) However it happened, the physical presence of Indians developed throughout nineteenth-century Australia, and we find the evidence of that here and there—growing maize in Gippsland or as hawkers throughout the rural districts, confused by undiscriminating Australians with Afghanistani camel-drivers.

The influence is detectable in other kinds of evidence, in the naming and making of Australia. Burra Burra, South Australia, in its day the richest copper mine in the Empire, possibly in the world, is named from Hindustani; a pastoralist in the region, James Stein, had Indian shepherds working for him. A more ubiquitous mark is the small blue square on the Ordinance Survey Maps, identifying the nine mile tank, or the twenty-five mile tank; as also in Joseph Furphy's *Such is Life*—the usage of tank meaning something more like a dam is directly from India.

The first Australian-born novelist, John Lang, born in Parramatta in 1817, did his writing in India, where he was by profession a lawyer. His first novel was *The Wetherbys*, or *Chapters of Indian Experience* (London 1853). The book for which he is remembered in Australia, also written in India, is *The Forger's Wife* (1855), also published as *Assigned to His Wife* and *The Convict's Wife*; and not to be confused with *Will He Marry Her?* (1858), suggestive of an antipodean sequel; nor with *My Friend's Wife*; or *York, You're Wanted*. Lang also wrote *Wanderings in India and Other Sketches of Life in Hindoostan* (1859)—having apparently run out of, if not on, wives. That title reminds me that there were any number of such books, travel memoirs or as we might now say private documentaries, personal travelogues in which the author recounts his experiences in the Cape Colony, Australasia, the Straits Settlements and India, Bengal, etc. etc. You get the idea. There seemed to be an indefatigable and, might I say, undiscriminating audience for this kind of book. Perhaps it was important for the writer. But it suggests a kind of circuit, and that circuit was also followed by touring companies—drama troupes, music hall, circuses, elocutionists, public lecturers and other entertainers. I suspect a modified version of that still operates—companies specially brought out for the Adelaide Festival start in Perth, and go on to Melbourne and Sydney. I doubt whether that loop now takes in South Africa and India. But it used to.

A different circuit was governmental. This field would be interesting to trace out. It appears a number of governors of the Australian colonies went on to appointments in India, as that suggests a hierarchy in Whitehall's scheme of civil service appointments, remembering the special estimation of the Indian Civil Service. Yet at some stage the pattern seems to flow the other way. Of course it is always possible in this case that the governors had misbehaved in India and were themselves in a sense being sentenced to a kind of punishment. Who knows? I am not entirely serious about that. A genuine and discernible consequence is that the architecture of various governmental residences reflect some features from India—that's another field to explore in detail. Alfred Deakin, three times Prime Minister of Australia, wrote a study of Indian irrigation and agriculture before becoming embroiled in local politics.

There have been other writers than Lang with substantial experience of India—Ethel Anderson immediately comes to mind, and of course Christopher Koch and Janette Turner Hospital in more recent times. I mean by this not writers who have visited India, as one might visit the Botanic Gardens, or the University on Open Day, but writers whose experience of and in India has changed their perception in some deep way. This is another uncharted region. And finally there are the family connections, such as Stephen Murray Smith speaks of, confessing that his family is one of those that dominated perhaps the single most substantial item of commerce between the two countries, the trade in horses. Horses were brought from India in the early days—Macarthur, for example, had a stud—and then eventually the Australian-bred horses were shipped back to the Straits Settlements and to India. The Duracks write of this, so does Katharine Susannah Prichard in *Coonardoo*.

The links are many and varied, and operate in all sorts of ways. We each find our own kinds and degrees of response to them. We enjoy reading India—and that can mean a number of different things. But there is a special Australian interest in, even attachment to, the rich variety of Indian culture, and not least because the evidence of it is everywhere about us, if we will only look carefully enough.

NOTES

1. The Australian Studies Centre, University of Kerala, S. India was established in August 1996.
2. This was the *Outside Images of Australia* Conference held in Perth, W. Australia in 1992.

Notes Towards Exploration of Australasian Bonds

C.D. NARASIMHAIAH
Asian Patron, AASA,
Dhvanyaloka, Mysore

I am afraid I don't have the credentials of Mrs. Alison Broinowski who, while an insider to Australia, has wide experience of Asian countries. And so, fellow Australasians, I feel greatly honoured to be the Indian patron of the Asian Association for Australia, which links two old giant continents together, or rather renews old links, reinforcing the compulsions of geography. Indians have traditionally perceived the seven continents including Asia and Australia as seven islands comprising the Great Earth as *sapta dvipa vasundhara*, also known as *Vasudhaiva Kutumbakam*, the Earth Family.

I am an Asian by birth but have looked upon Australia as my second country ever since my first visit to it in 1963 and subsequent visits have only deepened that faith. Experience of a new country helps one to respond to one's own country as never before and thus imparts a wholeness to life. The Patronship, if I may say so, is some kind of public recognition of a private experience for which I am beholden to Dr. Cynthia vanden Driesen and Professor Bala Kothandaraman. Cynthia is the moving spirit of this great enterprise and we cannot thank this ethereal spirit too much—ethereal in appearance but most substantial in her sense of purpose and determined pursuit of her mission.

Standing here at this historic moment when two continents meet on the edge of hospitable shores, I must confess to a feeling of a euphoria as though I am being called upon to second Jawaharlal

Nehru's resolution on holding the Asian Conference exactly 50 years ago to which a special significance was added by Australia and New Zealand sending observers. That was a measure of the importance the invitees, as well as Jawaharlal Nehru, attached to his view that the Pacific was destined to be the nerve-centre of the world in future. How prophetic! It is at such a resurgent moment that we meet here and it is the pride and privilege of the people of India to welcome their fellow Asians and their Australian neighbours to the enlarged family and to suffuse politics and poetry.

I shall start with our common ancestors, the Aborigines. When the fairskinned nomadic Aryans came to India in search of green pastures for their cattle, they set their eyes on the snow-clad Himalayas and the majestic Ganga and felt inspired to apostrophise the unknown deities who presided over the elements of earth, air, fire, water and ether to seek their protection—these became the hymns of the Rig Veda. The original inhabitants of the land, our dark-skinned ancestors, quietly moved down south of the Vindhyas (exactly as their progeny in Australia withdrew into the outback later when the fairskinned settlers came) and in their wander-lust, researchers are convinced, some of them must have left the Indian shores, and moved out stepping on successive islands of the Indonesian archipelago when the sea was shallow and kept going until they were greeted by the immense empty spaces between the land and the expansive sky and felt welcomed into the new continent of Australia. Once they were there the 'tyranny of distance' was transformed into what Patrick White calls the 'omnipotence of distance'. When they sighted plenty of fruit, fish and fowl around they may have killed them for food and asked their forgiveness exactly as the progeny of the earliest inhabitants of India still do in the hills and forests of the South. Indeed there is a remarkable resemblance between them and the Aborigines. They dreamt their dreams and in their 'dreamtime' saw visions of their ancestors who guided their movements and advised on how to live. They celebrated their sacred sites in the manner of their Indian ancestors for whom the earth was *Punyabhumi*, sacred site. They composed their rhythmic lines as they moved from water source to water source. Their footprints construct what Bruce Chatwin calls a musical map of Australia in his book *Songlines*. I first encountered the work as Chairman of the Commonwealth Literature Prize Committee in 1989 and lived in expectation for a whole month longing to meet the Prize-winning author and know the mystique of the old continent at the Prizegiving ceremony in London. I gathered he was either dead or dying in hospital. Yes, he was dead but the book lives, exuding what is beyond dispute, a magic which evokes the whole reality of an unknown past. And yet the Aborigines Chatwin brings to light are said to have had an 'earth-bound philosophy,' a term which ignites a prosaic fact, glows with a philosophical meaning as the author says the Aborigines trusted the Earth as the giver of life, language, food and protection—the reason why they thought 'they were the land's' and didn't care to assert 'the land belonged to them.' If they are today thought of as belonging to the Stone Age, I should lament our own sorry state.

'What a fall from the Stone Age!' Is there no way of returning to those times—if not the whole say at least part of the way—the way India has done through the ages. Consider Nehru's geological metaphor *Palimpsest* for India which is best spelt out in his own words:

> She was like some ancient palimpsest on which layer upon layer of thought and reverie had been inscribed and yet no succeeding layer had completely hidden or erased what had been written previously. Such a view should help to place the wisdom of the Aborigines in a larger and fairer perspective.

We would do well to listen to Charles Darwin, who writes after his visit more than 150 years ago; 'Farewell, Australia, you are a rising child and doubtless someday will become a great princess in the South. You are too great and ambitious for affection, yet not great enough for respect'. Nevertheless Darwin hastens to add his tribute to Australia for transforming vagabonds most useless in one hemisphere into active citizens of another thus giving birth to a new and splendid country, a grand centre of civilization. 'A grand Centre of civilization' is what we *Australasians* must visualize for our two continents in days to come.

Chatwin has something to say on this. It seems the Aborigines believe if there is a future for mankind it is an ascetic future, or what Vivekananda called *Vairagya*, renunciation. He said no civilization is likely to endure unless it practises the spirit of renunciation.

Let me add the testimony of Jawaharlal Nehru who can evoke the past of Asia so persuasively:

> It was here that civilization began and man started on his unending adventure of life. Here the mind of man searched unceasingly for truth and the spirit of man shone like a beacon which lighted up the whole world—he meant the Buddha.

It is good also to recall Lawrence for whom Australia has, as yet, made no great mistakes, humanly speaking, the great human mistakes of Europe and probably even the worse human mistakes of America.

I am surprised that Chris Wallace-Crabbe who rightly commended to Indians more than 30 years ago the 'masculine strength' of Furphy, should not have chosen to correct his own countryman. Geoffrey Dutton, who loftily pronounced that 'the artist who may have meant much to Australians and Australian literary history may well be a pigmy alongside Fielding or Wordsworth'.

Was Dutton so naive as to let his boyhood brainwashing by his kindergarten schoolmasters of Wordsworth's poetry to persist into his adult life when a lesser known Australian poet like Shaw Neilson could give a lesson or two to this high-priest of Nature as to how a poet can react to Nature. Perhaps Keats had lines like this in mind when he observed poetry does not 'support or dispute' but whispers as among neighbours. Look, how Neilson can carry it off buoyantly: 'I can give love-talk to you, you little blue flower of the spring'. Did the T.S. Eliot Prize-winning Les Murray recall this when he pleaded for the 'Boetian strain' as against the 'Athenian'?

Neilson had the daring to seek to win God Himself over to his side when he says God was beguiled by the 'wile' of a woman 'when he made his summer thirsty and unconsoled like her love'. Or listen to that priceless line: 'In every leaf is a glory caught from the Woman's hair' reminding Indians of the myth of Creation of Woman in which God borrowed the rotundity of the moon, the tenderness of the creeper, the cunning of the jackal, the cruelty of the tiger, and the vanity of the peacock and made woman out of them and gave her as companion to lonely man.

Neilson who seemed to have a better grasp of the life of poetry accepted his country's uncouth lizard even as the Indian novelist brought the inauspicious cat into his midst because the cat was for him the embodiment of Feminine Principle and a veritable mother and so could ask: "Trust to the mother cat, then, (for) 'have you ever seen a Kitten fall?' The cat carries its young ones by the scruff of their necks to safety."

Shaw Neilson presses forward unlike his British counterpart who is content to accept sentimentally 'If winter comes can spring be far behind?' For Neilson, 'Autumn is less than a twitter' and feels fortified by the folly of spring to live by. He wouldn't care to go after the nightingale in 'farthest Hebrides'. The lizard is more than a substitute, because

> My friend has the face of a wizard
> And tells me no desolate thing.

No one could suspect wizardry in a lizard, perhaps the gift of a good sense of rhyming. The Australian poet. A.D. Hope, did touch a tender chord in everyone as he wrote about a female bird which joined the seasonal migratory group in search of warm weather—and separated from its mate, memory became a passion, it could hold no longer and so dared to think it could return alone. It got lost in 'the blue unfriendliness of space': the cosmic design mocked at its small wisdom; its instinct winked and failed. It fell. And

> The great earth received the tiny burden of her death
> With neither grief nor malice.

This poet functioned precisely as his epic predecessor in India did while taking the cue from the death of a male bird by the hunter's arrow and transformed soka into sloka, suffering into rhythmic song that was the epic of *Ramayana*.

The animal world plays a glorious role in this epic. A Vulture fights the abductor of the heroine and dies; the monkeys help to build a bridge across the sea and help to restore her to her husband from the demon's clutches. This spirit of the air (Hanuman) here does not demand its 'freedom' but unlike Ariel hymns the master's praise in life after life. In the other epic, *Mahabharata*, the hero declines entry into heaven unless his dog can accompany him.

There must be something in the very soil and sky of this region that the Australian novelist Patrick White should have chosen Gandhi's remarks on suffering for an epigraph to his first novel *Happy Valley* and all his subsequent novels are a variation on the theme of suffering. As if to suggest there was a shared assumption, from the collective unconscious, A.D. Hope felt impelled to contemplate the then vanishing breed of deer 'in the high jungle where Assam meets Tibet' as though this poet had either received silent intimations of Buddha's teaching or read the Indian play *Nagananda* which must have rent the air of the Australasian region and have been deeply moved by the 'hundred thousand or so' deer that were killed each year for their musk. Alec Hope writes in 'Moschus Moschiferus', ironically a poem for St. Cecilia's Day, of the hunters' recourse to music to lure the deer to their net:

> The little musk deer slips into the glade
> Led by an ecstasy that conquers fear
> Then as the victim shudders, leaps and falls
> The music soars to a delicious peak.

The poet ends with a heart-rending dedication:

> Divine Cecilia, there is no more to say
> of all who praised the power of music few
> knew of these things. In honour of your day
> accept this song, I too have made for you.

It is significant that the other major Australian poet, Judith Wright, should also have been touched, in this case, by the sad plight of the Aborigines, to write her 'Nigger's Leap, New England'. She is full of remorse for the white man's actions against the Aborigine:

> The song is gone, the dance
> is secret with dancers in the earth
> the ritual useless and the tribal story
> lost in an alien tale.

Does this poet hear echoes of the songs sung by the Aborigines? To crown it all comes Bruce Chatwin with his *Songlines*, for he knows how music permeates all aspects of Aboriginal life. The Aborigine, he writes, believed music increases the fertility of trees, animals and creates rain. Almost 50 years ago the eminent Indian scientist Jagadish Chandra Bose, dubbed an occultist by Western scientists dwelt at length on this aspect of traditional Indian life to which scientists are now giving much credence.

A.D. Hope who opens his important poem 'Australia' on a negative note reverses his unsuspected stand in the second half as if he used the negative to enhance the value of his affirmation of faith: 'still from the desert prophets come'. The poet turns away from the lush jungle of modern thought.

Finally I come to Patrick White, for me the foremost practitioner of the literary art in the English speaking world. He brings a German explorer Voss to the Australian desert, puts him in touch with an educated young woman who refuses to take notice of the funereal landscape, instead takes delight in solving mathematical equations for a pastime now learns to affirm her faith in the efficacy of what she had earlier denied as she placed her head 'on the ugliest rock and feels rested'. And she who started, like the heroine of a Jane Austen novel, talking of parties, paying and receiving visits and serving wine in proper glasses in the opening pages, by a leap of imagination, rises to meteoric heights in adopting her convict servant's child, calls her Mercy and visualizes fulfilment for herself and her country. The novelist puts something in her mouth which can work like 'transfusion of the poem's blood' as she tells her uncle, 'My future, it's in the hands of God' and speaks not only for Voss but for all of us in her affirmation: 'The country is his by right of vision' gives expression to man's greatest need today caught up in the hole of the nation-state of which Jawaharlal Nehru, leading an agitation against the British rule, could nevertheless bring himself to say 'nationalism is an antifeeling, it feeds and fattens on hatred of other countries'. As if to reinforce it White writes in *The Twyborn Affair* out of deep anguish about the general breakdown of life's meaning:

> History burst over me and I dissolved into fragments. I woke to find myself scattered over the four quarters of the globe linked by every nerve in me to each and every individual. All my ideals and values were turned upside down; even the pursuit of happiness lost its importance. My life was no longer an autonomous project.

I begin to feel strongly such profound thought may well have come from the same part of the world in which 2500 years ago a young prince walked out of the palace at the dead of night leaving wife, babe and kingdom to find out the cause of man's sorrow, what the existentialists call 'the human condition' and walked away to a place of no return, intent on knowing the cause of all human suffering. Three hundred years after, Emperor Asoka, the beloved of the gods, was overcome with remorse that he was the cause of so much misery in the Kalinga War he had fought and embraced Buddhism. He sent his brother and sister to the neighbouring island of Sri Lanka to spread the Master's word. The sister took with her a sapling of the pipul tree under which Buddha received the Enlightenment. A Sri Lankan Chronicle, *Divyavamsa* records Buddha visited the island in spirit thrice after Enlightenment in the course of eight years. One of Asoka's successors, Chandragupta Maurya, who withstood the great Alexander, is said to have renounced his Kingdom and retired to a hill near Mysore to sit and meditate, as a Jain monk. Yet another Emperor, Harsha, wrote a play called *Nagananda* set in the spell-binding beauty of Malay Hills so the lovers, the Prince and his bride, could wander care-free. The Prince discovered that what he saw as a beautiful mountain was not a mountain of snow as he had imagined but mounds of bones of thousands of nagas—snakes killed by the vultures. In the play the Prince is shocked that the King should not have given protection to the serpents and violated Buddha's Law while the vulture was killing a snake every day. Overcome with sorrow, the Prince offers his own life to the vulture that day and thus saves a snake from the vulture's jaws. While the Prince Jeemutavahana is half eaten by the vulture, his young wife and old parents are seen in uncontrollable grief which moved the vulture's heart and in an act of expiation the vulture falls into the flames and kills itself.

Now look at the beginnings of Australian poetry against the background of what I have described; especially the play *Nagananda*; the story of a prince who offered himself to the vulture in place of the snake. Why? even the well-known Indian novels like *The Guide, Sweet Vendor* and *A Tiger for Malgudi* by R.K. Narayan and *The Serpent and the Rope* and *A Cat and Shakespeare* by Raja Rao and Ananthanarayan's *The Silver Pilgrimage* metaphysically enact the ascetic element in them. Hence the belief that if the individual is pure like a crystal he can build a staircase to Sirius. May it be true of the Australasian region which we should be proud to belong to. And may this Association do everything in its power to further this noble ideal of spiritual kinship.

WORKS CITED

Bruce Chatwin. *Songlines* (London: Cape, 1987).

A.D. Hope. *Collected Poems* (London: Anderson Robertson, 1977).

R.K. Narayan. *The Guide* (New York: Viking, 1958).

______. *The Sweet Vendor* (London: Bodley Head, 1967).

______. *A Tiger for Malgudi* (New York: Viking, 1983).

Shaw Neilson. *Collected Poems* (Melbourne: Lothian Book Publishing Co., 1934).

Raja Rao. *The Serpent and the Rope* (New York: Pantheon Books, 1963).

______. *Cat and Shakespeare* (Delhi: Hind Pocket Books, 1971).

Patrick White. *Happy Valley* (London: Harrap, 1939).

______. *Voss* (London: Eyre and Spottiswood, 1957).

______. *The Twyborn Affair* (London: Cape, 1979).

Judith Wright. *The Moving Image* (Melbourne: Meanjin Press, undated).

Looking West and Looking East

ALISON BROINOWSKI
Australian Patron AASA
Australian National University, Canberra

It is clear from the numbers of people from South Asian countries and Australia who have been attracted to attend this conference and to give papers that its organisers, Dr. Radha and Dr. Cynthia vanden Driesen, and their committee, have responded in a most timely and tasteful way to pent-up demand.

Tasteful, because no better place could have been chosen than Kerala, for centuries a State of navigators, international traders, intellectuals, readers, diverse culture, and strong women. Timely, because the conference provides exactly the follow-up that is needed to ensure the effectiveness of recent initiatives—among them the India Today program in Australian cities in 1994, the establishment in 1995 of the Australia-India Council, and in 1996 the Australia-India: New Horizons program.

In the history of Australia's relations with India since 1947, the fireworks of enthusiasm have too often fizzled out in exhaustion or indifference. Let us use this meeting to strengthen the Asian Association of Australian Studies and support its hard-working members to keep the bonfire burning steadily.

I take stoking of the fire to be part of my task in return for the honour of being the Co-Patron of the Association with Professor Narasimhaiah. I think I am less its stoker than its Matron. I imagine the Australian experience of Asia—or of this South Asian part of it—as one of my young patients, sent to the sick bay weakened after various bouts of fever. I want to talk today about what ails the patient, and to suggest some ways for us to get her back to classes and help her graduate. Or perhaps I am the Association's Matriarch, and the Australian experience of Asia is a gathering of several generations of my relatives, among whom there are enemies with old scores to settle and friends with communications to improve. So I want to think about our issues and our problems of communication.

It's not the job of either the Matron or the Matriarch to take sides on these issues. The patient may complain to the Matron of symptoms neglected for years, or of a continuing 'blind spot', or of not getting enough attention. The relatives may complain to the Matriarch that all was going well fifty years ago, and then a great falling-out occurred, which was all someone else's fault, and from which they have never really recovered.

We all know the historical issues: Australia's restrictive migration policy, India's pro-Soviet association, opposing stances in the past on South Africa, China, Vietnam and the American alliance, differences over military sales to Pakistan, Indian Ocean affairs, and recently, the issue of membership of ASEAN and APEC. We all know that with so much goodwill and commonality, the relationship should have gone better. But we are concerned with creativity at this conference, so we don't have to do more than note the political and economic issues as grudges between relations that are symptoms of an underlying condition.

Australia and the South Asian countries, even if their relationship has appeared until recently to be more off than on, do keep discussing it most articulately, as they have done for years. In 1957 Frank Moraes of the *Indian Express* (Moraes, 1958: 166-67) and Durga Das of the *Hindustan Times* both visited Australia. Das found a 'positive lack of interest in things Asian and Indian' (1958: 67-76). The clocks in the Hotel Australia, he complained, showed the time in no Asian country. 'How time ran in Asia and Africa was a matter of indifference to Sydney,' he wrote, 'for life in Australia is not integrated to anything that happens in those continents'. In 1961 Peter Hastings toured several Asian countries and found the same problem in reverse. He reported to *The Bulletin* (11 November 1961: 20) that Australia was viewed with 'utter indifference, or ignorance'. Australia was 'distant, insignificant' to most

Indians, wrote Neil McInnes from India in 1960, and White Australia was 'the first thing an Indian thinks about Australia [and] also probably the last' (*The Bulletin*, 28 December 1960: 25).

Moraes thought about much more than that while he was in Australia, but he wrote that the immigration policy was 'not only anomalous but dangerous'. *The Times of India* in 1976, after the White Australia policy had been dead three years, called Australia 'a white-dominated country this side of Suez a historical freak'. A few years earlier the same paper declared that Australia under Menzies was 'the last camel of the western caravan in Asia'. Durga Das thought Australians themselves were not racists, but that they applied too little pressure to their politicians to change the infamous policy. Both journalists reported with approval the views of Australians who told them the country was underdeveloped and could greatly expand its population.

Australians and South Asians share a habit of judging each others' countries by the presence or absence of news or pictures from home. Durga Das wrote: 'We looked in vain in the coffee lounge at Sydney airport for pictorial representation of Indian life and scenes among the pictures adorning the walls'. Australian travellers have made similar complaints then and now. Every so often we are half amused, half outraged, to see maps with Australia left out of the Asia-Pacific region, as *Time* and *Air France* both did in the 1980s. It is a form of homesickness, or insecurity, to judge another country's media by how much they report of your own, but we all do it.

The themes had scarcely changed in 1981 when Sunanda Datta-Ray of *The Statesman* (India) and Mervyn de Silva of *The Lanka Guardian* spoke at a conference, Australia, Asia and the Media in Canberra, at which a succession of Australians deplored the range and quality of Australian media reporting of Asian affairs. Between Australia and India Datta-Ray detected a 'furious baffling kind of empathy'. If Indians thought of Australia at all, he said, it was as 'the country where good Anglo-Indians go before they die'. But surveying news coverage of each other in the two countries, he found Australia had more grounds, on balance, for complaint of neglect and prejudice than India. He put this down to the inability of Indian media organisations to assign correspondents to Australia: *The Times of India* covered Australia at that time from Kuala Lumpur. 'We look inwards', he said.

De Silva, the Sri Lankan journalist declared that 'Australia in the Sri Lankan media equals cricket'. But he added that Australia was seen to have lost interest in Asian countries since the first Asian conference in Delhi in 1949, to have identified itself with United States policy in the Indian ocean, and to have failed to deal successfully with Aboriginal and refugee issues.

These are not the problems we want to discuss. But they arise from the fundamental question, one which I can't hope to answer in twenty minutes, but one which keeps being asked because its answer can only emerge over time: Is Australia Asian? The common answer these days is that Australia is Australian, a 'Western' country in the Asia-Pacific hemisphere settled by people from many countries. This is based on the short view of history. A novel answer with which I am experimenting within my present work is to take the long view and to say: Yes, Australia was always Asian, before the indigenous Australians reached it from their South Indian and Southeast Asian origins. when it was part of Gondwanaland. Professor Narasimhaiah, I was delighted to hear, anticipated this idea in his opening speech yesterday. The continent is even now moving towards Asia at the rate of 6 centimetres a year. As the anthropologist Tim Flannery writes, 'Australia is a member of a great family of lands. Distant relatives include India and Africa, more recent ones New Zealand, New Caledonia and South America. Our intimate family, however, consists of Antarctica, New Guinea, the eastern part of the Indonesian island of Sulawesi and a few other smaller Indonesian islands' (Flannery, 1994: 20, 26). In the long view, all Australians are boat people, and the latest arrivals, having been there only for 200 years at most, are still adjusting to their new home. The better that is understood, and the more people whose ancestry is of the region join them in becoming Australians, the more smoothly the transition process will be achieved. With the help of our regional neighbours—who, Flannery argues have, like us, tended to continue to see things from the point of view of the colonisers—the adjustment should progress at a faster rate than 6 cm a year.

Our writers have always given us the cultural vision and the long view that our politicians and economists lack. Let me list a few examples in relation to this part of the world. Novelist and poet Rodney Hall told me years ago that Kochi (Cochin) was one of the world's great intersections. Professor Radha's paper will expand in detail on what Hall sought to do in his 'progression of poems', The Law of Karma. This was the result of his travels in India and his interest in Hindu and Buddhist teaching about the transmigration of souls. Christopher Koch told me about Chaudhuri's writing on the cross-fertilisation of Indian and Western culture, and he and the Australian poet Les Murray developed a thesis about Australians and Hindus being 'cattle people' and hence culturally related: 'our brothers under the skin—not the British', as Koch put it, 'We have turned out to share a similar destiny'. Vicki Viidikas turned her India experience into poetry in 1984 (where is she now?). Mudrooroo (Colin Johnson), about whose indigeneity Lucy Frost spoke yesterday studied Buddhism in Thailand and India and in 'Four Aboriginal Poems from India', urged Aborigines and oppressed Indians to seek common cause in improving their lot. David Foster wrote in 1989 of being overcome with something like culture shock in Calcutta and told a nightmare story of being chased through its streets. It was a city in which, nevertheless, he declared he would wish to live and die. (How many South Asian writers, I wonder, would describe themselves as addicted to Australia as Foster said he was to India?) David Malouf admitted that he first came to India with comfortable Raj-based nostalgia in his cultural baggage. This, he said, was displaced on his first visit by fear, which came in many forms: 'fear of dirt, fear of illness, fear of people; fear of the unavoidable presence of misery' (Malouf, 1989: 105). Cricketers can smell fear from far away, and the Sri Lankan press had a nose for it when the Australian team chose not to play there after terrorist attacks in Colombo a couple of years ago. (This will be my last mention of cricket).

The list of Australian writers who have been fascinated or frightened by South Asian countries is longer than the list of politicians or economists. I could tell you of more. We all, of course, know Janette Turner Hospital's *The Ivory Swing* (1983), part of the action of which takes place in Kerala, making it required reading for being here, whether or not it accurately reflects the place that Kerala people know and love. But these 'Anglo' Australians writing of Asian experiences have recently been displaced by the cross-cultural Australian-Asian talents of novelists from South Asia like Yasmine Gooneratne, Adib Khan, James Goonewardene, Chitra Fernando, and playwright Ernest McIntyre. Their ear for the languages within English, and their eye for the double vision of migration, prejudice, and xenophobia has rendered 'Anglo' Australian writers in the 1990s virtually speechless and tone deaf by comparison. We look forward to more of their views through the two-way mirror, showing us a new Australian face, and sounding off in a different voice.

Fiction, of course, is not required to be 'true' or even 'authentic' or accurate, but fiction about another country by someone who is steeped in two cultures is more interesting, engaging, revealing, and ultimately more satisfying, than fiction by a mono-cultural outsider looking on. With the greatly increased mobility of the modern world and the access that technology brings, we can expect much more of this enriched bicultural writing from Australia.

What we lack to complete the vision is more writing from South Asia about Australia. Students, journalists, travellers, scholars: your experiences are valuable and your account of them reveals us to ourselves. In spite of what I have just said about the outsider's limited vision, I personally want to hear from you. Lack of deep knowledge about Australia need not be an inhibition: it has never inhibited Australian writers. As Meg Gurry pithily says in her 1996 study of India-Australia relations, from which I have drawn much help for this paper: 'Context-free images have always played a large part in shaping Australian attitudes to different Asian states' (Gurry, 1996: 51).

Meg Gurry denies the charge that our countries have neglected each other. But for so much interest, there is still less to show for our long association than there should be. One can always tell when nothing real is happening: politicians start using figures of speech rather than talking of figures in balance sheets. When Mrs. Gandhi visited Australia in 1968, the press enthused about 'converging paths', and the Prime Minister herself suggested that Australia could act as a 'bridge' between the two worlds of Pacific Asia and South Asia. In 1995 as Deputy Prime Minister, Kim

Beazley was still talking of 'sharing an ocean' with our large and important neighbour, and in 1996 Prime Minister Howard revived the old image of India as a 'blind spot' for Australian companies. The 'stop-start efforts' which Howard proposes to displace had been criticised by an Australian High Commissioner in the late 1980s, who argued to Canberra that Australia should no longer use the excuse of limited resources for not paying sufficient attention to India, and this produced a substantial package from the Hawke government. Now the talk is of Australia 'putting India into Asia'. For my part, I find that a strange expression, given where both countries stand on APEC and ASEAN and given their relative historical standing in Asia.

In 1992 I heard Kirpal Singh, a Singaporean academic who is with us today, address a conference in Perth on the subject of 'Australia in Southeast Asia: Eliminating Stereotypes'. In spite of the aim declared in his title, he gave a comprehensive account of Australia's image abroad, which he said was 'not very impressive'. He concluded that the only way for Australia to deal with its serious image problem in his part of the world was by means of a consistently funded, properly managed promotional organisation. He said: 'If there were an Australia Council present in every Southeast Asian capital imagine what the impact would be in terms of creating a truer awareness of what Australia really is and stands for'. We will not get, and may not need, the Australia Council—the Federal Government's arts funding and advisory body—in that role, but when our critics offer advice as constructive as this, we should listen.

I would prefer something more tangible from our politicians than imagery about bridges, links and oceans. I have four proposals about what is needed, to leave with you for your consideration during the conference. First: we need a fund to support Australians and South Asians who want to travel in and write creatively about each others' countries. Second: we need to bring together all the people who teach Australian Studies world-wide, in Australia in 2001. Third: we need a reverse Colombo Plan, to ensure that as many young Australians go to study in Universities in Asian countries as Asian students do in Australia. And fourth: we need a dedicated organisation that promotes Australia abroad through education, information, and culture.

If we can put consistent effort into such projects, there's a chance that with South Asian countries looking East and Australia, according to Paul Keating's 1995 initiative, looking West, our eyes may meet across a crowded region and something wonderful may happen, if not in this anniversary year of India's independence, then in that of Australia in 2001.

WORKS CITED

'Australia Back to Old Role', *Times of India* (Bombay), 13 August 1976, p. 8. *Times of India* (Bombay), 4 April 1970, p. 8.

Meredith Borthwick, *India's Economy at the Midnight Hour: Australia's India Strategy* (Canberra: DFAT, 1994).

Durga Das, 'India and the World,' *Hindustan Times*' (New Delhi), 1958.

Sunanda Datta-Ray, comment on 'Australia in the Asian Media', in Alison Broinowski, (ed.) *Australia, Asia and the Media*, Centre for the Study of Australia-Asia Relations (Nathan: Griffith University, 1982), pp. 53-56.

Tim Flannery, *The Future Eaters: An Ecological History of the Australasian Lands and People* (Melbourne: Reed Books, 1994).

David Foster, 'The Eye of the Bull' in *Hitting the Wall* (Vic.: Ringwood, 1989).

Meg Gurry, *India: Australia's Neglected Neighbour? 1947-1996*, Centre for the Study of Australia-Asia Relations (Nathan: Griffith University, 1996).

Christopher Koch, 'Crossing the Gap', in *Crossing the Gap: A Novelist's Essays* (London: Chatto & Windus, 1987).

David Malouf, *12 Edmonstone Street* (Vic.: Ringwood, 1989).

Frank Moraes, *Yonder One World: A Study of Asia and the West* (New York: Macmillan, 1958).

Mudrooroo, *The Song Circle of Jacky and Other Poems* (Melbourne, 1986).

'The Quandary of an India Addict', *Times Sunday*, 8 March 1987, p. 24.

Vicki Viidikas, *India Ink: A Collection of Prose Poems Written in India* (Sydney, 1984).

Poetry, Prophecy and Vestiges

CHRIS WALLACE-CRABBE
University of Melbourne

"What the past and the future have in common is our imagination, which conjures them. And our imagination is rooted in our eschatological dread: the dread of thinking that we are without precedence or consequence. The stronger that dread, the more detailed our notion of antiquity or of utopia." (Brodsky, 1995:269)

Of all the arts, those pleasurable creations or counter-creations of mankind, it is the especial distinction of poetry to be Janus-faced. It is a Oneness that is also a Both, as in Judith Wright's celebrated lines about a new world setting (a New England setting): "Your trees, the homesick and the swarthy native/ blow all one way to me, this southern weather/ That smells of early snow." Wright's past and present were also north and south. Poetry gazes back over the rich, devastated centuries of the past, but it also turns its gaze resolutely forward. Again and again it iterates Dryden's melancholy when he wrote, "Let me retire, betwixt two ages past/ The first of this, the hindmost of the last." Dryden was thinking of his place as a dramatist, but his situation is the place of every new poem.

Poets are linguistically aware, intensely aware, of the pathos of our situation as sentient beings, swimming in time. Nowhere is this pathos more tellingly spelt out than in a short poem by the contemporary American, Richard Wilbur; it is called "To the Etruscan Poets":

> Dream fluently, still brothers, who when young

> Took with your mothers' milk the mother tongue,
>
> In which pure matrix, joining world and mind,
> You strove to leave some line of verse behind
>
> Like a fresh track across a field of snow,
> Not reckoning that all could melt and go.

Between the obscurity—the Etruscanness, if you like—of our common past and the presentness, I won't say presence, of our language we try to make something which has form and meaning at once.

For a few poets, bolder or more naive than their late-modern contemporaries, a rhetorical and rhythmical raid on the Absolute eases the pain of this common situation; others retain some—often oddly slanted—connection with older, fading religious systems and denominations. Vincent Buckley paid close attention to the latter stream in his 1968 study, *Poetry and the Sacred*. In a chapter entitled "The Persistence of God" he writes

> What, of course, all these poets are doing, is using their imagistic power to suggest that the world may be *au fond* innocent; hence the ambience or radiance of innocence which tends to surround their images, and to infuriate readers of a less optimistic cast of mind. Actually no deception is being practised; there is no pretence that, if you say the world is innocent, it will become so. Rather, there is something midway between sympathetic magic and a quite sophisticated sacramental view of the representative nature of language: in other words, the implicit suggestion is that if a world of innocence can be created in poetry, it may come to reveal something which corresponds to it in the 'real' world, and the existence of which has not been fully appreciated. The stress is put on the capacity of poetry at once to represent and to reveal qualities in experience which are not apprehensible except by its means. (1968:62)

We can note the caution which accompanies Buckley's traditionalism here, in his "midway between" and "may come to reveal". His sense of language is by no means that of a transparent or easily mimetic substance, but as something which must resort to poetic "means" (whatever "means" means) to do its job. Later, he warns us about the dangers of transcendent hunger, saying that the common poetic task in our time is

> to test those privileged places—and privileged persons, moments and events as well—for sacredness: . . . Will the testing of their specific feeling, the exploring of their possible significance, open them up towards the transcendent, or will it merely return the poet to the involuted rounds of his own consciousness? (75)

Many readers now will pause over the shimmer of "transcendent", while yearning for a little of what it means. And many writers of our time (especially those who quiver at their marginalization on grounds of ethnicity or gender) would be likely to concur in William Empson's wry reflection that

> All those large dreams by which men long live well
> Are magic-lanterned on the smoke of Hell.
>
> ("This Last Pain")

Religious traditions may just seem a poisoned trail. A very common intermediate position in Australian poetry is that of examining a landscape in a finely impressionistic way and letting it speak in sacred terms: visually, as it were, with its own Wordsworthian voice, edited back to bare stones by the imagist tradition. Robert Gray is a notable practitioner of such poetry, finely sensible of detailed immanence.

It is in Gray's poetry that I glimpse, or think I see, something in tune with Kevin Hart's account of non-metaphysical theology, but that is altogether too difficult a question for me to explore, being neither a philosopher nor a mystic, and certainly not a Heideggerian. I should add, though, that I've been intrigued by the implications of Judith Beveridge's comment that "I'm extremely interested in detail and texture." (Digby, 1996: 211). It is not a surprising observation about a poet's concerns, but it opens up a fascinating epistemological field.

Being Janus-headed, poets live inside history, however much they may be tempted to render the lyrical moment ahistorical: the pure lyrical cry rising off a page which itself vanishes. Whatever their inescapable material condition, they attempt to make something outside time—like Hope's pharaohs and their pyramids—in the creative moment, "the instant of success" when even the heart stands still. In terms which Andrew Taylor has brought to bear on Francis Webb, such poems

> register the desire of the subject to rid itself of its own enabling and ineluctable desire, and . . . to be at one with the transcendental signified and thus cease to be a subject at all. (Taylor, 1987:111)

But, the moment over, we are back on the hinge of Janus, keeping an eye on the time. "We are all ex-children" (Peter Steele's phrase) and create our texts within that awareness. Nobody comes ex-nihilo.

Some poets drape themselves in a flag of pastness, silkily, dramatically or ironically. In our recent poetry I bring to mind Dorothy Porter's *Akhenaten*, Geoffrey Lehmann with *Nero's Poems*, Fay Zwicky addressing the Indian gods, Peter Rose's *Catullus* and Diane Fahey's *Metamorphoses*. The ancient world is extremely malleable, hence attractive: distant enough to be played across with a kind of freedom which a poet can't use dealing with settler history or with memories of her grandparents' generation. Antiquity, classical or biblical, becomes an arena in which the poet can struggle with mighty forebears, not too much crippled by the anxiety of belatedness, still feeling like an Original. Ken Bolton, demurring from tradition, has written sardonically that "Many, maybe most, who flock to poetry/pastiche the past/in their effort to evade the future." (McCredden and Trigg, 1996:131)

So, if our poetry is very light on actual prophecy, it is saturated or peppered, with vestiges: the remains and ruins, as we have seen, of the history of English poetry, of the classical world, the Bible, ancient musical rituals and holy dances. The signs and discourse of the past—of many pasts—turn up everywhere. Like the engineers who, trying to push a traffic underpass beneath the Castel San Angelo, are impeded by the buried buildings of ancient Rome, they run across history whether they will or no. As Judith Wright has put it, "Many roads meet here/ in me, the traveller and the ways I travel." And our junctions resemble hers.

This encounter with remains, or with old pathways, occurs both at the level of tenor and of vehicle. Some poets address themselves deliberately to the causal occasions of history. I have already mentioned younger exemplars of the latter practice, but Peter Porter and A.D. Hope are the most obvious exemplars of this, Porter jauntily ransacking what Stevens called "the dump" of western culture for occasions and topoi from the arts, especially those of Renaissance Italy.

More direct vestigialists, from the viewpoint of the modern nation-state, were the so-called Voyager poets; between the 1930s and the 1950s these Sydney-based male poets set out to write longish works in celebration of explorers, Columbus, Tasman, Cook, Scott, Eyre, Leichhardt.

From the point of view of teleology, all of these figures—except for Scott of the Antarctic—could be held responsible for our being what and who we are; they attained to the now-unfashionable role of heroes: tarred, alas, with the colonial brush. As Slessor ended the most crudely causal of these poems, "So Cook made choice, so Cook sailed westabout,/ So men write poems in Australia."

Slessor, it may be noted, was not fond of women: mermaids, wenches and nymphs perhaps, but not actual women.

Our loosely democratic literature (democracy is always loose, of course) is particularly weak in prophecy, in deliberate judgement, and in diatribe. This is partly the result of decades of "repressive desublimation", to re-use Marcuse's telling phrase about not telling. It is also affected, I have no doubt, by Australian writers' anxiety about whether they are going to get government funding (now regarded by a great many writers as their due, and not improperly so, given the present rules of the game); also by the incumbency of so many of our writers within the cloisters of universities, communities which are implicitly hostile to excess, prone to classification and measurement. (see Hazel Rowley, *The Australian*, 18/12/97) As James McAuley wrote, long before the arrival of serious managerial nonsense on our campuses, that is to say long before the present philistine assault upon our intellectual lives,

> The scholar-teacher's approach is not that of the working poet. The latter falls upon an author who attracts him as a beast of prey upon a victim, tears him open and consumes whatever will nourish his own vitality—heart, liver or lights—and leave the rest scattered in abandon. The former must sit down to a systematic meal, whatever his appetite. (1959:126)

The hedging passivity of weak postmodernism could only be sustained within academic life, or along its fringes: it is in the light of such a *camera oscura*, indeed, that one can understand some of the strong excesses of Les Murray, in his blasts and philippics against a confection of urban intellectuals, those whom Clem Christesen called "our hedgers and ditchers".

Murray combines prophecy with dark comedy in his four-part poem, "Futures Exchange" from *Ethnic Radio* (1977). It begins thus, as dramatic monologue:

> I am a cleaner in the Faculty of Production, South Sydney Campus. We are subtechnics staff; next year we'll be allowed to wear blue denim and take our orders only from postgraduates. At night, our seminar scrubs the assembly building where the undergraduates assemble cars. Untidy, scruffy young people, but have to pity them, not being allowed to pair-bond till they graduate. All degrees are masonic, my son told me one time. He doesn't live with us. He has triple Honours and hopes one day to become Dean of a region. He took me on a tour of the Central Chancellery once; it was enormous there: the halls, the sculptures. I asked to see the Chairs, and he was kind—that kindness hurt: I guessed I'd been naive. They had the last farmer there, preserved in Plexite.

Murray calls in question a world of academicization and abstraction; his last line holds against the fading georgic values, what he elsewhere defines as the Boeotian, rather than the Athenian spirit. He stands resolutely for the position characterized, a little ruefully, by Philip Mead when he writes that "the institutionalization of poetry in the wider literary culture still relies heavily on the Romantic, universalising, humanistic character of the Poet." (McCredden and Trigg, 1996:198) And if the Poet stoutly exists, so does the substantiality of poetry. I think in this context of Peter Beilharz's recent comments on postmodern abstraction even if he, unlike Murray, comes from the political Left. In Beilharz's words,

> one wonders about the surrealism of a great deal of radical argument since Marx. The more central issue, in this context, concerns the conceptual inflation of money and abstraction in modern culture. Alongside the overwhelming ghosts of abstraction and reification are the ghosts we ourselves generate, of scholasticism, of surplus abstraction, too much time spent with books or, rather, failing to place and distance texts in the world we actually also inhabit. (*Thesis Eleven*, 46, 1996:30)

The poet is, like all of us, both a function and a being; located in modern history and significantly determined by economic circumstances; identifiably part of a particular linguistic culture; given to making a particular, overdetermined product out of words and their melodiously-patterned syntax; and standing in that transient doorway which we call the present. It is perhaps to assert their *presentness* (which is, I suppose, one form of presence) that our poets so often resort to the Present Portentous, or simple present tense, in their lyricism. Thus Jill Jones,

> You carry me through ground level hands scoop up the fall the air of my doubt and Dorothy Hewett. An aerogramme arrives, "The Prince is dead!" I take up seances, each night we couple, circling the empty ballroom to "Moscow Nights". Cockroaches rustle, my thrombosed knee reeks of its vodka bandage, the dust settles from the chandelier on his bald head.

Jones's verbs are used thus to intensify the presented emotion, while Hewett's turn a comic-erotic narrative into a sort of myth, colourfully outside time. Often, too, poets use this curt tense merely to convey the imagistic impression of a moment *in situ*. Indeed, rural imagism is still one of the staple genres of our poetry.

Neither in the buoyant 1980s nor in the downsizing decade of the nineties do Australian writers seem willing to stick their necks out, except in sexual matters (where it is not exactly their necks which are exposed): a game long since won, by and large. Sex is easy.

Again, you can't easily savage a government which your fellow-citizens have elected. Indeed, prophecy and satire may be in direct opposition to democratic systems. Would any Australian poet, coming savage and scarlet from the desert, now dare to write something as ferocious as Hope's "A Commination"? Would any now dare to pour scorn on popular forms of entertainment as he does with such brio here?

> Now let this curse fall on my enemies,
> My enemies, Lord, but all mankind's as well,
> Prophets and panders of their golden calf;
> Let Justice fit them all in their degrees;
> Let them, still living, know that state of hell,
> And let me see them perish, Lord, and laugh.
>
> Let them be glued to television screens
> Till their minds fester and the trash they see
> Worm their dry hearts away to crackling shells;
> Let ends be so revenged upon the means
> That all that once was human grows to be
> A flaccid mass of phototropic cells;
>
> Let the dog love his vomit still, the swine
> Squelch in the slough; and let their only speech
> Be Babel; let the specious lies they bred
> Taste on their tongues like intellectual wine;
> Let sung commercials surfeit them, till each
> Goggles with nausea in his nauseous bed.

Such use of the swinging lash is very rare; it is uncool. It is not what we practice in a time when, as Fay Zwicky says, "the margins of freedom are becoming blurred, pushed away from the concept of social responsibility." (1986:2) It is in every way at odds with the masochistic aesthetic of post-modernity.

Hope once complained that "Nobody today really expects a poet to know anything about anything." (1974:92) Like the metaphysically romantic Gwen Harwood and the communist John Manifold, he insists that poetry engages with human and material subject- matter. His interest in the French symbolists never rid him of this anthropo-mimetic view of his art. He would be amazed at John Forbes's claim that Manifold's sonnet on the death of Stalin is not about things that happen in "the real world" but merely a linguistic construction of "almost Pop-Art beauty." (1996/4:693) He would certainly baulk at the hollow flippancy of Forbes's reading of the future in "Lessons for Young Poets":

> it's important to be major
> but not to be
> too cute about it—I mean
> it's the empty future
> you want to impress,
> not just the people
> who'll always be richer
> & less talented than you.

Despite the witty syntactical cut of the antepenultimate line here, the verse doesn't offer us much in the way of provender, and that's exactly the point. Don't overdo things. Moderate cuteness is all.

A proper stance in time, an attitude in the teeth of the future (when, after all, we will all die) is more important than this. For the Romans, Janus was "the god of gods", a deity of beginnings as well as of arches and doorways. And every lyric moment is also a new beginning, the fresh poem being, to borrow Dennis Haskell's words a "sensation of syllables sweeping you and your friends/ across the bar of technique, of grieving, of consolation." The past that a writer borrows from is also the foundation material for a foothold, the ground of possibility; what we have been, however regrettable, gives muscle to what we are.

We shape words, syllables, pulses, into poetry so that we will not be miserable. Poems give the reader joy, whatever else they may do: the joy of musicality, the joy of overdetermined language, a dance of rhythm.

Now, the backward-looking poet is the one who has given us what Roland Barthes has called the text of pleasure, while a radical, dismantling poet gives us the dangerous text of bliss. He goes on to define a third writerly self who can transcend this dichotomy. This is the poet we can truly admire. Barthes writes:

> Now the subject who keeps the two texts in his field and in his hands the reins of pleasure and bliss is an anachronic subject, for he simultaneously and contradictorily participates in the profound hedonism of all culture . . . and in the destruction of that culture: he enjoys the consistency of his selfhood (that is his pleasure) and seeks its loss (that is his bliss). (1975:14)

Here, exactly, we can see the Janus-vision; for in these terms, pleasure is a secure relation with an imaginatively adequate past, and bliss a bracing plunge into the future—into its towering, unknowable surf.

In our poetry, in the poetry of this anaemic decade, what are the circumstances which so prey upon a poet's imagination that they drive him or her to a keen awareness of how the future scrapes against the edges of the past?

One such circumstance is that of death or of serious illness. All elegies have the task of making sense of the arch between life and death; more subjectively imperative are those tense poems written by people who have some realistic grounds to fear that they might soon cease to be subjects. I refer, of course, to the poetry of serious illness. This may be mythologized into art, as it was in Yeats's Byzantium poems, but more often in our own time, and at best, it generates a poetry of courageous bleakness. Such writing we can find in the first section of Doris Brett's *In the Constellation of the Crab*, made up of lyric stages confronting cancer in which, as she puts it, "I wrote my way through the experience." This is the latter part of "Operating Theatre":

This is the room that God lives in
with his single eye
staring down from the ceiling.
This is the room
you will be born in,
do not ask why.
If you close your eyes
you will see again
they tell you
and, in the end, remember
after the sacrifice
comes the ascension.
They are coming for you now
in their loose green gowns
and masks . . .
Soon they will reach over you
green and leafy as hearts.

The language of this, ostensibly plain as a hospital wall, plays with birth and sacrifice, with an open eye and two closed ones, with remembering and telling; one is asked to "remember" something which is putatively in the future. The surgeons wear the "green gowns" of sexual love. And in a last, remarkable line, they are "green and leafy as hearts." We end this threatening, half-consoling poem with an image of doctors transformed into fertility gods.

Such poetry displays itself as what Seamus Heaney called "an exercise in the virtue of hope." (1995:4) And, it goes without saying that hope is one way of interacting with the future. Hope entails the hope that the rushing future will do something good for us before it roars into the past.

Politics is another area in which the past and the future fit. The patient becomes agent, engaged in having to make decisions, each of them dependent on past experience, and each having social consequences, for the polly and for the citizens at large. But very little of our poetry attends to that moment, to the instant of choice-making. The Voyager poets of mid-century were, but they dramatized existential moments long past, their generic mentor being

Browning; and most of our political poets, from Lesbia Harford to Bruce Dawe, concentrate on depicting the present, lamentable state of things.

Murray, despite his occasional swatches of darkly comic prophecy, is chiefly concerned with a long sweep of history gone and with an often deplorable modern world—in this he resembles F.R. Leavis. History is change, accelerating change, and commonly bad; as he writes, "The Nineteenth Century. The Twentieth Century. There were never any others. No centuries before these./ Dante was not hailed in his time as an Authentic/ Fourteenth Century Voice." Murray invokes a past which was not dynamic, but stable—with its milk jugs and picnics, its encaustic tiles and masonite—which has been jostled out of place by tumultuous modernity; and unlike Yeats he discreetly elides the "bitter violent men" for the builders and grazing families. For all that he writes inventively about helicopters, machines, technology, the abiding things for Murray are the home, the farm and the nuclear (funny adjective!) family.

Although Murray claims he "decided a while back to change everything," the most any of us appear able to do in the way of prophecy is to project present discontents a little way into the future. Thus I have written several poems comically developing sado-monetarism and lunatic managerialism into the next century: bitter poems, but with no real gift of prophecy. I am not a successful visionary; few are. A salient point to add here is that nobody seems poetically interested in the Millennium. The republicans have somehow lost heart in anything imaginative or patriotic happening, and the Christian fundamentalists don't write poems these days. We are all going to look pretty silly if the world comes to an end in 2001.

Among Australian poets who are practising now, Kevin Hart has a peculiarly keen awareness of time's hinge, of what it is to be poised in the present. Back in the 1970s he was already using one set of terms to envisage a valueless future. "The Twenty-first Century" is a wistful, anti-materialist poem about a future when "our hands will be empty, we will have nothing to give, only our stories".

By the time of his beautifully-shaped collection, *Peniel* (1991) Hart has reached a point where religious questioning and the shimmering prospect of individual identity are one. As an historian of silence in "a world of things with nothing at all to say", the poet keeps approaching boundary conditions, edges of consciousness, hiatuses, the brink of sleep. Things are always slipping or changing, but to what end? The self loses its name, the letter has no address; in parody of Voltaire, "This is the strangest of all possible worlds."

The poetry of *Peniel* has detached itself from the nationalist aesthetic, from any specifically Australian agenda. The poems are formally held in place, against disintegration, by their steady form: twenty-seven lines of tercets each, a Dantesque rigour. But the gift, the letter, the telephone call, approaching ambiguously, problematizes all our certainties about where we stand in human time. (In choosing such hinging moments, Hart stands close to his near-contemporary, John Foulcher, who dramatizes the turning-over times of dusk and dying, of sunrise and beginnings, experiences grasped in the rip of time.) Hart presses towards the via negativa, the path on which one empties oneself of possessions, familiar images, the whole social envelope. His is a metaphysical questioning/questing, but in anti-metaphysical terms. In his writing, St John of the Cross meets Jacques Derrida, outside history.

It is with a poem from *Peniel* that I should like to finish. This verbal gift is called "The Gift" and it celebrates lyric time, the poem's time, which is both inside and outside history. It and the four poems which precede it in the book are about eloquent silence, about Bergsonian duration, about art's impersonality: they press towards the existence of the poem as anonymous, inconceivable gift; I note, at this point, that a gift is a **present**:

> One day the gift arrives—outside your door,
> left on a windowsill, inside the mailbox,
> or in the hallway, far too large to lift
>
> Your postman shrugs his shoulders, the police
> consult a statute, and the cat miaows.
> No name, no signature, and no address,
>
> only, "to you, my dearest one, my all . . . "
> One day it fits snugly in your pocket,
> then fills the backyard like afternoon in Spring.

Monday morning, and it's there at work—
already ahead of you, or left behind
amongst the papers, files and photographs;

and there were lipstick smudges down the side
or have they just appeared? What a headache!
And worse, people have begun to talk:

"You lucky thing!" they say, or roll their eyes.
Nights find you combing the directory
(a glass of straw-coloured wine upon the desk)

still hoping to chance on a forgotten name.
Yet mornings see you happier than before—
after all, the gift has set you up for life.

Impossible to tell, now, what was given
and what was not: slivers of rain on the window,
those gold-tooled *Oeuvres* of Diderot on the shelf,

the strawberry dreaming in a champagne flute—
were they part of the gift or something else?
Or is the gift still coming, on its way?

The lyric is thoroughly assured, with all the authority of its simple present tense, but the self who seeks to inhabit it is provisional, has no name, is passive ("nights find you"; "mornings see you") and was dismantled long ago in the writings of Diderot. The poem itself is: that is to say, it has little in common with the causal fluency of narrative or instructive prose; its discursiveness is broken by dashes, dots, exclamations and question marks. The It, that is to say the gift, stands outside clock time, "already ahead of you, or left behind." Only the Janus-faced poet can hope to apprehend it, or at least take note of its traces in the cloud-chamber. And the poem somehow remains, "like a fresh track across a field of snow."

WORKS CITED

Roland Barthes, tr. Richard Howard, *The Pleasure of the Text* (Hill & Wang, 1975).

Peter Beilharz, *Thesis Eleven*, 46, 1996.

Ken Bolton, "Untimely Meditations (Excerpts)", in Lyn McCredden and Stephanie Trigg, eds., *The Space of Poetry* (Melbourne: Melbourne University Press, 1996).

Joseph Brodsky, *On Grief and Reason: Essays* (New York: Farrar Straus Giroux, 1995).

Vincent Buckley, *Poetry and the Sacred* (London: Chatto & Windus, 1968).

Jennifer Digby, *A Woman's Voice: Conversations with Australian Poets* (St. Lucia: University of Queensland Press, 1996).

John Dryden, "Prologue to Aurung-Zebe", *The Works of John Dryden* (London: University of California Press, 1969).

William Empson, "This Last Pain", *Collected Poems* (Harcourt Brace, 1955).

John Forbes, "Lessons for Young Poets", *New and Selected Poems* (Sydney: Angus & Robertson, 1992).

Kevin Hart, "The Twenty-First Century", *New and Selected Poems* (Sydney: Angus & Robertson, 1995).

_____, "Gypsophila", *Peniel*, Golvan Arts, 1991 .

Seamus Heaney, *The Redress of Poetry*, Oxford Lectures (Faber, 1995).

Dorothy Hewett, "Miss Hewett's Shenanigans", in Chris Wallace-Crabbe, ed., *The Golden Apples of the Sun: Twentieth Century Australian Poetry* (Melbourne: Melbourne University Press, 1980).

A.D. Hope, "A Commination", *Collected Poems 1930-1965* (Sydney: Angus & Robertson, 1966).

_____. *Native Companions* (Sydney: Angus & Robertson, 1974).

Jill Jones, *The Mask and the Jagged Star* (Hale & Iremonger, 1993).

James McAuley, *The End of Modernity* (Sydney: Angus & Robertson, 1959).

Philip Mead, "*Ut cinema poesis*: Cinematism and John Tranter's *The Floor of Heaven*", in McCredden and Trigg.

Les A. Murray, *Ethnic Radio* (Sydney: Angus & Robertson, 1977).

_____, "The C19-20", *Collected Poems* (Sydney: Heinemann, 1994).

Kenneth Slessor, "Five Visions of Captain Cook", *One Hundred Poems* (Sydney: Angus & Robertson, 1944).

Peter Steele, uncollected essays.

Wallace Stevens, "The Man on the Dump", *The Collected Poems of Wallace Stevens* (New York: Knopf, 1978).

Andrew Taylor, *Reading Australian Poetry* (Sydney: Angus & Robertson, 1987).

Judith Wright, "For New England", *The Moving Image* (Meanjin Press, 1946).

Fay Zwicky, *The Lyre in the Pawnshop* (Perth: University of Western Australia Press, 1986).

Beyond Identity: Australia's Post-Colonial Future

BILL ASHCROFT
University of New South Wales

An inaugural conference of the Asian Association for the Study of Australia raises some very interesting questions: What is the significance of studying Australia in Asia in 1996? What might India and Australia have in common? What is the pre-history of this conference? What does the emergence of such an association mean for Australian cultural study in general? These questions are not adequately addressed by the fact of Australia's increasing identification with the region, through diplomatic efforts and economic and cultural exchanges. Rather I would locate the establishment of this Association itself at a particular moment in the development of literary and cultural analysis throughout the post-colonial world. What we are seeing is nothing less than a restructuring of intra-national relations in post-colonial countries, a restructuring of relations which has proceeded from the increasing scope and penetration of post-colonial theory.

My approach to these questions was focussed by the simple task of getting airline tickets from Australia to India. Whereas flights from both countries to London are more frequent, more direct, comparatively cheaper and easier to book, flights between them arise as challenges of heroic proportions for travel agents. The reason for this, as for the questions I asked above, lies, quite simply, in a shared experience of colonialism, through which a continual privileging of the centre/colony binary reinforces the perpetuation of the hierarchical structure of imperial cultural power. The experience of colonialism has been vastly different in its local manifestations and practices, but similar in the way different societies have responded, through strategies of opposition, appropriation and change. It is this intersection of cultural experience which stands as the most productive line of analysis in these countries, an intersection which exists with many other cultures at many levels, an intersection which creates a rhizomic complex of cultural identities and practices (see Ashcroft 1997).

The Asian Association for the Study of Australia promises to further the post-colonial study of Australian literature and culture. But this raises the intriguing fact that of all post-colonial countries, literary studies in Australia shows the greatest resistance to the idea of its *post-colonial* status. Why is it that Australia appears to have been so resistant to the concept of post-colonial alliances and interventions, that is, resistant to the idea of its post-coloniality? Why is it that anti-establishment critics in particular have been stuck in the identity binarism? The answer lies, I think, in the dualistic nature of colonialist discourse and the way it problematizes resistance. This is the same colonialist discourse which both India and Australia have experienced, but the nature of its operation has been quite different in the two countries.

One of the most valuable ways of observing the operation of this discourse and of the ways in which countries such as India and Australia share its effects lies in the emergence of the discipline of English. For it is in the formation of the discipline of literary study that India's and Australia's histories are most strikingly linked. Of course I am talking about the development of English as the pre-eminent mode of colonial control throughout the empire. It is in understanding the origins and nature of this discourse, the most privileged discursive mode of the civilizing mission, that we can gain some insight on a number of things: the history within which this Association has now come into being; the nature of the intersections between India and Australia; the function of English in 'civilizing' both countries; and the reasons for the prominence of nationalism as a dominant mode of cultural dissent in both countries.

When we examine the surprisingly recent development of this field called English Literature we discover how firmly it is rooted in the cultural relationships established by British imperialism. Not only is the very idea of 'Culture' a result of the European political subjugation of the rest of the world, but the construction of Europe itself is inextricably bound up with the historical reality of colonialism and the almost total invisibility of the colonized peoples to European art and philosophy.

Virtually from its inception English existed as a promotion of English National Culture under the guise of the advancement of civilization. The founding document of the discipline is Lord Macaulay's Minute to Parliament in 1835. This document, Gauri Viswanathan tells us, signified the rise to prominence of the Anglicists over the Orientalists in the British administration of India. The Charter Act of 1813, devolving responsibility for Indian education on the colonial administration, led to a struggle between the two approaches, ultimately resolved by Macaulay's Minute, in which we find stated not just the assumptions of the Anglicists, but the profoundly universalist assumptions of English national culture itself. "We must educate a people who cannot at present be educated by means of their mother-tongue", says Macaulay, with breathtaking confidence,

> The claims of our own language it is hardly necessary to recapitulate.
>
> It stands pre-eminent even among the languages of the west. It abounds with works of imagination not inferior to the noblest which Greece has bequeathed to us; with models of every species of eloquence . . . with the most profound speculation on metaphysics, morals, government, jurisprudence, and trade. . . . Whoever knows that language has ready access to all the vast intellectual wealth which all the wisest nations of earth have created and hoarded in the course of ninety generations. (Macaulay 1836)

The advancement of any colonized people could only occur, claimed Macaulay, under the auspices of English language and culture and it was on English literature that the burden of imparting civilized values was to rest. It worked so well as a form of cultural studies because "the strategy of locating authority in the texts of English literature all but effaced the sordid history of colonialist expropriation, material exploitation and class and race oppression behind European world dominance." English literature "functioned as a surrogate Englishman in his highest and most perfect state" (Viswanathan, 1987:22). One could add that without the profoundly universalist assumptions of English literature and the dissemination of these through education, colonial administrations would not have been able to invoke such widespread complicity.

It is this moment in 1835 which also marks a key moment in the pre-history of the relationship between Australia, India and all other post-colonial countries. The title of this essay "Beyond Identity" is not meant to imply that Australia's future lies in the amorphous globalism which appears so irresistible, but to suggest a way out of the settler-colonial fixation with identity which has so clearly characterised Australian cultural history, and to suggest a better resistance to globalism than in the fixation with the concept of nation. I believe a key to this fixation lies in understanding the peculiar nature of Australian culturalist discourse, which is nowhere better metonymised than in its vexed and complex relationship with the emergent discipline of English.

Centripetal and Centrifugal

The Viswanathan narrative of the development of English is an engaging and influential one, but my contention is that this is only one aspect of a complex dynamic in the construction of imperial discourse. The establishment of English as the prominent mode of cultural study in India is an example of what might be called a *centrifugal* movement, the movement of cultural authority outwards towards the periphery. But a key to understanding the power of imperial hegemony is to understand that this centrifugal movement is always accompanied, and often preceded, by a *centripetal* movement in which the colonized not only comply with the process of colonial enculturation, but initiate and encourage it. Recent critiques of Viswanathan by Indian historians have suggested that there was significant support from indigenous elites for the establishment of English in India, that is, a centripetal movement towards imperial discourse without which imperial hegemony would not have been so consummately naturalized in the discipline of English.

This centripetal movement is shared by all colonized countries and can be seen operating in the discourse of English through the establishment of Rhetoric and *Belles Lettres*, the forerunner of English, in Scotland. Robert Crawford points out that in the eighteenth century, Scotland is drenched in an ideology of 'improvement' in all areas of cultural life. "The concept and vocabulary of improvement, of turning the primitive into the civilized, governed manifold areas of Scottish life at this time, from agriculture, economics and chemistry to poetry and fine arts." (Crawford, 1992: 16). Even the economist Adam Smith, whose *Wealth of Nations* discusses the circulation of capital in terms of the civilizing of the barbaric regions of the world, lectured on Rhetoric and *Belles Lettres* in Edinburgh.

In other words the seeds of the development of English are not planted but *propagated* by Macaulay's Minute to Parliament. It represents the beginning of the powerful *centrifugal* dynamic of imperial discourse through the civilizing mode of English. But the seeds of English lie in a centripetal movement in Scottish cultural life which emerged to resolve the deep conflict between the desire for cultural independence and the desire to be 'acceptable' and 'civilized'. For the Scots, the monumental, subtle and constant denigration of English culture led to a centripetal movement within which modern English literature became privileged. "Civilization in Scotland was largely a linguistic concept establishing a terrain in which vocabulary and syntax distinguished the refined and civilized from the vulgar and savage" (Crawford, 1992: 18).

The establishment of English as the prime civilizing mode of empire in all colonies made them sites for the fetishism of imperial cultural icons such as Shakespeare which operated as a primary focus of the civilizing mission. A history of theatrical activity in Calcutta in the eighteenth and nineteenth centuries, or Sydney or Melbourne in the nineteenth, gives a very good indication of the cultural arrangements in the society (Singh, 1996: 120-52). The iconic and evocative operation of Shakespeare as a signifier demarcating the civilized and barbaric, tradition and modernity, established in both societies a clear sense of what Culture might be. Shakespeare is an invention of the idea of Culture which in turn, operates as a powerful centripetal attractor in both India and Australia.

The 'Centripetal' and Australian Radical Nationalism

My argument is that the progress of imperial control always occurs by means of this dualism of centripetal and centrifugal forces in *all* societies. Despite the ideology of resistance we find in Australian nationalism, it was the constant and powerful centripetal movement, the desire of Australians and Australian institutions to privilege the models of English culture, what A.A. Phillips has called the "Cultural Cringe" (1958: 89), which has continued to be the strongest impulse in the Australian desire to be seen to be civilized, and continues to be the most problematic for cultural dissent. The centripetal movement in colonized societies actively constructs the centre, constructs and perpetuates the idea of Home.

Now despite the assumption that radical nationalism in Australia was a response to the dominance of what we might now call the 'centrifugal' movement of imperial discourse, I believe it maintains its very resilient hold on Australian cultural dissent precisely because the stronger mode of imperial discourse in Australia has been centripetal, Australians actively constructing the dominance of Empire. The anomaly of Australians being simultaneously empire loyalists and nationalists comes from the strength of this filiative energy towards the construction of a cultural prehistory. This anomaly continues in the dualism of a sometimes strident image-nationalism on the one hand and an apparent inability or refusal to become a republic, on the other. But this species of confusion underlies a much broader and insidious enslavement to the dominance of the 'international'.

The progress of English studies in Australia is a good example of this dynamic. The Australian branch of the English Association, established in 1864 is the oldest continuous branch of that decidedly imperial institution. In Australia Mungo Macallum, an empire loyalist and the first Professor of English at Sydney University, was the first President of the Australian branch of Henry Newbolt's English Association. The fact that both he and people like Le Gay Brereton were relatively enthusiastic supporters of Australian writing had no effect upon the fundamentally imperial conception of English itself. Christopher Brennan, Australian classicist and poet, saw Australia as being constructed by writers who inherited an "art whose beginnings are lost in the mystery that envelops the origins of the white race" (1927: 374-75). He hotly rejected advice to turn away from his (and our) Greek heritage. Brennan claimed that our inheritance in art is as unalterable by the artist as "the blood in his veins [or] the colour of his skin and hair", and believed that "through [the poet's] long and . . . deep intimacy with his [new] home, will his art take on a 'national' tinge and come to be expressive of what is most true and real in the world that his imagination prefers" (377). The most interesting aspect of these kinds of comments is that people like Brennan who believed they were initiating some kind of cultural independence for Australian art and letters, were actually confirming its dependent and supplementary status through concepts such as the 'national tinge'.

Judith Wright's "The Upside-Down Hut" demonstrates the fervour of the nationalist rejection of positions such as Brennan's, claiming that wherever reasoning such as his prevailed, Australia would always be the other of Europe (1961: 31). This centripetal movement, which emerged even in writings such as Brennan's, had a profound impact on intellectual history in Australia, *absorbing* much of the energy of intellectual dissent and resulting in an important distinction between the British and Australian left intelligentsia. Where "the language of class has provided the former with much of its central political vocabulary," says Andrew Milner, "the latter has more often found a roughly equivalent resource in the language of nationality. Where [Raymond] Williams privileges class over nation . . . Australian radical culturalisms have more typically privileged nation over class. The characteristically left wing variant of Australian culturalist discourse has thus emerged as a form of radical nationalism" (Milner, 1991: 36).

Thus the dominant note of Australian left culturalist discourse becomes radical nationalism. As far as English was concerned, where radical cultural discourse in Britain tended to move into cultural studies, particularly after the establishment of the BCCCS, Australian radical nationalists were marooned on a battlefield in which the claims of Australian literature were constantly and futilely promoted against the prejudices of the literary establishment while questions about the nature of literature itself were left unasked. This is a tendency which begins at least as far back as Frederick Sinnet in 1856 who, in "The Fiction Fields of Australia" proudly asserts that Australian novels are both possible and desirable because Australian individuals and society share those universal values and characteristics which are the very substance of novel writing (Barnes, 1969: 8-32). This situation is one in which Australian literary discourse remains stuck even when it rejects the nationalist stridency of the fifties. Because unless the universalist notion of Literature itself is questioned, Australian criticism has nowhere to go, it remains a branch of the British tree. Although there are very few card carrying radical nationalists in Australian criticism today, the legacy of its identity politics is deeply embedded in Australian literary study. In simple terms, then, the centripetal movement of imperial discourse in Australia explains why so much of the energy of radical dissent is absorbed by identity politics in general, and nationalism in particular. The legacy of this remains a continuing resistance to post-colonialism which is erroneously perceived as a global and internationalist discourse, a hegemonic 'grand narrative', rather than a vibrant and pluralistic network of cultural affiliations.

Post-colonialism and Globalism

So we need to address this issue of globalism. If nationalism has been a trap for Australian cultural analysis because it has bound Australia into a binary relationship in which the terms of the relationship fail to be questioned, then what of globalism? What of the possibility of re-imagining oneself into a world community? Much recent criticism urges the construction of a theory of the global. Globalism, it seems, is inevitable. We have lived since the sixteenth century, says Wallerstein (1980), in a single world system, that of global capital. Could the most promising avenue for the Australian analysis be to see it as part of a global system of capital, of profit and exploitation? Might globalism loosen the ties to a map inherited from the century of colonialism? In some respects this makes sense. The detection of a global system of capital may put the destiny of both Australia and India in a different light.

But the capacity of globalism to have any real effect on Australian Studies would lie in its ability to disrupt the idea of Australia inherited from the history of European imperialism. Not only does it not disrupt this notion, it entrenches it because imperialism is the aggressive outworking of this very world system. Just as global capital is the new diffused centre, so the doctrine of internationalism is the new cultural imperialism. We no longer look to London or Paris or even New York but to an amorphous circulation of power to which we want to belong. This we call the international. The opposition to this amorphous internationalism is not nationalism, which is always unerringly co-opted to the project of global capital, but a theory of the local. Not only is post-colonialism not a globalist discourse, it is one of the few ways of approaching cultural production as a local event operating in response to global discourse, because it sees the ways in which globalism extends the values and rhetoric of imperialism. Vast as the differences between particular local cultures and local experiences may be, their development lies in shared strategies in their response to imperial dominance.

Post-colonialism: Ontology or Strategies

The issue of cultural strategies is crucial because the most consistent mistake made by critics is that the terms 'post-colonial', and its subsidiaries such as 'hybridity', 'ambivalence', 'ethnicity' are *ontological* categories. Post-colonial discourse then becomes a "shimmering object of desire", a category to be inhabited rather than a tool to be used. But words such as "post-colonial" do not describe a universal form of experience but forms of talk about experience. If the term "post-colonial" seems to be homogenizing in the way it brings together the experiences of colonialism in a wide variety of situations this is because it is mistaken for an ontology. Once we see the term "post-colonial" as representing a *form of talk* rather than a *form of experience* we will be better equipped to see that such talk encompasses a wide and interwoven text of experiences. The responses of colonized societies to colonialism have occupied a continuum from absolute complicity to violent rebellion, all of which can be seen to be "post-colonial." If we see post-colonial discourse in the Foucauldian sense as a system of statements within which a particular knowledge of the world becomes possible, a space of enunciation, the rules which govern the possibility of statements about the field, we discover that this discourse operates upon a principle of interventionary and transformative strategies.

A theory of post-colonial creative response rests firstly on the recognition that the colonizing process triggers a wide range of responses in all colonized societies. So the post-colonial response is never simply unitary, either in object or design. Once we shake off the burden of ontology we see that the strategies shared by societies as diverse as India and Australia represent an intellectually and culturally productive alliance. For the most interesting features of this shared response are those strategies of transformation, by which the dominant discourse itself is invaded, appropriated and used, by which various post-colonial subjects construct a voice that can be heard by the widest audience. This is, by the very nature of the exercise, first achieved by creative artists, as they seize control of representation, and in this respect it is the post-colonial artists who may be leading the way for other forms of post-colonial social transformation. But it is, crucially, the transformative energy of these strategies which represent their most powerful capacity for change.

A Poetics of Transformation

The power of transformation can be seen in the engagement with language, with literary writing and the whole range of imperial cultural media. But the discipline of English is useful as a model of cultural engagement because it shows how a relevant oppositionality is bound to a strategy of transformation. One can either accept the orthodoxy of English literature with its huge edifice of disciplinary and cultural assumptions, as is often still the case in Australia, one can reject it and leave altogether or one can interpolate a post-colonial view of cultural textuality. This does not mean adding some different courses and different texts to the curriculum, but engaging the underlying assumptions, the ideology and the status of English as a moral technology.

The poetics of transformation examines the ways in which writers and readers contribute constitutively to meaning, how colonised societies appropriate imperial discourses, how they interpolate their voices and concerns into dominant systems of textual production and distribution. A poetics of transformation recognises the myth of parent and child, trunk and branch, stream and tributary by which the post-colonial is marginalised and replaces it with a perception of the rhizomic nature of discursive power and resistance. Transformation recognises that power is a critical part of our cultural life and copes with binary opposition by assuming new forms. But above all, a poetics of transformation recognises the transformative way in which post-colonial texts operate, even those which pose as simply oppositional.

The politics of transformation works constantly within existing discursive and institutional formations to change them, rather than simply to attempt to end them. Ultimately a poetics and politics of transformation effects a transformation of the disciplinary field. So it is this transformative energy of post-colonial textuality which offers the greatest promise from an Asian Association for the Study of Australia: a perspective which re-contextualizes Australian culture, which can compare local inflexions of a shared predicament of colonialism, and which, through an examination of post-colonial strategies, may yet re-configure the study of Australia.

WORKS CITED

Bill Ashcroft, "The Rhizome of Post-Colonial Discourse," in Roger Luckhurst and Peter Marks (eds.) *Literature and the Contemporary* (London, Longmans, 1997).

John Barnes (ed.) *The Writer in Australia 1856-1964* (Melbourne: Oxford, 1969).

Christopher Brennan, "Some Makers of Australia" (1927) in *Terry Sturm* (ed.) Chtristopher Brennan (St. Lucia: UQP, 1984).

Robert Crawford, *Devolving English Literature* (Oxford: Clarendon, 1996).

Thomas Macaulay, "Minute on Indian Education" (1836) in Bill Ashcroft, Gareth Griffiths and Helen Tiffin (eds) *The Post-Colonial Studies Reader* (London: Routledge, 1995), 428.

Andrew Milner, *Contemporary Cultural Theory: An Introduction* (Sydney: Allen & Unwin, 1991).

A.A. Phillips, *The Australian Tradition: Studies in a Colonial Culture* (London: Cheshire, 1958).

Jyotsna G. Singh, *Colonial Narratives/Cultural Dialogues: "Discoveries" of India in the Language of Colonialism* (London: Routledge, 1996).

Gauri Viswanathan "The Beginnings of English Literary Study in India", *Oxford Literary Review*, vol. 9, nos. 1 & 2, 1987.

Immanuel Wallerstein, *The Capitalist World Economy* (Cambridge: Cambridge University Press, 1980).

Judith Wright, "The Upside-down Hut", *Australian Letters*, vol. 3, no. 4, June 1961.

Australian Popular Culture: Models of Cultural Influence and Originality

DAVID CARTER
Griffith University (Brisbane)

Australia can be defined as a post-colonial, immigrant, settler nation, federated and highly-urbanised but widely-dispersed. Given which, the question of just what constitutes Australian culture has been the subject of intense debate from as early as the 1820s. These debates have produced different models of cultural development, cultural influence and importation, cultural originality and authenticity. In broad terms I want to outline three stages in the development of these models: first, to the 1950s/1960s when the dominant framework was the British-Australian relationship; second, the 1960s to the 1980s, dominated by the notion of 'Americanisation'; third, in the 1980s and 1990s, when a new model of cultural influence and originality has emerged. This new model will be my main focus.

1. Britain-Australia

In the century between the 1850s and 1950s the unavoidable question for understanding Australian culture was its relationship to British culture, British civilisation. This was so for nationalists and republicans no less than for conservatives or imperial patriots. Was Australian culture a young branch of the old oak tree, as one model expressed it, or was it a vigorous eucalypt sapling, growing up quite independently, as in another model. Any list of canonical works of cultural or social commentary from the period will establish the point: from Marcus Clarke's essays to A.A. Phillips's notion of the 'cultural cringe'.

This is not at all surprising, although it was perhaps always too simple. Both republicanism and imperialism in fact sponsored their own forms of internationalism. Cultural influences were always more diverse than British alone. There were enthusiasms for the new democratic culture of America and the new aesthetic and poltical movements in France; strong links to Irish culture; 'trans-colonial' connections in the nineteenth century to South Africa; German influences in music culture, and so forth. The framework for cultural modelling, nevertheless, was dominated by the British colonial connection.

What is surprising, I think, is how suddenly and completely this issue dropped out of view and became altogether irrelevant to the contemporary Australian sense of contemporary Australia (thereby also affecting how we understand the past). So thorough and sudden was the shift that I suspect we, in Australia and in Australian studies, are yet to take full account of it.

In the space of a decade, between the early 1960s and early 1970s, the British connection ceased being a source of anxiety, envy or even interest to writers, artists and intellectuals. Of course these shifts are always uneven—in Raymond Williams's terms, residual, dominant and emergent forces co-exist at any one time. But, from the early 1970s, the relationship to Britain was scarcely the issue around which cultural politics would be fought out; it would no longer produce manifestos or movements. Perhaps that is why our famous cultural expatriates in London (Barry Humphries, Clive James, Germaine Greer) often seem rather like stranded whales, frozen in a bubble of time *circa* 1969. At least, they seem that way from Australia.

In the 1980s and 1990s, Britain is scarcely on the horizon of influence for Australian artists and writers. I suspect it would rate behind the USA, France and Italy, S-E Asia, Latin America and Ireland—for example—as a place that 'mattered' culturally. I am not sure where India belongs in such a list, but for many artists, writers and intellectuals it would figure before Britain.

I do not have space to explain in full the reasons for this sudden change. But a few points can be mentioned briefly.

1. The generation reaching maturity at this time were Australia's first television generation. Television was introduced to Melbourne and Sydney in 1956 and to other major centres over the following few years. If we add in the influence of pop music and teenage radio, there is a sense in which this was the first modern 'popular culture generation', although Hollywood had long been with us. This modern popular culture was largely American. Britain had its moments of influence, of course, but youth culture was marked by its sense of contemporaneity rather than its sense of tradition. The meaning of London as a source of popular culture had almost nothing to do with older models of London as an imperial centre.
2. The late-1960s—early-1970s period also saw the development of local TV and film industries. A point that will be relevant to my later argument, both American *and* Australian influence increased at the same time. Australian TV drama rated highly, in terms of viewer preferences, for the first time in the late-1960s, and the variety of locally-made TV genres increased widely. In cinema the Australian Film Development Corporation was established in 1970. This body underwrote many of the films of the Australian film renaissance.
3. In the early 1970s Australia also began to be an exporter of culture. From Sidney Nolan and Patrick White to *Neighbours*, a TV soap opera, and pop/rock performers (Kylie Minogue, AC/DC, INXS), the map of cultural flows has been dramatically redrawn. We are no longer surprised to find Australian programs on television *anywhere* in the world.
4. In cinema, TV, literature, art, popular music, the institutions which define a complex local market began to be established in Australia. This 'market density'—involving training institutions, reviewing and criticism, magazines, local venues, local fans etc.—meant that cultural work could take its primary bearings from its relationship, real or imaginary, to a local audience. Careers could be forged in the local setting.

For many of the younger generation, popular culture was their *first* culture—we might say, their first language. 'High' culture was learnt as a foreign language or approached via popular culture—

from pop to poetry. The changes in the 1960s and 1970s thus grew out of the modern, mass media cultures, helping to produce that breakdown of the barriers between high and popular culture that has been called 'post-modernism'. Most contemporary Australian writers and artists can move happily back and forth across popular and high cultures, as well as across local, national and international cultures.

2. Americanisation

The rise of new forms of popular culture or media culture brought a new problem into view—the problem so often perceived as 'Americanisation'. America in Australian culture has always signified both positive and negative possibilities, and usually at the extremes. It has symbolised 'both the best and worst capitalism can offer': freedom and unlimited consumption, on the one hand, competitive individualism out of control, on the other. 'A mythologised America is routinely deployed in media constructions of utopian *and* dystopian futures for Australia' (Turner, 98-99). America has also symbolised both the best and worst that modernity can offer: 'the gleaming promise of *modernity* or the barbarism of an economically driven consumerism' (Bell and Bell, 203). Perhaps the commonest fears associated with the idea of Americanisation are, first, commercialisation (i.e. the sacrifice of quality or local authenticity for profit) and standardisation (i.e. the breakdown of local cultures, their replacement by a uniform Hollywood, Kentucky Fried, Disneyland culture).

The anxieties about Americanisation and modernity had been heard from intellectuals or middle-class moral guardians since at least the 1920s, although Australian consumers had readily embraced American popular culture. Radicals and conservatives alike shared the fear of Americanisation as a threat to the national culture, for the former, or to cultural tradition, for the latter. A new strand was added in the 1960s and 1970s, a new left-wing critique of US cultural imperialism developed during Australia's involvement in the Vietnam war.

Indeed, there were good reasons to be concerned about US domination of the TV and film industries, and it took government intervention in the 1960s to kick-start local production. With rock'n'roll, television, and mass publishing US popular culture was more readily available (or unavoidable) than it had ever been. But as a model for understanding the post-war explosion of media cultures *in* Australia, the notion of Americanisation was inadequate. It produced a simplistic opposition between Australian and American culture—on the one hand, the local, authentic, down-to-earth, democratic and decent Australian; on the other, the slick, superficial, commercial and decadent American. In this model, American influence could only be perceived negatively, as a threat to the integrity, authenticity and distinctiveness of Australian culture. Australian culture could only be defined as that which was purely, wholly and solely Australian.

Such arguments are misleading in a number of ways, many of which have affected Australian studies. For example, until recently the study of popular culture within Australian studies has worked with the simple opposition between imported and authentic in which Australian popular culture—the real thing, the culture of the people—has been romantically opposed to the mass-produced, imported commercial product. Early cultural studies, with its metaphors of dominant and repressed cultures, often reproduced this same simple opposition.

But let me quickly suggest some reasons why the simple, negative formulation of 'Americanisation' is flawed. For a start, American popular culture has been *part* of Australian popular culture since at least the 1920s; and certainly, since the 1960s if not before, through TV, pop music, radio and cinema, it has become part of the everyday culture of Australians. Second, the assumption that exposure to American popular culture will lead to 'Americanisation'—that is, Australians becoming more like Americans, Australian culture more like American culture—is based on a naive sense of audience reception or cultural consumption. There are similarities and influences of course, and these will increase and decrease over time; but 'Americanisation' will not explain the processes of consumption and transformation whereby Australian culture is thus constituted. Later, for example, I will argue that American popular culture has been a direct cause of Australia's cultural renaissance since the 1970s. Third, a little bit of historical work will show that American influence has been markedly uneven across time and across different cultural domains and sectors of the society. The thesis of 'increasing Americanisation' (to the critics, it's *always* increasing) won't stand up to analysis.

The new models of cultural influence and originality which have developed over the last decade have been attempts to respond to precisely these issues.

3. Positive Unoriginality

I have given this section the puzzling title 'Positive Unoriginality' for reasons I hope will become clear a little later. In the 1980s, the increasing sophistication of the Australian television system, the rise of a local popular music industry and the success of Australian cinema (not least movies like *Crocodile Dundee* and *Mad Max* which seemed to outdo the Americans at their own game) compelled cultural analysts to look for new models of explanation.

Graeme Turner addresses the question in his recent book *Making it National* through a brief analysis of Movie World, a Hollywood theme-part situated on Queensland's Gold Coast, a mixture of working movie studio and scaled-down Disney-style theme park. Run by Warner Bros, Australian film is virtually absent. If anything were an example of vulgar Americanisation, this is it!

Rather than dismissing it, however, Turner wants to take seriously the pleasures which Movie World offers its Australian visitors. Rather than seeing them merely as victims of American cultural imperialism, or seeing 'bad (American) culture' driving out 'good (Australian) culture', he wants to locate Movie World more substantially in its social context. After all, it's beside the point to criticise Movie World for its Americanness as this is the *whole* point—it offers Australians the opportunity to 'immerse themselves in the culture of American popular cinema'. It offers 'an idealised, timeless America' through the reiteration of movie references throughout the park.

The key point, for Turner, is that for the Australian viewer 'this is extremely pleasurable because it manages to be both exotic and familiar at the same time'. Hollywood on the Gold Coast is exotic but the pleasure of recognition is also strong, for Hollywood is also familiar, part of Australians' own cultural experience. Participation involves a recognition of one's *own* formative cultural influences, as well as the thrill of participating in something 'foreign'. Turner even sees the unavoidable sense of 'fakeness' at Movie World as part of its (serious) meaning for its Australian audience.

In a move typical of this new phase of cultural modelling, Turner also breaks down the simple Australia-America opposition by drawing attention to actual industry effects. In other words, he is not interested in essentialising generalisations such as Australian culture or Australian popular culture—at least not without breaking these down into their component parts: industrial, economic, governmental and so forth. The Movie World studios, for example, although part-American owned, have in fact played a substantial role in establishing a local, Queensland film production industry. American and Australian, in other words, can be complementary rather than in conflict.

Notions of American cultural imperialism or domination cannot explain the experience, the meanings, of something like Movie World in Australia. Audiences or visitors are not simply seduced or dominated; the pursuit of the real pleasures which Movie World offers need not imply gullibility. What's involved, rather, is what John Caughie has called 'playing at being American'. That is, enjoying the sense of recognition and 'insidership' re American culture but always with a sense of difference or distance from it, an 'ironic knowingness'. (A common expression of dissatisfaction with a popular culture experience in Australia is to comment, where appropriate, 'It's too American'.)

This is not to deny the power of American mass culture to influence cultural identities, but it does suggest that the cultural transactions which occur between Australian consumers and American cultural products are more complex, and in a sense more *creative*, than the simple model of Americanisation allows.

The movie *Crocodile Dundee* has been analysed by Meaghan Morris as a perfect example of this 'ironic knowingness'. The film and its lead actor have been taken, overseas and in Australia, as typically Australian. Crocodiles are now an inseparable part of every northern tourist promotion. But what is more interesting is that in Australia the film was also criticised, and for two apparently contradictory reasons: for being 'too American' and for being 'too Australian'. As to the latter, it was said to be a mere recycling of the old nationalist myths, the bushman, the larrikin, the outback. As to the former, it was criticised for having 'sold out' to Hollywood. It was yet another sign of (increasing) Americanisation, merely imitating American models (the western, Tarzan) in an attempt to break into the US market.

By contrast, Morris suggests the film is doing much more than simply imitating American models. Her argument turns on what she calls the film's 'positive unoriginality'. The term sounds like a paradox because our aesthetics since romanticism values originality in culture above all else. What does she mean? Morris contrasts three models of 'unoriginality'. The first, the most orthodox, assumes it is a bad thing, a product of cultural imperialism, giving rise to second-hand imitations in Australia against which critics value 'positive authenticity'—films like *Breaker Morant* perhaps. Australian literature is often celebrated by readers outside Australia rather in this manner, as if it were the last purely original literature in the world!

The second position holds that 'unoriginality' is the only thing, the natural and necessary thing, in modern times. Australia is just one part of an international western (Hollywood) culture, so the quest for cultural specificity is old hat. From this perspective, film-makers would attempt to make Hollywood movies in Australia without feeling any need to reference the local cultural context. The third perspective is 'positive unoriginality'. The position she describes goes beyond the kind of Australian-American opposition into which the other two views are locked. It rejects neither Hollywood nor Australian contexts.

In the case of *Crocodile Dundee* she refers to the way the film knowingly, ironically, exploits familiarity with Hollywood film styles and the Hollywood marketplace. In many ways it is wholly inside these Hollywood styles. But rather than simply imitating them, the film uses and re-works them for its own purposes, for creating a series of meanings specifically for its local Australian audience. Not least among these are jokes at the expense of America, and American popular culture. As Morris suggests, the film's pale imitations of Davey Crockett and Tarzan have the effect of 'disadvantaging the original'. The whole film in a way is a joke at Hollywood's expense.

Morris isn't necessarily celebrating the film. In fact she doesn't like its politics much at all. What she's doing rather is attempting to describe the cultural conditions which made it possible and how the film so successfully manages these cultural conditions. As Turner suggests, *Crocodile Dundee* takes 'deadly aim' at both its major markets, US and Australian. Whereas for American audiences it provided a new story of frontier, for Australian audiences the point was in part the film's 'ironic knowingness' about American gullibility while satisfying the audiences's desire for America or for 'playing at being American'. It was, Morris suggests, a kind of 'takeover fantasy', reversing the usual direction of cultural and commercial flows.

The *Mad Max* films are another example of positive unoriginality. The concept turns around our pre-conceptions about cultural originality. Borrowing or 'poaching' styles is not seen as the opposite of originality. Australia's long-standing insidership to American popular culture can therefore be seen as, potentially, a positive rather than negative condition, enabling certain forms of creativity rather than simply being destructive. Rather than predicting ever-increasing American domination, the term allows for a model of Australian originality (as it were) within a transnational cultural system—interdependent rather than wholly independent.

Other critics are even more up-beat about this reading of Australian culture. McKenzie Wark has written that 'the great virtue of Australian culture is its unoriginality—that it borrows shamelessly from all manner of foreign sources, that it adapts and collages'. For Wark, a healthy national culture is one which 'borrows what it chooses from what the global economy would thrust upon it'; and one which can sustain a dialogue with foreign and local at the same time, where the global influences but does not determine the local. 'That Australian content is assisted, but nevertheless has to compete for attention with imported product, means that Australian artists genuinely seek out audiences locally, and . . . find their images and stories resonate more subtly with the range of desires within this culture than their competitors'.

Again, the idea of importation or borrowing is not seen as the opposite of originality or even cultural distinctiveness. Australia's 'adoption and adaptation of other cultures is precisely its strength'. And this applies both to 'high' and 'popular' cultures. In this new mode of cultural modelling, certain perspectives from popular culture and popular culture studies have, as it were, infected how we might understand Australian literature as well. Borrowing, repetition and appropriation have long been recognised (and celebrated) in popular culture and cultural studies in contrast to the realm of high art with its celebration of originality and uniqueness. Such neat distinctions no longer make much sense of the world.

A more sober and sustained analysis is provided in Tom O'Regan's book, *Australia's Television Culture* (and his more recent book, *Australian National Cinema*). The charge of Americanisation has been strongest in relation to TV, so one of the book's main questions is: 'Does Australia have a distinctive television service?' O'Regan's answer is yes, but this answer is always relative. Note again the tendency to resist generalisations in the name of the national culture: 'Australia's television culture is distinctive but shares much with British, US, Canadian and New Zealand systems. Its distinctiveness is best understood as a point somewhere between two seemingly opposed positions: Australian television as a particular *invention* of television and Australia's television as simply an *imitation* of the transnational form of television. . . . These two positions may seem mutually exclusive but are, nonetheless, complementary. Some aspects of Australian television are original, others are a copy or close adaptation, while others—perhaps the majority—are a mixture of originality and adaptation.' This position in between is what defines its distinctiveness. Australian television functions 'in an *interdependent* fashion within a larger transnational television system'.

O'Regan carefully 'disaggregates' the question of American domination. First, at the level of institutions, he describes Australia's mixed commercial and public television structure (two of the free-to-air networks are government owned, three are commercial). While this resembles US models in some respects and UK models in others, it has produced a distinctive set of institutions, policies and practices. Structural similarities do not equal 'Americanisation'.

Second, he dissolves the simple opposition between local and imported (Australian and American) by arguing that Australian TV operates on four levels: local, regional, national and international. There is no simple contradiction between the levels—the local might sometimes support the national, sometimes contradict it; so too the international. And audiences move easily between the four scales on a nightly basis. O'Regan concludes that national cultures 'are formed at the intersection of international, national, regional and local scales'.

Third, at the level of programming, he shows that there are good economic reasons why US programs are imported. In the high-budget production areas (drama and comedy series) they are cheaper, and in fact they can be used to cross-subsidise Australian production. The situation is quite complex and varied. US imports comprise about 50% of programming, but its spread is very uneven. It is clustered into certain time bands and certain kinds of programs. On the other hand, many Australian-made programs are based on US programs. Sometimes this is a formal arrangement; Australian producers purchase a US program format and then make a local version, adapting it to fit local tastes, using local talent etc. Other borrowings are less formal, for example, attempts to replicate or rather invent Australian versions of US successes like *Melrose Place*. Other similarities arise because of the family resemblances in the television cultures.

Given this situation, it's not surprising that Australian TV has been criticised both for being too American (too many US imports and copies) and for not being American enough (our copies are only second-rate imitations). O'Regan's response recalls the idea of positive unoriginality. Like Morris, he stresses adaptation and borrowing as creative acts, as programs are given an Australian inflection regardless of their similarity to the imported model. Critics are mistaken, he says, to continually label Australian differences as flaws, and equally mistaken to label cultural similarities as evidence of 'endemic Australian unoriginality'. Australian programs have differentiated themselves from imported models as a way of inserting themselves into the local TV market—this is clear in drama series, police shows, soap operas etc.

Finally, at the level of audiences, he argues that exposure to

US programs has not made Australians more American per se but it has endowed them with a particular 'imagining' of America. As the idea of 'playing at being American' suggests, part of the pleasure might indeed be the sense of distance (and distinctiveness), an ironic sense of how different the world on the screen and the world all around the screen really are. Australians, he suggests, take television a lot less seriously than do Americans. We use TV differently.

Recalling McKenzie Wark, O'Regan concludes that 'Australia is a good place to watch television' with its mix of imported and local programming and mixed commercial-public structure. Imported programming is both competition to local programming and complementary to it. Australian audience allegiances attach in equal measure to both. It is a more open TV service than the American, British or Japanese, which are self-contained, even parochial. Satellites and cable change that less than we might imagine.

The distinctive nature of Australia's television culture comes from its status as a medium-sized television service, with imports central rather than marginal to its operation, although in fact Australia has a remarkably strong TV export business. Like the other writers discussed, O'Regan does not see importing or borrowing, on one hand, and originality and distinctiveness, on the other, as mutually exclusive. He does not see resemblances as signs of unoriginality (in the negative sense!). America is a structural condition of the Australian culture's operation not its inevitable doom.

4. Conclusion

In all these arguments, the opposition between American and Australian cultures is disaggregated into a much more complex, varied, open-ended and *mundane* process of cultural exchange and transformation. The influence of American culture is acknowledged, but this is broken down into its specific component parts—economic relationships, policy, institutions, cultural production, and audience reception or participation. The global charge of 'Americanisation' doesn't make much sense when seen in this light (or these many lights). Further, this enables us to argue that American influence has not been wholly destructive or disabling; it has been productive both for cultural producers and consumers. The attributes which have traditionally been seen as Australia's cultural disadvantage—its lack of a local ancient cultural tradition (at least a European one), its youth, its vulnerability to outside influence—are seen instead as cultural advantages.

Australia has developed a distinctive popular culture out of its mix of local and imported ingredients but this will continue to have close family resemblances to US and to a lesser extent British models given their dominant place in the transnational English-language cultural system. Australia's position, at once inside and outside these two cultures, gives it a necessarily mixed, hybrid, modern culture. (There are parallels here with post-colonial theory which I have not explored.) What the new models of cultural transference have done is to understand this position in positive terms as defining Australia's distinctiveness rather than taking it as a sign of mere derivativeness or domination. Australia's 'unoriginality' in this sense is the very condition of its originality. And this has not just been in popular culture. American popular culture also played a crucial role in the Australian *literary* renaissance, for example, in the 1970s.

Indeed, rather than being a force for Americanisation, I would strongly argue that TV in Australia, to take this one instance, has over the last two decades been a major force for 'Australianisation' if we can invent the word for the moment. Through its wide range of local programming, from soap operas to historical mini-series, travel and lifestyle programs, and nature or landscape documentaries, Australian television has played a central role in creating and redefining a national identity, even a series of national identities for Australians. Television, it has been said, is always an essentially local medium.

We don't need to be pleased with all the versions of Australian identity which have thereby been put forward but I think we do have to recognise the extent of TV's role in teaching Australians that they live in a distinctive country geographically, ethnically and culturally, and in heightening awareness of the differences between Australian and British or American societies. Television, above all, is where the nation happens. Literature, today, has *another* role in contemporary society, a role for which we have scarcely begun to find the right words.

WORKS CITED

Philip Bell and Roger Bell. *Implicated: The United States in Australia*. (Melbourne: Oxford University Press, 1993).

David Carter. 'The Wide Brown Land on the Small Grey Screen: Television and Australian Nature,' *Journal of Australian Studies* (forthcoming), 1997.

John Caughie. 'Playing at Being American: Games and Tactics' in Mellenkamp, ed., *Logics of Television* (Indiana: Indiana University Press, 1990), 44-58.

Meaghan Morris. 'Tooth and Claw: Tales of Survival, and Crocodile Dundee' in *The Pirate's Fiancee: Feminism, Reading, Postmodernism* (London: Verso, 1988), 241-69.

Tom O'Regan. *Australia's Television Culture* (Sydney: Allen & Unwin, 1993)

______. *Australian National Cinema* (London: Routledge, 1996).

Graeme Turner. *Making it National: Nationalism and Australian Popular Culture* (Sydney: Allen & Unwin, 1994).

McKenzie Wark. 'Media Law and Policy to Suit All', *Australian*, 6 December, 1995.

Post-Humanities: Re-Configuring Disciplines and Connecting Knowledges

DAVID MCKIE
Edith Cowan University, Western Australia

Cyborgology is proliferating as profligately as its subject, but it is still a small enough field to be treated comprehensively. Cyborgology as an academic attitude started with her [Donna Haraway's] 1985 'Manifesto'. (Gray, Mentor, & Figueroa-Sarriera, 1995: 7-8)

A discipline, and I'll justify my use of that term as I go, as currently fashionable as COKOCO ('Constructing the Knowledge of Cybernetic Organisms'), can transform, or more appropriately morph, 'academic discipline' into 'academic attitude' with ease. Aggressive as a Schwarzenegger-style Terminator from 21st century Los Angeles, cybergologists effortlessly meld the medieval, even ecclesiastical, frames of traditional knowledge with new science and new academic fields as well as old science fiction.

Instead of dismissing the cyberologist position as yet another postmodern, and high-tech, liberty, I want to track back to earlier days at two time-hallowed western universities, detour through recent campus wars in the USA, and then track forward to a reconfiguration of disciplines via a postcolonial perspective on the role of English studies in relation to imperialism in India. En route I expand the cyborgology position to challenge Cardinal Newman's famous 19th century 'idea of a university' as 'that true enlargement of mind which is the power of viewing many things at once as one whole, of referring them severally to their true place in the universal system' (Newman, 1852/1947: 23). The itinerary has two main aims: to show how attitudes to education, even at the heartland of the higher education system which has so influenced Australia and India, stamped subsequent claims to universal knowledge with specific local markings; and to sketch out a new alignment for humanities in the Australian university system in the late 1990s.

A brief history of academic attitudes

My first examples come from earlier days at Edinburgh and Glasgow Universities. All undergraduates at these ancient universities had, on matriculation, to make a solemn promise, known as the sponsio academica. At Edinburgh each undergraduate student promised to be 'dutiful and industrious' in their studies and graduands promised 'to abide in all due loyalty to the University' to their 'latest breath'; at Glasgow the equivalent undergraduate had to declare: 'I will not wilfully damage the fabric and furnishings of the University and will make good, to the satisfaction of the Senatus, any damage caused by me' (cited in Truscot, 1951: 199). At this point I should perhaps own up to being not only a graduate of Glasgow but someone who still sides with its ongoing tradition of rumbustiousness—albeit now directed towards the traditional tertiary webbing of knowledges rather than the physical campus fabric.

Perhaps that has some bearing on why I work within the rather disreputable, often termed 'Mickey Mouse', disciplines of cultural and media studies. Their canons tend to put Baz Luhrmann, director of Strictly Ballroom, on the curriculum before Patrick White, prefer the cyberian rhapsodies of VNS Matrix to Australian opera, and place queer theory ahead of straight criticism. By 1990 the success of cultural studies as a study configuration had drawn the acronym accolade of YUMDie, for 'young upwardly mobile discipline' (Hebdige, 1990: ix). By 1996 the strength of the backlash against the success of cultural studies left visible, and virtual—see documents available on the web at Sokal's home page (Sokal)—public traces in the Alan Sokal affair (the so-called science wars), and the struggles over political correctness (the so-called PC wars).

Identifying cybergology as a strong candidate for a future YUMDie award, I contend that its use of 'academic attitude' should be extended to encompass the very core of discipline constitution and reconstitution. In making the argument, this paper draws heavily on the work of a number of communication theorists (who have established criteria for re-classifying disciplines), looks at rationales for discipleship and questions my own personal and political rationalisations as one of the many academics operating within the lowest division of Australian universities. Finally, I will set those arguments amidst theoretical and practical concerns with the politics of disciplinarity configurations in relation to students as publics especially for cultural studies, English studies and business studies.

Disciplines and publics

Calling for papers for the Journal of Communication's special issue on 'The Future of the Field—Between Fragmentation and Cohesion', the editors claimed, 'Communication scholarship lacks disciplinary status because it has no core of knowledge. Thus institutional and scholarly legitimacy remains a chimera for the field' (Gurevitch & Levy, cited in Shepherd, 1993: 83). Now, given my Glaswegian origins, I am someone far from averse, at least theoretically, to illegitimacy and that particular exclusion may not seem much of a problem. Moreover, as a product of schools intended for the British general public and not the so-called 'public' schools reserved almost exclusively for the rich, I have no desire for discipline's historical-semantic connections with the seventeenth century description of 'strict discipline' as an art of correct training (Walhausen cited in Foucault, 1977: 170).

Where I do have problems is with the allegation that a lack of disciplinary status stems from the absence of a 'core of knowledge' or foundational set of ideas. That would make communication and cultural studies, for example, no more than parasites feeding off real disciplines. Instead, following Greg Shepherd, I take the view that 'disciplines are defined not by cores of knowledge (i.e., epistemologies) but by views of Being (i.e., ontologies)' (Shepherd, 1993: 83). That is to say more by attitude than by content. Etymological considerations lend weight to Shepherd's thesis. The word 'discipline' itself, derives from the Latin disciplina, or instruction of disciples, and disciples, in turn, are instructed in a doctrine or indoctrinated by doctors so that 'Berkeley could write that to be "undisciplined" is to be "nurtured to no doctrine"' (83). In short, therefore, academic disciplines have depended more on faith, indoctrination and training than on any core of knowledge, and are distinguished more how they look than by what they know.

My chosen territory for exemplifying Shepherd's thesis is the human body. In taking this topic and approach I echo Foucault's *Discipline and Punish* in more than my section heading: 'There can be no question here of writing the history of different disciplinary institutions, with all their individual differences. I simply intend to map on a series of examples' (Foucault, 1977: 139). Nevertheless, in humorous fashion, but with serious intent, I propose to map a series of micro examples of how different bodies of knowledge raise distinctly different questions about the same object, the human body. My intention is to illustrate how neither content nor knowledge make a discipline unique.

In practice, from anthropology through physics to zoology, the distinction of each discipline arises from the particular view of existence it adopts. So, anthropology, as the study of conscious human bodies in interaction across cultures, might pose the question of how similar or how different the tribal body is from the urban body? Astronomy, concerned with more celestial bodies, might consider the human body as infinitesimal fragments of planetesimals, and ponder the distance between extraterrestrial dust and flesh and blood. For chemistry, considering a body as metabolised carbon compounds, the key question might be how those compounds are constituted? Literary studies, less attached to the solid and more concerned with the imaginative, might be concerned to find out how representable the body is? On the other hand, physics, still searching for the God particle, might want to know how reducible? Cultural studies might wonder how the body means and, perhaps cruelly, I might pose the key public relations question as how influential the particular body might be?

Mother stuff and founding fathers

The one point I want to make in this extraordinarily crude exercise is that attitude to whatever is being studied is what distinguishes disciplines. Shepherd expands the point by posing a series of questions about the characterisation of disciplinary ontology:

> Is existence best understood as cultural, creative or chromosomal? Is the foundation for all best thought of as the molecule, a commodity, or time? Is ontology best viewed as rational, material, or governmental? (84)

From his standpoint disciplinary ontologies become imperfect approximations of how they look at the world: 'They depend on disciples acting as advocates for the ontology they put forward, making implicit and explicit claims that their view "matters" (i.e., is of the "mother stuff" from the Latin mater)' (84). Obviously this matters to new disciplines but why should they matter at this conference of 'creative configurations' in Kerala in 1996? Since this conference draws mainly from English and literary studies I think a great deal. English studies itself demonstrates how a discipline is capable of emerging and changing over time. Moreover, the formative attitude of English studies is intimately connected to historical happenings on this subcontinent. My understanding of this period derives from the work of Gauri Viswanathan (1989, 1995) who observed 'the irony that English literature appeared as a subject in the curriculum of the colonies long before it was institutionalized in the home country' (1989: 3). She convincingly locates 'its rootedness in strategies of sociopolitical control' (1989: 166), its role in attacking non-Christian religions and its support for grossly exploitative British imperialism.

But it is not just English studies which is undergoing a scrutiny of its myth of origin, so forgive me one last hyper-European retrospective. In accounting for the lack of status given to communication, various writers take us back to a core bifurcation at the birth of the modern as the 17th century with three key figures and processes: Galileo Galilei's trial defence; Descartes' deployment of scientific method; and John Locke's dethroning of the linguistic, other than as a carrier of the idea, as insubstantial, untrustworthy and valueless (see Peters, 1989). Acting as a kind of unconscious affinity group, this trinity's crucial break with the past was to separate the world into linguistic and nonlinguistic spheres with all the power residing in the latter. Working contre-Derrida, they saw the real as existing only outside of texts and, indeed, it is hard not to see poststructuralism and Baudrillardian postmodernism as the vengeful return of the repressed verbal. In concert these three historical figures laid special claim to 'reality knowledge' by distinguishing it from words, talk and rhetoric. That claim reduced communication to an immaterial and inessential status, to a process without any kind of legitimacy, and to no more than a shoddy secondhand vehicle for the 'real', whether that be material things or pure ideas.

This narrative of origins would not be complete without addressing the role played by the overarching, or more accurately undermining, metadivide between science and culture. This split organises different disciplines into separate camps of different status. And of course status, because it translates directly into differential resourcing and funding, is crucial. As late as the 1960s, in an article entitled 'Social factors in the origins of a new science: the case of psychology', two sociologists argued that the sheer quantity of human resources became the very basis of a scientific discipline: 'The uninterrupted growth of a scientific field depends upon the existence of a scientific community permanently devoting itself to the field' (Ben-David & Collins, 1966: 451).

Disabled by being, in theory and practice, the binary opposite of science, the humanities loses out in human and other resources: CSIRO, for example, gets more research money than the whole university system and science and medicine research budgets far exceed humanities ones. I do not have the Australian figures to hand but doubt if the situation is likely to be much better than Newfield's assessment of the US in the early 1990s:

> Financial incentives are vastly more influential in creating university policy than any group's programmatic desires. Likening the funding behind a university's government contracts or corporate partnerships to any potentially 'subversive' humanities projects is like comparing a TV station to a filing cabinet. The $10 million [$US] spent at my campus [University of California] last year [1992] through Department of Defense contracts equals the amount budgeted this year by the four national humanities agencies for all national humanities research fellowships. (Newfield, 1993: 311)

It is because of the prestige, and its associated funding, that, from the 'physics envy' of economists to the annual scientific conferences of the International Association of Media and Communication Research, there are more probably more aspirants to scientific status, or scientific wannabes, than there are Madonna wannabes.

Science rules and environmental exclusions

This prestige can be traced back to my trinity of dead white European males. First there is the role played by Galileo. Facing life-and-soul threatening religious prosecution for adhering to the avant-garde position that the earth moved round the sun, Galileo rested his defence on a crucial distinction between the language of words, as found in the bible, and the language of nature, as found in mathematics and scientific equipment. The former, he claimed as subject to interpretation; the latter as 'inexorable and immutable' (cited in Boorstin, 1985: 323). This cunning demarcation failed to carry his individual battle with the cardinals, but it did lead to a substantial, if posthumous, victory for future scientists.

On hearing the news of Galileo's defeat Descartes piously, or prudently, shelved his pro-Copernican writings. He also, methodically, set out scientific method as the methodology for deriving truth and an early giant TOE, or theory of everything. In this Cartesian project the secular version of the famed mind of God, supposedly still almost within the compass of recent physicists and cosmologists, would be sought in the God of Mind supported by mathematical and geometric principles. The third member of the trinity, philosopher John Locke, closed the door on communication as constitutive by making words mere conveyers of meanings, dangerous distortions of pure ideas. That triple matrix of idealists, allied with the physical and economic success of new science-based commerce and manufacturing, birthed communication into modernity as foundationless, as no more than a vehicle. The resultant offspring can be observed in ripe maturity when Stephen Hawking's (1988) *A Brief History of Time* complacently dismisses Wittgenstein's perception that 'The sole remaining task for philosophy is the analysis of language' with 'What a comedown' (175).

At this conference more participants would probably opt for Wittgenstein's view that to 'imagine a language is to imagine a form of life' (Wittgenstein, 1953: 19) than see the analysis of language as a 'comedown'. Nevertheless questions remain. How? and what? can we creatively configure which might arrest three centuries of devaluation? and how can we do it in a climate where technoscience-based commerce and manufacturing retains cultural, economic and political dominance? What disciplinary configuration and what distinctive perspective on reality can we offer in a climate of economic fundamentalism? From my experience, much of the best of English, cultural and communication studies at the tail end of the 20th century stems for their good attitude (to shift to the political rather than the disciplinary dimension), towards egalitarianism. But to retain disciplinary status, or more personally, my discipleship, all of them require a radical attitude shift towards including, rather than excluding, the nonhuman.

As I was unable through ill health to attend the conference in person, I do not know for sure but would be surprised if many papers engaged with environmental issues in general and non-anthropocentric ones in particular. This neglect is not the case in some other non-scientific disciplines. Recently, as part of a move into the academic discipline of public relations I attended various academic and industry practitioner gatherings and found the large scale attention to environmental issues a welcome change. To my pleasant surprise I found that the world's leading public relations academic, James Grunig, advocated the first of public relations' presuppositions as 'Humanity's relationship to nature' whereby 'unhealthy organizations see their relationship to the environment as one of dominance or subjugation' and 'healthy organizations treat the stakeholders in the environment as 'fellow human beings' and try to alleviate the impact of a crisis on them as well as on the organization (Grunig & White, 1992: 45). That kind of an anthropomorphism is commonplace to many in India but I doubt very much that it was a major concern of Australians at this or other conferences. After a decade of conference attendance I can safely claim that they tend to be embedded in the Western Intellectual Tradition, or TWIT, to use psychologist Robert Ornstein's suggestive acronym (see Jagtenberg & McKie, 1997). One of the more creative moves we Australians might make to improve our disciplinary attitudes would be to be more respectful of indigenous traditions and the religious and cultural traditions of ancient civilisations such as India.

Post-humanities: Students as publics

We must also play theoretical attention to our key stakeholders, the existing and potential student body. If the post-humanities arc not to resemble post-industrial cities that is to say to have virtually no humanities presence as many of the cities have virtually no industrial presence, that is one public all disciplines must acknowledge. To remain, without much government support, viable, as well as ethical, then disciplines will have to attract students in large numbers. As Grossberg put it, 'you don't win by being moral' but 'by being effective' (cited in Slack, 1994: 11). So, since the status quo becomes less and less an option in tertiary education, how are disciplines such as English, communication and cultural studies to retain or increase their attractiveness? At my present university, as in the rest of Australia, there has been a shift in student desires from the old humanities (e.g., classics and European languages) to the new humanities (e.g., communication studies and media studies). The shift has more recently been accompanied by a downturn in job opportunities and a vocationalism as discernible in school leaver preferences as in the talk of Liberal government spokespeople.

So what will this intensified public desire create? Will the growth of nakedly functional courses become exponential? I contend that severe attitudinal adjustments will be required to engage with student vocationalism and that a continued binary opposition to business is one of them. Otherwise the growth of nakedly functional, and rapidly changing, courses might become exponential. At my own institution I recently participated in a sparse little gathering called, rather grandly, 'The Second National Humanities Summit of the Humanities Australia Campaign.' I found myself almost completely out of sympathy with the main tenor of the summit. That can best be gauged by the call to celebrate the victory of a classicist called Homer for defending classics departments in Melbourne and the bemoaning of students who didn't recognise the value of 'the best that had been thought and said' in a range of disciplines within the old humanities. From my viewpoint the survival of classics too frequently depends on taking a disproportionately large share of resources, often generated by the new humanities, to serve a disproportionately small number of students. Moreover both old and new humanities lag behind business in the recruitment of students in general and overseas students in particular.

In his keynote address, Professor Robert Pascoe, Dean of the Faculty of Arts at Victorian University of Technology, and a member of the Humanities Australia Campaign secretariat, proposed the options of humanising business or demonising business with a decided preference for the latter. Is either case a viable option? or will new or renewed disciplinary projects work more explicitly to change consciousness in terms of less growth, greater job sharing and falling standards of living? These are big and relatively unaddressed questions at a meta level; at a micro level they have become part and parcel of many academics' daily concerns. I want to focus them around some of my present activities and sketch the beginnings of a justification for the grandiose use of post-humanities in my title.

In this context Pascoe, who is also from an institution which only recently crossed the tertiary binary divide into university status, made an interesting point. He observed that it was students from relatively deprived backgrounds, understandably seeking qualifications which would gain them some vocational purchase, rather than the offspring of the well-off, who needed to be persuaded to take the humanities. He went on to argue in favour of the humanities and for the 'demonisation' (Pascoe, 1996) of business in a way which, I suspect, would still gain massive support in humanities old and new.

The missing (cyber)link

Rather than see the humanities demonising business I would advocate introducing business students to humanities disciplines and humanities students to business disciplines. Once again Foucault's words seem apposite:

> 'Discipline' may be identified neither with an institution nor with an apparatus; it is a type of power, a modality for its exercise, comprising a whole set of instruments, techniques, procedures, levels of application, targets; it is a 'physic' or an 'anatomy' of power, a methodology. And it may be taken over either by 'specialised' institutions (the penitentiaries or 'houses of correction' of the nineteenth century), or by institutions that use it as an essential instrument for a particular end (schools, hospitals), or by pre-existing authorities that find in it a means of reinforcing or reorganising their internal mechanisms of power. (215)

Similarly, in early English studies in India, Viswanathan (1995) notes how, in 'a crude reworking of the Cartesian axiom, production of thought defined the Englishman's true essence, overriding all other aspects of his identity', especially 'the sordid history of colonialist expropriation' (436). Whether this paper's application of Foucauldian discipline to minor academic reshuffles/ reconfigurations/ rationalisations and the anxieties of one specific intellectual is as apt is another matter. Certainly my ordinary working experience of disciplinarity now concerns gaining a student public for the courses I and my colleagues construct and run. Since the idea that extradisciplinary considerations can be excluded from curriculum categorisation is manifestly unsustainable, then it makes sense to align intelligently with current trends. This becomes more critical as overt disunity, another word for democracy, rumbles invisibly beneath the managerial ethos promoted without debate by 'executive' deans in all faculties.

In a realignment as controversial in cultural studies as in English studies (but not in public relations), strategic alliances may include the formation of working partnerships with business studies. To retain the humanities component in a post-humanities time we might need to take down barriers to business as well as science and the nonhuman environment. While I remain committed to cultural degrees for the sake of the education itself I believe we have to rethink how these might be sustainable in the future and what we can and might offer our students to equip them for an increasingly harsh world. If we do not, people from the business side have already begun to colonise literature and film in new strategies of appropriation and containment.

In conclusion, therefore, I return to another variation on my initial cyborg theme through cyberbusiness, or 'the ever-closer harmonization of people, computer technology and organisational infrastructure' in 'the shared computer-mediated electronic realm of information and communications' (Barnatt, 1995: 5). Christopher Barnatt's (1995) book, entitled *Cyber Business: Mindsets for a Wired Age*, includes a bibliography which features more novels and movies than it does business literature, and throughout his book quotations from Management Today sit alongside analyses of Marge Piercy's (1992) *Body of Glass* and Paul Verhoevan's (1990) *Total Recall*. I believe we too may need to be open towards post-humanities configurations along these lines to survive and to continue offering other creativities as a crucial educational and life resource for students.

WORKS CITED

C. Barnatt. *Cyber Business: Mindsets for a Wired Age* (Chichester: John Wiley. 1995).

J. Ben-David, & R. Collins. 'Social factors in the origins of a new science: The case of psychology.' *American Sociological Review*, 1966, vol. 31, 4. 451-65.

D.J. Boorstin, *The discoverers: A history of man's search to know his world and himself* (New York: Vintage, 1985).

M. Foucault, *Discipline and Punish: The Birth of the Prison*, A. Sheridan, Trans. (Harmondsworth: Peregrine, 1977).

C.H. Gray. H.J. Figueroa-Sarriera, & S. Mentor. 'Cyborgology: Constructing the knowledge of cybernetic organisms.' in C.H. Gray, with the assistance of H.J. Figueroa-Sarriera & S. Mentor, ed., *The Cyborg Handbook* (London: Routledge, 1995), 1-14.

J.E. Grunig & J. White, 'The effect of worldviews on public relations theory and practice,' in J.E. Grunig, ed., *Excellence in Public Relations and Communication Management* (Hillsdale, NJ: Lawrence Erlbaum Associates, 1992), 31-64.

S. Hawking, *A Brief History of Time: From the Big Bang to Black Holes* (New York: Bantam, 1988).

D. Hebdige, 'Subjects in Space,' *New Formations*, vol. 11, Summer, 1990. v-x.

T. Jagtenberg, & D. McKie, *Eco-impacts and the Greening of Postmodernity: New Maps for Communication Studies, Cultural Studies and Sociology* (Seven Oaks, CA: Sage, 1997).

C. Newfield, 'What was political correctness? Race, the right, and managerial democracy in the humanities,' *Critical Inquiry*, vol. 19, Winter, 1993, 308-36.

J. Newman, *The Idea of a University* (New York: Longman-Green, 1852/1947).

R. Ornstein, *Multimind* (Boston: Houghton Mifflin, 1986).

R. Pascoe, The current crisis in the humanities. Paper presented at the Second National Humanities Summit, Perth, Edith Cowan University, October 1996.

J.D. Peters, "John Locke, the individual, and the origin of communication." *Quarterly Journal of Speech*, 1989, vol. 75, 387-99.

A. Sokal, Homepage, http://www.nyu.edu/gsas/dept/physics/faculty/Sokal/index.html.

J. Slack, 'The environment matters: Complicity, ethics, theoretical rigour, intervention.' *Australian Journal of Communication*, 213, 1994, 1-13.

B. Truscot, *Red Brick University* (Harmondsworth: Penguin, 1951).

G. Viswanathan, *Masks of Conquest: Literary Study of British Rule in India* (New York: Columbia University Press, 1989).

______. English literary study in British India. In B.Ashcroft, G. Griffiths & H. Tiffin, ed., *The Post-Colonial Reader* (London: Routledge, 1995).

L. Wittgenstein, *Philosophical Investigations* (Oxford: Blackwell, 1953).

In preparing this paper I gratefully acknowledge the generosity of my colleagues at Edith Cowan University, Professor Alan Black, Dr John Duff and Dr Brian Shoesmith, for not only drawing my attention to useful references but also providing sources used in this paper, and Dr Cynthia vanden Driesen for her understanding and support.

Portrait of a Nation? Children's Literature and National Identity

SHARRYN PEARCE
Queensland University of Technology

In an important article entitled 'Cultural Studies, New Historicism and Children's Literature,' Tony Watkins argues that myths of national identity are woven into children's literature. (Watkins, 1992:173-95) He alleges that *The Wind in the Willows* and *The Wizard of Oz* represent different national responses to fin de siecle changes in English and American society, and in particular to the development of industrialization and technology, and the concurrent changes in the relations between the social classes. According to Watkins, *The Wizard of Oz* is a quintessentially American text in that it presents a vision of a utopian society which is progressive, oriented to the future, and which is part technology and part pastoral (that is, in the kingdom of Oz which merges the industrialized world with the realm of nature). Because the great and powerful wizard turns out to be a common man from Omaha, and Dorothy, the ordinary girl from Kansas, is given a central role and allowed to act as an intrepid pioneer adventurer, while the Scarecrow, the Tin Woodman and the Cowardly Lion all find that they have powers that they had not realised they possessed, Watkins sees *The Wizard of Oz* as encompassing elements of the American national myth in which America is a place of progression where ordinary people—if they learn to be self-reliant—can prosper.

On the other hand, according to Watkins's analysis, the supremely English *The Wind in the Willows* represents a widespread nostalgia on the part of the professional middle classes for a lost rural arcadia, an unchanging England uninfluenced by contemporary events such as the agricultural depression and social unrest in the cities, together with the concurrently alarming changed into adults of desired ideological orientation or social conditioning. From the beginnings of children's literature in the nineteenth century onwards, children's novels have been heavily pedagogical and riddled with the moralism and values of their times. Clearly novels can operate as powerful shapers of children's imaginations and can transmit, consciously or otherwise, myth-like messages about national identity. In the words of one observer:

> Through myths the psychology and world view of our cultural ancestors are transmitted to modern descendants, in such a way and with such power that our perception of contemporary reality and our ability to function in the world are directly affected. (Watkins, 185)

Using Watkins' work as a reference point and base, I should firstly like to examine a text published in Australia in the 1890s—that is, at the same time as *The Wizard of Oz* and *The Wind in the Willows*—in order to examine how this text constructs national identity. This text will then be contrasted with an Australian text published in the last ten years, in order to examine the changing perceptions of national identity in novels aimed at young audiences, as well as the contrasting images of "home".

When Ethel Turner's *Seven Little Australians* was first published in 1894, it created a literary sensation. The Australian edition sold out in seven weeks, and it was reprinted every year for the next twenty years. It has never been out of print, and has spawned radio plays, an ABC television series in 1974 (when the Whitlam government inspired a renaissance in Australian literature), and even a musical. *Seven Little Australians* is probably Australia's best-known children's story—for instance, in a survey in 1980 Geoffrey Dutton found that if Australians read their own literature at all, they had read Australian children's books, notably those of Ethel Turner and her rival, Mary Grant Bruce. (White, 1988:50)

Seven Little Australians is very much a product of its time and place. Like England and America, Australia in the 1890s was undergoing a severe agricultural depression, while technology was producing permanent changes in its social demography. More pertinently, however, there were some factors operating which were unique to this country, and in the years leading up to Federation in 1901, there was a ferment of creative activity, with writers and intellectuals preoccupied with the future directions of the fledgling Australian nation, and the national debate being seasoned by contributions from utopian, socialist, racist and feminist ideas. In particular the 1890s were marked by an aggressive literary nationalism which was promoted particularly by the Sydney *Bulletin*, which advocated republicanism and furthered anti-British feeling, at the same time promoting the superiority of the Australian bushman—that mythic creature born of the yearnings of urban men. The so-called "Bushman's Bible", with its idiosyncratic mix of iconoclastic cartoon humour, radical politics, misogyny and racism, provided the starting point for Ethel Turner's literary career. *The Bulletin*'s Literary Editor, A.G. Stephens, was Turner's mentor, and he placed her as one of the leading figures in Australia's literary birth, alongside Henry Lawson and "the Banjo", announcing "Only one (other) Australian author since Marcus Clarke—Henry Lawson—has had such moving emotional art". (Cited in White, 1988:53) There is little doubt that Turner was heavily influenced by *The Bulletin*'s ethos, especially since it had such a huge impact upon the production of Australian literature and in dictating the tastes of the Australian literary public—in other words, her target readership.

Prior to *Seven Little Australians*, Australian children's literature came predominantly from the United Kingdom. Stories set in Australia showed transplanted British children who showed pluck, dogged tenacity, and an unswerving, implicit belief in Britain's imperial destiny. Australian children behaved like stereotypical products of an English public school. In *Queensland Cousins*, for instance, which is supposedly set on a cane farm in Far North Queensland, the hero Eustace aspires to become a "gentleman" and is appalled when, on a visit to England, someone asks if his family eats with the servants when they are in the colonies. He is equally disgusted when an ignorant English cousin declares that he has read in a book that there are no class distinctions in Australian life, and that men and women meet as equals:

> ". . . rot," said Eustace briefly. "I don't know how you could believe it. Our friends were all gentlemen and ladies. Australians are as particular as you are whom they have for friends" (QC:197).

In an earlier episode, Eustace and his neighbour Bob, a token Australian bushman, are captured by hostile Aborigines and fear for their lives. In these circumstances even the recognisably larrikin bushman loses his cheekiness in order to speak and act like a caricatured upper-class Englishman. Aware that like all heathens these black men have no knowledge of mercy—"They have no Great Example to follow like we have"—Bob turns to Eustace:

> "Buck up, old chap," Bob said softly; "One can only die once. Let's show these black-fellows how a Christian and an Englishman can do it. You'll get the strength right enough; I'm not a bit afraid of your funking" (QC:149).

The typical colonial children's novel is also sharply gender- differentiated. Colonial girls are denied access to these life-threatening but sinew-enhancing dramas, and have a very low profile in these romanticised valourisations of the exploits of juvenile empire-builders. They are not questers, and have no thorny road to womanhood comparable to, say, Eustace's path to manly self-definition. They remain indoors in almost purdah-like confinement, kept there by their male kin, fearful of their defilement by other, lesser races. Their destiny lies in their biology, as future receptacles for further generations of sturdy Anglo-Saxon stock, while their husbands carve a future out of the wilderness. And so colonial girls customarily get the short straw: they reveal that to be born female is to be born into a world which demands submission, passivity and dependency. In *Queensland Cousins*, moreover, the children, with Bob in tow, eventually return to England for good. They are last seen in their ancestral manor house, surrounded by loyal forelock-tugging family retainers:

> "The great house, standing grey, massive and strong in the evening light" makes the children's hearts thrill with pride:

> "This was something better than their own slenderly-built, iron-roofed house in Queensland" (QC:236).

Their heritage intact, Australia for these Queensland cousins recedes into little more than an exotic memory. It is certainly never "home". Unlike *Queensland Cousins*, *Seven Little Australians* is actually the genuine article: a novel written by an Australian (originally born in England) and about "real" Australians. Turner was inspired by *The Bulletin*'s ethos of ardent Australianness, and an identically aggressive nationalism/patriotism is apparent in her famous disclaimer on the first page of *Seven Little Australians* that children born in Australia, unlike those born in England, are ever perfect:

> It may be that the miasmas of naughtiness develop best in the sunny brilliancy of our atmosphere. It may be that the land and the people are young-hearted together, and the children's spirits not crushed and saddened by the shadow of long years' sorrowful history. There is a lurking spectacle of joyousness and rebellion and mischief in nature here, and therefore in children . . . the spirited, single-hearted, loyal ones who alone can "advance Australia" (SLA:7-8).

Turner's coupling of the land and the people is in keeping with the nationalist discourse of the time, in which Australia was regularly presented as a "young" country, immature but vital, eagerly awaiting a future without the strictures enforced by the "mother" country. In her novel there is more than a generation gap dividing Captain Woolcot, English-born and educated at Rugby Public School, and his unruly Australian offspring. Captain Woolcot personifies the rigid world of the English middle class: he endorses the values of correct etiquette, children who are preferably neither seen nor heard, and the imposition of discipline and plenty of it. His cultural outlook is literally worlds apart from that of his children, who are emblematic of the exuberant, informal country of their birth, happy inhabitants of the lawless house known as "Misrule". Whereas the New World children bond affectionately with each other, they have a dutiful but distant relationship with their

Old World father, who is remote, unsympathetic, and preoccupied with his own interests and pleasures (when he sends the children off to their step-mother's parents' property at Yarrahappini, for instance, he suddenly assumes "a jaunty air as if the prospect of two months' bachelordom was not without its redeeming points" (SLA:136). Turner makes it clear that the seven little Australians bring themselves up; their father intrudes upon their freedom only intermittently to reprimand, chastise or beat them, while their sweetly ineffectual stepmother Esther, the mother of the youngest of the seven, is barely older than they are. These children are indomitable, and it takes more than one hapless (perhaps this should read "hopeless") parent to fence them in.

In a collective fashion, the seven little Australians represent the joyous opportunities for life in Australia, and the novel encapsulates the hopes, dreams, uncertainties and fears of an unformed nation prior to Federation. Perhaps these uncertainties and fears are mirrored most closely in the figure of Judy, the lively and extroverted instigator of all the family scrapes, the one child who is contemptuous of authority and consequently most troubles her father:

> Judy always mystified him. He understood her the least of all his children, and sometimes the thought of her worried him. At present she was only a sharp, clever, and frequently impertinent child; but he felt that she was utterly different from the other six, and it gave him an aggrieved kind of feeling when he thought about it, which was not very often. . . . That restless fire of hers that shone out of her dancing eyes, and glowed scarlet on her cheeks in excitement, and lent amazing energy and activity to her young, lithe body, would either make a noble, daring, brilliant woman of her, or else she would be shipwrecked on rocks the others would never come to, and it would flame up higher and higher and consume her (SLA:28).

Towards the end of the novel, Judy, brimful of promise and life, is felled by a gumtree while saving the life of her smallest brother. In one sense Judy's death is one of the great set-pieces of Victorian writing, catering to established tastes for sentimentality and melodrama. Turner herself was quite cheerful about it all—"killed Judy to slow music" she wrote in her diary on October 18 1893. She certainly contrived an effective death scene, including the requisite references to rejoining her dead mother, the final prayers being said in a quavering voice by her older sister Meg, and Judy's last, lingering look at her soulmate and favourite brother, Pip. But there are significant differences from the usual scenario—in *Little Women*, for instance (a work upon which *Seven Little Australians* is quite closely based, with Turner even being promoted as "the Australian Alcott"), good, angelic Beth resignedly departs the world in a pious, self-effacing manner. In contrast Judy hogs the limelight, refuses to leave, and in her own characteristic way fights off the blandishments of death for as long as she can.

Why, then, does Judy die? Judy can be portrayed as a victim of a patriarchal society which ultimately punishes her (in the strictest possible way, it has to be said) for her unconventionality, her wilful disregard for the niceties of the traditional female role, her refusal to be typecast as a submissive female, forever following in the lead of her wiser, protective, brothers. Indeed, her position at the centre of the Woolcot family is then superseded by "Little Mother Meg", who has learnt through suffering, and particularly by witnessing her headstrong sister's death, to be more mature, gentler, and purer (in short, she becomes something of a martyr, with the typically Victorian air of other-worldly, self-sacrificing resignation). Actually Meg has learnt to be a perfect lady, in the Ruskin-like terms appropriate to nineteenth century discourse. In the course of time, Meg will become an ethereal angel-wife, and a caring, nurturing force in the correct domestic realm, maintaining the family unit and keeping the family happy and harmonious.

Yet there are some problems with this otherwise persuasive analysis. For Judy's "indomitable spirit and pluck" is certainly in keeping with a specifically "Australian type" of girl which was much celebrated in pre- and post-Federation times, and whose chief virtue lay in the fact that she was anything but a replica of her English counterpart. According to many contemporary writers and journalists the enviable climate ensured that the Australian girl enjoyed a much freer life than girls elsewhere, and as a consequence was more resourceful and lively. Judy is a literary embodiment of what journalists, in particular, were lauding as the most wholesome and splendid companion in the world—even, at times, a kind of surrogate mate (in the words of one enthusiast, "a really good pal"). (Garth, 1908:1006) According to the nationalist discourse of the times, which was then inextricably intertwined with notions of racial identity, this happy, hearty, and wholesome girl inevitably became the nation's hope for the future, the superb wife and mother of tomorrow, a glowing advertisement for White Australia. As one writer put it, the girl "whose qualities render her so eminently companionable from a masculine point of view" proves to be also "an ideal mother from a nursery point of view—and here nursery and nationality are interchangeable terms." (Garth, 1007) This same author was blunter elsewhere, when he noted that the Australian girl "almost inevitably makes a good housewife. Whatever the army of dyspeptic husbands who may choose to deny it, there are more girls per thousand in Australia who can cook an eatable meal than in any other English-speaking country." (Garth, 1009)

Certainly the special childhood freedoms deemed the privilege of all Australian children, regardless of their gender, stand in ironic contrast to the restrictions customarily placed on the nation's women. Yet some deft authors, Mary Grant Bruce included, managed to transform their tomboyish heroines into exceptional wife and mother material (and after all, years before, Louisa May Alcott did the same thing with Jo March, proving that biology will always win out over brains). More probably, perhaps, Judy is ousted because girls only have a limited time to share the nationalist space with their brothers. Nationalist discourse in the 1890s, as Susan Sheridan (1995) and Marilyn Lake (1986) have both shown, was controlled by the men, and the women were relegated to marginal positions within it. Significantly it is at Esther's parents' property in the bush (the "real" Australia) where Judy's brother Pip comes into his own. In this, the key nationalistic "centre" of the novel, Judy is not allowed, despite her pleadings, to participate in the campdrafting, but Pip does so: "clad in a crimean shirt and a pair of old serge trousers fastened around the waist with a leather belt, in which an unsheathed bowie knife, freshly sharpened, was jauntily stuck. No persuasions would induce him either to wear a coat or sheath the knife" (SLA:155). As he leaves, he shouts, "Hurrah, Fizz! . . . What 'ud you give to change places?" (SLA:155), and upon his return he signifies their future roles in life. He will become a stockman, and Judy will be relegated to the sidelines, becoming his aide-de-camp, "provided he let her stay in the saddle, and provided her with a whip just as long as his own" (SLA:159). It is now clear that Judy cannot contest the nationalist arena with her brother; and that from puberty onwards she must be content to play second fiddle. Already weakened from her previous exposure to the bush (when she walked seventy miles home from the boarding school where she had been sent by her exasperated father), Judy's end proves conclusively that the bush is no place for a woman. In keeping with the tradition of women being imprisoned in the bush (Judy's grave is on the station), Turner echoes the ideology of other nineteenth century writers, who routinely depicted women as being physically trapped in their rooms, attics or their father's or husband's houses, as if their very femininity is sanctioned by their incarceration in their future "realm". These metaphorical indications of women's physical, economic and emotional imprisonment are, in fact, a striking feature of the adult radical-nationalist literature of the 1890s, and are perhaps most evocatively seen in Barbara Baynton's *Bush Studies*, (1902) including the grotesque "Squeaker's Mate", where the woman is paralysed by a falling tree and left to fester in an outhouse while her worthless husband is free to squander her money and sell her possessions, or the even grimmer piece, "The Chosen Vessel", in which a brutal husband is miles away shearing while his terrified wife with a babe in arms is confined to the house as a swagman systematically tests the walls to find the most convenient way to enter the house in order to rape her. Significantly when she leaves her prison/sanctuary she is caught, violated and murdered. In Turner's discourse, too, the bush offers freedom to the men, but not, ultimately, to women (especially those otherwise decked out in masculine attire).

Moreover, it is instructive to note that while A.G. Stephens, literary lion and preserver of the masculinist tradition in Australian writing, was lavish in his praise of *Seven Little Australians*, a text in which maverick women are punished for overstepping the boundaries of *The Bulletin*'s separate male and female cultures, he was far less effusive when Turner turned her pen to more adult themes, and to analyses about the relationships between men and women in particular. He apparently preferred Turner to "prattle . . . pleasantly" in a charmingly girlish manner in her correct sphere of children's writing, rather than portray real-life situations about married life, and in so doing promoting an alternative image of masculinity, that of Domestic Man, fond of home and hearth, which was diametrically opposed to *The Bulletin*'s own model, the Bushman, who regarded domestic life as a burden, a drag on his spirit and independence. (Cited in White; 53) It has been alleged that *The Bulletin*'s savaging of her work, whenever she strayed from her circumscribed area, forced Turner into keeping with children's literature, even though she privately declared it worthless: "Never think that flagrant pile of rubbish books lying about the continent is in the least my 'something': they have just been bread and butter", she once announced at a particularly jaundiced moment. And so, although *Seven Little Australians* seems at first sight to be a very different novel to the colonial ones which it supplanted, the message concerning gender ends up as very much the same. Like their predecessors, nationalist children's stories were also orientated around a desire to enhance the continuation of certain values for the ultimate goal of racial preservation. The brave new world of the Australian Commonwealth would be inherited by the boys, and the girls would still at best be confined to the verandahs. Nationalist priorities meant the eventual glorification of male cultural heroes, and over-reaching women are noble failures, shipwrecked on the rocks that the others will never come to. And, as Turner's case reveals, this is identical to the manner in which women writers were also forced to adhere to rules which dictated that they never veered into serious or adult fiction, but remained always on the margins as writers of light romantic novels or children's stories.

In 1988, almost one hundred years after the ecstatic reception accorded to *Seven Little Australians*, Gillian Rubinstein's *Beyond the Labyrinth*—(1988) a bold, post-modern, post-colonial text, won the Children's Book of the Year (for Older Readers). Like Turner's novel, *Beyond the Labyrinth* is very much a product of later, different times, moulded by revisionist history, influenced by Reaganite cold war political ideologies, and anticipating the Mabo judgment concerning national sovereignty. *Beyond the Labyrinth*, in tone, outlook, structure and disposition, is worlds apart from the earlier novel, and provides a powerful deconstruction of the now established myths concerning national identity.

Rubinstein offers her readers a starkly depressing picture of Australian life and mores. As in *Seven Little Australians*, the focus is on family life, and the novel is set in an outlying part of a capital city. Chris and Geoff Trethewan, their children Shelley, Brenton and Michael, live on a hobby farm just south of Adelaide. Modern Australian life is seen through the eyes of Brenton, the family scapegoat who is sensitive, alert and intelligent, and therefore out of place in the society about him. Brenton is appalled by the materialism and hedonism that he sees everywhere about him, and by a world that he feels is doomed to be destroyed in a forthcoming nuclear holocaust. Life seems to offer little hope for the future and consequently he spends his time playing violent computer games and adopts a habit of rolling a dice to decide any further course of action—heads he will do something, tails he will not: "It's a game he has taken to playing lately. It amuses him to have to base decisions on chance. It seems to him quite a good approximation of what the universe is like—quite unpredictable and arbitrary" (BTL:90).

At the beginning of the novel, Brenton is the only misfit in this microcosm of Australian society. However he is soon joined by Vicki, daughter of a family friend who has spent the past five years with her family in Nigeria, but has returned to Australia to continue her high school education. Vicki is appalled by what she sees:

> Her life has been the opposite of sheltered; she has seen poverty, disease and death at first hand, but the people among whom she has seen them are reserved and inhibited. Even the most deprived of them do not drop obscenities around the way these golden-haired children do so lightly and casually.
>
> I suppose I'll get used to it, she tells herself. It just hits me at the moment because I'm on the outside looking in.

> When I'm a proper part of life here I won't notice it so much (BTL:60-1).

Yet Rubinstein offers little hope for those who do not fit the dominant norm. The society she depicts is consumer-oriented and spiritually impoverished (an aspect which is reflected in the linguistic impoverishment of many of the characters). According to Rubinstein herself, the novel "is about alienation and identity. It's full of despair about everything". Moreover the world of *Beyond the Labyrinth* is highly gender-differentiated, and dominated by a male culture of a hearty, blokey kind, with tall, blond, beer-swilling men and their progeny swaggering about in a kind of perpetual adolescence which is perhaps best summed up by Geoff Trethewen's habit of gunning his car up the drive, stopping in a screech of brakes just before he reaches the house. This is the culture which has inherited Australia, and Rubinstein appears to be shuddering with horror at the crassness of it all. Amidst these assorted bully boys of varying ages, Brenton can find few role models to aspire to. His own father Geoff is hostile towards him because he is not macho enough, and not a recognisable "beach" type. Unlike his brother Michael, who is a mirror image of his father and the other Aussie males about, Brenton is small, dark, intense—in short, a real worry for his parents. His mother is concerned about him—"I sometimes wonder if he's really all right" (BTL:124), and she fears that he might be a schizophrenic, while his father, annoyed beyond endurance by his irritatingly wimpy son, glowers at him, hits him, and threatens to crucify him as well.

White Australian society in *Beyond the Labyrinth* is characterised by transience and impermanence. The Trethewens and their kind hug the coast, never venturing inwards towards the dead heart, but forever looking outwards towards a treacherous sea which has already claimed three lives prior to the start of the novel. "Home" seems an alien concept for this nation of coastal dwellers, not seafarers, living precariously on the habitable margins of the continent, their eyes firmly averted from the centre. As a phantom graffiti artist wanders nightly through the sleepy town, spraying DEAD END on the town's walls, it appears likely that this is what will eventually happen to this civilisation as well.

The same masculinist discourse that ensured Judy's death in *Seven Little Australians* operates one hundred years further on, and this time there are few Judies around. The girls and women are subordinates, homemakers and followers of the men. As seventeen year old Shelley laughingly snaps to attention when her boyfriend Jason blows his horn outside their door, she also confesses to her predicament in being born female in this society:

> "I don't want to be in love with anyone yet. It's too soon. And I'm terrified—I want to be with him, and love him, and all that, but I don't want to get tied down to one person"—and at the same time I keep thinking, "I must make it work out with Jason, because who else is there?" (BTL:95).

In this culture femininity is defined as being inscribed with make-up, becoming pretty and therefore attractive to boys. When Vicki has her first period, Shelley "makes her over", ritualising her progress towards womanhood. Shelley enthuses, "That's really exciting! . . . It means you're growing up. You'll be having boyfriends next!", and she organises a little "girls own" party:

> Under the make-up Vicki's face feels slightly heavy and unfamiliar, as though she has after all become a new person, and has crossed some sort of boundary between childhood and adulthood.
>
> "Gee, you've got lovely skin, Vicki," Shelley observes. "I bet your nose never peels! There, look at yourself. How do you like that?"
>
> Her face stares back at her, mature and pretty (BTL:111).

There is little or no space reserved for "different" boys or girls in this culture. Rubinstein demonstrates this by including the figure of Cal, "a small dark alien of uncertain age, race and sex" (BTL:8), a time-travelling anthropologist from another galaxy who has landed in this part of the world in order to study the behaviour of primitive races. Cal remains (mostly) the objective scientific observer, examining twentieth century Australians as if they are biological specimens or elementary types of life forms (and in an amusing twist Cal gives Vicki and Michael the customary beads that one gives to the natives). When, midway through the novel, Vicki discovers that Cal is actually a female, the reader is as shocked as Vicki. She

> assumed the alien was a boy because of his manner of dealing with the world, so confident and assured. She had assumed people in any culture who were anthropologists and explorers were automatically male. She feels thrown off balance by having related to someone as a boy when all the time he was a girl. She sees all at once the limitations she places on herself, simply because she is female. And she feels very strongly a new resentment towards Michael who avoids her, not because he dislikes her, but because she is a girl (BTL:72-73).

Indeed, Cal is doubly Othered. Not only because she is female, but also because she is black, and therefore assumed to be Aboriginal and thus ignored or patronised by all of the characters with the exception of Brenton and Vicki. Vicki feels a rush of compassion for her:

> She looks at Cal, no longer protected by camouflage, a skinny, black kid in Brenton's old clothes, and she feels a rush of concern for her. Cal looks so confident and composed; she has no idea how vulnerable she is. She has no idea that in this culture she is just about at the bottom of the kicking order (BTL:74).

Rubinstein points to the arbitrariness of racial prejudice, for Cal herself has found it difficult not to condescend to these people; in her advanced society the only colour for people is brown, and she thought initially that blond Michael was suffering from a skin disease. Cal comments: "Occasionally our people grow without pigmentation, but they are not permitted to develop. The idea is so bizarre" (BTL:71). Bizarre or not, Cal suffers from prejudice throughout the whole story, enabling Rubinstein to make telling observations about sectors of Australian society which were largely erased from Turner's text. For many, including members of Brenton's own family, sophisticated Cal is simply "a bit weird . . . but a lot of Abos are" (BTL:51).

When Cal seeks information about White Australia, Brenton informs her: "You don't want to get a clear picture of this culture . . . . It would drive you mad. We have to distort it a little to be able to bear it" (BTL:100). Cal had originally time-travelled in order to carry out field work among the Narrangga tribe which remained in the same place for 40,000 years before becoming extinct after the arrival of the Europeans. A miscalculation landed her among this comparatively short-lived civilisation, one which many of Cal's contemporaries believed had never really existed, and was only a myth. White civilisation is clearly found wanting in Cal's eyes: she comments: "The things that made their society rich cannot be recorded by your society—you simply do not have the means or the approach" (BTL:109). And later she inadvertently blurts out. "Your culture is like a little backwater developing in such a strange way. I can understand why it comes to a dead end" (BTL:132).

At the end of the novel Brenton has to decide where his future lies: "I don't think the future belongs to men any more—not to Western men. They've fucked it all up too much. It's someone else's turn to have a shot at it—women, other races, other cultures" (BTL:142). In true post-modern style the reader is then offered two endings, depending on the throw of the dice. In either ending the author offers few answers for troubled teenagers, and has been accused of abandoning the difficult questions rather than resolving them. (Mills, 1991:24-29) In the first ending the hero Brenton sidesteps the action to live in another galaxy with Cal (an option not available for most adolescents). In the second, probably preferential ending (in the sense that it comes last of all), Brenton decides to live "as if", following the example of Vicki's plant geneticist father, "Live as if you will die tomorrow. Garden as if you will live forever" (BTL:169). In this favoured ending Brenton accepts the chaos about him, and thus goes beyond the labyrinth of modern life. A more positive viewpoint is presented: "The bombs have not yet started to fall. He has a strong sensation that he may be going to live to grow up after all" (BTL:169-70). This is despite the fact that we already know, via Cal's earlier, unguarded remarks, that this civilisation is eventually annihilated. Perhaps, in the end, Rubinstein has capitulated to the old adage of children's and adolescents' writing, that no matter how gritty and realistic the subject matter, you have to give them hope in the end.

Beyond the Labyrinth is a very bleak novel indeed, and despite the endings, offers little hope for the future. In its preoccupation with cultural identity, it deconstructs the myth of Australia as a paradise for the young. Unlike the youngsters in *Seven Little Australians*, the children in *Beyond the Labyrinth* are neither happy nor carefree (if they are sensitive, that is), and in spite of all their material possessions they are an unhappy bunch. As newcomer Vicki notices: "There seems to be too much of everything. Everything is too new, shiny and wealthy. The people's faces are too white and, in spite of the wealthiness, unhappy. She thought she was coming home. Now she realises the place she left is home."

The text consequently reveals myths of English national identity which are essentially backward-looking, embracing an idyllic past of a static, rural, non-industrial, properly hierarchical society in secure, thatched—cottaged surroundings situated somewhere in the South of England. This is a place where animals learn, like Dorothy in *The Wizard of Oz*, that true wisdom lies in accepting one's "home"; or, in this particular instance, their place in the class structure. "Home" for Toad, Ratty and Mole is linked with order, tranquillity and harmony—values which many felt were being destroyed by industrial progress (symbolised in this novel by the stoats, weasels and ferrets from the Wild Wood attempting to take over Toad Hall). And it is also interesting to note that contrary to *The Wizard of Oz* this is a society in which women are either absent or relegated to subsidiary roles like the gaoler's daughter or the bargewoman, and that the strongest emotion in the novel is that of male comradeship; things which Watkins allies with the male-oriented English public school system operating in Grahame's time. Watkins' argument about these contrasting myths of national identity and their place in children's literature is a persuasive one. While it goes almost without saying that extraliterary cultural formations shape literary discourse, this is also supplemented by the fact that much children's literature is imbued with the notion that children and young adults can be "feeling homesick!"

When the dying Cal also admits to being homesick, Brenton can only remark bitterly: "Better to be homesick away from home than at home" (BTL:87). If "home" can be defined as one's place in society, one's position in the class structure, then the alienation felt by these Australian children is surely highly significant.

According to contemporary children's literature, twentieth-century Australia is not a nice place to be. It may be argued that *Beyond the Labyrinth* is, in its own way, just as didactic as *Seven Little Australians*, but its message is much harsher, and much more depressing, in keeping with present day notions of what is suitable for young people. If it can be presumed that all our assumptions and understandings proceed from our own historically, socially and institutionally shaped vantage points, then contemporary Australian society, seen through children's literature, is in an awful mess, a mess inherited from a past generation's credo that Australianness was a mantle assumed principally by white, middle-class males. If Australia did invent itself mythically as "a man's country" in the 1890s, then according to Rubinstein we are reaping a very bitter harvest indeed.

WORKS CITED

Barbara Baynton, *Bush Studies* (Sydney: Angus and Robertson, 1902).

John Garth, "Our Girl", *Australian Magazine*, 8.11, August 1908, p. 1006.

E.L. Haverfield, *Queensland Cousins* (London: Nelson, 1908).

Alice Mills, "Dancing the Labyrinth: Gillian Rubinstein's Game Players," *Papers*, 2.1 (1991). Cited as QC.

Philippa Poole, ed., *The Diaries of Ethel Turner* (Sydney: Lansdowne, 1980), p. 98.

Gillian Rubinstein, *Beyond the Labyrinth* (Melbourne: Hyland House, 1988). Cited as BTL.

Susan Sheridan, 'Along the Faultlines: Sex, Race and Nation' in *Australian Women's Writing, 1880s-1930s* (Sydney: Allen and Unwin, 1995), and Marilyn Lake, "The Politics of Respectability: Identifying the Masculinist Context", *Historical Studies*, 22 (1986).

Ethel Turner, *Seven Little Australians* (London: Ward, Lock, 1894). Cited as SLA.

Tony Watkins, "Cultural Studies, New Historicism and Children's Literature", in Peter Hunt, ed., *Literature for Children: Contemporary Criticism* (London: Routledge, 1992), 173-95.

Kerry White, "'Blooming with Childhood's Fragrance': Sweet Words and Tough Times for Women Writers in the 1890s", *Australian Feminist Studies*, 7 & 8, 1988.

Crowds and Power: Number and Movement in Postcolonial Theory and Australian Literature

PATRICK WEST
Edith Cowan University, Western Australia

One of the impulses behind my decision to talk about the significance of 'crowds' in Australian literature is the current anxiety in Australia over racial identity and immigration. Predictably enough, the racist rhetoric of a wide range of influential community leaders (most notably the federal Member of Parliament Pauline Hanson) has, more or less explicitly, used a (paranoiac) image of 'hordes' and 'masses' threatening Australia from the north. The most common expression adduced to this image is that white Australians will be 'over-run' by Asians. But the 'engulfing group' is not the only one apparent in the current debate; although it is no doubt the most obvious. How might we interpret, for example, the crowd of parliamentarians who sat through Hanson's controversial maiden speech many of whom argued that they were simply following parliamentary protocol in personally congratulating her afterwards? Or how to understand the call by one member of the public for all citizens concerned not to be typecast as racists to wear an orange ribbon on their lapel? To ask these questions is to begin work on a *typology* of crowds, and to engage with the seminal thesis of Elias Canetti. In his view, a parliamentary meeting would be a good example of a 'closed crowd', while those who might chose to identify themselves with an orange ribbon are using a 'crowd symbol' to ensure group solidarity and the promotion of a specific meaning.

This is how Canetti describes the 'closed crowd', in the opening pages of his most famous text, *Crowds and Power*:

> The closed crowd renounces growth and puts the stress on permanence. The first thing to be noticed about it is that it has a boundary. It establishes itself by accepting its limitation. It creates a space for itself which it will fill. This space can be compared to a vessel into which liquid is being poured and whose capacity is known. The entrances to this space are limited in number, and only these entrances can be used; the boundary is respected whether it consists of stone, of solid wall, or of some special act of acceptance or entrance fee. Once the space is completely filled, no one else is allowed in. Even if there is an overflow, the important thing is always the dense crowd in the closed room; those standing outside do not really belong.
>
> The boundary prevents disorderly increase, but it also makes it more difficult for the crowd to disperse and so postpones its dissolution. In this way the crowd sacrifices its chance of growth, but gains in staying power. It is protected from outside influences which could become hostile and dangerous and it sets its hope on repetition. It is the expectation of reassembly which enables its members to accept each dispersal. The building is waiting for them; it exists for their sake and, so long as it is there, they will be able to meet in the same manner. The space is theirs, even during the ebb, and in its emptiness it reminds them of the flood. (Canetti, 1984: 17)

This seems to me to be a very accurate description of the parliamentary group, at least as it is manifested in Australia at both a federal and a state level. A chamber of parliament has a boundary; and it is typically a depressed space—something to be filled (as a vessel for liquid)—overlooked by people in the public gallery, who we might say "do not really belong." (Canetti, 17) Parliamentarians rarely, if ever, care to acknowledge these people (the former Prime Minister Bob Hawke being an exception). It "renounces growth and puts the stress on permanence." (Canetti, 17)

Despite the fact that the cost of government is not particularly high for the returns it brings, there is a general agreement that Australians are overgoverned, that there are *too many parliamentarians*. Finally, it lives through repetition and the "expectation of reassembly." (Canetti, 17) This might be seen as the role of elections.

Canetti's description of the 'closed crowd' thus seems remarkably apt for a study of one of the central institutions of Australian life. It allows us to comprehend those elements of the parliamentary group that seem peculiar in the light of common understandings of democratic representation. I have already alluded to one of these: that is, the failure of parliamentarians to recognise the electors in the public gallery. In addition, the elaborate procedure of calling for a division in the parliament, the 'ringing of the bells', the guarding of the entrances and so on, might be viewed as an intensification of the boundary of the 'closed crowd'. Or, by extension, as a mode of protection from 'dangerous', external forces. More to the point for our concerns, we might want to read the politeness extended by other parliamentarians to Pauline Hanson, after her maiden speech, as intimate with the dynamics of a 'closed crowd'. Something that maintains its fixed identity.

The example I raised of an orange ribbon as a 'crowd symbol' for those who want to display their distance from Hanson's position can also be related to a part of Canetti's thesis. 'National crowd symbols' allow a nation to represent itself to other nations, as well as to itself. Canetti argues that they always speak to a characteristic aspect of a nation's experience; for example, the sea for the English, the protective dykes for the Dutch, and so forth for every other case. The orange ribbon is not a 'national crowd symbol' like these ones, of course, but it can be distinguished from ordinary 'crowd symbols' because its wearers want to participate in a debate over Australia's national direction and identity. The original suggestion for the orange ribbon came in a letter to a well-known social commentator from a certain Susan Leith-Miller of Sydney, Australia, but it was related to its broader audience by its addressee, Phillip Adams, in these terms:

> Leith-Miller's letter describes how, in recent weeks, she had been feeling a growing unease. Then, while waiting for a bus,

> it had all become painfully clear. She was surrounded, as usual, by a multicultural crowd, by people of various hues and backgrounds. It was something she had always enjoyed, one of the reasons she loved living in Sydney. But this time she was conscious of tension in the air, of mistrust. It was as if her Anglo-Saxon features were branding her a bigot. She wanted to turn round and talk to the people, to explain to them that she was happy about a polychromatic Australia but, being Anglo-Saxon, was constrained.
>
> So she came up with an idea for people who want to stand up to be counted, a method that allows us to emphatically identify ourselves as people who celebrate rather than fear difference. She pinned a little piece of orange ribbon to the letter—and wants people to wear other pieces on their lapels. Why orange? Other colours signify other issues, other concerns. And obviously a black or white ribbon wouldn't, in the current circumstances, be appropriate. So it wasn't so much "why orange?" as "why not?"
>
> So I got a couple of rolls of orange ribbon and have cut them into little bits and have been handing them out for days. It's as good an idea as any, and a lot better than most. I like the way the idea came from a private citizen and not from a political or ethnic organisation, let alone from a politician or an ad agency. The idea doesn't require sophisticated, centralised organisation and couldn't be less expensive. Yet it's a method that allows people to identify a multicultural Australia, to quietly deplore the strident, vicious campaign being waged by ultra-Right organisations who are using Hanson as their Joan of Arc. (Adams, 1996: 2)

There are many things that could be said about this passage; we might want to question, for instance, the assumption that a "grass-roots campaign" is the best means to, as Adams puts it, "reinforce progressive attitudes." (Adams, 1996: 2) Or the notion that common sense allows access to a set of core, humanist values. But Canetti's thesis would have us notice another feature of this passage that very few other theorists would be sensitive to, something even more fundamental than concerns about the nature of political action, or the value of transcendental values (if I can put it like that). I am speaking of the opposition in Adams's article between silence and sight, between the ear and the eye. Canetti's 'crowd symbols', even his slightly less fanciful 'national crowd symbols', are full of noise: the bee swarm, fire, rain, the sea, wind and so on. He states that "mute knowledge [is] dangerous." (Sontag, 1980: 195). In this relation, Susan Sontag argues that

> Canetti claims to be a 'hear-er' rather than a 'see-er.' . . . [He] stresses the moralist's organ, the ear, and slights the eye (continuing to ring changes on the theme of blindness). Hearing, speaking, and breathing are praised whenever something important is at stake, if only in the form of ear, mouth (or tongue), and throat metaphors.
>
> What is heard is voices—to which the ear is a witness . . . . The ear is the attentive sense, humbler, more passive, more immediate, less discriminating than the eye. Canetti's disavowal of the eye is an aspect of his remoteness from the aesthete's sensibility, which typically affirms the pleasures and the wisdom of the visual; that is, of surfaces. To give sovereignty to the ear is an obtrusive, consciously archaizing theme in Canetti. . . . Implicitly he is restating the archaic gap between Hebrew as opposed to Greek culture, ear culture as opposed to eye culture, and the moral versus the aesthetic.
>
> Canetti equates knowing with hearing, and hearing with hearing everything and still being able to respond. . . . The voice for Canetti stands for irrefutable presence. To treat someone as a voice is to grant authority to that person; to affirm that one hears means that one hears what must be heard. (Sontag, 1980: 195-97)

With this material to hand, Leith-Miller's experience while waiting for a bus can be read as evidence of a 'blind' reliance on sight as the currency of social life and change in multicultural Australia. "Is not the maximum of light also the source of all obscurity?" asks Jacques Lacan somewhere. (Lacan, 1973:263) Leith-Miller cannot (or will not) speak to the people around her; nor does she hear them (let alone they her). All is silence and all is colour.

Canetti asks us to take his 'crowd symbols'—and his work on crowds in general—in a literal sense. He would point up the dangers of the "mute knowledge" implied by particular phrases like "people of various hues," "a polychromatic Australia" and the (visual) expression of the thought process: "it had all become painfully clear" (Sontag, 195; Adams 2). How ironic that Adams regards the orange ribbon as a form of 'emphatic identification' then! That he has in effect conceded to his opponents our best means for communication: speech and noise. (In fact, it is possible that the orange ribbon—as part of a visual, semiotic economy—panders to the same emotion that Hanson's racist rhetoric does: that is, the desire for an uncomplicated world, one unconstrained by logic.)

Canetti's approach would also have us question the choice of a silent colour as a '*national* crowd symbol'. The curious lack of care displayed by Adams with respect to the colour of the ribbon—'why not orange?'—is a symptom of the lethargy of colour as a force. And in terms of Australia as a nation it is an index of a larger anxiety over the choice of an appropriate national symbol, something most obvious in the current debate over the design of the Australian national flag. The orange ribbon points towards a fundamental silence in Australian national life.

In exploring the value of Canetti's work to what is probably the key issue in Australia today (the rise of racism on a quasi-official level), we have encountered two aspects of *Crowds and Power*: the attention to 'crowd symbols' and the idea of the 'closed crowd'. Both of these will be encountered again in the fictional text I will be looking at shortly, but the most important of Canetti's concepts remains to be fully explicated. I am talking here about the 'open crowd'. The 'open crowd' is everything that the 'closed crowd' is not. Canetti writes that the 'open crowd' is

> everywhere spontaneous. As soon as it exists at all, it wants to consist of *more* people: the urge to grow is the first and supreme attribute of the crowd. It wants to seize everyone within reach; anything shaped like a human being can join it. The natural crowd is the *open* crowd; there are no limits whatever to its growth; it does not recognize houses, doors or locks and those who shut themselves in are suspect. 'Open'

> is to be understood here in the fullest sense of the word; it means open everywhere and in any direction. (Canetti, 16)

Canetti sees this unfurling of the 'open crowd' as a cosmic rebuff to the exercise of *power*, which he understands as an entirely negative phenomenon, "predicated on the power of death and the corresponding destructive and self-destructive logic of totalitarianism." (Anarson, 1996:IV) To this extent, he parts company with theorists like Michel Foucault, who insist on "the creativity of power" that goes hand in hand with its effects of domination. (Hindess, 1996:146) For Canetti, the 'open crowd' is typically a challenge to the power of totalitarian leaders, who succumb to its force when they are unable to keep at a distance the mass of people that is also the condition of their power. The paranoiac dictator's self comes apart when the fine balance between the world outside—the eternal renewal of the 'open crowd'—and their inner world of obsession and fantasy, is disrupted. When the line separating the outside from the inside becomes queered. A dictator wants power over the people, yet hates them, and is therefore forced into an unstable compromise: a great quantity of imaginary people, or real or imaginary objects, stands in for the crowd as the dictator's object of desire, but the outside world inevitably merges with this inner fantasy world, and the paranoid's self collapses. (In this respect, we might say that 'closed crowds' are to be found in the mind of the paranoid, in the shape of a controlled group; and that certain 'crowd symbols' might also be located in the same place. I am thinking of those symbols that, like the orange ribbon, are not open to the world.)

To reach this and further stages in the unfolding of Canetti's thesis, however, two obstacles need to be overcome. Firstly, one must learn to interpret as he does: that is, in a thoroughly literal and empirical way. Canetti's achievement depends on naive readings of texts and practices that, not in spite of but because of their very naivety, turn into cunning interpretations. In addition, his whole study of crowds and power relies on his empirical observations of real crowds. This method allows Canetti to unearth the deep assumptions that serve to combine things seemingly distinct, or to separate things apparently alike. The second and closely related problem, concerns Canetti's "exceptionally hermetic and idiosyncratic" view of the world. (Anarson, 1996:86) One commentator argues that Canetti is two steps removed from mainstream social theory, and that "we are thus dealing with a deviation from a deviation, an outsider's heterodox response to a half-established heterodoxy. This double estrangement makes it difficult to bring Canetti's ideas into discursive contact with more conventional views." (Anarson, 1996:87) For both of these reasons, Canetti's significance for a host of disciplines has not been fully utilised to date; and the study of Australian literature is no exception here. It is appropriate to begin the task of redressing this situation with the fiction of the Melbourne writer Gerald Murnane, because the view of the world expressed in some of his texts resonates so much with Canetti's preoccupations.

The Plains is a novella that has attracted more critical attention than any other of Murnane's texts. It tells the story of an unusual nameless film-maker, who lives in an unusually strange world. First of all, he is a film-maker who never makes the film—entitled *The Interior*—that he spends all of his time writing notes towards and speculating about. Additionally, throughout the novel he is aided and abetted in this interminable project by the plainsmen and, in particular, by his patron, all of whom spend their time engaged in complicated and arcane investigations into the nature of the plains. A key element of the novel is the contrast between 'Inner Australia' (the plains) and 'Outer', coastal or 'Other Australia'. The plains are understood by their inhabitants to offer a richer experience of the world than is possible in the coastal regions of Australia. This potentially perfect experience, however, is always felt to be at least one remove from the various projects of the plainsmen.

Even from this brief description, it should be clear that Murnane's novella has much to offer post-colonial theorists in terms of its play with a distinction between the coast and the desert interior that has been so often decisive in Australian history, its engagement with problems of representation, its examination of the lone explorer who encounters an older civilisation, and so on. I have not, however, come across any analysis of this text that relies on Canetti's thesis. This strategy for reading *The Plains* would appear to be of great value in regard to post-colonial theory because the latter is always already engaged with what can be identified as 'crowd-like' issues: that is, for example, the violent displacement of peoples (not to mention the racist rhetoric of someone like Pauline Hanson). Such a project would have the effect of forcing us to reconsider *The Plains* in line with Canetti's argument that all fictional texts and critical positions contain a mostly implicit relation to, or judgement on the crowd—taken in the broadest sense.

This might be of only trivial significance with some fictional texts and some critical positions (although for Canetti's cosmic purposes this relation or judgement would be everywhere important: the latent content would not need to match with the patent content for this to be so). However, it strikes me as a crucial insight when placed alongside texts like *The Plains* and every position within post-colonial theory. What violence is enacted, for instance, when these things become active without being aware of the presence of what Canetti seeks to identify and classify? That is, specifically, of the very deep energy of the 'open crowd' and the potential it has to undo power. How might political options be tainted by this sort of deafness? What other arrangements of the post-colonial landscape (real and theoretical) might fail to come onto the scene?

The Plains displays its interest in the themes explored by Canetti from its first pages. Having just arrived on the plains, the film-maker exchanges his story for the stories of the plainsmen drinking in the hotel where he is staying. And the tale he relates sounds, in fact, like a close copy of *The Plains* itself, if not of all of Murnane's fiction:

> I told them a story almost devoid of events or achievements. Outsiders would have made little of it, but the plainsmen understood. It was the kind of story that appealed to their own novelists and dramatists and poets. Readers and audiences on the plains were seldom impressed by outbursts of emotion or violent conflicts or sudden calamities. They supposed that the artists who presented such things had been beguiled by the noises of crowds or the profusions of shapes and surfaces in the foreshortened landscapes of the world beyond the plains. (Murnane, 1982:14-15)

The reference to "outsiders" here is perhaps early notice of the totalitarian figure that, I will be suggesting, the film-maker of *The Plains* really is. (Murnane, 1982:14-15) Silent knowledge is in evidence in this passage too: another thing that Canetti finds dangerous. Not only will coastal dwellers make nothing of the story the film-maker tells—which makes it secret rather than expressive—but it is explicitly contrasted both with what is an extremely good description of the 'open crowd' ('emotional', 'violent', 'sudden' and 'calamitous') and, significantly, with the "noises of crowds" (Murnane, 1982:14).. It will be remembered that noise is crucial for Canetti as opposition to the virtual silence of the totalitarian leader (Murnane, 1982:14-15). Finally, this passage concludes with a move typical of Canetti, and one that we have already noticed. It points up a symbolic stand-in for the crowd: ". . . the noises of crowds or the profusions of shapes and surfaces in the foreshortened landscapes. . . ." (Murnane, 1982:14-15)

Murnane's text expresses, therefore, many of the topics that intrigue Canetti; however, *The Plains* ultimately—and very stridently—develops its own slant on Canetti's thesis. All the elements of his crowd theory are exploited by Murnane's text, and progressed in the one direction. The film-maker turns out to be a type of dictator. Still more provocatively, we could say he becomes an Australian dictator (one among many) to the extent that he becomes a plainsman like other plainsmen, all of whom hate the coastal dwellers. All the plainsmen were concerned that "the borders of the plains [would be] beset by a horde of exiles." (Murnane, 1982:37) Are we then dealing with an oxymoronic community of dictators? (if such a thing is possible anywhere, it could only be on the plains, where men can retreat at will, sometimes for years, to their private mansions).

This extreme reading is nevertheless paralleled by the circumstance that, in odd ways and at unpredictable moments throughout the text, a version of the crowd as pathologically violent and inherently bad, something to be controlled, raises its head. Any excuse seems good enough for this understanding of the crowd, precisely the one that repelled Canetti, to emerge in *The Plains*. For example, the members of a polo-playing team are represented with attention to their inherent perversity: "the very tilt of their bodies—low over the flapping manes—suggesting menace" (Murnane, 1982:32). In this respect, *The Plains* betrays an association with Gustave Le Bon's thesis—against which Canetti rebelled—that the crowd is pathologically perverse, violent and evil. Unlike Canetti, Le Bon did not distinguish between 'open' and 'closed' crowds, although effectively he only discussed 'open' crowds (but in a fashion diametrically opposed to Canetti, obviously). The polo-playing team here could perhaps be seen as an example of a 'closed crowd'; but, even if this is granted, I think the emphasis on the hatred of the crowd in this instance clearly indicates Le Bon's influence. (Canetti's dislike of the 'closed crowd' is always couched in very different terms from Le Bon's) (Le Bon. 1895). The general presence of dictators is therefore matched by the general and random hatred of the crowd in Murnane's novella. However, let us follow the trajectory of the film-maker himself in some more detail.

In *The Plains* the paranoiac film-maker spends much of his time in his patron's enormous library. In this second stage of the evolution of his totalitarian life, the hatred of the outsiders from 'Outer' or 'Other Australia' is complemented by his creation of a 'closed crowd' as a device for controlling the inhabitants of coastal Australia, who are now—in the film-maker's mind—threatening the very walls of his residence in 'Inner Australia'. This 'closed crowd' is made-up of books and the combinations of words within them, both of which at the same time comfort and threaten the film-maker:

> The countless volumes of this library are close-set with so much speculative prose, so many chapters after chapters appear in parentheses, such glosses and footnotes surround the thin trickles of actual text that I fear to discover in some unexceptional essay by a plainsman of no great reputation a tentative paragraph describing a man not unlike myself speculating endlessly about the plains but never setting foot on them. (Murnane, 1982:101)

The same idea of books as a paranoiac defence against the outside world is clear in this extract from an interview with Murnane conducted in 1992:

> I've often thought of my ideal life as a life of inaction. I don't mean lolling beside a swimming pool in Queensland—that would be hell. I mean staying for weeks at a time in a house filled with books and surrounded by empty grasslands—not even writing, perhaps not even reading, but just staring at the books. . . . Often, as a boy, I wanted to be a monk in a monastery surrounded by an immense wall. (Braun-Bau, 1996:45)

In a discussion between Canetti and Theodor W. Adorno in 1962, human desire for increase is countered by the fear that the earth will not be able to support its ever-increasing population (Canetti, 1972). So the desire for increase is itself an ambivalent one. In the following extract from the interview with Murnane, he taps into the fear that the world is not big enough for all it must contain. To this extent, he reflects, I believe, a totalitarian fear of the crowd overflowing the boundaries of the world (his world), which can be linked, by reversal, to his notion of the 'closed crowd' as a defence against the 'open crowd'. Murnane says to his German interviewer:

> I have a *strange* feeling about space and distance. When I look at a map—and I'm always looking at maps—I begin to worry that the places I'm looking at are not spacious enough. So I have to know the scale of the map. And then I have to do a sort of mental exercise to reassure myself. When I go home tonight, I'll look at a map of your country and try to convince myself that Melbourne and Bendigo can fit into it a few times over. I seem to have this need to know that there's plenty of space in the world, even though I don't want to leave my own part of the world. I looked at a map of Malta the other day and felt sorry for the people who live there with so little room to move, so little space around them. I don't think of the ocean as space. It's only land that counts. (Braun-Bau, 1996:44)

Elsewhere, Murnane talks of the "crowdedness" of Germany. (Braun-Bau, 1996:44)

I am not claiming that Murnane is in his own subjectivity a para-dictator; but I do think it is important to comprehend the reading of his texts that Canetti's thesis allows us to produce. Read at the intersection of post-colonial concerns and an emergent racist trend in Australia, *The Plains* offers a disquietening vision of power.

WORKS CITED

Phillip Adams, 'The Colour of Tolerance,' *Australian* 23-24 Nov. 1996, 'Weekend Review', 'Features': 2.

Johann P. Arnason, 'Canetti's Counter-Image of Society,' *Thesis Eleven*, 45 (1996): 86-115.

Susanne Braun-Bau, 'A Conversation with Gerald Murnane,' *Antipodes: A North American Journal of Australian Literature*, 10.1 (June 1996): 43-48.

Elias Canetti, *Auto-da-Fe*. (1935; London: Pan, 1981).

______, *Crowds and Power*, Trans. Carol Stewart (New York: Farrar, 1984). Trans. of *Masse und Macht* (Hamburg: Claassen Verlag, 1960).

______, 'Discussion with Theodor W. Adorno,' Trans. David Roberts, *Thesis Eleven*, 45 (1996): 1-15. Trans. of 1962 Radio Discussion in Elias Canetti, *Die Gespaltene Zukunft* (N.p.: Hanser Verlag, 1972).

Barry Hindess, *Discourses of Power: From Hobbes to Foucault* (Oxford: Blackwell, 1996).

Axel Honneth, 'The Perpetuation of the State of Nature: On the Cognitive Content of Elias Canetti's *Crowds and Power*,' *Thesis Eleven*, 45 (1996): 69-85.

Jacques Lacan, *Le Séminaire de Jacques Lacan*, Trans. Jacques-Alain Miller, I. Livre 1, 'Les Ecrits Techniques de Freud,' xix (Paris: Seuil, 1973).

Gustave Le Bon, *The Crowd: A Study of the Popular Mind* (1895; Atlanta, GA: Cherokee, 1982).

Juliet Flower MacCannell, *Figuring Lacan: Criticism and the Cultural Unconscious*, Critics of the Twentieth Century (Lincoln: U of Nebraska P, 1986).

Rousiley C.M. Maia, 'Elias Canetti's *Auto-da-Fe*: From the Antithesis of the Crowd-Man to the Madness of Power,' *Thesis Eleven*, 45 (1996):

28-38.
John McClelland, 'The Place of Canetti's *Crowds and Power* in the History of Western Social and Political Thought,' *Thesis Eleven*, 45 (1996): 16-27.
Gerald Murnane, *The Plains* (1982; Ringwood, Vic.: Penguin, 1984).
David Roberts, 'Crowds and Power or the Natural History of Modernity: Horkheimer, Adorno, Canetti, Arendt,' *Thesis Eleven*, 45 (1996): 39-68.
Susan Sontag, 'Mind as Passion,' *Under the Sign of Saturn* (1980; London: Vintage-Random, 1996). 181-204.
Max Whisson, Letter, *Australian*, 26 Nov. 1996: 12.

Fear of Passing

LUCY FROST
University of Tasmania

Any construction of identity, whether individual or collective, relies on narrative to produce a defining shape. The collective identity we call 'nationality' encompasses narratives endorsed as 'authentic' in a specific social space. These narratives are structured as paradigms, skeletons given flesh by particular stories. When the stories cease to fit the skeleton, another skeleton takes its place, another paradigm. The Howard government seems determined to change the paradigm for reading stories of Aboriginality in Australia.

When Howard came to office in March 1996, the previous Keating government had endorsed a paradigmatic narrative of Aboriginal/non-Aboriginal contact which went something like this: In 1788, the European settlement of Australia began. Lands occupied at that time by Aboriginal tribes were taken by European settlers under the auspices of the British government. Aborigines who resisted were driven off their lands by gun-carrying men on horseback; many Aborigines were killed; many more died from infectious diseases. Those who survived the period of colonial settlement continued to be subject to a degree of government intervention which would not have been tolerated by non-Aboriginal Australians. Until 1967 Aborigines were not included in the national census; their names were not on the electoral roles, and they could not vote. They were restricted in where they could live; what they could drink; where they could walk after dark. Until the 1970s, their children could be taken away. Although these policies of radical intervention no longer operate, the effects of two hundred years are manifest. Aboriginal Australians taken as a group (as they have consistently been taken since the moment of settlement in 1788) are disproportionately represented in jails, among deaths in custody, among deaths in childbirth, among all categories of death at an age earlier than the non-Aboriginal population.

The narrative I have just summarised features invasion, dispossession, and injustice. Its ethical dimension was accepted as inescapable during the Keating years. What to do about it was under constant debate, but broadly speaking, the goal was to effect closure to the colonial narrative by recognising Aboriginal claims upon the historical past from which the settler society constructed its 'nation', and to embrace a process of reconciliation between the indigenous peoples and the European settlers. The earlier assimilationist paradigm, in which white settlers authorised the speaking position for 'Australia', was to be replaced by a narrative of reconciliation establishing a dialogue which accorded full subject status to both indigenous and settler peoples. Within the parameters of this narrative of reconciliation, government policy was formulated during the early 1990s, court judgments were handed down, the representation of Aboriginality in public discourse was monitored, the policies and practices of instutitions such as universities were altered.

But simply because a paradigmatic narrative is endorsed by the authenticating agencies does not mean that it is universally acceptable. The extent of resistance to this particular paradigm is becoming apparent, as are the pressures for change. That's not the way the politicians would put it of course; they talk in terms of principles, not narrative paradigms. Principles of good management practice and the protection of public monies were evoked when, as one of its first actions, the new government instigated an investigation into the affairs of ATSIC (the Aboriginal and Torres Strait Islanders Commission). It was the democratic icon of free speech to which the Prime Minister appealed when pressured to disassociate himself and his government from the racist rhetoric of Pauline Hanson, a new member of Parliament elected as an independent after the Prime Minister's own party had disendorsed her.

Of course governments alone do not and cannot determine the

narrative paradigms within which cultural identity takes shape. The authorising agencies are spread throughout the institutions of a society. The processes by which these agencies endorse and dis-endorse paradigms are often intricate and difficult to disentangle. Conspiracy in the form of an articulated and mutually agreed arrangement is rare. Nevertheless, when individual stories are read within and against competing cultural paradigms, a politics may appear without reference to the conscious intention of the story-teller.

I want to look at one such case, a recent Australian newspaper story about an Australian writer. Using the methodology of textual analysis—the tools of my trade as a literary critic—I'll read this particular story intertextually, situating it within other stories leading to a paradigm which is American rather than Australian. The American paradigm in turn illuminates the process of narrative construction at work today in Australia.

On the 20th of July 1996 I read a story I had heard circulating for weeks as well-sourced gossip. It was published in the glossy magazine which accompanies the Saturday edition of the *Australian*, the country's one national newspaper, owned by the international media mogul and sometime Australian citizen, Rupert Murdoch. The subject of the article was the writer, critic and university professor, Mudrooroo. As written, there are two versions of his story, one told by his older sister, Betty (nie Johnson), and the second by Victoria Laurie, the journalist who shaped Betty's telling for national publication. The narratives, though entwined, serve different ends. Separated, they reveal a family politics of identity, and a cultural politics of race. Mudrooroo is under attack, but he is by no means the only target.

The Johnson telling: fear of passing

This is the story of a family—of Elizabeth and Thomas Johnson, their forebears and their descendants. One of these descendants is Betty, now aged seventy. It was her curiosity which sparked the story, and her diligent research into genealogical records which gave it direction.

Betty wanted to know how it was that her youngest brother Colin, who in 1988 changed his name to Mudrooroo, could be Aboriginal. How did his claims affect her identity? Like many researchers into family history, she seems to have had no background in historical analysis or theoretical modelling, and no inkling that this lack could make her vulnerable to narrative takeover by a political agenda. She was thinking in strictly personal terms, asking apparently simple questions. If Colin was Aboriginal, she and the other Johnson siblings must have been as well, but Aboriginality was not their experience:

> If, like him, she were Aboriginal, Betty should have obtained permission from Native Welfare authorities to marry a white man—but she hadn't. Frank should have been prevented by curfew laws from wandering around Perth's city centre after sunset in the fifties; he hadn't been.

Underpinning these personal questions lies a social model of racial identity in which power and space are deployed along a clearly demarcated divide. Everyone is on one side of the divide or the other. Either a person is Aboriginal and restricted (forbidden to marry without permission, forbidden to wander the city after sunset), or non-Aboriginal and free. Either Betty and Frank were non-Aboriginal, and entitled to the privileged positions they unthinkingly claimed, or they were Aboriginal and law-breakers, appropriating an identity to which they had no right. They were 'passing'.

'Passing' belongs to a political story of racial transgression. It is a story I know well because I grew up in the American South when the 'Jim Crow' laws of racial segregation marked every inch of space I walked through. There were drinking fountains with signs saying 'whites only', but mostly signs weren't needed, mostly people knew that swimming pools were for whites and not for blacks, knew which suburbs were white and which were black. Every institution I encountered was marked in this way. There were schools for whites and schools for blacks, 'separate but equal' we said, though I failed to notice that no school for blacks was accredited, failed to see the implication when I read in university handbooks that no graduate of an unaccredited high school was eligible for admission.

In this model of racial demarcation, the superiority of whites was assumed. Superiority justified privilege. It might also, whites feared, breed jealousy. Blacks might want what the whites had (never imagining that desire could flow in the opposite direction), might insinuate themselves into white space and appropriate a white identity. What if, by looking at a person, you could not see the black blood of the ancestor? What if a white-skinned black crossed over the white/black divide, 'passed'?

The boundaries had to be policed if 'whiteness' was to be protected, and 'whiteness' had to be protected because it meant power. This was a lesson learned during the slave era by the English actress Fanny Kemble. In 1834 she had married an American, Pierce Butler, but not until 1838 did she come with him and their child to his Georgia plantation. Writing to a friend, she describes being introduced to a slave woman as the master's new wife. The slave tries to ingratiate herself by commenting not on Fanny's beauty (as one might in other discourses of femininity) but on the colour of her skin:

> "Oh massa!" shrieked out the old creature, in a paroxysm of admiration, "where you get this lily alabaster baby!" For a moment I looked round to see if she was speaking of my baby; but no, my dear, this superlative apostrophe was elicited by the fairness of my skin: so much for degrees of comparison. Now I suppose that if I chose to walk arm in arm with the dingiest mulatto through the streets of Philadelphia, nobody could possibly tell by my complexion that I was not his sister, so that the mere quality of mistress must have had a most miraculous effect upon my skin in the eyes of poor Rose.

The connection Fanny Kemble makes between reading skin (whatever its actual colour) and acknowledging or exercising power underlies as well the quotation with which Victoria Laurie begins her article, a quotation from Mudrooroo's first novel, *Wild Cat Falling* (1965):

> I get up from the table and she notices my clothes.

> "Looks like you've been wrigglin' through that drain pipe again. You haven't been with those dirty Noongar kids I hope?"
>
> "It's no joking matter," she says. "If we get seen with that mob we'll be chucked out of this place quick smart."
>
> "Some of the white kids play with them."
>
> She starts packing up the plates. "That's different. They belong on the white side of the fence. You've got to prove you do."

Or, in my language from the American South, you've got to take care to 'pass'. Otherwise, 'we'll be chucked out of this place quick smart.' One member of a family can put the whole family at risk.

Surveillance must be unceasing. And along with surveillance comes denial. In James Weldon Johnson's *The Autobiography of an Ex-Colored Man* (1912), the narrator who has been passing walks along a Chicago street one night with his white fiance and sees his mother. He pretends not to know her. Next day he writes her a letter:

> Ma, I felt mighty bad about last night. The first time we'd met in public that way. That's the kind of thing that makes passing hard, having to deny your own family when you see them. . . .

Similarly, Betty's story of the Johnson story is permeated with denial and the accusations of denial. During her family research, she reads a booklet about the settlement of the West Australian town where her parents had lived. In this booklet 'she found her father's name under the entry, "T.C. Johnson (an American Negro).'" She was incensed and 'sent off a terse note to the author that her father was Australian-born; his birth certificate showed that Thomas Creighton Johnson had been born in York Street, Sydney, in 1874.'

Foreign birth she will not have, but 'Negro' blood she accepts, apparently on this evidence from the booklet, together with a copy of her grandfather's marriage certificate which says 'he was a migrant from North Carolina who had, in Victoria in 1868, married an Irish woman from County Clare.' She writes to 'a distant cousin in the US' who tells her that 'if Thomas Johnson was an "American Negro" born in 1833,' he 'would have been born into Southern slavery.' Betty is satisfied: she is not Aboriginal on her father's side. She then investigates her mother's family, traces it back to the first white child born on the Swan River in 1829, and is delighted. She is not Aboriginal, her Australian origins are pioneer white.

Erasing 'Aboriginal' as unauthentic, Betty the family historian can stop worrying that inadvertently she and her siblings have spent their lives 'passing'. None of them other than Mudrooroo ever identified as Aboriginal, and none has begun identifying as African-American. Betty's conclusions take visual shape in a photograph of four generations celebrating a reunion of family. Without the youngest brother.

The Second Telling: Who's Passing Now?

I would never have heard Betty's story, never have heard of Betty, if her brother had not been a recognised name in my world. Because Mudrooroo holds an eminent position in Australian writing and criticism, his unknown sister's amateur sleuthing has interested the national press, and the story has moved from family history in the private sphere to representative history in the public. The meanings are no longer personal; they are cultural, they are meanings directed at me as a reader of the *Australian* newspaper and a member of Australian society, and they contribute towards the pressures to change the narrative paradigm for reading Aboriginality in Australia.

The narrative with reconciliation as a closure to colonial history is, it would seem, to be replaced by a narrative determined to relegate the past to the past, and insisting that in the present everyone must be the same. No special favours for blacks. They can stop their wingeing, their pleading for a special deal, and get along like the rest of us. They can assimilate. The *Australian's* account of the Johnson story fits in nicely with the new narrative. Here's a family whose ancestry includes slave-blacks, but they aren't going on about that, aren't complaining or asking that history be redressed. They've assimilated (what's a little colour in multi-cultural

Australia as long as the colour keeps quiet and acts 'white'?). Mudrooroo, however, refuses to join his siblings in white space, and it is an attack on this defiance which structures Victoria Laurie's narrative.

Initially in the journalist's story, Mudrooroo is a powerful figure. The article's first words are his, those I quoted earlier from *Wild Cat Falling*. Laurie in her opening paragraph acknowledges him as a writer 'at the pinnacle of his literary career,' but from this moment, his literary reputation is questioned by bringing into doubt his Aboriginality. Laurie, like Betty and with the help of Betty, has done her own research, and from it she tells the story of the Johnson children, an impoverished family split up immediately after the death of their father and before the birth of Colin. Records generated for Colin at the Child Welfare Agency and the Clontarf Boys' Town confirm a childhood in which skin-colour is crucial to personal identity. Colin is described as 'a dark-featured lad, very promising in school'; later, he becomes a school leaver for whom it's difficult to find accommodation 'because of his fairly dark appearance (part-native blood)'; another welfare officer suggests 'Dash of Indian or Negro'. Then he's in court on assault charges. 'He claims he is a bodgie', says the arresting officer. An outsider without reference to skin. Victoria Laurie's narrative reinscribes him as outsider, outsider to the Johnson family, outsider to the Nyoongah community who 'invited Mudrooroo to put his case'. He didn't. By the end of the article, the words of the writer 'at the pinnacle of his literary career' have vanished altogether, and it is Betty who effects closure: 'I've got to say my bit, don't I?'

It's Betty's 'bit' that makes it possible for the journalist to convert a private narrative of anxiety over passing into a politically charged narrative about assimilation. Passing subverts the power grid; assimilation yields to its mapping. And it is to a paradigm of assimilation that the federal government has now shifted, rejecting the previous government's drive towards reconciliation.

Assimilate: that is the message underlying the telling of the Johnson family story in the *Australian*. The Johnsons in erasing their blackness are depicted as truthful, their stubbornly 'black' brother as a liar—because his identity is not the one uncovered by his sister. He's not Aboriginal black, he's African by way of

American slave black, so he's not what he claims to be, not a writer whose words are to be trusted. He says Mudrooroo, they say Johnson, sounding English by origin, sounding ordinary Australian today, mainstream, belonging. 'Johnson' is also the name they have inherited from a slave ancestor, a name used to erase Africanness, but Victoria Laurie doesn't mention this. Her article, attacking the integrity of Mudrooroo while supporting the integrity of his siblings, arouses suspicions about other 'so-called Aborigines', a phrase heard with increasing frequency in these days of the Prime Minister's new 'freedom of speech'. If Mudrooroo is unauthentic, only passing, the article by implication asks, how many more are doing the same? How many more are passing? The narrative of assimilation is shadowed by the unassimilated, the Other, and when the Other is Author, his words become vulnerable, subject to appropriation, denial, erasure. The future then looks like a past to which I hope we will not return.

The Subaltern in Shadow: Reading Aboriginal Women's Life-Stories

DEBJANI GANGULY
Australian National University, Canberra

The concept of subalternity, originally used by Gramsci to connote the condition created by class oppression, has had much wider ramifications in colonial and feminist discourse. Today, the term is materially underpinned not only by class but also gender and (post)-colonial oppression. This of course does not mean that 'all' women and 'all' colonized peoples are subalterns. The projects of the *Subaltern Studies* collective and of Third World feminist historiographers have problematised the concept of subalternity well enough to demonstrate how absurd such a notion is. However, when one looks into the inflexion of gender in colonial discourse, one finds that the subaltern, whether as the object of colonialist and / or nationalist historiography or as the agent of insurgency, is, almost invariably, male. Hence, Spivak's relegation of the subaltern as female to the 'shadows', from which it is well-nigh impossible for her to emerge. (Spivak, 1994: 83).

Much has since been written on the 'historically muted' subjectivity of the subaltern woman in colonial discourse. The difficulty of retrieving her agency, caught as she is, between colonial and indigenous patriarchal constructions of her role and identity, has been recognised early enough by post-colonial feminist theorists.

What then, of the politics of reception, when she actually does begin to decode her experience in writing, often with the help of imperialistic and / or patriarchal collaborators? What effect does homogenised concept of subaltern resistance have, on the voices of subaltern women? This is the issue my paper will look into, in its examination of life-stories written by Aboriginal women in Australia, such as Sally Morgan, Ruby Langford and Glenyse Ward.

In the last three decades or so, there has been a considerable "unpicking of the seams" (Goodman, 1994:49) of the traditional forms of Australian national history by New Left, post-modernist, feminist, and, not the least, Aboriginal interventions. And any discussion of Australian national identity in the Nineties has had to come to terms with this continent's Aboriginal heritage. Whether it is Paul Keating's assertion of the Aboriginal "as a defining element in the character of our nation", or Pauline Hanson's myopic exasperation at Aboriginal demands for rights and dignity, the fact remains that Aboriginality has blasted open the two-hundred-year-old white continuum of Australian history.

While white historians in Australia are only beginning to relativise and decenter Australian history, whether in theoretical response to modish academic trends or in atonement for causing generational pain to the Aborigines, the Aboriginal voice and consciousness itself is beginning to be increasingly circumscribed by notions of the authentic, the traditional—merely another version of the Eurocentric notion of unified and homogenised subjectivity. Significantly, the political potency of the authenticity construct is vehemently endorsed by a few Aboriginal activists and intellectuals themselves. Charges that any essentialist project eventually reifies and even commodifies identity are squarely met by a Fanonite argument such as the one given by Robert Ariss:

> Pan-Aboriginality is a politically necessary concept for Aborigines to present a unified and therefore, more efficacious front to a government reluctant to recognise their demands. The recourse to traditionality is perhaps as much politically induced as a felt reality in the minds of Aborigines. In emphasising traditional culture, its otherness, Aboriginal discourse establishes itself firmly in opposition to the dominant culture. It is only from this position that Aboriginal people can resist the seduction of assimilation and confidently work at rebuilding a unique identity. (Ariss, 1988:136)

Such conscious fetishization of the 'traditional', which is seen as empowering by some Aborigines themselves, brings to mind the white anthropological cannibalising of Aboriginal lived experiences as a means of continuation of Western European epistemology. The simplistic, yet self-serving evolutionary premises underpinning such anthropological work, which "traced the development of culture from simple oral forms to advanced cultural forms, especially the forms of literate societies" (Hodge-Mishra:1991, 76) constructed reading regimes that denigrated Aboriginal cultural forms. The Western anthropological focus on the mythical, the non-scribal, the traditional, in Aboriginal narratives has been part of an "overall discursive system or economy that has cumulatively served Australia and its Aboriginal peoples very badly." (Hodge, 1993:165) It gave rise to that overarching disciplinary formation, which Bob Hodge and Vijay Mishra termed 'Aboriginalism' and which Bain Attwood and John Arnold were at pains to dismantle (and herald the age of 'post-Aboriginalism') in their book *Power, Knowledge and Aborigines* (1992).

But what happens, when it is not the white anthropologist or the non-Aboriginal academic, but the Aboriginal intellectual or political activist himself (the use of the male pronoun is deliberate) who attempts to mobilise an essential Aboriginal identity by invoking what Paul Carter has called, in another context "the genealogical rhetoric of blood and property." (Carter, 1992:8)—that recourse to the mythical, the originary, the traditional, set in unmitigated opposition to the dominant culture? If the fetishization of the primitive-as-authentic in Western ethnographic discourse was seen as disempowering to the Aborigines, the Aborigines' own mythologizing of the authentic—what Mudrooroo Narogin calls "Aboriginality"—is seen by them to be an essential oppositional political strategy in—to invoke Fanon—"the murderous and decisive struggle between two protagonists". When Aboriginality functions as "a meta-text in Aboriginal writing, the latter serves as "a community gesture towards freedom and survival rather than the self-expression of an individual author" (Davis, et al, 1990:3). Or in the words of Mudrooroo, "Aboriginal literature begins as a cry from the heart directed at the whiteman. It is a cry for justice." (Narogin, 1990:1) Communal responsibility, in other words, ought to be the foremost preoccupation of the Aboriginal writer or artist. While such prescriptive notions of identity and cultural responsibility do constitute the moral first step of protest, the normative and exclusionary tendencies that are latent in these notions do begin to be manifested sooner than later.

I am especially concerned with the way in which the same notion of essential difference from the colonial culture—namely Aboriginality—which functions as such a potent weapon in the arena of (male?) oppositional politics, can become a repressive mode as soon as we raise questions about the Aboriginal woman's relationship to power and discourse. In my presentation, this tyranny of authenticity is seen to be manifested in Mudrooroo's critique of the life-stories written by Aboriginal women such as Sally Morgan, Glenyse Ward and Ruby Langford. The gist of Mudrooroo's critique is that, works like *My Place, Wandering Girl* and *Don't Take Your Love to Town*, function essentially as 'battler' genre, the kind of writing that focuses on an individual "who blazed a trail through a maze of prejudice and fear", and which, therefore, is not adequately 'communal'—that yardstick of pure Aboriginality—and hence, not politically confrontationist

It is seven years since Mudrooroo first made his reservations about Aboriginal women's writing, public. Since then, much ink has been exhausted in academic attempts to either extricate Morgan's and Langford's texts from the critical denunciations of a 'male' Aboriginal critic or, as in the case of Joan Newman's essay, "Race, Gender, and Identity" (1992), to reinforce Mudrooroo's critique by placing these texts in the "context of anxieties about the potential neo-colonising influence of individualistic and individualising European Australian literary forms" (Thomas, 1993:171).

Aboriginal women from all over Australia had their first ever formal meeting in 1980. A white-edited anthology, *We Are Bosses Ourselves*, published by the Australian Institute of Aboriginal Studies, Canberra, in 1983, is a record of the proceedings of this Symposium. Mudrooroo's comments on the gaps and highlights of the book are worth noting in the light of his judgements on the works of Aboriginal women published in the late 1980s. After commenting on the persistence of the community motif on the cover of the book—a group of women photographed with their children, with the 'absent male' crying out only too loud not to be noticed—Mudrooroo notes how the pictures of individual women in the pages, between the covers, shows these women in "typical female roles of 'nurturing': teaching and nursing". (Mudrooroo, 1990:156) What disturbs him is the absence of photographs of black women writers: "Woman-as-writer, especially black-woman-as-writer, has been written out of this text" (Mudrooroo, 1990:157). He reads into this ommission, the operation of white conspiracy where, as he says, "an ideology of group collectivity or solidarity of women has been maintained at the expense of truth" (Mudrooroo, 1990:157). He then asks, with palpable indignation, "If we are bosses ourselves, should we rely on a white woman to write us down?" (Mudrooroo, 1990:156-57)

There are two issues of significance that emerge from this critique. The 'truth' that Mudrooroo refers to, is an acknowledgement on his part that there is a commendable archive of Aboriginal women's literature (he himself cites the names of Roberta Sykes, Noonuccal, Gloria Brennan, Margaret Tucker, Faith Bandler and others) that merits attention. The second is that, the 'information-retrieval' approach of the white community towards the Aborigines persists till date and contaminates a substantial body of what purports to be Aboriginal discourse. He sees this contamination especially endemic to the 'life-story' genre, which, post-1988, seems to have become the most preferred form in which Aboriginal women inscribe their experiences.

The debate about compromised black-white collaborative publications is, of course, not new. As Carole Ferrier says, in her book, *Gender, Politics and Fiction*, "The process by which black writers become authors is still, by and large, in the hands of a small taste-making group" (Ferrier, 1992:216, emphasis original). And notwithstanding Stephen Muecke's innovative editorial strategies in *Gularabulu: Stories of West Kimberly* (1983), the idea of producing Aboriginal narratives that are faithful to the original narratorial voice, remains problematic (Ferrier, 1992:206).

Enmeshed in these debates, Mudrooroo's disapproval of Morgan's *My Place* and Langford's *Don't Take Your Love to Town* appears worth paying attention to. After all, both these texts have been worked through with white editors—Langford worked with

Susan Hampton and Morgan with Ray Coffey. At the same time it is also worth noting Sally Morgan's claim, in an interview, in 1992, with Delys Bird and Dennis Haskell, that she was quite happy to work with a white male editor (Morgan, 1992:4). As if that were not enough, the two interviewers along with Morgan herself, fall over each other in applauding the contribution of Ray Coffey to Western Australian writing. So we have Dennis Haskell's, "he's one of the great unsung heroes in literature" (Haskell, 1992:4), and Sally Morgan's, "he's one of the best in Australia" (Morgan, 1992:4)—statements not exactly cocking a snook at Mudrooroo's reservations, but pointing to editorial interventions that do not exactly fit in with Aboriginality's white-victimiser-black-victim paradigm. The conscious charge that Morgan took of her own manuscript—"I had worked over a lot of it. . . . I just kept working at it" (Morgan, 1992:5)—and her equal and intense working relationship with her editor, contrasts sharply, for instance, with the condescending tone of the non-Aboriginal editors of Elsie Roughsey's (Labumore) *An Aboriginal Mother Tells of the Old and the New* (1984):

> It became apparent that some editing would be required in order for it to be acceptable for commercial publication, and accessible to the average white Australian reader. . . . Despite the changes to the text, we feel that we have preserved the flavour and flow of Elsie's work (1984:241).

Editorial stances such as these do hark back to the appropriative gestures of white social anthropologists towards indigenous cultural productions. But to claim from this evidence that the life-story genre remains and will always remain compromised, as Mudrooroo does, is to subject interventionist texts, such as Morgan's and Langford's to a doctoring, a surveillance that is, to say the least, discomfiting. These texts not only fracture the anthropological paradigm of black-informant-white-writer, but also produce reading effects that slice through, if not transcend, attempts at homogenisation and authentication of Aboriginal modes of resistance.

Mudrooroo uses *authenticity* as a 'gate-keeping concept' (Appadurai, 1986:357)[1] when he also claims that *My Place* and *Don't*

Take Your Love to Town are written in the 'battler' genre mode and hence, valorise individual effort and expression at the expense of communal responsibility. His implication is that autobiography as a classic expression of white bourgeois individualism, is unlikely to be politically cogent in the hands of these Aboriginal women writers.

A similar reservation was voiced by the African-American novelist, Toni Morrison, in 1985, in her article, "Rootedness: The Ancestor as Foundation": "The contemporary autobiography tends to be 'how I got over-look at me—alone—let me show you how I did it'." (Morrison, 1985:339-40). What both Mudrooroo and Morrison fail to recognise is the difference between two modes of autobiographical production. They have tended to circumscribe autobiography within the bourgeois-male mode, which articulates white liberal humanist views of individuality and achievement. However, when the autobiographical mode is appropriated by oppressed groups to narrate their life-stories, the genre, more often than not, "opens out to shared experience that is of ritual significance to the contests on hand. It is the typical and not the exceptional that is of interest" (Tharu, 1996:2020). In India, for instance, the primary subaltern mode of expression is the life-story and it is found, to give just two examples, in 'Gramin' and 'Dalit' literature in Marathi and the 'Bandaya' in Kannada.

There have been impressive critical attempts to rescue and rehabilitate the works of Morgan and Langford from attacks branding them as flawed, compromised self-centred. An Aboriginal critic, Jody Brown, for instance, has exposed Mudrooroo's reading of *My Place* as "minimalist" for failing to acknowledge the preponderance of historical and political issues in the text (Brown, 1992:23-31). Carole Ferrier shows how, the possessive personal pronoun in the title of Morgan's text notwithstanding, the title and Morgan's epigraph together, foreground the politically confrontationist stance of the text:

> In the light of a history of Aboriginal people having been often forced to know their place in the white coloniser's scheme of things (this bitter pun is also present in Morgan's text), finding a place within the dominant institutions from

> which to speak and resist, becomes one strategy of opposition. (Ferrier, 1992:213)

And at least half a dozen critics have commented upon and demonstrated the palimpsestic, multi-voiced narratorial strategy used by Sally Morgan, as against Mudrooroo's claim that *My Place* is dominated by a single authorial voice and, hence, in some sense, is not authentically Aboriginal.

What the critical attempts outlined above have not done, however, is to extricate Morgan's and Langford's texts from the tyranny of authenticity. They have, on the contrary, only reinforced Mudrooroo's notion that only those texts which solely address racial and communal issues, can be authentically Aboriginal. Such essentialist interpretive strategies shut off reading effects that are not ineluctably aligned with ethnic dissimilarities. In other words, an overarching emphasis on racial or nationalistic issues, often gloss over issues of gender, class, even caste, to structure reified identities that can serve the cause of cultural nationalism. And where Aboriginal women's writing is concerned, "blindness to the gender subtext can be as occluding as blindness to the racial subtext. . ." (Henderson, 1994:258). Or as Tracey Moffatt, the Aboriginal film-maker, puts it: ". . . making art is not about exploring black issues all the time" (Quoted by Rowse, 1993:93).

Ruby Langford's *Don't Take Your Love to Town* exposes the authenticity myth by showing how Aboriginality itself, far from being a monolithic ideological construct, has sources and dimensions that can hardly be ranged hierarchically on an authenticity-scale. For lack of space, I shall briefly touch upon two manifestations of Langford's problematisation of the Aboriginality construct.

In the first place, for all her assertions that her text is, first of all, an attempt to delineate the Koori experience (see her interview with McGrath and Sawyer in *Meridian*, May 1994), various aspects of the book compel us to conclude that it is her identity as a woman that seems far more problematical than her identity as a Koori. The kinship and community network that forms the cornerstone of any attempt to define traditional Aboriginal society, is seen to rupture time and again, in Langford's text, as she describes her struggle to bring up nine children in a familial context of irresponsible, unfaithful, abandoning males. As she says, after just about managing to rescue her son, David, from drowning:

> I felt like I was living tribal, but with no tribe around me, no close-knit family. The food-gathering, the laws and songs were broken up, and my generation at this time wandered around as if we were tribal, but in fact living worse than the poorest of poor . . . and in the case of women, living hard because it seemed like the men loved you for a while and then more kids came along and the men drank and gambled and disappeared. One day they'd had enough and they just didn't come back. (Langford, 1988:96)

The 'wandering' of her generation that she refers to, in the above passage is, as sociologists have pointed out, a fall-out of the "massive post-Depression urban migration of New South Wales Koories" (Rowse, 1993:94). Thus, while non-Aboriginal hegemony and the weight of colonial history do constitute the racial subtext of Langford's book, her overwhelming struggles as a woman can be attributed more immediately to "the contingencies of kinship, fractured by rural-urban migration, and by the fickle vulnerabilities of men" (Rowse, 1993:103). Does this make her text more or less Aboriginal? Isn't it more significant to see texts like Langford's "contain within themselves strategies of recuperation towards distinctive feartures of *difference* in the cultures of Australian Aboriginal peoples"? (Griffiths, 1994:77, emphasis original). How can the delineation of the "gendered contingencies of Koori experience" (Rowse, 1993:103) compromise the cause of Aboriginal autonomy?

These questions lead me on to the second manifestation of splintered Aboriginality in Langford's text. This is her visit to Uluru or Ayers Rock with a group of twenty-seven Aboriginal women. Uluru, which according to anthropologists documenting traditional Aboriginal culture, is a conjunction of several sacred sites (which in turn are the focus of several spatially coincident Western desert myths) (Rowse, 1993:86), has, over the years, been at the centre of a white-appropriation-black-retrieval tussle. On the one hand, was the slogan—"The rock belongs to everyone"—which opposed the handing over of the Rock to its 'traditional' owner. On the other hand, enough flak has been directed at the process of appropriating it as "the sacred centre of a rapidly developing settler cosmology" (Marcus, 1988:254). Today, much to the chagrin of the Aboriginal community, Ayers Rock or Uluru has become an indispensible land-form attraction in brochures promoting Australian tourism. It is interesting to note that Langford's reaction to seeing Uluru for the first time is not unlike that of the quintessential tourist. She uses clichéd terms such as 'big', 'rugged', 'huge animal asleep in the middle of nowhere', in her description of the magnificent Rock. And she herself (along with twenty-seven Aboriginal women) has allowed the white gaze in the form of the ABC team, to fix her as the commodified Aboriginal in quest of a spiritual centre of sorts. The team's acceptance of ABC sponsorship and Langford's concern with her television appearance—"It was the first time I'd been interviewed for TV. I was wearing a Land Rights coloured hat, dark glasses and I hope it showed up good on film" (Langford, 1988:234)—jostle with moments of illumination that have not so much to do with the Rock per se as with connecting with a primal, yet dynamic past:

> It made me think of our tribal beginnings, and this to me was like the beginning of our time and culture. Time was suddenly shortened to include all of history in the present, and it was also stretched to a way of seeing the earth that was thousands of years old. (Langford, 1988:234)

Her momentary desire to reclaim the tribal past is, however, immediately offset by visions of modern-day comforts "like not having to boil the billy for a cup of tea or having to make a fire to do that. . ." (Langford, 1988:236).

It is only a "black intellectual totalitarianism" (to use Mulvaney's words), that will condemn Langford's non-traditional response to Uluru as 'inauthentic', as a whitening of Aboriginal values.

Since so much of my presentation has been taken up by the 'proprietary rights' that are often claimed by an 'oppressed discourse' (Suleri, 1994:251), I cannot but conclude my presentation by asking, what happens, when the proprietor of the oppressed discourse himself, is hounded by charges of tainted, even false, genealogy. I refer, of course, to the furore caused, in the Nyoongar community and in academic and literary circles, by the revelation of Mudrooroo's non-Aboriginal parentage, by his siblings, no less. Such charges take on ominous dimensions, especially because, for such a while now, Mudrooroo has set himself up as the indisputable arbiter of what is, or is not, Aboriginal. If one goes by the last published reports on this issue, Mudrooroo has yet to clear the air. Instead, as Tom and Lorna Little say, in their brief write-up in the Spring'96 issue of *Westerly*, "Mudrooroo appears to have gone to ground." (p. 7) The ramification of this rather disconcerting affair can hardly be accommodated within the scope of this paper. But, whatever the outcome of this unseemly controversy, it, along with the Demidenko affair, has ripped apart, perhaps forever, the complacent contours of Australian literary space.

NOTE

1. In his brief write-up on how anthropologists traffic in 'otherness', anthropologist Arjun Appadurai of how "a few simple theoretical handles become metonyms and surrogates" for complex civilisations. Among the examples he gives are, 'hierarchy' for India and 'filial piety' for China. He calls such theoretical handles as "gate-keeping concepts in anthropological theory, concepts . . . that seem to limit anthropological theorising" of the place or civilisation in question.

WORKS CITED

Arjun Appadura, "Theory in Anthropology: Centre and Periphery," *Comparative Studies in Society and History*, Vol. 28, 1986.

Robert Ariss, "Writing Black: The Construction of an Aboriginal Discourse," in Jeremy Beckett, ed., *Past and Present: The Construction of Aboriginality* (Canberra: Aboriginal Studies Press, 1988).

Jody Brown, "Unmaking White Myths:Your Laws, My Place," in Delys Bird and Dennis Haskell, ed., *Whose Place?—A Study of Sally Morgan's My Place* (NSW: Angus and Robertson, 1992).

Paul Carter, *Living in a New Country: History, Travelling and Language* (London: Faber, 1992).

Jack Davis, Muecke, Narogin, Shoemaker, ed., *Paperbark: A Collection of Black Australian Writings* (St. Lucia: University of Queensland Press, 1990, 1993 reprint).

Carole Ferrier, *Gender, Politics and Fiction* (St. Lucia: University of Queensland Press, 1985, 1992 reprint).

Fay Gale, *We are Bosses Ourselves* (Canberra: Australian Institute of Aboriginal Studies, 1983).

David Goodman, "Australian Identity, Postmodernism and History," in Livio Dobrez, ed., *Identifying Australia in Postmodern Times* (Canberra: Bibliotech, 1994).

Gareth Griffiths, "Myth of Authenticity: Representation, Discourse and Social Practice," in Alan Lawson and Chris Tiffin, ed., *De-scribing Empire: Post-colonialism and Textuality* (London: Routledge, 1994).

Mae Gwendolyn Henderson, "Speaking in Tongues: Dialogics, Dialectics and the Black Women's Literary Tradition," *Colonial Discourse and Post-Colonial Theory*, Patrick Williams and Laura Chrisman, ed. (Hertfordshire: Harvester Wheatsheaf, 1994).

Bob Hodge, "Theory and Practice in the Age of Post-Aboriginalism," *Meridian*, Vol. 12, No. 2, October, 1993.

______, and Vijay Mishra, *Dark Side of the Dream: Australian Literature and the Postcolonial Mind* (Sydney: Allen and Unwin, 1991).

Ruby Langford, *Don't Take Your Love to Town* (Melbourne: Penguin, 1988).

______, Interview with Caitland McGrath and Philippa Sawyer, *Meridian*, Vol. 13, No. 1, 1994.

Tom and Lorna Little, "The Mudrooroo Dilemma," *Westerly*, No. 3, Spring, 1996.

Julie Marcus, "The Cultural Appropriation of Ayers Rock," in Anna Rutherford, ed., *Aboriginal Culture Today* (Sydney: Dangaroo Press—Kunapipi, 1988).

Sally Morgan, *My Place* (Fremantle: Fremantle Arts Centre Press, 1987).

______, Interview with Delys Bird and Dennis Haskell, in Bird and Haskell, ed., *Whose Place?—A Study of Sally Morgan's My Place*, (NSW: Angus and Robertson, 1992).

Toni Morrison, "Rootedness: The Ancestor as Foundation," in Mari Evans ed., *Black Women Writers* (Pluto, 1985).

Mudrooroo Narogin, *Writing from the Fringe: A Study of Aboriginal Literature* (Melbourne: Hyland House, 1990).

Joan Newman, "Race, Gender and Identity," in Bird and Haskell, ed., *Whose Place?—A Study of Sally Morgan's My Place* (NSW: Angus and Robertson, 1992).

Elsie Roughsey, *An Aboriginal Mother Tells of the Old and the New* (Victoria: McPhee Gribble, 1984).

Tim Rowse, *After Mabo: Interpreting Indigenous Traditions* (Melbourne: Melbourne University Press, 1993).

Gayatri Chakravarti Spivak, "Can the Subaltern Speak?," in Patrick Williams and Laura Chrisman, ed., *Colonial Discourse and Post-Colonial Theory* (Hertfordshire: Harvester Wheatsheaf, 1994).

Sara Suleri, "Women Skin Deep: Feminism and the Postcolonial Condition," in Patrick Williams and Laura Chrisman, ed., *Colonial Discourse and Post-Colonial Theory* (Hertfordshire: Harvester Wheatsheaf, 1994).

Susie Tharu, "A Critique of Hindutva Brahminism." *Economic and Political Weekly*, July 27, 1996.

Sue Thomas, "Positioning Sally Morgan," *Meridian*, Vol. 12, No. 2, October, 1993.

Presenting Colonisation: Teaching Post-colonial Theory and Practice in the Australian Secondary English Classroom

COLIN KENWORTHY
Edith Cowan University, Western Australia

ABSTRACT: Texts that construct European colonisers as 'normal' and the colonised as 'strange' are a universal legacy of colonialism. This paper shows how teaching upper secondary English students to make post-colonial readings of hegemonic Australian texts that represent Aborigines and Aboriginality as 'other' and Anglo-Australian culture as 'normal' can develop their capacity to read the world. The paper describes a pedagogy based on discourse theory and 'new left' Marxism which enabled a group of Year 12 students to rethink Anglo-Aboriginal relations and the place of Aborigines in Australian society. The pedagogy outlined in this paper enabled the students to: consider the ways in which writing from a Eurocentric perspective hides or distorts indigenous experience understand that texts and reading practices draw on existing discourses to produce meanings develop the capacity interrogate written texts and to challenge their authority understand that acceptance or rejection of the reading positions offered by dominant texts changes the meaning which can be produced for a text. Discourses are not about objects; they do not identify objects, they constitute them and in the process of doing so conceal their own invention (Foucault, 1972: 49).

[Reading] is the child's understanding of the teacher's culture, as it is made available in the teacher's commentary on the text and the teacher's description of what counts as reading of the text (Baker and Freebody in Castell, Luke and Luke, 1992: 278).

Australia, like India, is a country in which European colonial discourses still operate; but, unlike India, Australian culture is ninety-eight per cent European. As Wilkes has shown in *The Stockyard and the Croquet Lawn* (1981), Australian cultural identity has been informed by writing that explores the tensions between a centre which values education, social class distinctions, high church Anglicanism, the monarchy and Imperial connections and margins where new ways of thinking and behaving are developed around experience, practical work, the bush, free-thinking utopianism and even republicanism. As Graeme Turner has noted:

> Throughout its white history, Australia has obsessively defined itself in opposition to Britain; Australia was what Britain was not and even those traditions we shared—our 'common traditions'—were inflected differently in an Australian context.' (Turner, 1996: 128)

Australia's national consciousness has, like India's, been developed partly by seeing, thinking and behaving in ways that resist the power of the Imperial centre (Lawson, 1995). But the resistance to the Imperial centre in the writing of whites in Australia and the other settler societies of Canada, South Africa and New Zealand has never been directed at an object or a discursive structure which can be seen as purely external to the self. The Second-World writers, the Second-World text, that is, have always been complicit in colonialism's territorial appropriation of land, and voice, and agency, and this has been their inescapable condition. (Slemon, 1995: 110)

Because of the colonisers' belief in the doctrine of terra nullius, the dominant culture has remained Anglicised to a much greater extent than in India where other traditions were drawn on to shape the national identity. Australian writing, therefore, reveals an ambivalence towards colonial discourses. Australian institutions and persons on the margins of the Empire have invoked Eurocentric discourses to displace and marginalise indigenous institutions and peoples. As a result, the othering of Aborigines has always been more complete and less compromising than the othering of the English.

In the Australian context, therefore, the postcolonial project of dismantling the centre/margins binarism of colonial discourses is a twofold task. On the one hand, the literary canon of Australia's emergent national identity can be explored for its resistance to colonial authority and for its development of an ambivalent subjectivity which is at once colonial and anti-colonial. On the other hand, this canon can be explored for its misrecognition and misrepresentation of Aborigines and Aboriginality. Part of the task of post-colonial criticism, then, is to locate and describe the absence of the Aboriginal in historical and contemporary texts because, as Macherey claims, 'An ideology is made of what it does not mention; it exists because there are things which must not be spoken of' (Macherey, 1978, p. 132). In many texts—literary and non-literary—from the first European contact until today, indigenous peoples have provided a convenient other for the production of a Eurocentric sense of self. Fanon (1963), Memmi (1974), Said (1978, 1984) and Bhabha (1990) have explicated the role of colonising discourses in excluding the colonised from participation in the economic, social, political and cultural life of European colonies and their successor states. These discourses are invoked daily in contemporary non-literary texts.

While postcolonial theorisation has had some impact on both texts and teaching in several university disciplines, it has had little effect on primary and secondary curricula and pedagogy. If 'the rereading and rewriting of the European historical and fictional record are vital and inescapable tasks' (Tiffin, 1987, p. 95), then they are tasks that should begin in our primary and secondary schools. An equitable society depends on all Australians understanding the nexus between the production and interpretation of dominant texts and the maintenance and reproduction of versions of reality that exclude Aborigines—and other minorities—from full status as Australians.

This paper will show how teaching postcolonial reading practices to a group of secondary school students enabled them to challenge ideas about race encouraged by the hegemonic discourses. It will show how, by drawing attention to changes in nineteenth century Eurocentric constructions of Aboriginality, students were enabled to interrogate the discursive construction of the Aboriginal as 'Other' in current print media texts.

English teaching in Australian schools has been profoundly altered by the development of curricula and professional development programs that have drawn on the theorisations of 'new left' Marxist structuralism (Althusser, 1984; Jameson, 1991; Barthes, 1975; Eagleton, 1981, 1983, 1984, 1986, 1990); on discourse and social reproduction theories (Kress, 1985; Fairclough, 1989; Gee, 1990, 1992; Luke, 1988, 1991; Lemke 1995; Bourdieu, 1977, 1991); and on postcolonial theories (Fanon, 1963; Memmi, 1974; Said, 1978, 1984)—all of which have led to new ways of 'doing reading' in the classroom.

These theorisations of reading have, to a greater or lesser extent, underwritten books for the teaching of reading that have become popular since the mid eighties-books like those by Janks (1993, 1993), Mellor et. al. (1984, 1984, 1987, 1991), Mellor and Paterson (1996), Martino (1994), Moon (1990, 1992), Comber (1993, 1995) and Morgan (1994, 1996). Through these books, students have been taught to regard texts not as creations of individual gifted writers but as instantiations of existing discourses: not as carriers of meaning but as sites for the contention of meaning; not as transparent media for catching images of the world but as constructions which legitimate particular versions of reality. None of these activity-based books for teaching reading, however, contains textual material dealing specifically with Aboriginal issues.

This paper will report on a four-hour seminar given to group of 22 Year 12 students, who attended an inter-school conference in preparation for University Entrance examinations in English. The seminar outcomes were dependent both on the choice of texts and activities and on the prior reconceptualisation of secondary English that has resulted from a focus on cultural critique rather than on the cultural canon.

The pedagogy used in the seminar required students to work in pairs and small-groups on activities designed to unmask the attitudes and values embedded in both texts and reading practices.

The resources for the seminar included transactional texts, that were chosen to help students recognise different hegemonic discourses that, over the last 250 years, have marginalised Aborigines; to help them identify these same discourses in contemporary print media: and to help them to see how these texts contain political and social advantages and disadvantages for particular groups in Australian society. The seminar built on the understanding that most students already had of terms like 'text, 'context', 'reading', 'ideology', 'dominant reading' and 'resistant reading'. It was designed to lead students to see that texts on Aborigines—like all other texts—offer reading positions which readers can accept or reject; that readings of texts are affected by a reader's subject position which is contingent on factors like social class, age, ethnic background; that reading can involve challenging hegemonic versions of society.

The seminar was designed to clarify the students' understanding of 'discourse'; of 'dominant discourses' as those which tend to legitimate, support, maintain and reproduce the status quo (Kress, 1985); of the idea that discourses operate most successfully when they are seen by those who speak, write, read and listen to them as 'common sense'; of the connection between 'knowledge' and power that Foucault points to when he writes:

> Discourses are not about objects; they do not identify objects; they constitute them and in the process of doing so conceal their own invention' (Foucault, 1972, p. 49).

By focusing on variations in colonial discourses about Aboriginality that resulted from changes in the social, economic and political needs of the colonisers, the activities destabilised the students' hegemonic assumptions about Aboriginality as a fixed entity outside the pale of Australian national identity. The seminar created an environment in which students learned that what counts in reading texts are issues of representation, sources of power, reading positions promoted by texts, and reader responses. It encouraged them to step outside the discourses that have formed their own subjectivities and it invited them to develop a national consciousness free of Anglocentric exclusivity.

Learning about Three Colonising Discourses

Time constraints limited the number of discourses that could be taught in the seminar to three—the 'noble savage', the 'aggressive savage' and the 'dying race'. It could be argued that European settler societies created other discourses—both positive and negative—about Indigenous peoples. But the use of the chosen discourses offered students alternative perspectives on the mythology of settlement; it presented the concepts of discourse and dominant discourse to them in a simplified form; it limited the quantity of printed material they needed to read; it provided data for the development of a theoretical framework with which to view the operation of these discourses in contemporary texts.

Getting secondary students to understand how historical texts invoke discourses that support colonising ideologies was a first step on the path of understanding how contemporary texts use similar discourses to maintain European power and privilege. Starting with texts distant from their own experience, helped the students to recognise how these texts maintained and reproduced assumptions of European colonial supremacy.

After a brief introduction to European colonial expansion and to the 'settlement/invasion' of Australia, students were given simplified descriptions of three discourses and of the historical contexts in which they developed. The discourses were not named. The students were asked to discuss the descriptions outlined below with a partner and to offer labels for each discourse for the whole class to consider.

Historical Contexts of Three Discourses for Constructing Aborigines

Discourse 1 was developed during first contacts between Europeans and Aborigines. In this early stage, the colonisers had relatively little power over much larger numbers of Aborigines. They relied on Aborigines who knew more about the territory than they did. The ideology of these early texts is often marked by the following features:

> Aborigines are constructed as living in harmony with nature; they are presented as 'noble savages' who lead happy, moral lives;
> their lifestyle is like that of Adam and Eve in the Garden of Eden;

> they are shown as not having to worry about work.

Discourse 2 was developed as a result of conflict over control of the land. This discourse was used by some Europeans in Australia even before 1788. It intensified after the crossing of the Blue Mountains in 1813 and the 'opening up' of the continent for European pastoralists and European animals.

As the frontier of European settlement moved out from the capital cities, the struggle for land led to negative descriptions of Aborigines. Even today, texts produced by whites who want control of land for mining, pastoral or tourist purposes often construct Aborigines as difficult or obstructionist. The ideology of these texts is often marked by the following features:

> Aborigines are dangerous, violent criminals with no respect for life or property;
> their religion is based on superstition;
> they should be trained to work for white land owners;
> they should be taught to respect whites and white laws;
> it is reasonable to drive Aborigines into the outback or to place them on reserves because they don't use the land to produce goods which are valued by the European market economy and because they are happier in their own environment.

Discourse 3 was developed by colonisers as they increased control over all aspects of Aboriginal life. It is estimated that there were between 300,000 and 1,000,000 Aborigines in Australia in 1788. By 1900, there were only 70,000. Their numbers fell because they had no immunity to European diseases like smallpox, measles, influenza and syphilis, because they were killed or forced off their lands. These changes often led to the collapse of Aboriginal law and society. Texts written and read between 1860 and 1960 often constructed Aborigines as:

> a race who would eventually die out and who should therefore be studied by anthropologists the most primitive form of humanity on earth; physically and socially similar to Neander-

> thal man a different species, mentally inferior to the rest of humanity in need of protection and control by white administrators people who should be kept separate from whites and should not be allowed access to white schools, hospitals or welfare because they did not pay taxes.

These three discourses about Aborigines and Anglo-Aboriginal relations developed and became popular at different stages because of:

> the moving frontier of European colonisation, the needs of the European settlers, changes in European writers' and readers' understanding and opinion about Aborigines.

In small groups, and then as a whole class working with the teacher, they named the three discourses. They found the labelling of the first discourse difficult because it was furthest removed from their own experience. They suggested: 'paradise', utopia', 'idealistic', perfectible'. They discussed 'golden ages' of mythology and sifi/fantasy and initial contacts between European and 'primitive' societies. Eighteenth century European drawings of Aborigines helped them to understand the Enlightenment concept of the 'noble savage'.

Their labelling of the second discourse included the terms: 'wild', 'dangerous', 'criminal', 'backward' and 'aggressive'. Their experience of films that dealt with the European conquest of North America led them to quickly agree that 'aggressive savage' fairly described the colonisers' view in this second stage of colonisation. Several students, who had seen Dances with Wolves, argued that the 'natives' were only constructed as 'savage' or 'aggressive' by white discourses.

Though closest to them in time, the third discourse seemed strangest to them. They agreed that the media presented Aboriginal welfare as a 'drain on the taxpayer' and argued that some Aborigines 'don't fit into white society'. They suggested the labels of: 'outsiders', 'misfits' and 'primitives'. Some argued against these labels by saying that Aborigines had developed a high level of skill in practical farming tasks. Others debated the reasons for low rate of academic success among Aborigines. This was challenged by two Aboriginal students, who argued that tribal Aborigines had their own forms of reading and writing that would be difficult for Westerners. They discussed the effects of Western food, alcohol and diseases on Aboriginal body chemistry. Despite all of this knowledge, they were surprised by the social Darwinism of the label 'dying race'. But they accepted it as a historical reality and readily debated its positive and negative effects for Aborigines.

This extended discussion around the contexts in which the texts they were about to read were originally written and read constructed a different cultural context for their own reading. The teacher-led talk had shaped a redefinition of what would count as reading (Baker, 1992); a redefinition based on the role of reader as analyst of both text and context (Freebody, 1992).

They were then instructed to read seven historical texts and to fill in a chart showing ideas from the three discourses that were drawn on to produce each text. The selection of only seven texts does unavoidably simplify the past, but, in this case, it allowed students to interrogate discourses of settlement that have had the effect of hiding the dispossession of Aborigines (Reynolds, 1981, 1984, 1987, 1989); and helped them to understand the ideological effects of uncritical reading practices.

For the sake of brevity, only parts of four of the seven texts are included in this paper. The students were instructed to read the texts individually, making notes on:

(i) assumptions about race that the original readers might have accepted, but which you might want to question; (ii) fallacies in the argument of the text that the original readers may not have noticed; and (iii) techniques in the texts that position the reader to accept the values endorsed by the texts.

and then to discuss their notes with a partner.

TEXT 1: The Natives [of Australia] go quite naked both men and women without any manner of Clothing whatever. . . . These people live wholly by fishing and hunting. . . . We never saw one Inch of Cultivated land in the Whole Country. . . . The Natives of New

Holland . . . are far more happier than we Europeans; being wholly unacquainted with the Conveniences so much sought after in Europe, they are happy in not knowing the use of them. They live in Tranquillity which is not disturbed by the Inequality of Condition: the Earth and sea of their own accord furnish them with all things necessary for life: they covet not Magnificent Houses, Household stuff etc. . . They live in a fine warm climate and enjoy wholesome Air. . . . They [seem to] think themselves provided with all the necessarys of Life. (Description of Australian Aboriginals from Captain Cook's Journal, 1770)

TEXT 2 We see daily in the midst of us numbers of the former lords and ladies of the soil in almost their native costume marching about with the lordly air which so distinguishes them and apparently taking stock and diligently spying out the nakedness of the land and the weak points, maybe, of its holders. It [therefore] becomes us as invaders to enforce submission to our laws on the part of the conquered. We have . . . hitherto done this by recourse to powder and the ball. . . . We must not cease to be firm and must take special care to show our black neighbours that whilst we are willing to hold our hands from slaughter, we are at the same time determined to enforce at all hazards and by any means submission to our laws. (Letter to the *Port Denison Times* 12 June 1869).

TEXT 3 A description of the Myall Massacre from a Letter to *The Townsville Herald* 14 February, 1907

TEXT 4 An unsigned article suggesting that Aborigines are a different species from 'whites from 'Savages and Civilised Men.' (In *Science of Man* 21 March, 1903)

TEXT 5 Another article suggesting that Aborigines are a different species by D. Macalister, 'The Australian Aborigines,' *The Melbourne Review*, 3 (1878)

TEXT 6 If the Government is desirous of having the native race in existence for many years longer . . . and wishes to do away with the seemingly never ending trouble and expense pertaining to it, why not emasculate all initiated native offenders and indenture them to settlers? As Eunichs [sic] they would make good, useful, law-abiding servants. Cattle stealing, sheep-stealing, hut robbing, and murder would soon be offences of the past, and peace as far as niggers are concerned would reign in the land. The uninitiated boys could then—under penalty of castration if they became initiated—roam about with the gins, each in their own district, clear of the townships, or be indentured to white people. . . . Native offenders among the initiated for the first offence would suffer partial castration. It is improbable they would appear on a second charge to have the operation completed. The old crawlers could be fed and clothed by the Government or follow their emasculated sons to the stations. Under this system . . . the Aboriginal race would be much more contented and consequently more useful, and the benefit the Government would derive in the way of curtailing expense and saving trouble can only be estimated by those who know the seriousness of the native question.

Castration has a wonderfully soothing and beneficial effect on all creatures with wild and vicious blood—it is like lancing a boil or tumour. It seems to quieten and cow them once and forever. . . . I am confident in a very short time after it had become known that natives in each district had become eunuchs, that not only would the depredations cease, but also the horrible and cruel ceremony of initiation [would] gradually come to an end.

> H.G Mason, (1907) Darkest West Australia: a Treatise bearing on the Habits and Customs of Aborigines and the Solution to 'The Native Question': A Guide to Outback Travellers.

TEXT 7 An article suggesting similarities between Aboriginal behaviour and that of wild animals from R. Cilento & C. Lack (1959) Triumph in the Tropics, Brisbane, p. 179:

They were then required to fill in the chart below in order to better understand the effects on both the colonised and the colonisers of the texts that they had considered.

Tick the texts which encourages the idea that Aborigines are socially and morally superior to Europeans,
don't need to work and are therefore better off than Europeans,
are not interested in making useful things like extra food or houses,
are 'wild' and therefore unwilling or unable to adopt European cultural patterns of behaviour,
are barbaric and therefore likely to be violent and dangerous to white settlers,
the idea that Aborigines are likely to be criminal and therefore have to be controlled or punished by settlers belong to a different species or a lower kind of race,
the idea that the Aborigines are dying out,
are socially and morally inferior to Europeans.

Filling in the next chart enabled them to discuss the way in which each of the seven texts drew on the discourses of the 'noble savage', the 'aggressive savage' and the 'dying race' to develop stereotypes of Aboriginality that were politically useful to the Europeans at different stages in their colonisation of Australia.

Tick the square that shows which discourses each text draws on and discuss your ideas with a partner 'noble savage' 'aggressive savage,' 'dying race'. When they began talking about stereotypes, I defined stereotypes as: useful short cuts to communication that have built-in advantages for groups of people who use them, because they provide simplified images of groups of people and attribute these simplified group characteristics to all people in the group thereby providing judgments without seeming to do so.

Filling in a further chart enabled them to interrogate the 'common-sense' beliefs about Aborigines which were developed in the three discourses and to see how each discourse provided political or economic advantages for colonisers and disadvantages for the colonised. This chart contained all the stereotypical ideas they had already worked on. For brevity's sake, it has been truncated. The first example was completed for them. How Eurocentric stereotypes disadvantaged Aborigines. The stereotypical idea that Aborigines has these advantages for the colonisers and disadvantages for the colonised are not interested in producing useful things like extra food, clothing or houses. This justified European takeover of land for agricultural and pastoral purposes. It allowed the Europeans to feel superior because they produced more material goods which they could trade for money.

This devalued Aboriginal uses of the land which for thousands of years had carefully conserved animals and plants. It also devalued Aboriginal art, music and dancing which were part of their spiritual relationship to the land. are socially and morally inferior to Europeans are dying out.

The process I have outlined may seem laboured, but for these students it provided an effective scaffold for learning to read for issues of representation, for sources of power, and for positions promoted by texts. It also allowed them to consider their own responses within a carefully controlled context. At this halfway point in the seminar, it was clear that the interrogation of the historical texts had developed their capacity to understand:

> that discursive constructions of the colonised change over time
> that the idea of 'race' as stereotype served the colonisers' needs
> that texts present versions of reality rather than mirror some pre-existent reality
> that reading involves looking for inconsistencies in the arguments of texts and consideration of information that texts exclude
> that texts play a role in creating just or unjust societies.

This preliminary work on historical texts had also prepared them to read the contemporary media texts in the second half of the seminar.

Reading Colonial Discourses in Contemporary Texts

The second half of the seminar began with a discussion of Aborignal academic, Marcia Langton's assertion that:

> Stereotypes of Aborigines have a long and changing history. After being depicted as noble savages in the eighteenth cen-

> tury and as a dying race in the nineteenth, we must come to terms with the stereotypes of the late twentieth—the drunken brawler, the development defeating land rights activist, the dole dependent neglecter of children, the improvident and squalid fringe-dweller. The point about such images is that non-Aborigines create and use them for their own purposes. For example, the environmentalist s now vaunt tradition-oriented Aboriginal groups as the original conservationists; Marxists speak of them as proto-communists.

In small groups, students were asked to reflect on Langton's ideas and on the work they had done in the first session and to develop definitions of race and racism. Each group's definitions were displayed and discussed and then I gave them the following definitions:

> RACE is a cultural construct rather than a biological one. Although there are some superficial physical differences between different groups (such as hair colour and texture, skin colour, facial features etc), the biological differences between people of different 'races' are minimal. The genetic material that makes up human beings is ninety-nine per cent the same across all racial groups. It is a scientific fact that there are far greater differences between individuals of the same race than between different races as a whole.
>
> RACISM is an ideology that is used to justify the exploitation of colonised peoples. It generally succeeds where the whole population, both the colonisers and the colonised, can be persuaded to believe that people who belong to one 'race' are superior to people who belong to another.

Persuading people to believe that certain groups are different in some way (inferior, violent, greedy, lazy or 'dying out') makes them easy to control.

This process of constructing a group in society as 'the other' has been used with disastrous effects throughout world history. Sadly, there are many examples more recent than Hitler's elimination of over 6 million European Jews in the 1930s and 40s, including the 'ethnic cleansing' practised in the former Yugoslavia and in Rwanda in the 1990s.

These definitions established a datum from which students were invited to identify racism in texts from their own cultural context. By defining racism in Australia—as in most postcolonial situations—not as 'prejudicial feeling which blacks and whites alike harbor towards one another as well as other groups [but as] institutionalized white supremacist domination' (Hooks, 1995), students were unable to assert, 'Blacks are just as racist as whites.'

The activities included simple tasks like: transferring information from specially marked texts to charts; reading the 'gaps and silences'; finding inconsistencies and biases in texts; pointing to illogical or unsubstantiated arguments; making comparisons. These tasks were designed to enable students to:

> identify in contemporary texts the discourses they had already explored
> understand why these discourses are still employed
> interrogate the conflation of Aboriginality and criminality by media texts
> understand how hegemonic representations of minority groups can lead individual members of those groups to become alienated.

Their first task was to quickly read five recent newspaper reports, and to note:

(i) their use of the discourses of 'noble savage', 'aggressive savage' and 'dying race'
(ii) their use of stereotypes
(iii) discourses which oppose Eurocentric perspectives on any of the issues
(iv) any links between the arguments of these texts and those in the historical texts
(v) the use of techniques to position readers to accept a particular version of reality (title, choice of words, the words used to describe people's actions, the uses of quote—including the

quoted opinions of experts etc).

For brevity's sake, only the headlines and parts of each article are included in this paper. Working in groups of four, the students were quick to recognise the 'noble savage' discourse in LAND RIGHTS WILL BRING LANDCARE by Geraldine Capp from 'Earth 2000' in *The West Australian* 31/7/95.

> Aboriginal people will help stop environmental degradation of Australia's northern pastoral lands as they win more land rights, according to a Northern Territory educator. 'Only when Aboriginal people have land rights are they in a position to be managers of the land.' Mike Carmody, Aboriginal land-care education coordinator said in Perth last week . . .

the 'dying race' discourse in ABORIGINAL CHILDREN SNIFF THEIR LIVES AWAY by Tony Barrass, *The West Australian*, 28 February, 1990

> With glazed eyes and numb brains, a generation of Aboriginal children are stumbling into oblivion. They are children who have become dependent on the fumes of petrol and glue. They sniff to get away from their heritage; they sniff to get away from the boredom of unemployment and racial hatred and most importantly, they sniff because they want to. Aboriginal worker Marian Kickett believes an entire generation of Aborigines could be crippled by this deadly craze which began when American servicemen showed Aborigines in the Top End how to get high during World War II. She says the craze then filtered down through the Northern Territory and into WA. It has already reached epidemic proportion in WA and is slowly taking a stranglehold on a youth already devastated by crime, poverty and unemployment.
> If the tide can't be held back a white man's substance will have succeeded in putting another nail into the coffin of a race already struggling to survive in a white man's world.

The 'aggressive savage' discourse in ABORIGINAL GANGS

> TERRORISE SUBURBS by Helen Winterton from *The West Australian*, 28 February 1990
>
> Aboriginal gangs with members as young as seven are terrorising Bayswater residents and police fear the situation is getting out of control. With racial tension rising in the area, police have launched a big crackdown. . . . Local hoteliers . . . have threatened to take matters into their own hands if the gangs are not stopped. . . . Aborigines . . . continually damage their premises and steal goods and money. Anyone who stands in their way is assaulted. In recent weeks there has been a spate of window smashing and house break-ins. In the most serious instance of violence a couple were viciously assaulted by a gang of stone-throwing Aboriginal youths. . . . Chief Superintendent Harry Riseborough said Aborigines refused to obey the law. 'I don't like picking on the Aborigines, but they are creating the problems.'

and the same discourse in TRAGIC END FOR TEEN CAR THIEF from *The Sunday Times*, August 1994, and a new discourse of Aboriginal authority in DEATHS BLAMED ON COCKTAIL by Karen Brown from *The West Australian* July 1994.

Having identified the main discourse in each article, groups were assigned one article for close analysis. They enthusiastically debated the effect of reader positioning on the readings that most Australian readers (i.e. Europeans) would make for these texts. When they reported back to the whole class, they articulated their understanding that if people were surrounded by texts like these and talked to each other in the ways encouraged by these texts, they would see the ideas constructed by the texts as 'normal', 'natural' and 'true'. Some held that the texts were merely reflecting reality and others maintained that they were definitely providing a version of reality.

They were then asked to read and discuss an excerpt from *Rites of Passage* (Beresford and Omaji, 1995, pp. 24-26) that I entitled 'Media Influence on Public Attitudes'. This excerpt analyses changing versions of Aborigines in the media, from the 1960s-70s, benevolent paternalism to the 1980s and 90s, representation of young

Aborigines as dangerous, violent criminals who pose a threat to law and order. It points out that two days after the story, 'Aboriginal Gangs Terrorise Suburbs' appeared, forty-five ABC journalists wrote to the editor of *The West Australian* to complain that the story contained no identifiable link to any event in the past twenty-four hours.

'Media Influence on Public Attitudes' refers to a study of *The West Australian*'s reporting on young people for the period April 1990 to March 1992, that identified 275 separate articles dealing with Aboriginal youth—eighty-four per cent of which dealt with crime. It also argues that the police are advantaged by such reporting because it justifies a strong police force and distracts attention from the Government's inaction on the recommendations of the Royal Commission into Aboriginal Deaths in Custody.

The students were asked to reconsider the ideas presented in 'Aboriginal Gangs Terrorise Suburbs' in the light of their reading of 'Media Influence on Public Attitudes'. They were asked to address these questions:

(i) In 'Aboriginal Gangs Terrorise Suburbs', which groups speak and which group doesn't have a voice?
(ii) List the ways that the research done by Stockwell and Mickler quoted in 'Media Influence on Public Attitudes' challenges the claims made by the article 'Aboriginal Gangs Terrorise Suburbs'.
(iii) 'Media Influence on Public Attitudes' suggests that the police have benefited from sensationalising the link between Aboriginality and crime. Explain this.
(iv) What reasons are given by 'Media Influence on Public Attitudes' to explain why the newspaper has published many more negative than positive articles about Aborigines?
(v) List the ways the article 'Aboriginal Gangs Terrorise Suburbs' is different from the expository text, 'Media Influence on Public Attitudes'. (You must give examples. Focus on use of language, organisation of material, audience, purpose, argument, use of evidence to support claims etc.)

With the understandings they had gained from their comparison of 'Aboriginal Gangs Terrorise Suburbs' and 'Media Influence on Public Attitudes', they were asked to read again the two newspaper accounts of the car chase death. The type in these articles was altered to make it easy for them to locate the discourses and the sources of information used to construct the two very different versions of the incident. They read first: 'Tragic End for Teen Car Thief'; and in pairs filled in the chart below it:

> TRAGIC END FOR TEEN CAR THIEF from *The Sunday Times*, August 1994 by Nick Taylor and Matt Trinca
>
> A young car thief killed in a horror smash yesterday was wanted for questioning over the savage bashing of a man left for dead in Northbridge last weekend. Joseph William Isaacs, 18, was killed in South Guildford after slamming a stolen car into another vehicle after an 8 km wild drive on the wrong side of the road. The young woman driver of the other car, who has asked not to be named, escaped with cuts and bruises. Isaacs was convicted of attempted murder after trying to run down two policemen three years ago. Yesterday, Isaacs, of Balga, had been driving the stolen Ford Falcon on the wrong side of a stretch of Roe Hwy and almost the length of the Great Eastern Hwy by-pass. The accident happened just after 2 a.m. . . . Acting Inspector Eddie Giumelli said the stolen car was seen travelling at high speed, flashing its lights. It had been driven the wrong way up an off-ramp onto Roe Hwy and then off the wrong ramp onto the by-pass. Isaacs was taken to Royal Perth Hospital but died soon after. . . . It is understood Isaacs' relatives and friends are blaming police for his death. Officers have been warned to be vigilant. Acting Inspector Giumelli said: "His death was not the result of a police pursuit. This was not our fault. This has happened because the person drove the vehicle the wrong way." The driver of the other car called her father on her mobile telephone from the crash scene.
>
> Her father said yesterday: "My daughter is probably the luckiest girl alive. She got out of it with bruises and cuts . . . . You read about these things but never expect them

to happen to your family." Isaacs who had dozens of convictions was also involved in a high-speed chase in April when a stolen car was driven on the wrong side of two highways. He was 15 years old and on the run from Longmore Remand Centre in 1991 when he was charged with attempting to kill two officers by ramming their vehicle with a stolen car during a pursuit. It is believed Isaacs was the first youth to face an attempted murder charge as a result of a high-speed chase.

"Tragic End for Teen Car Thief" *Sunday Times*: Words and phrases: The way the text positions us to regard this person, group; Words and phrases used to construct Isaacs *teen car thief, savage bashing, slamming, irresponsible*; Words and phrases used to construct the girl and her father; young woman driver, Words and phrases used to construct the police, police have been warned. They were asked to contrast the way the article positioned the reader to view the experience and family background of Joseph Isaacs and of the girl in the other car. While most students, drawing on their reading of 'Media Influence on Public Attitudes' saw the article as news construction, four students argued that the article was a true reflection of social reality.

They were then told that 'Deaths Blamed on Cocktail' appeared a few days after Joseph Isaacs' death. They were asked to read that article and to fill in the chart below it making use of the modified typeface to extract the information from the text.

DEATHS BLAMED ON COCKTAIL by Karen Brown from *The West Australian* July 1994

A lethal combination of drugs, bravado and fear of police has been blamed for the recent deaths of two Aboriginal juveniles in high-speed crashes. Aboriginal Legal Service executive director Rob Riley said the deaths were a tragic indictment of the inadequacies of the government's juvenile justice policies and the use of intimidation by an element in the police force. Mr. Riley said the ALS would meet Police Commissioner Bob Falconer next week to discuss the force's policy on high-speed chases and police-Aboriginal relations. "While we can't

> hand over the roads, I believe that if the police didn't chase these kids then there would be no challenge or novelty," he said. Mr Riley claimed he had heard too many stories not to believe that some young people had a genuine fear of police and thought a small, over-zealous section of the force was guilty of taking the law into their own hands. Mr Riley appealed to the Government to look beyond quick-fix policies and involve rather than ignore the Aboriginal community in addressing the problems of juvenile justice. He said more young Aborigines would die if government did not adopt a more compassionate practical approach and attempt to address the social problems confronting the Aboriginal people. It is still not known whether the two young Aborigines in the past fortnight were amphetamine related. Christopher Clarence Pickett, 16, of Coolbellup and Joseph William Isaacs, 18, of Balga died in separate accidents in which they drove stolen cars down the wrong side of major suburban roads. But Mr Riley said the use of drugs such as amphetamines and alcohol is a deadly combination responsible for the overwhelming number of youngsters involved in the criminal justice system.
>
> The Nyoongar Alcohol and Substance Abuse Service said there had been an increase in the number of Young Aborigines experimenting with amphetamines or using them regularly. Social worker Nancy Hampton said. . . . Youngsters often mixed amphetamines with other drugs, including marijuana and alcohol. It's a chemical cocktail which is the end result of social problems affecting most young Aborigines. These kids have very low self-esteem, low education, poor health and low rates of employment.

'Deaths Blamed on Cocktail' The West Australian Words and phrases: The way the text positions us to regard this person, group; Words and phrases used to construct Aboriginal youth and the struggles faced by this group, fear of police, number of youngsters, Aboriginal youth belong to a severely disadvantaged group in society, Words and phrases used to construct the police *intimidation*, Experts quoted Nancy Hampton, social worker.

Filling the charts revealed the way words and phrases were

used to position readers of each text. All students expressed great surprise at the fluidity of the categories of 'right' and 'wrong', 'lucky' and 'unlucky', 'perpetrator' and 'victim' and of 'hero' and 'victim'.

The sudden realisation of the extent to which the writers', editors' and newspaper owners' representations of 'good' and 'bad' can mould a community's beliefs and values impressed and dismayed them. They were shaken by the recognition that the status of 'victim' could be awarded by a text to either the white girl or the black boy. They understood, several of them for the first time, the power of media texts to 'other' members of minority groups by constructing versions of reality that have profound personal and social consequences. They discussed the power of the media to position readers so that they feel included in or excluded from society. When asked to write a critical reading of 'Tragic End for Teen Car Thief' which challenges the dominant Eurocentric reading, all students were able to write a short response that drew attention to what was foregrounded and what was marginalised in the article. By using the information from 'Deaths Blamed on Cocktail', they were able to point to the gaps and silences in 'Tragic End for Teen Car Thief'. Philip's resistant reading shows a clear understanding of the discursive construction of reality and a good command of the critical language the seminar was designed to enhance:

> The headline, 'Tragic End for Teen Car Thief', suggests that the writers, Nick Taylor and Matt Trinca care about human life. But their sympathy does not extend to Aborigines, especially not to Aborigines who break the white laws imposed on them. Their article foregrounds the things that Isaacs has done wrong. By repeating the word 'wrong' six times, it constructs Isaacs as a dangerous and violent criminal. It twice says he attempted to murder two policemen and that he 'was wanted for the savage bashing of a man left for dead'. The article marginalises the fact that Isaacs is dead and that his family are grieving.

The words 'savage' and 'wild' could bring the dominant discourse of the 'aggressive savage' to the mind of uncritical readers. The article draws on the negative stereotype of Aborigines as criminals to construct the boy who was killed by the police chase as a danger to society and totally evil. An alternative view of Isaacs is given by Karen Brown's article, 'Deaths Blamed on Cocktail'. This article uses information provided by knowledgeable and articulate Aborigines from the Aboriginal Legal Service and the Nyoongar Alcohol and Substance Abuse Service. By foregrounding the low self esteem and the high unemployment of Aboriginal youth, this article puts the death of Joseph Isaacs into a larger social context and positions the reader to see him as a victim of society and of 'over zealous' police, who 'take the law into their own hands.'

Nearly all the information in 'Tragic End for Teen Car Thief' comes from the police who are constructed like Jedi Knights as protectors of the innocent. The article's preferential representation of the police is most evident in the last sentence which could have said, 'Isaacs is the second Aboriginal youth to be murdered in the last two weeks as a result of unnecessary police chases.' It actually distracts attention from this view of reality by saying that Isaacs was 'the first youth to face an attempted murder charge as a result of a high speed chase.'

Philip While Ben's reading shows less control of the critical jargon than Philip's, it still reveals his capacity to go beyond a simple reading of the text to a reading of the world (Freire, 1972, pp. 64-65)

'Teenage Car Thief' constructs the white girl as a victim. She was unlucky to be 'slammed' into by the 'savage' 'young car thief'. Her caring father and her mobile phone are things readers of the article would like to think they could have and so they identify with her. This encourages them to empathise with the girl and not with the boy who was tragically killed. Isaacs' parents are not mentioned. The article does not quote any source for information about Isaacs. It just says, 'It is understood Isaacs' relatives and friends are blaming the police for his death.' Because the rest of the article makes the girl look like an innocent victim and the police look like law abiding protectors of the public, this one sentence makes Isaac's [sic] relatives seem like an unreasonable black backlash.

The girl's father says she is 'the luckiest girl alive'. And she is. She owns a car and mobile. And her father can tell his side of the story in the paper. Because the article does not quote the dead boy's father, readers could think that Joseph Isaacs does not have parents or that he has parents who do not care. His parents are silenced by this article. 'Teenage Car Thief' misrepresents the reality of Aboriginal life because family is central to their culture.

The readings by Ben and Philip show that by building on a critical apparatus with which they were familiar from activity-based texts by Mellor and Paterson, Moon, Martino and others, the students in the seminar were able to step outside the discourses that construct hegemonic versions of Australian society. By challenging them to the intellectual game of paying attention to the discourses that writers and readers draw on in the production and reception of texts, the seminar enabled them to 'read the world'—a world in which individual subjectivity, social relationships and national consciousness are, to a very large extent, influenced by texts that marginalise Aborigines and Aboriginality. By comparing two very different versions of Joseph Isaacs' death, the seminar led them to understand that texts are able to construct contrary versions of Aboriginality—one in which Aborigines exercise power in antisocial ways and another in which Aborigines are relatively disempowered. By scaffolding their learning with visual charts and with pair and small group work, the seminar gave them social practice for a form of reading that their written responses showed they had begun to internalise. One seminar with 20 students can do little to change the power of Eurocentric discourses to construct versions of Aboriginality that justify European assumptions of moral and material superiority that have had such profound social, economic and political effects on both the colonised and the colonisers. But the talking and the writing within the seminar show that the careful selection of texts and reading practices and the teacher's commentary on their understanding of texts and contexts (Baker and Freebody 1992, p. 278) can enable secondary students to develop post-colonial reading practices. The pedagogy employed in this seminar is a 'vital and inescapable task' (Tiffin, 1987, p. 95) that should be undertaken in secondary and primary classes as well as in universities. Unless the powerful Eurocentric discourses that have othered Aborigines and Aboriginality (Broome, 1994) are deconstructed, the Aboriginal studies programs planned for all Australian schools in 1999 will have a limited effect on national consciousness. Understanding the bias of Eurocentric discourses is a precondition for the appreciation of Aboriginal culture and writing.

WORKS CITED

Louis Althusser, *Essays on Ideology* (London: Verso, 1984).

Roland Barthes, *S/Z* (London: Cape, 1975).

Quentin Beresford and Paul Omaji, *Rites of Passage* (Fremantle: FACP, 1995).

Homi Bhabha, *Nation and Narration* (London: Routledge, 1990).

Pierre Bourdieu and Jean-Claude Passeron, *Reproduction in Education, Society and Culture* (trans. from the French by Richard Nice, with a foreword by Tom Bottomore; London; Beverly Hills: Sage Publications, 1977).

Pierre Bourdieu, *Language and Symbolic Power*, ed. John B. Thompson (trans. Gino Raymond and Matthew Adamson; Cambridge: Polity Press in association with Basil Blackwell, 1991).

Richard Broome, *Aboriginal Australians: Black Responses to White Dominance 1788-1994* (Sydney: Allen and Unwin, 1994).

Barbara Comber, Classroom explorations in critical literacy, in *Australian Journal of Language and Literacy*, 16 (1) (1993).

______ and A. Simpson, Reading cereal boxes: analysing everyday texts, Texts: the heart of the English curriculum, Series 1, Department of Education and Children's Services, South Australia, 1995).

De Castell, A. Luke, and C. Luke, ed., *Language, Authority, and Criticism: Readings on the School Textbook* (London: Falmer Press, 1975).

Terry Eagleton, *Walter Benjamin, Towards a Revolutionary Criticism* (London: Verso Editions, 1981).

______, *Literary Theory: An Introduction* (Oxford: Blackwell, 1983).

______, *The Function of Criticism: From the Spectator to Post-Structuralism* (London: Verso, 1984).

______, *Against the Grain: Essays 1975-1985* (London: Verso, 1986).

______, Fredric Jameson and Edward Said, *Nationalism, Colonialism, and Literature* (Minneapolis: University of Minnesota Press, 1990).

Norman Fairclough, *Language and Power* (London: Longman, 1989).

Frantz Fanon, *The Wretched of the Earth* (trans. by Constance Farrington with a preface by Jean-Paul Sartre; New York: Grove Wiedenfeld, 1991).

Michel Foucault, *The Archaeology of Knowledge* (trans. from L'archeologie du savoir; London: Tavistock, 1972).

Peter Freebody, A socio-cultural approach: resourcing four roles as a literacy learner, in Alan Watson & Anne Badenhop, *Prevention of Reading Failure* (Sydney: Ashton Scholastic, 1992).

Paulo Freire, *Pedagogy of the Oppressed* (trans. Myra Bergman Ramos [from the original Portuguese manuscript; Harmondsworth: Penguin Books, 1972).

James Paul Gee, *Social Linguistics and Literacies: Ideology in Discourses* (London, England; New York: Falmer Press, 1990).

______, *The Social Mind: Language, Ideology, and Social Practice* (New York: Bergin & Garvey, 1992).

Bell Hooks, *Killing Rage: Ending Racism* (New York: Holt, 1995).

Fredric Jameson, *Postmodernism*, or, *The Cultural Logic of Late Capitalism* (Durham: Duke University Press, 1991).

Hilary Janks, *Language, Identity and Power* (Johannesburg: Hodder Stoughton in association with Witwatersrand University Press, 1993).

______, *Language and Position* (Johannesburg: Hodder Stoughton in association with Witwatersrand University Press, 1993).

Gunther Kress, *Linguistic Processes in Socio-Cultural Practice* (Geelong: Deakin University Press, 1985).

Colin Lankshear & Peter Mclaren, *Critical Literacy: Politics, Praxis and the Postmodern* (with a foreword by Maxine Greene; Albany, New York: State University of New York Press, 1993).

Bill Lawson, "The discovery of nationality in Australian and Canadian literature," in Bill Ashcroft, Gareth Griffiths and Helen Tiffin, *The Postcolonial Studies Reader* (London & New York: Routledge, 1995).

Jay Lemke, *Textual Politics: Discourse and Social Dynamics* (London; Bristol, PA: Taylor & Francis, 1995).

Alan Luke, *Literacy, Textbooks, and Ideology* (New York: Falmer, 1988).

______, Peter Freebody and Pam Gilbert, *Reading Positions and Practices in the Classroom Curriculum Inquiry*, 21 (4), (1991).

Pierre Macherey, *A Theory of Literary Production* (trans. Geoffrey Wall; London: Routledge and Kegan Paul, 1978).

Wayne Martino and Bronwyn Mellor, *Gendered Fictions* (Cottesloe, WA: Chalkface Press, 1994).

Bronwyn Mellor, *Making Stories* (London: ILEA English Centre; Scarborough, WA: Chalkface Press, 1984)

______, *Changing Stories* (London: ILEA English Centre; Scarborough, WA: Chalkface Press, 1984).

______, *Reading Stories* (Scarborough, WA: Chalkface Press, 1987).

______ and Annette Patterson, *Investigating Texts* (Cottesloe, WA: Chalkface Press, 1991).

Bronwyn Mellor, Annette Patterson and Marnie O'Neill, *Reading Fictions* (Scarborough, WA: Chalkface Press, 1991).

Albert Memmi, *The Colonizer and the Colonized* (trans. from Albert Memmi, Portrait du colonise precede du portrait du colonisateur by Howard Greenfeld with an introduction by Jean-Paul Sartre, afterword by Susan Gilson Miller; Boston: Beacon Press, 1992).

Brian Moon *Studying Literature: Theory and Practice for Senior Students* (Scarborough, WA: Chalkface Press, 1990).

______, *Literary Terms: A Practical Glossary* (Scarborough, WA: Chalkface Press, 1992).

Wendy Morgan, *Ned Kelly Reconstructed* (Cambridge; Melbourne: Cambridge University Press, 1994).

Wendy Morgan with Pam Gilbert, *Critical Literacy: Readings and Resources* (Norwood, South Australia: Australian Association for the Teaching of English, 1996)

Henry Reynolds, *The Other Side of the Frontier: An Interpretation of the Aboriginal Response to the Invasion and Settlement of Australia* (Townsville, Qld: History Dept., James Cook University, 1981)

______, *The Breaking of the Great Australian Silence: Aborigines in Australian Historiography 1955-1983* (London: University of London, Institute of Commonwealth Studies, Australian Studies Centre, 1984)

______, *Frontier: Aborigines, Settlers and Land* (Sydney: Allen & Unwin, 1987).

Henry Reynolds, *Dispossession: Black Australians and White Invaders* (Sydney: Allen & Unwin, 1989).

Edward Said, *Orientalism* (London: Routledge and Kegan Paul, 1978).

______, *The World, the Text, and the Critic* (London: Faber, 1984).

Stephen Slemon, *Unsettling the Empire: Resistance Theory for the Second World* in Bill Ashcroft, Gareth Griffiths and Helen Tiffin, *The Postcolonial Studies Reader* (London & New York: Routledge, 1995).

Helen Tiffin, *Imagining Countries, Imagining People: Climate and the Australian Type*, in William McGraw, ed., *Inventing Countries: Essays in Post-Colonial Literature*, Papers delivered at the fourth conference of the South Pacific Association for Commonwealth Literature and Language Studies. Massey University, February 1987.

Graeme Turner, *American Dreams*, in Wenche Ommunsden and Hazel Rowley, ed., *From a Distance: Australian Writers and Cultural Displacement* (Geelong, Vic.: Deakin University Press, 1996).

G.A. Wilkes, *The Stockyard and the Croquet Lawn: Literary Evidence for Australian Cultural Development* (Melbourne: Edward Arnold, 1981).

Racist Acts and Human Rights

SUSAN KENWORTHY
St. Brigid's College
Perth, Western Australia

The 1905 *Western Australian Aborigines Act* (based on the 1897 Queensland Aborigines Act) was used as a blueprint for the establishment of Apartheid in South Africa. The Western Australian Act while ostensibly aimed at improving the welfare of Aboriginal people, actually resulted in disempowering them by setting regulations that controlled every aspect of their lives. For example, Aborigines were not allowed to live in towns, to enter towns at night, to own property, to attend government schools or to bring up their own children. This paper by comparing the Act with the Universal Declaration of Human Rights, shows how the Act still governs the perceptual frame-works that affect social policy and practice in Australia. It also outlines and reports on the effectiveness of a number of strategies for teaching secondary school students to develop critical readings of texts like the Act that embed conflicting discourses of welfare and control. It shows how postcolonial readings of the Act and of the *Universal Declaration of Human Rights* can equip students to develop resistant readings of contemporary racist texts and to challenge racist assumptions and language in dominant texts.

It is easy to teach about racism and human rights abuses that happen in someone else's country. I have always found my students to be very receptive to the suffering of non-whites in South Africa under the Apartheid regime and of African Americans in the USA. They feel keenly the injustices shown in films such as *Cry Freedom*. they sympathise with the Logan family in *Roll of Thunder Hear My Cry*; they are shocked at the jury's verdict in *To Kill a Mockingbird*; and disgusted at police corruption and brutality in *Mississippi Burning*. However, the real challenge for all of us is to accept that racism and human rights abuses occur in our own backyard.

For Australians, this means the treatment of our Aboriginal people. I remember as a postgraduate student in the 1970s, being struck by the comments of a visiting South African Fellow, Professor Kathleen Hill, who was an outspoken critic of the racist regime in her own country. At the time there were strong student protests in Australia against Apartheid. Her response was that there were no conditions in South Africa as disgraceful as the Aboriginal Reserves in Western Australia.

What has changed since the 1970s? Unfortunately very little. The life expectancy of Aboriginal Australians is among the lowest in the world (over 20 years lower than non-Aboriginal Australians). They are severely disadvantaged in the areas of health, education, housing and employment. Further, Aboriginal Australians, a mere 2 percent of our population, are imprisoned at 40 times the rate of non-Aboriginal Australians. Why is it so difficult to treat this group with justice in such a rich country?

There is hope, however, and that hope lies in changing the understandings and attitudes of our young people through education (Lankshear, 1987, 1989; Eagleton, 1990). It would not be fair to paint a picture of Australia as a shockingly racist country. Australia has often been called the most successful multicultural society in the world and there are good reasons for this. For example, at the school where I teach—St Brigid's College, a girls' Catholic Secondary College in a middle class Perth suburb—the majority of students are from an Anglo-Celtic background, but there is also a healthy multi-cultural atmosphere in the school. There are approximately thirty Aboriginal students, boarders from the north-west of the state; 30 overseas students, mainly from Indonesia; students of Chinese, Indian, Filipino descent; as well as those from a wide variety of European ethnic groups. Most of our students were born in Australia and many come from families where there has been intermarriage between different groups who have migrated from Europe and Asia. On the whole, the students are easy-going and tolerant; they take people as they come and treat students of other races with respect. There are many close friendships between students from different racial backgrounds. Head girl is the most prestigious position in the school. In the nine years I have taught there, one head girl was a Malaysian Buddhist of Chinese descent and one was an Australian of Indian descent. Also in that time there have been at least three Aboriginal girls elected to the Year Twelve Student Council. There are many other examples that show that leadership positions and the popularity and power of students within the school are unrelated to racial, ethnic or religious differences.

Aboriginal culture is celebrated in many ways. We have an Aboriginal Liaison Officer who organised kangaroo stew, crocodile kebabs, Aboriginal story-telling, face painting and dancing during NADOC Week. Also, on Holy Thursday we had an Aboriginal Stations of the Cross.

To a certain extent the school is a microcosm of our society. People in Australia are usually accepted on their merits and the children of first generation migrants of non-Anglo background rise above the social and economic status of their parents at a significantly higher rate than that of the general population.

However, despite all of the above, I have often met a blank wall of resistance in trying to teach Aboriginal issues in the English curriculum. The reasons for this are many and complex. I will attempt to give a brief explanation of the reasons for this.

First, in the cases of Aboriginal Australians, there is a high level of ignorance in the general population both about Aboriginal culture and the history of Aboriginal people since the European invasion. Despite the many books that have documented alternative histories of Australia (Bain, 1989; Reynolds, 1981, 1984, 1987, 1989; Green, 1984, 1984, 1995; Haebich, 1988), most Australians are more familiar with mythologies of settlement (Blainey, 1982; Clark, 1981; Crowley, 1960; Portus, 1959). Our education system is full of gaps and silences (Iser, 1978) about the effects of colonisation on Aborigines. As always, history has been written by the victors and the story of the colonised has been told mainly by oral history (Gilbert, 1977). Not surprisingly, racist acts, the sexual abuse of Aboriginal women by white men, the exploitation of Aboriginal labour, the massacres, the high rate of imprisonment and the use of neck chains did not feature in Australian history when I was at school, nor are they a part of our current social studies curriculum.

One of the reasons for this silence in our history is the deep conflict between the cultural myths of the two groups exemplified by the *settlement/invasion* controversy. There are two very different versions of history based on the different mythologies that underlie them. It is necessary for Eurocentric culture to cherish the myth of the pioneer who established farms on unoccupied land, battled with the harsh environment of the bush, and also with the often hostile Aborigines in order to civilise the wilderness. Overall, the official version alleges that Australia was 'discovered', 'explored' and 'settled' with very little bloodshed. Thus it has suited the interests of the white colonisers to construct Aborigines as passive victims of colonisation—the sad losers in the battle for control of the land.

Aboriginal history constructs a very different version. Aborigines enjoyed a peaceful idyllic life until the white invaders armed with guns and ships took their women and their land, and killed or imprisoned anyone who dared to resist (Gilbert, 1977). Thus according to this version, many Aborigines were skilful warriors who challenged the invader at every opportunity and engaged in an inter-racial war over control of land (Miller, 1985; Wilkes, 1995). In the unofficial version some of the pioneers become murderers and rapists, rather than heroes. Not surprisingly, many of the descendants of pioneer families deeply resent any challenges to the official version. The depth of feeling about this issue was recently shown by the fact that an historian received death threats when he published a book documenting a brutal massacre in Australia which is still denied by the official version. (I believe it would not be safe for me to reveal his name in this paper.)

Largely unaware of the Aboriginal version of history, current Australians see only the present social and economic conditions of this the most marginalised and disadvantaged group in our society. As often happens, a 'blame the victim' mentality has developed. Many Australians strongly resent any perceived or real advantage given to Aborigines in an attempt to improve their unacceptable levels of health, education and housing. Fred Chaney, the leader of the Senate in the Fraser Government and now Chancellor of Murdoch University summed up the problem like this:

> In a bizarre paradox, Aboriginal people manage to be in trouble with their fellow Australians for being disadvantaged and privileged at the same time (Chaney, 1994, p. 51).

People holding these contradictory views are represented by Independent MHR, Pauline Hanson. Under the umbrella of the discourse of 'equal rights for all Australians', adherents of this philosophy propose that Aborigines should not get preferential treatment to help them to gain economic self-determination and to allow them to reach the same level of affluence as their fellow Australians because this is unfair to non-Aboriginal Australians.

A further problem has been caused by the economic changes of the 80s and 90s in which the middle classes have been squeezed. The economy has been restructured; many people have lost their jobs; and feelings of anxiety and uncertainty about the future have increased. Interestingly, although these changes have resulted in a huge redistribution of wealth in favour of the rich, it is the marginalised groups in society that have been blamed for these problems: migrants (especially those from Asian countries), Aborigines and the unemployed.

These changes are related to the increasing level of political conservatism in Australian society. A move to the right is shown in John Howard's recent statements in the press in which he rejected the 'black armband view of history'. Supporters of this view assert that it is wrong to teach Australian children about past horrors and to bombard them with guilt and depression; that the present generation has nothing to be guilty about and that we have a fine history that we should be proud of.

For all of these reasons, it is difficult to challenge the racism in our own society. Racism is always a delicate subject that requires careful handling. Within any classroom, there is always a range of opinion ranging from racist to very tolerant—reflecting the society outside. Shock tactics, preaching and too strong an emphasis on the horrors of the past will inevitably provoke feelings of guilt and denial. and resistance both to the teacher and to the subject being taught. Thus an overly direct approach can often be counter-productive in producing subtle changes in students' attitudes and understandings about racism.

This led me to search for new ways of leading students to discover how racism operates in our society through the reading and writing of texts (Longley, 1994). With help and advice from Hilary Janks (1993) and Wayne Martino (1995), I have developed strategies which encourage students to construct postcolonial readings of texts. This is done through carefully structured activities Before, During and After the reading of texts that allow students to discover the naturalised (Eagleton, 1983; Moon, 1990) racist assumptions and discourses embedded in the texts and to challenge them. This has proved to be a far more effective and less exhausting way of teaching about racism.

The activities are carefully constructed so that racist readings are not possible. Otherwise, some students would fill in the gaps with negative stereotypes taken from the racist discourses which are part of our culture. The use of these activities could be criticised for being manipulative on the grounds that they do not allow racist readings. I would counter this argument by contending that all education is value laden; and I make no apologies for foregrounding the values of tolerance of differences and of respect for minorities. This teaching-learning approach helps to reveal inequities in our society which are usually naturalised by dominant discourses, which too often cloak racism, classism and sexism (Gilbert, 1989, 1991; Davies, 1995). The dangers of allowing racist discourses to flourish in the name of free speech in Australia have been made clear recently to the whole world when Pauline Hanson's attacks on political correctness in the area of race legitimised the racist lunatic fringe and resulted in an unprecedented spate of verbal and physical racist assaults all over Australia.

In order to illustrate the teaching approach I have trialed with Year Ten students, I will outline some of the activities I have devised to lay bare the racist discourses that operate in *The Western Australian Aborigines Act of 1905*. The Act is a suitable text to start with for many reasons. First, it serves as background material to fill in some of the important gaps in the education of our students. Mainstream society remains almost completely unaware of racist Acts of Parliament and the ways in which they have contributed to the current social, political and economic marginalisation of Aborigines.

A further advantage of using the text of the Act is that it is over 90 years old and therefore it is easy for students to see clearly its ideology based on the assumption of the superiority of British language and culture.

The stated aim of the Act was to 'make provision for the better protection and care of the Aboriginal inhabitants of Western Australia' (5 Edward VIII, No. 14 of 1905 quoted in Haebich, p 83). It was designed to protect Aboriginal people from various kinds of exploitation—especially in the North-West of the state. In this frontier society, women were used as sex slaves and the labour of both men and women was exploited in the pearling and pastoral industries. Also, there was widespread abuse of alcohol and opium (Haebich, Chapter 2). The *Western Australian Act*, based on the *Queensland Act of 1897*, incorporated and extended some existing policies of protection and of rigid segregation of Aborigines for their own physical protection. And to check the decline in their numbers, Aborigines were to be forcibly removed from the wider community and kept indefinitely on segregated reserves (Haebich, pp. 59-67). Similar legislation was passed in South Australia in 1910 and the Northern Territory in 1911 and strongly influences discriminatory legislation passed in South Africa (Haebich, 1988, p. 58). The Bill was challenged in the State Parliament as introducing 'slavery' (Western Australian Parliamentary Debates 28, 1905; 314; quoted in Haebich, p. 81). But, despite protests, it was still passed into law (Haebich, p. 81).

Under the terms of the Act, Aborigines were not allowed to own guns or to drink alcohol; they had to live in reserves and were not allowed to enter towns without a permit; they were under the control of the Chief Protector of Aborigines, they could not marry a white person without permission. The Chief Protector was the legal guardian of all Aboriginal children; and employers needed a special permit to employ Aborigines.

Haebich (Chapters 4-10) documents in tragic detail the devastating effects of the administration of the *Act* on the Aborigines of Western Australia—particularly in the South-West of the state. It destroyed any chance of Aboriginal people making a healthy adaptation to the new circumstances presented to them by invasion and colonisation. In the early twentieth century many Aborigines were an integral part of colonial society. Several were working their own small farms in the South-West and were keen to educate their children to take their place in the new society. Some were making a living from hunting and trapping possums and kangaroos and selling their fur, while others worked as farm labourers (Haebich, Chapters 1-2).

The *Act* worked to segregate Aboriginal people completely from the wider community. Welfare and control was administered largely by the same agency—the police. The police had special powers under the Act and had control over most matters relating to Aborigines including control over the ration system. Some police abused their powers to dominate local Aborigines. Police-Aboriginal relations centred on alcohol and gun control. Breaches of the *Act* resulted in Aborigines being imprisoned for six months and the high rate of imprisonment of this group dates from this time.

From 1911, Aborigines were systematically excluded from state schools which prevented their social and economic advancement. The permit system and their exclusion from towns meant that they were not able to find employment. By prohibiting their use of firearms, their participation in the fur industry came to an end. Aborigines were obliged to turn to the Aborigines Department for all their needs. They had little choice but to be dependent on welfare. Perhaps the most cruel and destructive result of the *Act* was the removal of children from their parents and their placement in institutions. This policy operated for several generations and tore thousands of families apart. The severe psychological trauma resulting from this practice still haunts the Aboriginal community today. Haebich (p. 356) claims that

> By the 30s most [Aborigines] were trapped in a cycle of poverty characterised by long periods of unemployment, deplorable living conditions, malnutrition, disease and premature death. Their children were growing up without schooling or

> vocational training and they had few prospects of breaking out of this cycle. Discriminatory laws and a repressive administration had shaped them into second class citizens and rejected and despised by the white community, they had become outcasts in their own land.

But few Australians know of the marginalisation, degradation and brutalisation of Aborigines that resulted from the *1905 Act*. Because late twentieth century school students know nothing of the Act, it provides an ideal text for laying bare the racism that is reproduced by other dominant texts and reading practices (Bourdieu, 1977; Tiffin, 1995).

Activities on the Act

The activities outlined below were trialed by four classes at St Brigid's College last year. The activity Before reading the *Act* worked very well as a whole group discussion on the use and abuse of power. The students were led from a consideration of situations and roles with which they are familiar to a consideration of the specific powers enjoyed under the *Act* by the Chief Protector of Aborigines. They were encouraged to see the title of 'Chief Protector' as very ironic.

The teachers reported that, after using these activities, the students seemed less racist and were much more comfortable about the assigned tasks of developing resistant readings of racist texts. The teachers started the process by introducing the concept of use and abuse of power and linking it to the power differences that always exist between the colonisers and those they colonise, with a spiel like this:

> Everyone is involved in relationships of unequal power throughout their lives; for example, relationships between student and teacher, child and parent, child and adult, patient and doctor, teacher and principal, employee and employer, child and police officer
>
> Those with more power in a relationship always have the opportunity to abuse this power. Children are more vulnerable

than adults with regard to abuse of power because in most situations in life, adults have more power than children.

For the most part in our society, adults use their power appropriately for the benefit of children. However, in some cases, adults can use the power they have over the children in their care in ways that hurt them. This is abuse of power. Everyone experiences situations of use and abuse of power in their lives. If an adult continually humiliates, exploits or harms a child (physically or emotionally), this would be regarded as abuse of power by most people in our society. Of course, use and abuse of power occurs over a wide spectrum of human situations, some of which have far more serious implications and consequences than others.

Discuss in groups your experiences of the use and abuse of power. What is appropriate use of power in our society? When have people abused their power over you? Can you think of times in your life when you have felt powerful? Are there situations when you have had power over others and not used it appropriately? Examine the following cartoons which show a series of different situations involving the legitimate use and the abuse of power and then complete the chart on the next page:

Cartoon	**Situation/roles**	Who holds the power	Is the power legitimately used or is it abused?	What would be the effects of challenging the power in this situation?
1	Cafe dispute between waitress and manager			
2	First consultation between a psychiatrist and a rich lady: "I'm sure I can help you. You will need to see me twice a week for five years."			
3	A teacher who shouts to a pupil: "How dare you question me? You don't think you are going to pass do you?"			
4	Lecherous university lecturer and young female student: "Come back after class and I'll show you how to get better marks."			
5	Mother and child in dispute over pocket money and chores.			
6	Father and child in dispute over homework and the right to watch television.			

The teachers then moved the students from the consideration of power and abuse of power in the cartoons which had presented situations close to their own lives to the colonial situation (Said, 1978) with which they are much less familiar:

> Like the situations depicted in the above cartoons, there is also an unequal distribution of power in colonial situations, wherever they occur in the world. **The coloniser** always has much more power than **the colonised** and has the means to enforce it—usually through the army or the police; and also through control of discourses, genres, texts and of reading and writing practices. Thus the process of colonisation itself is a form of abuse of power.
>
> In colonial relationships, the colonised are always constructed as essentially different—as **"the other"**. It is always a case of **"them and us"**. The colonial logic goes something like this:
>
> They are different from us; they look different; they act differently. They have different clothing, food, customs and a different lifestyle. They don't speak a civilised language but a kind of gibberish. They are heathens—not civilised Christians like us. Therefore, they are not really human beings who need to be treated with consideration and respect like we do.

The next activity uses the following questions to draw attention to the irony of the title "Chief Protector" to describe the bureaucrat who enjoyed almost unlimited power over the lives of Aboriginal people in the first half of the twentieth century.

Protection or Persecution?

- What are the connotations of the word "Protector"?
- Is it right to give one man so much power over another human being or group? What are the dangers of giving people too much power?

- Imagine that there was a person appointed by the government with a great deal of power over all adults and children in WA, including the power to:

1. Decide whether or not you have permission to have a job.
2. Make decisions about where you are to work and for how long.
3. Move you anywhere in the state without giving a reason.
4. Make all decisions about your money and your property.
5. Take your children away from you permanently and for no reason and send them to an orphanage.
6. Make all decisions about your food, clothing and education.
7. Have you arrested without a warrant.
8. Stop you marrying the person you want to marry.
9. Send you to gaol for six months if you:

   drink alcohol
   leave your job
   own a gun
   enter a town after dark
   leave the place he's sent you to
   resist having your children taken away

- Brainstorm in groups an appropriate title for such a person.
- Share your group's titles with the class.

The questions above led students directly to an examination of the 1905 Act which established the power of the Chief Protector. In the next activity, the students used bubble questions to interrogate the *Act* itself. By answering the questions, they were encouraged to make a resistant reading of the *Act* and to expose the gaps and silences in the document. They were enabled to uncover the conflicting discourses of welfare and control which have had such long-term destructive consequences for Aboriginal people in Western Australia.

When I was puzzling over how I might begin to develop strategies to achieve my aims, Hilary Janks helped me by suggesting the use of bubble questions about the Act as a strategy to encourage students to disrupt the text. In *The Critical Language Awareness Series* (1993), Hilary established this critical tool as a powerful and effective part of a pedagogy for disrupting dominant readings of texts.

It is often very difficult for readers to see as strange the texts that are drawn from discourses in which they themselves are implicated; the texts that construct their own sense of identity and their own version of reality. The bubble question strategy helps students and teachers to get outside the Act and to see how its discourses worked to establish a society of 'haves' and 'have-nots' based on skin colour.

Students were instructed to:

> Read the following clauses of the *Aborigines Act of 1905*. The questions in the bubbles will help you to produce a particular reading of the Act:

The Aborigines Act 1905

What is the stated aim of the Act?	**An Act to make provision for the better protection and care of the Aboriginal inhabitants of Western Australia . . .**
	2. In this Act . . . "Chief Protector" means the chief protector of Aborigines appointed under this Act . . .
Why couldn't their parents look after them?	4. There shall be a department under the Minister to be called the Aborigines Department and to be charged with the duty of promoting the welfare of the aborigines—providing them with food, clothing, medicine and medical attendance when they would otherwise be destitute, providing for the education of aboriginal children, and generally assisting in the preservation and well-being of the aborigines.

Why were Aboriginal children removed?

8. The Chief Protector shall be the legal guardian of every aboriginal and half-caste child until such child attains the age of sixteen years (later extended to twenty one years).

Aboriginal culture is based on identification with a particular area of land. How would moving Aborigines from one place to another affect Aboriginal people? Who they wanted to?

12. The Minister may cause any aboriginal to be removed to and kept within the boundaries of a reserve, or to be removed from one reserve or district to another reserve or district and kept therein.

Family and extended family are central to Aboriginal culture. What effect would this clause have on families?

Were white people moved from their homes like this?

Did this help Aborigines to get jobs?

17. It shall not be lawful to employ any aboriginal . . . except under permit and agreement.

Why weren't Aborigines paid with money like whites?

22. (An employment agreement must stipulate) for the supply by the employer to the aboriginal or half-caste of substantial, good, and sufficient rations, clothing and blankets and also medicines and medical attendance when practicable and necessary;

Could 22 and 25 be read as legalising slavery?

25. Any aboriginal who without reasonable cause . . . shall refuse . . . to work in the capacity in which he has been engaged, or shall desert or quit his work without the consent of his employer, or shall commit any other breach of his agreement shall be guilty of an offence against the Act.

Why weren't Aborigines allowed to look after their own money and property?

33. The Chief Protector may undertake the general care, protection and management of the property of any aboriginal or half-caste, and may . . . take possession of, retain, sell or dispose of any such property, whether real or personal . . .

What effect might this have had on Aboriginal/police relationships in the long-term?

37. . . . a protector may cause any aborigines or half-castes who are camped . . within or near the limits of any town or municipal district to remove their camp . . . as he may direct; and all police officers shall assist the protector in carrying out the provisions of this section . . . Any aboriginal or half-caste neglecting or refusing to obey such an order shall be guilty of an offence against this Act.

How were the police used to enforce colonialist practices?

38. Any justice of the peace or police officer may order any aboriginal found loitering in any town . . . forthwith to leave such town . . . any aboriginal neglecting or refusing to obey such an order shall be guilty of an offence against this Act.

Why weren't Aborigines allowed in towns?

Why couldn't they marry who they wanted to?

42. No marriage of a female aboriginal with any person other than an aboriginal shall be celebrated without the permission in writing of the Chief Protector.

But under Australian law, isn't it true that no person can be arrested for a crime without a warrant?

58. Every person convicted of an offence against this Act shall be liable to **imprisonment** with or without **hard labour**, for not exceeding **six months**, or to a fine not exceeding fifty pounds.

What—just for leaving a job you don't like?

Isn't it a parent's job to have custody of their children and to care for them?

60. The Governor may make regulations

. . .

(c) Providing for the care, custody and education of the children of aborigines and half-castes;

(d) Enabling any aboriginal or half-caste child to be sent to and detained in an aboriginal institution, industrial school, orphanage;

(e) For the control, care and education of aborigines and half-castes in aboriginal institutions, and for the supervision of aboriginal institutions.

If you had a 'dog licence', you had to agree not to associate with Aborigines. You had to live and act like a white. What does this suggest about white attitudes to Aboriginal culture?

63. The minister may issue to any aboriginal or half-caste who in his opinion ought not to be subject to this Act, a certificate . . . that such aboriginal or half-caste is exempt from the provisions of this Act.

Why do you think Aborigines call them 'dog licences'?

- In small groups discuss the answers to the questions.
- Make a list of:
  (i) what Aborigines were not allowed to do as a result of this Act
  (ii) what all other Australians were allowed to do as a result of this Act.
- What does this document suggest about differences in power between Aborigines and other Australians in 1905? Whose interests does this document serve?

The questions and the discussion they generate served to make clear to students the total disempowerment of Aborigines by the Act. The students were then required to fill in the chart below:

The stated aim of the Act was the welfare of Aborigines. Find words and phrases which suggest care and concern.	The Act gave the government enormous control over the lives of Aborigines. List words which suggest control and punishment.

By focusing on specific use of language in the *Act*, the chart emphasises the conflicting discourses of protection and control and thereby makes clear to the students—without the teacher having to say it directly—that there are many more examples of the language of control than of protection. Students were generally amazed to see how the *Act* served to control almost every aspect of Aboriginal life: to make Aboriginal people totally dependent on white society; and to diminish their drive, initiative, self-reliance and motivation.

The next activity again directs the students to make a particular postcolonial reading of the *Act*. It provides a series of readings which encourage the students to read the Act more closely and support the postcolonial readings with evidence from the *Act* itself. Again, the activity enabled the students to make a resistant reading. By working through the questions, the students began to interrogate their own prejudices.

Complete the chart below. In the left-hand column, several readings of the Act are provided which direct attention to the ways in which colonial rulers violated the rights of Aboriginal people. Find textual evidence form the Act to support these readings.

Readings	Textual evidence
Colonialists used the Act to impose their values on Aboriginal people.	
Aborigines are constructed as incapable of bringing up their children.	
Colonialists used the legal system to oppress and control Aboriginal people.	
Aborigines were considered incapable of managing money and property.	
Aborigines were discriminated against socially and economically.	
Aborigines were not treated fairly by the legal system.	
Aborigines were treated as second class citizens.	

Hilary Janks also suggested the next activity which requires students to read *The Universal Declaration of Human Rights*, and to compare its provisions with what they knew of the *1905 Act*.

By doing this activity, which again asked them to go back to the *Act*, they discovered the human rights abuses embedded in the *Act*. They were thereby empowered to see and to reject the racist assumptions underlying the *Act*.

Human Rights for First Australians

The following text is a summary of the provisions of the Universal Declaration of Human Rights adopted and proclaimed by the United Nations in 1948.

- Read the text and consider to what extent the Aborigines Act breaches human rights.

The Universal Declaration of Human Rights

- All human beings are born free and equal in dignity and rights regardless of race, colour, sex, nationality or religion.
- Everyone has the right to life, liberty and freedom from fear and violence.
- No one shall be used as slave labour.
- No one shall be tortured or be given a degrading punishment.
- Everyone has the right to the protection of the law without discrimination.
- No one shall be subjected to arbitrary arrest, detention or exile.
- Everyone has the right to a fair and public trial. Everyone charged with a penal offence has the right to be presumed innocent until proved guilty.
- No one shall be subjected to arbitrary interference with his privacy, family, home or correspondence, nor to attacks upon his honour and reputation.
- Everyone has the right to freedom of movement within his own country and abroad.

- Adult men and women have the right to marry and to found a family regardless of race or religion.
- The family is the natural and fundamental group unit of society and is entitled to protection by society and the State.
- Everyone has the right to own property. No one shall be arbitrarily deprived of their property.
- Everyone has the right to vote for the government of the country.
- Everyone has the right to work and to just and favourable conditions of work.
- Everyone has the right to equal pay for equal work.
- Everyone has the right to fair pay to enable their families to live with self-respect.
- Everyone has the right to a standard of living adequate for their health and well-being including food, clothing, housing and medical care.
- Motherhood and childhood are entitled to special care and assistance. All children, whether born in or out of wedlock, shall enjoy the same social protection.
- Everyone has the right to an education.

It would be naive to claim that any country has not abused human rights at some time in its history. One of the aims of this chapter is to increase awareness of how the human rights of our indigenous population have been abused as part of the process of colonisation.

Re-read the Aborigines Act. Complete the chart below by either providing a quote from the Aborigines Act in the left-hand column or a quote from the Universal Declaration of Human Rights in the right-hand column.

ABORIGINES ACT	HUMAN RIGHTS VIOLATION
8. The Chief protector shall be the legal guardian of every aboriginal and half-caste child until such child attains the age of sixteen years (later extended to twenty one years).	Motherhood and childhood are entitled to special care and assistance. All children, whether born in or out of wedlock, shall enjoy the same social protection.

	The family is the natural and fundamental group of society and is entitled to protection by society and the State.
	Everyone has the right to equal pay for equal work.
	Everyone has the right to the protection of the law without discrimination.
52. In every prosecution for an offence against this Act . . . the complaint that any person referred to therein is an aboriginal or half-caste shall be deemed to be proved guilty in the absence of proof to the contrary.	
	Adult men and women have the right to marry and to found a family regardless of race or religion.
	Everyone has the right to work and to just and favourable conditions of work.
33. The Chief Protector may undertake the general care, protection and management of the property of any aboriginal or half-caste, and may . . . take possession of, retain, sell or dispose of any such property, whether real or personal . . .	

	No one shall be subjected to arbitrary arrest, detention or exile.
	Everyone has the right to freedom of movement within his own country and abroad.

- The power of the Aborigines Act of 1905 lasted until 1967 when Aboriginal people were granted full citizenship rights by a national referendum. How do you think Aboriginal people have been affected by being controlled by this Act for 62 years? How do you think it may have affected other Australians' perceptions of Aborigines?
- The West *Australian Aborigines Act* of 1905 was based on the Queensland *Act*. Similar Acts were passed in all Australian states and territories. **These Acts were used by the South African Government as the model for establishing the apartheid system in South Africa**.
- How does this knowledge affect your attitude to Australian colonialist practices towards Aborigines in the first half of the twentieth century?
- Australian social studies textbooks often condemn the South African apartheid regime as an example of extreme racism and abuse of human rights. Can you suggest some reasons why these textbooks don't present the treatment of Aboriginal people by Australian governments in the same way?

Having these discussion questions at the end of the chapter focuses the students' attention on the links between racism in South Africa, which they are always willing to condemn and racism in Australia which they find difficult to see.

Activities like those outlined in this paper are central to the approach taken in our book, *Changing Places: Aboriginality in Texts and Contexts*. We hope that these activities will enable teachers who use the text in their classrooms to step outside the discourses and literacy practices that have naturalised dominant texts that speak so many Australians into relationships and structures that are unjust and inequitable.

The great advantage of these activities is that they enable the teacher to avoid preaching and they enable the students to "discover" their own understandings of the ways in which texts position readers to accept the views of the colonisers or the colonised. Post-colonial theory has done much to make academics and tertiary students conscious of the ways in which colonial discourses and reading practices have worked to maintain social structures and relationships based on inequalities of race and class and gender. What I have shown in this paper is how those understandings can be made available to secondary school students.

Beyond National Territories: A Study of Yasmine Gooneratne's *A Change of Skies* and Bapsi Sidhwa's *An American Brat*

SUMAN BALA
University of Delhi

There is a considerable body of fiction in English written by immigrant writers based on their personal experiences. The exiled writer usually benefits from his or her uprooting: what is left behind is seen more clearly from a distance; and the new abode is seen in a sharper focus than can be done by indigenes. The statement is very relevant in the case of two writers from Sri Lanka and Pakistan respectively: Yasmine Gooneratne who migrated to Australia twenty five years ago and Bapsi Sidhwa who settled in the USA in 1984. Yasmine Gooneratne's *A Change of Skies* juxtaposes two societies and two cultures, Sri Lankan and Australian; Bapsi Sidhwa's *An American Brat* delineates the clashes the divergent cultures generate between the families 'back home' and their progeny groping their way in the New World.

Bharat Davasinha and his wife Navaranjini in *A Change of Skies* and Feroza Ginwalla in *An American Brat* leave their own culture and enter another. Their old values come into conflict with the new ones. The tremendous difference between the two ways of life leads to feelings of depression and frustration. Both the novels employ stories which highlight strengths and shortcomings on both sides. The characters in both the novels are placed in familial, cultural and ideological positions that prevent them from stepping outside their fixed assumptions and attitudes. Yet both novels suggest that breaking away from one's ethnicity and absorbing the new culture is the only way for survival.

A Change of Skies is a sparkling debut novel by Yasmine Gooneratne that describes in tragi-comic fashion the experiences of a Sri Lankan couple who come to reside in Australia. The novel, published in July 1991, was reprinted in November 1991 and has been reprinted six times since then. It received the 1992 Marjorie Barnard Literary Award for Fiction, was shortlisted for the 1991 Commonwealth Writers Prize and has been recorded for the library of the Royal Blind Society.

The story could reflect some authentic experience—the writer herself being an immigrant to Australia. Currently, Gooneratne is Professor of English at Macquárie University, New South Wales. She settled in Australia with her physician husband and their two children in 1972. She has published extensively on migrant writers like V.S. Naipaul and Ruth Jhabvala. So, the theme of migration came in handy to Gooneratne when she took up creative writing.

Bapsi Sidhwa is a Pakistani writer, settled now in the USA. She was born in Karachi in 1939 and was brought up and educated in Lahore. She graduated from Kinnaird's College for Women in Lahore. At the age of nineteen she fell in love with a Bombay businessman and married him. However, this marriage did not last long. She was allowed the custody of her daughter but was forced to part with her son who returned to her later at the age of sixteen after his father's death. At the age of twenty five, she married Noshirwan, twelve years her senior.

Bapsi Sidhwa started writing at the age of twenty-eight after the birth of her children—two girls and a boy. She has written four novels to date. These are: *The Crow Eaters* (1980), *The Pakistani Bride* (1982), *Ice-Candy-Man* (1988)—published as *Cracking India* in the USA—and *An American Brat* (1993).

Bapsi Sidhwa has won international acclaim for her work. Her works have been translated into French and German and are taught as part of the academic curriculum in some American universities. Both Pakistan and America have honoured her for her writings. In 1991, she received the *Sitara-i-Imtiaz* award. In Pakistan, this is the highest honour in the arts bestowed on a citizen. Sidhwa's *Cracking India* was named a Notable Book of 1991 by *The New York Times* and won the Literature Prize of the 1991 Frankfurt Book

Fair. In 1993, she received an award of US $ 105,000 from the Lila Wallace-Reader's Digest Fund. This is perhaps one of the largest grants in the country for writers. She received this award in three annual instalments of thirty five thousand dollars. When I met her in June 1994 on the occasion of the release of her latest novel *An American Brat* by Penguin at the India International Centre, New Delhi, she said that she planned to build a home in the Rice University area with her prize money.

An active social worker among Asian women, Bapsi Sidhwa represented Pakistan at the Asian Women's Congress in 1975. She has taught creative writing at Rice University in Texas and the University of Houston. She was a Bunting Fellow in 1986-87 at Radcliffe College, Harvard, where she also wrote her novel *Ice-Candy-Man* or *Cracking India*. In the early nineteen eighties, she and her husband Noshirwan went to the US and settled in Houston in 1984.

A Change of Skies centres around the life of a Sri Lankan couple—Bharat Mangala-Davasinha, a solemn young Asian linguistics expert, and his wife Navaranjini. Bored by his life in Colombo, Bharat answers an advertisement for a visiting professorship at Southern Cross University in New South Wales and is invited to join it for a five-year term. The two eventually fall in love with the country and decide to stay on. In a very deft manner, Gooneratne weaves into this naration the experiences of Bharat's grandfather Edward who reached the Australian shores on the *S.S. Devonshire* in 1882. The novel includes many extracts from the journal maintained by Bharat's grandfather Edward and later published by Bharat as *Lifeline. The Journal of an Asian Grandee. 1882-1887.* Edited by his Grandson. The parallels in the experiences of Edward with that of Bharat and Navaranjini suggest a continuity. Navaranjini perceives "a link, a firm (though hidden) connecting line between past events and future possibilities." (*CS*, 9) The novel thus attains a kind of universality

Initially, Bharat and Navaranjini's decision to go to Australia for five years is not seen in any favourable light. When their families learn about the plan, there is a vigorous reaction to it. Bharat reports that his younger sister Vera writes from New York: "You must both be out of your minds . . . it's a provincial version of the American Midwest. Maybe you can't imagine what *that* must be like. You'll be miserable. There's nothing there but koalas and kangaroos, sheep and (I think they call them) wombats. . . . And what about the White Australia Policy?" (*CS*, 33) She drives some consolation from the fact that their exile will be only a temporary one: "Well, Bharat, it's only a short-term visit: just a five-year sentence, after all." (*CS*, 33) After the Sinhala-Tamil riots a few years ago, many of Bharat's colleagues had left for academic posts in Canada, Britain and the United States. But going to Australia was unimaginable: "Vera . . . couldn't see any point in our going to Australia. America, yes. Britain, certainly. But *Australia*? Certainly not. Nor, it was made clear to me, could Baba see any point in it either." (*CS*, 341) In a similar vein, Navaranjini's mother tells Mr. Doraisamy: "Her husband has doomed her to spend five years in a cultural desert." (*CS*, 57)

Fed on English literature since school days and having a number of relatives going to and returning from England, whole generations of Indians and Sri Lankans are familiar with London, its Dickensian fog and murky Thames "sweating oil and tar." But Australia is by and large an unknown country. The word "Australia" summons up in Bharat's mind a picture straight out of the *Philip's Atlas* he had used as a schoolboy. On Philip's map of the world, the huge areas colonised by the British were shown in pink and this included India, Ceylon (now Sri Lanka) and Australia. Other ideas and memories pertain to Australia being a country of kangaroos, emus, koalas and sheep—and of course cricket and Don Bradman.

Navaranjini's meagre knowledge of Australia is based on a poster pinned up on the wall of the Geography room in her school. In it, a fair-haired pink cheeked little girl stood smiling in the middle of a field of golden grain, with a bunch of wild flowers in her right hand and a woolly lamb tucked under her left arm. She remembers that the poster said invitingly: "Come. . . . To sunny Australia." (*CS*, 18)

Despite their ignorance of the country, both Bharat and Navaranjini are strongly determined to make a great success of their five-year stay in Australia. Navaranjini tries to equip herself for the stay by taking driving lessons and obtaining a driving licence. Marina, one of her former schoolmates, reminds her that Australians are fond of swimming. She therefore takes swimming lessons at the Colombo Swimming Club because it seemed to her that "an ability to swim would be as important to us in Australia as an ability to play bridge or tennis had been to my parents in their outstation days: it was, obviously, a social necessity." (*CS*, 64-65)

While editing the diary maintained by her husband's grandfather Edward throughout his journey to Australia and his stay there, Navaranjini discovers the common threads, that underlie all expatriate experience. As she says at the very outset, even before leaving for Australia: "A hundred years ago, I thought, this man made the same journey that we are making now. What can I learn from it? What can it teach me?" (*CS*, 64) Again, right in the middle of the novel, we come across another significant statement about the expatriate experience: "He who crosses the ocean may change the skies above him but not the colour of his soul." (*CS*, 67)

The first encounter with Australia leaves Navaranjini breathless. The fast traffic, the stickers on the rear windows of the vehicles, being winked at by the ginger-haired driver of a monster truck, the slogans "ASIANS OUT" and "BASH A PAKI A DAY" make her feel "that the welcoming smile on the face of that little girl in the poster at school had been meant for someone else. Whoever it was that she had held flowers out to so invitingly, it could not have been me." (*CS*, 69)

The first look at Sydney traffic makes her wonder if she would ever be able to drive there and exchange her Sri Lankan driving licence for an Australian one. She finds people driving very fast—with tense and grim faces, shoulders hunched, eyes focused straight ahead and not glancing sideways, mouths unsmiling. She is attracted by the stickers on the rear windows of the vehicles which are quite varied; while one proclaims to the world "I'd rather be sailing," another states in a humorous vein, "If you can read this, thank a teacher"; still another has a warning, "If you toucha my truck, I breaka your face." Then there are stickers with contradictory messages: while one says invitingly "Move up a little closer, honey," the very next warns in tiny letters and numerals "U R 2 close." (*CS*, 66) While looking out eagerly on that first day for clues of one kind or another that might help explain Australia to her, Navaranjini begins to watch the stickers which seem to her "like the flags run up by ships at sea, being in this case signals of friendship and a shared sense of fun." (*CS*, 68)

Navaranjini reflects that the traffic in Colombo may be crazy but it is not death-oriented. There are no multiple traffic lanes, no purposeful forward movement of streams of vehicles. There it is merely swirl and muddle. People hang out of bus windows and stand on the footboards; nobody takes any notice whatever of zebra crossings. With traffic moving at under five miles an hour, there are frequent traffic jams at crossings. Later in the narrative, Navaranjini recalls a bad traffic jam as the exact context of their decision to move out. Bharat and Navaranjini had been held up at a railway crossing on General's Lake Road long after the train that was being waited for had come and gone. The cause of the delay was a lorry loaded with flour bags that had wandered out of the line and then developed engine trouble. There were lines of cars and lorries, with the drivers continuously honking the horns. The ear-splitting noise on the terribly hot day added to Bharat's discomfiture and made him announce: "Baba, you must do as you like. You must please yourself. But I have had enough. And I am getting out." (*CS*, 158, author's italics) The incident does act as a catalyst for Bharat and Navaranjini to leave Sri Lanka "Until things improved." (*CS*, 158)

The theme of immigration is quite prominent in Bapsi Sidhwa's *An American Brat*. In an interview with Naila Hussain, Bapsi Sidhwa says that "the book deals with the subject of the 'culture shock' young people from the subcontinent have to contend with when they choose to study abroad. It also delineates the clashes the divergent cultures generate between the families 'back home' and their transformed and transgressing progeny bravely groping their way in the New World." (1993: 19)

Whereas the first three novels of Bapsi Sidhwa are set in the Indian subcontinent, her fourth novel is set partly in Pakistan and partly in the USA. The time is the late seventies. Zulfikar Ali Bhutto is in jail and Islamic fundamentalism is growing in Pakistan. The heroine of the novel, Feroza, a sixteen-year-old girl has been carefully brought up in the small but prosperous Parsi community in Lahore. Her parents think that she should be saved from being further influenced by the Muslim government. Her mother Zareen is perturbed because Feroza is becoming more and more backward everyday. Feroza has stopped answering the phone because "what if it's someone I don't know." (*AB*, 10) The un-Parsi like orthodoxy in Feroza's attitude and outlook alarms her mother who tells her husband that Feroza objects to her wearing a modern dress:

> I went to bring Feroza from school today. I was chatting with Mother Superior on the veranda—she was out enjoying the sun—and I had removed my cardigan. Feroza pretended she didn't know me.
>
> In the car, she said: "Mummy, please don't come to school dressed like that." She objected to my sleeveless sari-blouse! Really, this narrow-minded attitude touted by General Zia is infecting her, too. I told her: "Look, we're Parsi, everybody knows we dress differently."
>
> When I was her age, I wore frocks and cycled to Kinnaird College. And that was in 59 and 60—fifteen years after Partition! Can she wear frocks? No. Women mustn't show their legs, women shouldn't dress like this, and women shouldn't act like that. Girls mustn't play hockey or sing or dance! If everything corrupts their pious little minds so easily, then the *mullahs* should wear *burqas* and stay within the four walls of their houses! (*AB,* 10)

Zareen admits that things have changed in Pakistan, the claustrophobic atmosphere of Zia's islamization is quite alarming:

> Could you imagine Feroza cycling to school now? She'd be a freak! Those *goondas* would make vulgar noises and bump into her, and the *mullahs* would tell her to cover her head. Instead of moving forward, we are moving backward. What I could do in '59 and '60, my daughter can't do in 1978! Our Parsi children in Lahore won't know how to mix with Parsi kids in Karachi or Bombay. (*AB,* 11)

Zareen feels that Feroza should go to the USA during the summer vacation where her brother Manek, a graduate student at M.I.T., can look after her: "Travel will broaden her outlook, get this puritanical rubbish out of her head." (*AB,* 14) Considering the fact that the farthest Feroza or Zareen had ever travelled was across the border to Bombay, the suggestion to send Feroza off by herself to the US is quite audacious. But Cyrus accepts it because he remembers how timidly Feroza had behaved with a young boy in their drawing room a week ago.

Feroza's joy knows no bounds as the plans for her trip to the USA are finalized:

> Feroza slipped under her quilt fully dressed, her eyes wide open, her mind throbbing with elation. She was going to America! She found it difficult to believe. She repeated to herself, "I'm going to America, I'm going to America!" until her doubts slowly ebbed and her certainty, too, caught the rhythm of her happiness.
>
> To the land of glossy magazines, of "Bewitched" and "Star Trek," of rock-stars and jeans . . . (*AB,* 27)

How eager and excited she is to go to America!

Throughout her journey, Feroza behaves as instructed by the elders but as soon as she reaches America she is a changed person. As the plane lands at Kennedy Airport, Feroza is triumphant and glowing. She is dazzled by the orderly traffic of rushing people, the bright lights and warmed air, the extraordinary cleanliness and sheen of floors and furnishings, the audacious immensity of the glass-and-steel enclosed spaces.

Feroza is subjected to rather inhumane treatment by the custom officials. There is a moment of confusion as her Pakistani passport opens from the wrong end. Unlike English, Urdu is written from right to left and not vice versa. And then there is a barrage of questions—how long would she stay? where would she stay? who would support her? how old was her uncle? what did he do? was he a US citizen? resident or visitor? Feroza's answers do not seem satisfactory to the hostile officer and she is directed to go in for secondary inspection after collecting her luggage.

Feroza tries to cope with the different life-style of the Americans and the modern technology used by them. Feroza is quite unfamiliar with the moving staircases, escalators, which one finds in abundance in even the small stores in the USA. An elderly American couple help her to cross this hurdle—the man takes the duty-free packages from her hand and the woman takes hold of Feroza's arm to help her get on and off the escalator.

The next problem Feroza faces is of carrying her outsized suitcases. Approaching an immensely tall porter with a large cart evokes no response. Thrown on her own resources, Feroza finds people carrying the luggage on carts and asks a gray-haired woman where she had gotten her cart. Directed to a shining caterpillar of stacked carts, she struggles to extract one but fails. She finds youngmen coming and taking away carts one by one after inserting a dollar bill in a slot. As the next man hustles up with the same intention, Feroza steps right in front of the box, barring access and says: "It's my turn." Jolted by her somewhat rude and strange behaviour, the youth comes to an astonished halt. Feroza explains in a manner which is half-apologetic and half-appealing for help: "I don't know how to get this, . . . Can you show me?" (*AB*, 57) The man smiles flirtatiously and shows her how to insert the dollar bill. As she loads her suitcases and hand luggage on the cart, Feroza's mind is filled with images of the slender young American and his candid admiring eyes: "How easily he had talked to her, his gestures open, confident. She wished she could have responded to his readiness to be friends, but she was too self-conscious." (*AB*, 58) She realizes that this was the word which could define her new experience. The people around her were busy with their own concerns; none of them had even bothered to glance her way or stare at her as they would have in Pakistan.

Feroza's wide-open eyes soak in the new impressions as she pushes the cart. A strange awareness seeps into her: she knows no one and no one knows her. It is a heady feeling to be suddenly so free of the thousand constraints that governed her life.

Feroza feels reassured to find Manek waiting for her in the lounge. But the worst is still to come. A woman in blue uniform looks sternly at Feroza and reminds her that she must go in for a second inspection. The immigration officer leads Feroza to the ominous place where weary passengers stand before their disarrayed possessions with subdued looks. The absorbed customs inspectors take their own time, checking each and every item in the suitcase which makes each passenger look unaccountably guilty.

Feroza's interrogation starts with a simple query: "Are you a student?" (*AB*, 59) However, Feroza is so nervous by then that her answer does not reach the inspector who gets impatient and feels irritated at her response. In a cold, calculating manner he explains to Feroza that the sworn statements she was going to make in a few minutes's time should be "the truth, the whole truth, and nothing but the truth." (*AB*, 60) Otherwise she can be fined two thousand dollars or imprisoned for not more than five years or both. This is followed by routine questions about her name, address, date of birth etc. till the officer comes to the crucial question: "How long do you wish to stay in the US?" (*AB*, 60) Feroza's answer "Two or three months" does not satisfy him and he wants her to be more specific. It is at this moment that Feroza blurts out that she will stay with her uncle who is "a student. But he also works at two other jobs to make extra money." (*AB*, 61) Evidently, she does not know that it is a crime for foreign students to work. She is told that her uncle would be hauled before an immigration judge and most likely deported. She too would have to go back on the next available flight. He accuses her of being a liar—she has no uncle in America and her so-called uncle is actually her fiancé.

Feroza finds it difficult to believe her ears, Her eyes begin to smart. To this is added the inspection of each and every item in her bags—the shoes, the toiletries, the underwear, a sanitary pad. Tears roll down Feroza's burning cheeks at the humiliation.

Feroza is relieved to find Manek around, not knowing that he has been paged, his name announced over the loudspeakers in the reception lobby and interrogated. She realizes that she has unwittingly incriminated him with her naive answers to the questions fired at her and is petrified. In a composed, reliable and trustworthy manner, Manek assures the officer that he is indeed Feroza's uncle, studying chemical engineering at M.I.T. and receives enough money from home for his education and living expenses. The odd jobs he does are for the university which are permitted.

The officer reverts to his aspect of demon prosecutor as he turns to Feroza and tells her: "You are not eligible to enter the US. You and your uncle have concealed the truth. You're both lying. Isn't this man your fiancé? Aren't you here to marry him?"

(*AB*, 64) The officer holds up between his fingers a lacy pink nylon nightie he has fished out of the bag and triumphantly announces: "Ah-ha! . . . The wedding negligee!" Both immigration officers leer at the nightgown as if it was an incriminating weapon discovered at the scene of a crime. The comment "It's no use, you're lying. Here's the evidence" rouses Feroza who snatches the nightgown from the officer's stubby, desecrating fingers and shouts: "To hell with you and your damn country. I'll go back!" (*AB*, 64)

Feroza's immigration officer realizes that he has exceeded his bounds and has surprise stamped all over his soft, shiny face. He accepts Manek's guarantee that the girl will go back at the end of three months or whenever her visa expires and asks Manek to provide proof of his assertions as soon as possible. The officer who had treated Feroza so vilely just a few moments back is now conciliatory. Shaken by the yellow blaze emanating from the eyes Feroza had inherited from Khutlibai, her maternal grandmother, and confounded by the fierce dignity imparted to her by Soonamai, her paternal grandmother, he even helps Feroza in stashing her belongings into her suitcase. However, the doubt and suspicion of the officer do prove right: Feroza does not go back to Pakistan after three months, her three-month visit turns into a four-year stay!

Gooneratne describes in the course of the narrative many of the misconceptions one has about the host country. In his journal, Bharat's ancestor Edward describes the hostile crowd they faced on reaching the alien land. When the *Devonshire* approached the wharf at Mackay, Edward saw a considerable crowd assembled which appeared to be waving their arms and shouting as if to welcome them. However, as they drew nearer, quite large stones started falling into the water. Sensing trouble, the captain dropped anchor some distance from the wharf and the passengers got off only at daybreak when the crowd seemed to melt away. The stone-throwing at Mackay seems a mere skirmish in comparison with "The Battle of Bundaberg" which soon followed. When the drays were fully loaded with their expected complement of labourers and started to move away from the landing point, members of the Anti-Coolie League (which had organised the stoning of *Devonshire* at Mckay) rushed at them waving sticks and clubs in their hands. While the employers threatened police action, the Sinhalese formed a tight group among themselves and drew the knives from their belts and rushed upon the Leaguers with truly blood-curdling cries, flourishing their knives above their heads. Since the Leaguers were unarmed, they had to retreat.

Having read about the stoning of the *Devonshire* in the journal, Navaranjini mistakes a hail storm on the first night of their arrival in Australia to be a similar attack on them. This is how she describes the situation to her husband: "It's the Australians! . . . the Australians have come. They're throwing stones on the roof, and breaking all the windows." (*CS,* 81) Later, this is how she narrates the incident to Mrs. Koyako:

> The stones struck the roof of our new house with a tremendous clatter. Then they hit all the front windows. The panes were shattered into great big jagged pieces, the carpet was covered with splinters of broken glass. (*CS,* 81)

With the loud banging on the door Navaranjini grabs a kitchen knife in her hand, in case somebody attacked her husband. They are dumbstruck when they are informed by their neighbour Bruce Trevally that it was a hail storm which had caused all that devastation.

Feroza's initiation to the USA in Baspi Sidhwa's *American Brat* cannot be complete till she sees the ugly side of New York too. On Eighth Avenue, she walks past small dark video parlours flashing lewd advertising, interspersed by grubby pawn shops, cheap hotels, and bars. Later, Manek directs Feroza's attention to male prostitutes, elegant transvestites—the American-style *heejras*—the pimps and miniskirted prostitutes. He also tells her about "lookouts, runners, and drug dealers." (*AB,* 80) Feroza is shocked to see the Port Authority bus terminal "the infested hub of poverty from which the homeless and the discarded spiralled all over the shadier sidewalks of New York. Ragged and filthy men were spreading scores of flattened cardboard boxes to sleep on in the bus terminal." (*AB,* 80)

Feroza was used to the odour of filth, the reek of poverty: sweat, urine, open drains, rotting carrion, vegetables and the other debris. She was accustomed to these sights and smells in Pakistan and had developed a tolerance for them. However, she finds it hard to accept the poverty and stench of filth in the USA. The smells of New York repel her:

> This was an alien filth, a compost reeking of vomit and alcoholic belches, of neglected old age and sickness, of drugged exhalations and the malodorous ferment of other substances she could not decipher. The smells disturbed her psyche; it seemed to her they personified the callous heart of the rich country that allowed such savage neglect to occur. The fetid smell made her want to throw up. She ran out of the building, and, leaning against the wall of the terminal, began to retch. (*AB,* 81)

She understands that "America is not all Saks and scyscrapers." (*AB,* 81) A little further down, she sees a couple of shifty-eyed young men selling stolen goods.

Feroza has another unpleasant experience when she confronts a sex maniac at the YMCA bathroom. While using the facilities in the women's bathroom, Feroza feels uneasy, menaced, as if she were being observed by someone or something dangerous. As she raises her head to look into the mirror, she stands transfixed. A man's bloodshot eyes are staring at her, hideously examining her not as a woman but as a specimen of the female gender. As Feroza whirls around, the man's face suddently breaks into a cunning, lewd, brown-toothed grin and he says: "How ya doin', baby? Ya wanna poke?" As Feroza tries to save herself from this dark man, another one moves in to block her path: "Howja like it if I rub it up against ya?" (*AB,* 70) As Feroza swerves and dodges past him, banging against one of the half-doors, the man's hand brushes her back. She reaches her room completely out of breath after taking several wrong turns. As a precaution, the next few days Manek stands guard outside the bathroom whenever Feroza goes in.

Again, Feroza has a horrifying experience when she is locked out in the YMCA fire-stairs. Returning from shopping around one o'clock, Feroza is surprised by the long lines of people waiting for the elevators. Wondering which line to stand in, Feroza sees one line being rapidly absorbed through open doors into an elevator and joins it. Only when the elevator sails past the fifteenth floor where she is staying does she realize that the different elevators are meant for different floors of the building. The elevator stops on the twenty-second floor, the level reserved for women and she steps out, not knowing what to do. A sympathetic soul asks her to go down again, get into the correct line, and then take the elevator that goes to the fifteenth floor, the numbers being marked on the top. Feroza feels that this will take a long time and the amiable woman shows her the fire-stairs—she can run down to the fifteenth floor.

Feroza steps inside the door hesitantly. As the woman shuts the door at her back, Feroza has a feeling that she has been shut out of New York. She feels disoriented—the air is rank with the smell of stale cigarette smoke and food. She gets a whiff of urine and of decaying refuse too. After a minute or so, she tries to open the door but fails to do so.

Forced to take the stairs, Feroza looks at the accumulated debris in a corner—cigarette butts, food cartons, grimy plastic bags. The atmosphere is weird enough—the shallow steps dissolving in the darkness. At certain places, the banister is loose in its moorings and wobbles beneath her hand. What if some part of the balustrade were missing—as happened in nightmares—or a section of it comes away where the concrete has crumbled, and she is plunged into the void? An unsettling weakness creeps into her legs. She tries the doors on different floors but all of these are locked. She shouts for help but no one listens. She prays to God but it does not help. It seems to her nothing exists outside the stairwell.

> America assumed a ruthless, hollow, cylindrical shape without beginning or end, without sunlight, an unfathomable concrete tube inhabited by her fear. She was sure something monstrous was crouched in the impervious shadows that patrolled this alien domain—ferocious sewer rats, a brutish Doberman—breathing softly, waiting patiently. (*AB*, 90)

The fear of somebody coming up the stairs makes Feroza fly up the steps. Her heart pounding, she runs up flight after flight of stairs till she feels her lungs would explode and flings herself at a door. Banging on it with her fists, with the palms of her hands, rattling the rod and the handle, she screams: "Open the door . . . For God's sake, open the door! Can't anybody hear me? Please, somebody . . . " (*AB*, 92) Her scream finally attracts a Japanese man who opens the door with a sharp metallic click. Like an uncle or a family friend, he scolds Feroza for her irresponsible act and warns her: "Never do that . . . Never! You could be murdered . . . No one would know. All kinds of shitty people . . . drugs!" (*AB*, 94) It is only later that Feroza realizes that she had been marooned in that hell for only half an hour.

As a linguist, Bharat becomes aware very early in his sojourn that the Australians are lazy in their speaking habits and they find the long Sri Lankan names almost impossible to pronounce. He becomes very self-conscious about it when T.V. sports commentator, reporting a one-day cricket match between Australia and Sri Lanka, refuses to pronounce the Sri Lankan captain's name:

> "It's written up on the SCG scoreboard, mate," he told his co-commentator. "Have a look—there it is—and as you can see it's taking up all the available space and more. You want me to give it air-time too?" (*CS*, 96)

Bharat notices that in Australia, all proper nouns are quickly trimmed or truncated. Creuzoither becomes 'Crew,' Padapopulos becomes 'Pad' and Hashimoto becomes 'Hash.' Even Mr. Koyako who loves to be known by his full name—the pompous-sounding Mekaboru Kiyanahati Belapan Koyako—is forced to shorten his name for the convenience of the Australians. When Bharat introduces him to Bruce, the latter ironically refers to his name as "Almost a short story." Unused to such directness, Koyako rallies himself quickly and says: "Just call me Kojak." (*CS*, 97)

In seeking ways to be assimilated in their new surroundings, a change of name seems to be the first step to Bharat. Each time he is introduced by name to someone new and that someone assumes the blank bright smile of total incomprehension, Bharat finds himself becoming more and more embarrassed and apologetic. When he is repeatedly referred to as "Dr. What's-his-name" by his neighbours and "Dr. Er-hum" by Professor Kingsley Fysshe, he seriously considers shortening his surname. Mangala-Davasinha which poetically combines words meaning "Wedding Day" with a complimentary description of the person being an all-conquering lion is first shortened to Mangala Dy and then Mundy, thus retaining neither the sound nor the sense of the original name. Bharat, which means 'India,' was named thus to commemorate his grandfather's scholarship in Indian languages, becomes Barry and the musical Navaranjini is chopped to Jean. Initially, Navaranjini does not like their new names: "There are problems attached to waking up with Barry when you've gone to bed with Bharat." (*CS*, 124) However, she soon finds the new names very handy and convenient. She finds it much easier to say "Mrs. Mundy here" when she rings up people to fix things. Nobody asks her to spell her name or to repeat it. Nevertheless, she sounds quite bitter when she tells Professor Blackstone that in Sinhala, the word "bari" means "incapable . . . impotent." Just on the other extreme is the connotation of the name to the Australians who know Barry Mundy to be a kind of enormous fish.

Slowly but steadily Barry and Jean start to get adjusted to their new surroundings. Jean actively participates in the English School's Open Day Exhibit which turns out to be a big success. Jean takes up complete charge of the book display. Having a diploma in librarianship, she is the right person to do the job. She immediately sets to work organizing display cabinets, collecting staff publications, writing labels and designing posters and notices. Jean also suggests that there should be an entrance charge for the exhibition; this would help meet the expenses. She pleads with Maud: "And literature, after all, is the word of God, created by His breath—it should be worth paying to hear and read it." (*CS*, 137) Maud however, finds the suggestion funny: "Against tradition. . . . Never done. And for a very good reason. Who's to pay to hear a poetry reading? The Aussie Undergrad? His mum and dad?" (*CS*, 136)

Maud is proved wrong. Despite the charge there are long queues to enter the exhibit area. The Chaucer readings are such a sensational success that two additional performances are put on. They earn ten thousand dollars from the Open Day activities. Most of the money comes from the Book Display. Jean comes up with the brilliant idea of cancelling the flat rate and charging the visitors by the minute. When Maud congratulates her on the phone, Jean says, quite simplistically: "Liteature is the breath of God. That's worth paying something to receive." (*CS*, 140) The reality dawns on Maud only when Angel tells her that Jean had included some Indian erotica in the book display; that the book that drew the maximum crowds came from Mundy's own library—Limited edition of the illustrated copy of the Kama Sutra, containing "Every single position." (*CS*, 140) She now understands the real significance of Jean's simplistic last words on the telephone: "They are thirsty for knowledge, . . . And we provided it. Isn't that what universities are supposed to do?" (*CS*, 140)

In his letter to his mother, Bharat voices his concern about preserving their ancient culture and traditional ways of life: "The Asian community here, though it is not as large as the one in Melbourne, is very much aware of the cultural hazards, amidst which we live." (*CS*, 87) He writes about the children of Sri Lankan families who have become infected with Australian values. In a tragicomic manner, he describes Mr. Koyako's efforts to preserve his national identity. As Mrs. Koyako tells Navaranjini: "My husband . . . is very very keen that our children who are growing up overseas should not lose touch with the traditions of their forefathers." (*CS*, 92)

On the invitation of Mr. Koyako, Barry Mundy starts writing a book for the use of Asian migrants in Australia. Barry is, of course, the fittest person to write *The Guide*. Mr. Koyako refers to his "Cambridge background" (*CS*, 144) and Jean to his reputation as "the scholar in our family":

> Indeed, if Barry's Grandfather Edward had written his journal in Greek or Latin (and not in English as, fortunately for me, he did), Barry would have translated his observations about the new world he encountered as easily as he once translated—through a pair of binoculars—that Latin inscription about the Dutch Governor Johann Gideon Loten which is carved high up on a wall in Westminster Abbey. (*CS*, 156)

Earlier, Barry had published the biography of his grandfather Edward in book form entitled *Lifeline*. By writing *The Guide* now, Barry feels he will be carrying his family's traditional pursuit of translation and interpretation into a new country.

In *The Guide for the Asian Migrants to Australia*, Barry writes that one question which haunts him still, even after spending so many years in an alien country, is: "when is it exactly that the immigrant throws overboard every other idea, every other possible destination, and decides that here, and in no other place, he will make his home?" (*CS*, 151) In every expatriate's experience, he feels, "There must surely have been a moment, a small space in time for all of us who are now here, when the anchor was let down, the sails folded, the landing made." (*CS*, 151) Barry goes on to ruminate about his own case and that of his grandfather Edward and comes to the conclusion that "we do not choose the moment of departure or settlement. We are chosen by them. And also that those moments, once they have touched us, make us different persons from the persons we were before, and place ceases to matter." (*CS*, 152)

The change started when Bharat and Navaranjini stepped out of the exit door of the plane at Sydney Airport. As Barry writes in his *Guide*: "One conclusion I have reached that is sadly, but I think incontestably, true is that people, like all material things, undergo change." (*CS*, 154)

Jean also considers the question of immigration in the course of her narrative. She talks of the various reasons given by her acquaintances from India and Sri Lanka, Pakistan and Bangladesh:

> "The educational system there is in ruins, ... The mobs burned our house during the riots in 1958." Or "we saw our books burned, our furniture broken, and our china smashed by vandals. We escaped with the children over the garden wall into the house next door, or we would have been killed." (*CS*, 155)

Barry and Jean had none of the above reasons to migrate: they had no children to educate; nor was there any racial or religious discrimination against them which made them flee to Australia. They were leading a comfortable, even a luxurious life in Colombo.

Occasionally Barry did grumble about the university not funding his research properly or about the social and political life in

Sri Lanka—about the photography of the prime minister greeting His Holiness Sri Bhansi Ram, the guru from South India, splashed in full colour on the front page of the *Daily News*.

The novel is a witty tale of culture clash and adaptation which never becomes sentimental about either country. It is totally devoid of hatred and self-loathing. The book explores the tensions between the migrant feeling for the old country and the new. Both Gooneratne and Sidhwa deliberately avoid the immigrant writer's temptation to fall into the trap of glorifying his/her country of origin and belittling or degrading the adopted country.

WORKS CITED

Yasmine Gooneratne, *A Change of Skies* (Penguin India, 1991). Abbreviated *CS*.

Naila Hussain, *The Nation, Midweek*, 26 May 1993, p. 19.

Bapsi Sidhwa, *An American Brat* (Penguin India, 1991). Abbreviated *AB*.

A Passage to Australia: Three Novelists in Search of a Homeland

LAURIE CLANCY
La Trobe University, Melbourne

Over the last 25 to 30 years, Asia, from being initially neglected as a source of interest to our novelists, has become an object of almost continual focus. Alison Broinowski in her study of *The Yellow Lady* points out that the two decades between 1965 and 1985 'saw the publication of more than fifty Australian novels set in Asian and Pacific countries, which reassessed and mostly rejected the images of the past.' (Broinowski, 1992) The decade since then has probably produced just as many.

As with any new species of narrative, from the American western to the Australian colonial novel, the genre developed its own motifs and tropes with remarkable rapidity. Broinowski has pointed to some of these, especially in dealing with what she calls the 'journalist' novels of writers like Christopher Koch, Robert Drewe and Blanche d'Alpuget. There is the Australian's first encounter with an Asian country and the experience of arrival. As she says, 'The airport scenes are virtually interchangeable with accounts of Asian harbours half a century earlier.' (Broinowski, 1992:199) There is the retreat to the bar (especially if the journalist is a male), the journey inland and uphill into the mountains, the sexual encounter with an Asian and usually the subsequent retreat from radiance as the Australian protagonists (usually though not always male) discover the Asians (usually though not always female) as 'the codifiers of enlightenment and the releasers of dark mysteries.' (Broinowski, 1992:194)

As with any genre, too, the themes and tropes exhaust themselves and need to be constantly renewed, sometimes by parody and satire, as in the novels of David Foster, Gerard Lee and Kevin Brophy, since these constitute the most extreme forms of subversion and inversion. Eventually the genre becomes imploded and Asian writers turn our scrutiny back upon ourselves. This paper examines the views and attitudes of Asian writers who have come to Australia.

This kind of scrutiny is not a completely new phenomenon. Mena Abdullah wrote a beautiful collection of stories, *This Time of the Peacock*, about an Indian family in Australia back in the nineteen sixties. But it is really only in the last decade or so that a literature which documents the experience of Asians in Australia has become widespread. A number of writers have been associated with this development—Brian Castro, Don'o Kim, Sang Ye, Beth Yahp and even the Englishman Alex Miller—but in this paper I want to look at three of them: Yasmine Gooneratne, Adib Khan and Dewei Anggraeni—in order to see if one can't find some elements they have in common.

Yasmine Gooneratne's *A Change of Skies* (1991) is the story of a Sri Lankan couple who arrive in Australia, expecting to stay in exile for only five years, but who eventually fall in love with the country. The Prologue contains the first of several selections from a book called 'Lifeline. The Journal of An Asian Grandee in Australia 1882-1887. Edited by his Grandson.' The 'Grandee' is Edward, whose narrative voice (with the extracts italicised) is interspersed with a number of others. One of these is his grandson who tells us, 'Edward had grown up (as I grew up too, though in a later generation), in a country where the line between fact and fiction, history and legend—if such a line exists—tends to blur until it fades to nothing.' (Gooneratne, COS, 1991:4)

Gooneratne uses the technique of Robert Drewe (*The Savage Crows*) and Brian Castro (*Birds of Passage*) as well as others, of alternating a contemporary story with a past one with which it has considerable parallels in order to suggest the continuity of the experience of displacement, as well as providing an ironic commentary on both the forms that contemporary exile can take and the fact that people taken as *arrivistes* are in fact as much settlers as the white people.

The novel alternates the voices of Bharat Mangala-Davasinha and his wife Navaranjini, whom he calls Baba. He is Sinhalese: she is Tamil. Bharat is an academic in linguistics who is bored by his life in Colombo and answers an advertisement from the Southern Cross University in NSW for a visiting Professor in Linguistics, a five year appointment, beginning in 1964. He had known almost nothing about Australia before seeing the ad. He comments only that he had seen the country on a map: 'To the east of India and the island of Ceylon (also pink), south of Borneo and Sarawak, there Australia had been, a blank pink space shaped like the head of a Scotch terrier with its ears pricked up and its square nose permanently pointed westwards, towards Britain.' (COS:11) Not surprisingly, such images of cartography abound in postcolonial literature.

He speaks ironically of the country's 'doggy devotion' to Britain. Their friend Mr. Doraisamy warns them before they leave of 'that ancient legend of Asia, according to which a sage warned seafarers questing in lower latitudes for a Great South Land to beware lest they be sucked into a great emptiness, and have their spirits drained away.' (COS:57) The point is often made in these novels that Australia is lacking in myth and oral story-telling. This alleged thinness manifests itself even in the manner and the structure of these novels. For instance, as several reviewers pointed out, Adib Khan's *Solitude of Illusions* starts almost in a mode of Rushdie-like magic realism but particularly in the scenes set in Australia resorts to a kind of social realism that fits the limited rationality of his protagonist. We are told of the protagonist that 'His reward for spending time with Munir was a privileged insight into a secret world populated with invisible beings—*buraks* and *nagas*. *Djinns* and *pories*' (SI:87) but it is an insight from which he is unable to profit; he cannot see with his heart, as Munir accuses him. (It is noteworthy, incidentally, that Adib Khan does not feel impelled to translate the Indian words in either novel, even though he uses them liberally. The writer can now take some familiarity with Asia among his readers for granted).

This incident shows up the limitations of Khalid's rationality. He is unable to enter into Munir's imagined world. White and perhaps Peter Carey aside, the climate of Australia has proved too thin to support the kind of inventiveness that magic realism and similar modes demand. Dewi Anggraeni, too, complains several times in her novels on precisely these grounds. The oral traditions she is accustomed to in Indonesia, she says, are not appropriate for Australia. Adib Khan's protagonist Iqbal observes, 'I now live in a world where myths are wafer thin and commercialised, without mystery or a multiplicity' (SI:7). When writers do resort to modes approximating to magic realism they tend to set their novels entirely outside Australia, as Beth Yahp does with *The Crocodile Fury* and Fotini Epanomitis with *The Mule's Foal*.

On the other hand, Australia is noteworthy for its egalitarianism. To return to Gooneratne, we are given a quotation from Edward's diary: '*Every man here is, or expects one day to be, his own master; a way of thinking which gives rise in the majority of men to a spirit of marked independence.*' (COS:103) Shortly afterwards, we are told, 'His first name used by a secretary to her boss? This had not been the practice at Cambridge, nor was the practice, by any means, in Colombo.' (COS:103) This seems to be meant straightforwardly even if in general the mode of the novel is satirical, built around the mutual misunderstandings inherent in the clash of eastern and western cultures.

That satire in the novel is broad and even-handed, to the point of being almost promiscuous. Sometimes it is conventional academic comedy, of the kind we get in Australia in novels like *Busy in the Fog* and *The Wild Life Reserve*. For instance, the university display is successful because Bharat's wife Navaranjini, who has now become Jean, puts some Indian erotica in it, thus giving her husband Bharat, who has now become Barry, an undeserved reputation as an expert lover. 'There were rows of Japanese students,' we are told at one point, queueing up to learn English, and rows of Australian students 'queuing up to learn Japanese.' (COS:120) At one point the novel even, in a post-modern display of self-referentiality, turns in upon itself. Here is 'Jean' writing to her mother, Amma: '*. . . according to Bharat there is a whole new literary genre developing in south Asia now called 'Gulf Sorrow'—poems, songs and stories about love and loss and separation, composed by people who have left their homes and children behind them in order to earn money quickly in Saudi or Baghdad or Kuwait.*' (COS:179) Or Australia.

Most often, though, the essential theme of the novel is division. Where Broinowski's so-called journalist novels concerned the contact between a more or less innocent Australian and an alien Asian culture on which the protagonist impinges only briefly and shallowly, the characteristic protagonist in the Asian novel is caught between two cultures, crossing back and forth between them, constantly comparing them and finding neither of them satisfactory. While Australia is continually if benignly satirised, the land of origin does not escape either; after five years Barry and Jean return to Colombo briefly to find there poor teaching conditions, snobbery about Australia, arranged marriages and a sense of Sri Lanka's so-called 'distinguished' history that is largely a history of violence and injustice.

Gooneratne's second novel, *The Pleasures of Conquest* (1996), is more pointedly satirical than her first. The de-bunking intention is announced on the first page with a reference to the mythical country Amnesia, an island postcolonial state which is very recognisably Sri Lanka, and which the American novelist Stella Mallinson is visiting. Once again a map is involved: the visit is inspired by her glimpse of a mariner's chart commissioned in 1720 by the Dutch East India Company and executed by Gerard van Ryckman the Elder. The novel is really looking through a series of intricately related stories which employ some of the same characters, at different white attitudes towards and mostly exploitation of Amnesia, and in particular the exploitation of women. Academia, too, comes in for a fair whipping, through the person of Professor Philip Destry who, it becomes clear, has built a highly successful career around the labours of his (predictably female) research assistants. Destry, 'Phil the Philanderer, you dog, you!' (POC:116) is obviously a highly risible character.

Australian characters exist only on the periphery of the novel; for the most part, although not always, they are treated sympathetically. We are told at one point of Australian men that they knew how to treat their women: 'Maybe it was because they were closer to the cave than civilised Americans, Philip thought, but he had often found that Aussies know better than any other race how to treat their women. In fact, they could teach American sophisticates a thing or two.' (POC:136) Given what follows, it quickly becomes clear that this is meant ironically, as evidence of sympathy in Destry's mysogynistic eyes. A few moments later Caroline's brother Ray turns the hose on a mistress who has come to plead with him.

But Destry's first wife Caroline was Australian, the descendant of convicts. So is the sympathetically treated Professor Colin Matthews, a fellow scholar of Destry. Leila Tan, a former lover of Destry and the research assistant whom he barely acknowledged, becomes Australian also. As one character noted in *A Change of Skies*, 'Australian people can be endlessly surprising. One surprising thing about them is, that deep, very deep, a long way down, Australians are true Orientals at heart' (POC:117), which perpetuates a stereotype (about Orientals) by challenging another one (about Australians): underneath our rough exteriors we have hearts of gold. The Australians generally figure surprisingly favourably as against the Americans and English, perhaps because they are not part of the colonisers or at least are situated ambiguously between the colonisers and the colonised. There is a certain naivety about even Matthews, who is outwitted by the calculating Destry, perhaps because he does not even realise that he is engaged in a battle of wits.

Destry is deeply and devotedly hostile to women even as he exploits them. He denies the possibility that they have brains even as he profits from them. As he puts it succinctly at one point, 'We have feminists in our department the way Hamelin Town had rats.' (POC:218) Much of the novel deals with the violation of women by men although we have to remember the balancing opening section, in which a young boy is violated by an older woman.

Once again there is a kind of ur-text involved. Destry's major work is a biography of the remarkable Sir John D'Estery, nineteenth century diplomat who fell in love with Amnesia, and whom Destry regards as a kind of original version of himself. On the flimsiest evidence he builds a case around his being a spy for the British, instead of a man who went to seed in the tropics, but eventually we learn the truth about him—that he had come to reject all his colonial attitudes and recognise the quality of the Amnesians and their way of life.

Although the satire in *The Pleasures of Conquest* is sometimes uncertainly directed, the essential theme is the oppression of women, which in turn is related to the oppression of colonial cultures in general, and their resistance to it. Gooneratne spells out the connection in perhaps the most significant passage in the novel. The Amnesians believe that their Inner Kingdom can never be conquered until men bored a hole in the mountain, and in this they prove to be right. We are told:

> Well, they forced their way through that rock, did they not, those English engineers. They violated the land with the urgency of a bridegroom on his wedding night. And though they made love to her afterwards as all men do . . . she can never hear the mournful sound of the engine-driver's whistle echoing down the valleys without recalling the pain of her own marriage night and the helpless anger with which she had lain in silence, suffering her husband's embraces. (POC:328)

Colonial *conquest* (the word which resonates in the title of the novel) is directly equated here with rape of women and in turn with patriarchal structures generally, even in postcolonial societies.

Dewi Angraenni's first novel, *The Root of All Evil* (1987), opens in Melbourne with the narrator, a Sudanese woman named Komala, having just decided to return to Indonesia after nine years of absence with her Australian family, in order to see her father, who she has just learned from her sister Narsih has suffered a stroke. Once again, therefore, the protagonist is postulated as a site of division. She has been inside both cultures for a considerable period of time but is now going back to her original home to view it from the relatively distanced perspective of her long absence. This sense is reinforced when she first lands in Jakarta and goes through the same experience Alison Broinowski describes. She is treated rudely by the customs officers, she cannot stand the heat and humidity of the place, having lost her natural conditioning to it. She is terrified by the traffic. 'The walk was acclimatising my body and mind to the new situation,' (RAE:8) she tells us, and again, 'Conversation was interrupted by my gasping at the closeness of a vehicle to our bodies and my sighs of relief when we escaped unscathed.' There is no air conditioning. 'My body had not adjusted to the humid climate.' Inevitably, like Adib Khan's

Khalid and Angela Barrett she is appalled by the changes that have taken place in the city since her absence, to the point where she does not recognise her own street *Jalan Jambu Monyet* (RAE:10) as well as by the change in fortune of her family. She finds that her mother now has to take in boarders in order to pay for her invalid husband's full-time nurse. He had no superannuation or pension, unlike the situation in Australia.

The Root of All Evil starts off in one kind of genre—the stranger home from abroad and the implied comparisons of two cultures—but transfers to another, that of Janette Turner Hospital's *The Ivory Swing*: the question it poses is that of how far and on what terms should an outsider interfere in what she perceives as injustice. The question Adib Khan's protagonist asks himself in *Seasonal Adjustments* is one which Komala could also ponder: are they merely 'bumbling agents of change who spread themselves across the globe and unwittingly seek to impose their hybrid perceptions on closeted cultures'?

It is also a very explicitly feminist novel. Shortly after Komala arrives back in Jakarta, Australia almost disappears from the novel and the concern becomes the very obvious contrasts between rich and poor, between the old and the new as sections of the cities are torn down to make way for modern high rises, and above all, between the situations of men and women. Everywhere Komala is confronted with the spectacle of fearful and helpless women. There is the new 'happiness exercise,' designed for women to keep their weight down and allow them to retain their sexual appeal to their men. This is the first sounding of the theme of the humiliations into which women are forced in order to compete for or retain a man.

The males crowd into a cafe rather than eat outside, so that they won't be seen with their mistresses. Narsih spells out more of the rules: 'Our society at large, especially the married women, don't like divorcees. They think divorcees, especially the young ones, are a threat.' (RAE:64) Tati, the sister of one of Komala's friends, has had two children by a husband who subsequently died. Financially helpless, she becomes the mistress of a rich married man but his wife throws acid in her face and the man disowns her. Not only are women placed in a subordinate role but they turn in upon themselves and blame other women for their husbands' infidelity. Anggraeni sums all this up through her protagonist Komala in an important speech half way through the novel. She is considering the predicament of a male friend Roby Tjoa, who married a divorced woman but then found that she trusted him so little that she began to divorce *him* and take all his money:

> I began to get a clearer picture of life in Jakarta now. Its pressure on women. If you are single and not suitably employed, you will have to wait around for a man to offer you security in the form of marriage. Once married, you have to summon all your wits and energy to keep your man happy and occupied, so that he will not be tempted by other "loose" women, who are only after his money, which you also need. If you're not good enough he dumps you, then you become a "loose" woman. Then you have experienced being dumped, you become wiser and realise your precarious position, your disposability. So you dig for gold and you dig hard. Every opportunity could be your last: Robby's wife was an extreme example. Her obsession was motivated by her fear of being dumped again, eventually. Unfortunately her obsession had also made her blind to Robby's genuine love for her. (RAE:76)

Anggraeni goes on to develop her theme in one of three novellas, "Uncertain Step," she published collectively as *Stories of the Indian Pacific* in 1992. It opens on that situation, familiar from her earlier fiction, of the woman who is without a man and hence the object of derision or despair to her family. Like many of Anggraeni's heroines, Aryani is spoken of as 'plain' yet in the course of the narrative proves herself exceptionally attractive to a number of the male characters and is spoken of as having a strange kind of beauty in many ways. Like many of the author's heroines, also, she displays talent as a writer. More or less out of a sense of having no alternative she accepts what seems at first to be an almost flippant proposal: 'At thirty-four, she knew the chance had passed, and had more or less resigned herself to it. Even when Steve Dunne, the Australian teacher she worked with at the English Language Institute unconventionally proposed to her, shė took it as a joke.' (Angaraenni, SIA:1)

When she changes her mind and, in one of the story's most moving moments, rings him up to confirm that he is serious, it turns out that he is indeed. Without loving him, she enters into the marital state, gives her virginity to him before they are married, and struggles to come to terms with an Australia that is immensely foreign to her. What is new about the novella is the way in which Aryani eventually becomes empowered, growing in strength and confidence to the point where her husband is in danger of being left behind by her, as he was by his first wife.

Though there is one extended scene—the traditional Indonesian version of the wedding—that is set in Jakarta, most of the novel is placed in Adelaide and it contains some barbed observations of Australia. Although she is highly educated, speaks perfect English, recites English poetry beautifully and knows a great deal of it off by heart, Aryani is constantly mistaken for a mail-order, Filippino bride. Steve himself is in many ways a quintessentially Australian male, a very decent, tender man but with many limitations and a fear that he has to learn to overcome of allowing his wife to have a life and search for fulfilment outside himself.

With the encouragement of a kindly older man, Vincent Wilkes, whose Samoan wife left him, Aryani writes a screenplay and has it accepted. In the closing scene of the novella, the predatory producer of the film makes an ugly pass at her and she realises why Wilkes lost his wife. The ending is sudden but the observation of the early stages of a rocky but finally successful marriage is well done and the portrait of Steve is one of an average, essentially decent Australian who learns to grow with his wife.

That sense of division of which I have spoken is most evident in the two novels of Adib Khan. *Seasonal Adjustments* (1994) concerns a man from Bangladesh named Iqbal Ahmed Chaudhary, member of a highly distinguished family, who has lived in Australia for eighteen years. After his marriage to an Australian breaks up he returns home with his young daughter for the first time, in a search for restoration. Adib Khan cuts back and forth between the two countries and between past and present in a kind of structural enactment of the protagonist/narrator's sense of divided identity as he becomes occupied, as he says in '*painstakingly piecing together the shards of my earliest memories.*' (SA:1)

As the novel cuts in time and place, so it makes incessant commentaries and comparisons on the two cultures, in a more or less equitable fashion. The first real mention of Australia comes with the headlines of a newspaper Iqbal had bought at the airport. His is a curiously nostalgic view: 'The woes of a once carefree, larrikin nation are reflected in the sombre headlines' and again, 'I cannot help feeling sad for the generous country I stepped into as a confused young man. . . . Australia, as I once knew it, was too good to be true. It was a huge dream full of sharply defined rainbows and realisable wishes for those who cared to pursue them. The transition to an imperfect reality is painfully difficult.' (SA:32) The sentiment is repeated later: 'It is difficult to be positive about the Australia of the 1990s. Had he asked me fifteen years ago,' he says of a friend's inquiry, 'I would have given him an unequivocal answer. It was a rich country in more ways than Iftiqar could have imagined.' (SA:114) Iqbal sees it as a country that has lost the innocence and generosity of youth and now 'stands tottering on the brink of adulthood, enmeshed in the process of finding its soul and learning about the traumas of maturity.' Perhaps the kindest statement is the concluding one: 'The country is slowly teaching itself the difficult task of being humble.' (SA:115)

On the other hand, he is deeply critical of his native country on such grounds as the obvious suppression of women in Bangladesh (SA:19, 24), the excessive eating of the Chaudhary family, and the harsh contrasts of rich and poor, the patriarchal history of the family and its oppression of the villagers. Adib Khan is careful to de-romanticise *Khush Manzil*, pointing to its origins in the sexual and financial oppression of women. (SA:150) The binary opposition here is the very traditional one between the village (Modhunagar) and the forest. 'It was accepted in Modhunagar that the forest was the abode of supernatural beings who were benign enough, during daylight hours, to allow mortals to benefit from the bounty of firewood, wild fowls and fruits.' (SOI:87) A trip in the Grampians is juxtaposed against a tiger hunt. Iqbal, who has rather too much of a tendency to abstract statement, to spelling out the themes of the novel sometimes, informs us, 'There are occasions when I regret my exposure to the diversity of cultural radiation which has bleached my individuality . . . I have a house. A job. A country . . . let's say I possess a passport. What I lack is the weight of emotional anchors. There is nothing which binds me to a place.' (SA:9)

Like Gooneratne, Adib Khan is delighted by ironic contrasts and incongruities in a culture. At one point, he tells us, 'I am saved by the screeching brakes of an old van announcing the global influence of Coca-Cola.' (SA:14) Images of binary opposition run through the novel, enacting the condition of the protagonist. He says of himself, for instance, that 'Caught between Catechism and Koranic lessons, I was like a young Everyman in a variation of a morality play. Instead of the good and bad angels fighting for my soul, the principal antagonists were the Brothers of the Holy Cross and the Peshawari *mullah*.' (SA:89) These divisions culminate in a bizarre fantasy in which Iqbal imagines a war between Islam and Christianity in which he acts as referee. In a passionate but unspoken monologue, Iqbal spells out his feelings: '*Do you know what it means to be a migrant? A lost soul forever adrift in search of a tarnished dream? You live in a perpetual state of conflict, torn between what was and what should have been.*' (SA:143) This silent monologue, proceeding out of rage and the 'self-righteous insularity' of his former friends, is probably the most important passage in the novel. For Adib, the condition of expatriation is one of division and unfitness, of not belonging completely anywhere and being lost in more than one world. He tries, though, to see what is positive about it: '*But out of this deprivation emerges an understanding of humanity unstifled by genetic barriers. No, I wouldn't have it any other way.*' It is a highly rhetorical speech, that has a slightly desperate note to it but the authenticity of the emotion is felt. The 1300 years of tradition and culture to which his family appeal have become imprisoning things: 'I value the agony of free thinking and freedom of choice above the cosiness of belonging. I am a free floater. I take and adapt what suits me. I have been indelibly tainted with a diversity of experiences embracing a cross-current of customs and behaviour. I am a composite of lifestyles and rituals. I can never blindly follow.'

Seasonal Adjustments ends on a note of almost Chekhovian elegy as the family house in which Iqbal grew up is being destroyed to be replaced by a refinery. Adib Khan's second novel, *Solitude of Illusions* (1996), makes it even clearer that you can't go home again. His protagonist in this novel is Khalid Sharif, a 76 year old man living temporarily in Melbourne with his son's family and, unknown to them, under sentence of death. Again the novel is dominated by memory, with the massive weight of a lifetime's failure of nerve bearing down on Khalid. In particular, he had fallen in love with the courtesan his family had sent him to in order to acquire social skills but when he tried to marry her he had allowed his family to destroy the relationship.

Juxtaposed against the story of Khalid is that of Angela Barrett, Khalid's neighbour and a representative of the old Anglo-Indian order. They form a curious friendship and become another useful device by which the author can explore and resolve differences because Khalid forms a friendship with Angela's grandson, with whom she has been lumbered by her daughter's aspirations for freedom and escape from an unhappy marriage. Angela Barrett represents the opposite of Khalid. She evokes and attempts to inhabit a world that no longer exists and that was, in any case, founded on illusion. 'She did not,' we are told, 'think of herself as being anything but English.' (Khan, SOI:28) 'Angela had been raised to ignore the Indian connections in her life, so that the term *Anglo-Indian* was never a cause for a conflict of identities and had no bearing in determining the cultural boundaries of her life. She adopted propriety, correctness and boundaries of her imperial heritage.'

Juxtaposition, contrast, comparison are all central to Adib Khan's quest in both novels. *Solitude of Illusions* works in a less obviously satiric way than the earlier novel to place two cultures side by side and explore each of them. There is no single, privileged point of view although Khalid is the dominating character. Both novels are preoccupied with a personal quest and crisis on the part of the protagonists and although one cannot say that questions of nationality, identity and so on are not central to these they do not dominate them. The political/national drama is subservient to the personal, in the now 76 year old Khalid's case the time he spent in *Khush Manzil*.

We are shown the machinations to get Khalid to give up his

property. If Khalid is shown as being broken by his cowardice in giving up the courtesan he loved, the new generation is treated even more harshly. Javed and his family are materialistic and bound together by hardly more than ties of convention. Javed is having an unpromising affair, which he is trying to break off, under cover of his squash games. Javed's sister Nasreen pursues her father's money because under Islamic law she is disadvantaged in comparison with the males.

Ron Shapiro has asked the question in *Crossing Cultures* of the limitations of postcolonial modes of criticism. He says: 'The underlying question being asked is this: 'How adequately can the postcolonial mode help answer these more 'personal' or 'human' or 'existential' questions?' (45) It's a question that I think Adib Khan's work raises more explicitly than most. Apart from the problem of the kind of language that postcolonial criticism frequently employs, the postcolonial mode seems to limit the fiction and reduce it to the status of sociological investigation.

I'm not sure whether Adib Khan is aware of this but I suspect he is in his second novel and that this is the reason for the constant references back to Tolstoy and *Lear*. Like Tolstoy's Levin, Khalid thinks constantly upon the afterlife: 'What if there was no afterlife? No angels or devils? No meeting of souls? Suppose the deceased in his family could only be reached as a reflection in the ripples of his memory while he was alive? Was life ultimately no more than a despairing creation of an unreliable imagination?' (SOI:66) More than anything, *Solitude of Illusions* is a deeply sympathetic portrait of old age in which the question of country and cross cultures becomes increasingly less important than dilemmas that preoccupy all human beings, in all cultures.

WORKS CITED

Dewi Angraenni, *The Root of All Evil* (Melbourne: Indra Publishing, 1987). Abbreviated RAE.

______, *Stories of the Indian Pacific* (Melbourne: Indra Publishing, 1992). Abbreviated SIA.

Alison Broinowski (Melbourne: Oxford University Press, 1992).

Yasmine Gooneratne, *A Change of Skies* (Picador, Sydney: Pan Macmillan, 1991). Abbreviated COS.

______, *The Pleasures of Conquest* (Vintage, Sydney: Random House, 1996). Abbreviated POC.

Adib Khan, *Solitude of Illusions* (Sydney: Allen & Unwin, 1996). Abbreviated SI.

______, *Seasonal Adjustments* (Sydney: Allen & Unwin, 1996). Abbreviated SA.

Ron Shapiro, "Critical Areas of Uncertainty" in Bruce Bennett, Jeff Doyle and Satendra Nandan, ed., *Crossing Cultures, Essays on Literature & Culture of the Asia-Pacific* (London: Skoob Books, 1996).

Multicultural Impact on Music Learning in Australia

BASIL JAYATILAKA
Edith Cowan University, Western Australia

Multiculturalism is now an everyday fact of life in Australia. The dramatic increase of migrants to Australia has resulted in an impact of great diversity, diffusion and awareness of different cultures upon music education in Australia. Such a situation will open new and fresh avenues for music learning in Australia which, hitherto, has had a monoculturally chauvinistic and essentially eurocentric direction.

Appreciation of diverse and different artistic music traditions tends to enhance social interaction, cooperation, trust, respect and understanding (Santos, 1994) particularly with all those who see international and global education as almost established features of education in Australia (Morris and Hudson, 1996). The changing face of multicultural classrooms in Australia will present many new challenges. In order for Australian music pedagogy to internalise the realities of multiculturalism, teachers will have to deal with the unfamiliar in order to survive or flourish in this new learning and teaching environment.

This paper seeks to outline perceptual differences and different learning processes and patterns music students from different ethnic backgrounds bring to bear on learning music. It also suggests principles and strategies for multicultural music education in Australia.

In the last 50 years Australia has changed from being a predominantly European and monocultural populace to one which reflects a kaleidoscopically changing mosaic of international migrants, 40% of whom have one parent who comes from a non-

English speaking background. Such a situation may have the potential for cultural incompatibilities which so often appear to be at the heart of many conflicts in other multicultural communities and countries (UNESCO International Commission on Education). Australian music educators, however, take a different and more positive view of such situations. Like some African and Asian educators and musicologists, they posit that "intercultural education through music may be one way of raising people's level of tolerance for that which is different" (Oehrle, 1996: 95). The validity of this supposition seems to be embedded in the shared psychological and spiritual commonality of the "collective conscious" of all peoples in which "nothing is precious, except that part of others which is in you" (Mabry, 1994: 22). Or, in the words of Teilhard, "the age of [individual] nations has passed. Now unless we wish to perish, we must shake off our old prejudices and build the earth . . . by correcting our errant perception of reality as being made up of separate units" (1962: 25).

This paper proposes that for Australia, like other countries that are increasingly multicultural in their make up, **education through music** rather than music education ought to be the preferred mode of accomplishing the aims and objectives of music curricula in multicultural settings. Such an approach tends to illuminate and educate the whole person through the study and performance of the various ethnic musics now available in Australia. Furthermore, this approach not only goes beyond the mere transmission of the knowledge and skills of particular musics but is also tied up with whole cultures to include performance and socialisation as part of music making as is the case with many Asian and African cultures (Chernoff, 1979: 154). It can become a unifying force with social significance (Leonhard, 1989: 5). When education through music functions as culture rather than music per se music, it may then be seen as humanistic with the "potential to change prejudicial attitudes and behaviours" (Elliott, 1989: 14: see also Swanwick, 1988).

For many new Australian ethnic migrants difficulties in assimilating and adjusting to their new surroundings are often compensated by a recourse to their respective artistic traditions which naturally sustain them morally and aesthetically. They come from cultures widely separated by experience, values and environments which invariably develop musical systems that emphasise different aspects of expertise and learning modes. For example, most Asian and African cultures are more tuned to micro-tonal melody and intricate rhythmic structures than harmony which appears to be the basis of Western tonalities. Thus, the implications for music learning in Australia will invariably traverse quite different routes before arriving at the same destinations.

In multicultural Australian classrooms many children with highly diverse learning patterns face teachers who do not give this phenomenon much thought. How do Asian, African and Latinos formulate their music learning patterns? Are these patterns necessarily the same as those of their European or American counterparts? There is nothing to indicate in the research literature that music educators in Australia are aware of differences of the prior musical training some of their migrant students have experienced. Pedagogy in contemporary music education in Australia faces new challenges and has yet to internalise the realities of music in cultural education.

In examining and exploring the music of some of the dominant migrant cultures represented in certain schools in Australia, useful insights may be gleaned of the culture's music learning patterns. For instance, the greatest impact made in the study and performance of musics of other cultures is on the affective rather than the cognitive or psychomotor domains of music. Campbell (1986) suggests that instruction in the music of other cultures may provide students with a useful flexibility of approach to the study of music and puts them in a better position to make intelligent value judgements concerning future style selections. She, however, cautions that "tolerance [for the music of other cultures] and preference [for any type of music] are truly not synonymous" (p. 160). She also suggests that selecting and studying the music of more than one ethnic group enables students to realise the "depth and breadth of human expression through music" (Campbell, 1992: 32).

According to Taylor (1970), students share common neurophysical constants that predispose them to use certain musical procedures despite cultural differences. However, Taylor does not discuss the process of music learning. This author disagrees with Taylor who, like so many anthropologists, sociologists and ethnomusicologists, often appear, unfortunately, to be insufficiently sensitive to the viewpoint of ethnic groups who supply the information and who subsequently disassociate themselves from the study. Furthermore, trying to establish commonalities in the world's music systems for the purpose of detecting similarities and differences between them proves to be more an ideal than a viable practice (Engle, 1993). For example, a study by Kessler, Hansen and Shepard (1984) which compared perceptions of Balinese and American music by participants from both cultures revealed how the participants attempted to explain the other's music in terms of their own cultural experiences. Results indicated that the Balinese were more successful at identifying Western 'tonal hierarchies' than the Americans were with Balinese music! It soon becomes evident that even a cursory examination of this subject reveals how differently the musical practice and thought of different cultures are taught and learnt. For example, European civilisations use teachers to instruct whereas in parts of Asia and Africa, peers, senior peers or the community assume the role of teachers and where song, dance, participation and socialisation are inseparable strategies and components of music making. Some other cultures derive their method and music from dreams, visions and the supernatural, as is the case with the Blackfeet American Indians (McAllester, 1985).

In several non-European approaches to music making, the fundamental values of these cultures are mediated through music which appears to be an indispensable necessity to life itself. Swanwick is noticeably thought-provoking here when he advocates a breaking out of "restricted worlds of culturally defined reality" (1988: 112). He promotes, instead, "imaginative criticism" where the strength of an individual's comprehensive education lies in "the possibility of creating new values in transcending [the pervading] culture, in critical reflection and going beyond the first ways of looking and thinking.

Multicultural music education is obviously "value-laden, reflecting a set of beliefs, principles and ideas that . . . govern the relationships of people of diverse cultures [where teachers may] evaluate people, things and behaviours in terms of those cultures, groups and experiences that produce them" ((Standifer, 1990: 7).

Such a perspective enables students to view "cultural and group differences . . .[as] assets that simply involve alternative ways of looking at, and doing things, and these differences are not absolute or mutually exclusive" (ibid: 60).

Music is culture to many non-European nations. The concept of the right of ownership to composed music in some contexts has more to do with "usage rather than rights which may be conferred by creation" (Wiggins, 1996: 13), and whether it is "good to dance to rather than whether the pitches used are correct" (ibid: 22). One is reminded of Henry VIII who, in accordance with the custom of the day, altered popular recorder compositions by merely improvising or adding other voices to them and then palming them off as his own creations.

In Australia as with other European countries, having a complete mental image of the music to be performed and sounded is extremely useful though separate from the skill needed to perform it. For most Asian and African music teachers these separate strategies are integrated. The very act of internalising the music by its nature implies the skill. Furthermore, in Western instruction teachers help children to analyse and then encourage their players to study and perform the music typically with correction so as to bring the study and performance of music to more acceptable levels of musical excellence.

In non-European cultures, like Ghana, for instance, the teachers play and then leave their pupils to imitate and understand the music in their own way. Thus, the pupils' conceptualisation of the study and performance of music is basically constructivist and metacognitive in its approach. Imitating the master/s with approximate sounds appears to be a normal, acceptable procedure. Students in these situations have a different understanding of wrong notes and mistakes. For them, music learning appears to be more enjoyable and less inhibiting. "Ideas for what is possible in this context appears to be far more helpful than directives about what should be done" (Wiggins, 1996: 29).

The study and performance of new musics will foster the development of children's creative abilities. As one African writer has stated "our simultaneous contempt for, and seeming acknowledgment of, the indispensability of Western European influence has [had] a stranglehold on artistic activity in Africa" (Flolu). If the musics of most ethnic communities in Australia are practised as an integral part of social life, "there is the danger that musical activities in the classroom—an artificially created musical [environment]—may be unrelated to the experience in society" (Nketia, 1966: 231). Nketia asserts that "music serves as a means of teaching the values of society, as an avenue for literary expression and as a means of social cohesion" (ibid: 233-34).

The following are some principles by which the new music curriculum may be guided:

1. an awareness of musical procedures that apply to the particular cultures chosen for study;
2. understanding of the structures and learning processes that the music requires; and
3. socio-musical context and psychology of the peoples and their musics chosen for study but never at the expense of their artistic standards, resources or domains.

As a first step, it is imperative for music educators to be aware, informed and prepared to move away from the notion that there exists only one universal view of music and music education. It is just as needful to make students globally aware and receptive to cultures radically different from their own.

This new multiethnic music syllabus will not consist of an amalgam of world musics. Nor will the music systems of any one culture be permitted to dominate or eliminate the musics of available migrant cultures in Australia. Music educators will need to reflect this change within the context of a national music syllabus which will need to be approached more gradually and designed more carefully.

The curricula will thus see a juxtaposition or accommodation rather than an integration of various musical aesthetics and disciplines of available world musics in Australia. Such a curriculum, according to Leglar (1992), should encourage pre-service teachers to think of all musics as valid forms of human expression rather than as adjuncts to Western art music. Furthermore, although the various systems of different musics will reflect their uniquely individual aesthetics, practices, pedagogy and compositions, no one system must be made to explain the uniqueness of the other. Each will define its own boundaries of significance and specific music repertoires. Each will have its own process of transmission and methodologies based on its own musical and extra musical concepts. For instance, many occidental and African cultures emphasise direct interactive teaching strategies like listening and familiarisation of tonal systems, imitation of singing and playing techniques, most of which do not appear to be verbalised (Brennan). Even drawing on the available resources of local instrument makers from within some minority migrant communities will help to throw much light in understanding the subtle, tonal nuances and sonorities of the global musics studied.

The cultural implications of the music and aesthetics that motivate their creations are often beyond the experience and inauguration of prospective music teachers. Thus, despite careful preparation and efficient training, teachers will always remain limited in their knowledge, performance and expertise of the new musics. Improvisation, the development of the 'seeing ear' and 'listening eye' which are important foundational corollaries to the study of the musics of other cultures will feature predominantly in the new syllabus which will involve more practical classroom music making.

In Australia there are many rich cultural traditions and musical styles which permeate our lives. As music educators strive to create a syllabus with a multiethnic base, there will be insurmountable hurdles to overcome. There will be initially an almost unending battle of overcoming faculty resistance to change and narrow departmental traditions which die hard.

Experimental research supports the contention that multicultural education and world musics should be an integral part of the entire curriculum for music teachers (Leglar). Furthermore, length of exposure to multicultural teacher education correlates positively to use of multicultural materials in the school classroom (Sleeter, 1988 cited in Grant & Secada, 1990).

The case for pioneering reform in music education in Australia does not argue for a mere substitute of different musics in place of western music. The new curriculum will stress the need for the study of both western and occidental music and their music's social and musical values carried to their highest artistic levels possible. Nor ought any attempt be made to integrate both music systems with their inherent pre-suppositions and distinct methodologies into some kind of hybrid synthetic whole. Although group activity and community-oriented approaches to music learning are stressed in occidental cultures, the European emphases upon the personal development of individual talents should be no less predominant. The curriculum will naturally be selective and reflective of only those aspects of music and culture deemed to be worthwhile. It may draw on the expertise and contribution of local musicians. Both India and Australia have, therefore, much to contribute to an enriched multicultural music syllabus which in turn will enrich the musical lives of our children.

WORKS CITED

P.S. Brennan, 'Design and implementation of curricula experiences in world music: a perspective.' In H. Lees, 25-34.

P.S. Campbell, 'Towards tolerance and taste: preference for world musics'. *British Journal of Music Education* (1986). vol. 3 (2), 153-63.

______. 'The world of music through American eyes: a case for multi-ethnic consciousness in teaching the world's music traditions'. In H. Lees, 32-42.

J.M. Chernoff, *African rhythm and African sensibilities: aesthetics and social action in African musical idioms* (Chicago: Chicago University Press, 1979).

Teilhard De Chardin, P. *L'Energie Humaine* (Paris: Editions du Seuil, 1970).

D.J. Elliott, 'Key concepts in multicultural music education'. *International Journal of Music Education* (1989), vol. 13, 11-18.

R. Engle, 'Intercultural impact on music learning'. *Update: Applications of Research in Music Education* (1993), vol. 12 (1), 22-25.

J. Floflu, A dilemma for music education in Ghana. *British Journal of Music Education* (1993), vol. 10, 111-21.

C.A. Grant, & W.G. Secada, 'Preparing teachers for university'. In W.R. Houston (ed.). *Handbook of Research on Teacher Education* (New

York, Macmillan, 1990).

E.K. Kessler, C. Hansen & R.N. Shepard, 'Tonal schemata in the perception of music in Bali and the West. *Music Perception* (1984) vol. 2 (2), 131-65.

H. Lees, ed. *Proceedings of the 20th World Conference of the International Society for Music Education* (New Zealand: University of Canterbury, 1992).

M.A. Leglar, 'Towards sharing world musics: Some research-based perspectives for teacher education'. In H. Lees, 207-14.

C. Leonhard. 'Music education: a unifying force with a social significance'. In Rice, T. & P.M. Shand, (eds.), *Multicultural Music Education; the 'Music means harmony' Workshop* (Toronto: University of Toronto, Institute for Canadian Music, 1989).

J. Maybry, 'Cyberspace and the dream of Teilhard de Chardin'. *Creation Spirituality* (1994), vol. X, 11, 22-28.

D. McAllester, 'Becoming human through music'. *The Wesleyan Symposium of the Perspectives of Social Anthropology in the Teaching and Learning of Music* (Reston, Va., Music Educators National Conference, 1985), 1-5.

S. Morris, & W. Hudson, 'International education and innovative approaches to university teaching'. *The Australian Universities' Review* (Published by NTEU, 1995), vol. 38 (2), 70-74.

J.H. Nketia, 'Music education in African schools: A review of the position in Ghana.' *International Seminar on teacher education in music* (Ann Arbor: University of Michigan, 1966).

E. Oehrle, 'A South African perspective'. In Comte, M. (ed.), *Music education: international viewpoints* (Nedlands: University of Western Australia, Australian Society for Music Education, 1994), 133-39.

______. 'Intercultural education: Towards a culture of tolerance', *British Journal of Education* (1996), vol. 13, 95-100.

R.P. Santos, 'Authenticity and change in intercultural music teaching'. In H. Lees, 25-34.

J. Standifer, 'Multicultural education in action: musical and intercultural guidelines for the humanities'. In Oehrle, E. (ed.), *Proceedings of the third National Music Educators' Conference*, 1989 (Durban, University of Natal, SAMES, 1990).

K. Swanwick, *Music, Mind and Education* (London: Routledge, 1988).

G.F. Taylor, 'Culturally transcendent factors in musical perception' (Doctoral dissertation, Florida State University, 1969). *Dissertation Abstracts International*, 30, 5022A (1970).

T. Wiggins, 'The world of music in education', *British Journal of Music Education* (1996), vol. 13, 21-29.

Multiculturalism and the New World (Dis)Order

G.S. JAYASREE
University of Kerala, India

In this paper I want to consider two things. First, what I shall call the Benettonisation or rather, the extension of a capitalist mode of living through the virtual power of metaphor. The background to this is the fall of the Soviet Union and the establishment of a unipolar world; a New World Order based on the principles of capitalist modes of production. In the first part of the paper I wish to look into how capitalism through strategic positioning of systems of signs makes this possible. I have chosen the term 'Benettonisation' because the Benetton logo 'United Colours of Benetton' is a fine trope to exemplify this process. In the second part of the paper, I wish to examine how multicultural societies like India or Australia, caught between the either/or isms of resistance/acquiescence, negotiate the universalisations implied in such an ordering.

Before I set out, I must clarify that I have, within the scope of this paper, touched on just one aspect of what constitutes the New World Order. I use the term to refer to a post-industrial society that is now fast becoming a global phenomenon. In the West it follows the first Industrial Revolution that devalued muscle work and the second, that devalued routine mental work; where a combination of energy, resources and technology were the transforming agencies. In the present phase we find that knowledge and information are fast becoming the strategic resources; labour and capital, the central variables of the industrial society being replaced. It follows that those who have control over systems of knowledge and the effective dissemination of these systems control the world, just as in the earlier phases mastery of advanced levels of technology facilitated colonial control. Past societies were primarily space-bound or time-bound. They were held together by territorially based political and bureaucratic authorities. In contrast, we find that in the society where information technology prevails, space and time are compressed. The Gulf War which brought Scud missiles into our drawing rooms is perhaps the best example we can think of. It proved the inevitability of being caught in the drama, being affected in our day-to-day lives by something happening thousands of kilometres away. But the role of the IT is not confined to the war front. Just as the West's world-wide military role provided both the motive and the opportunity for the development of more and more sophisticated systems of communication, so did the world-wide expansion of the transnational corporations. Both were faced with similar command and control problems. As enterprises spanning the world, both live by communication; computers and satellites are as essential to their operation as the workers or plants that produce their goods.

What concerns us here in this paper is not how this all-encompassing information technology functions, but how it is put to use in the construction of meta-narratives of commercial interests obliterating the interests of individual nations or even the communities that make up these nations. In this context 'nation' or 'nationalism' has to be understood by aligning it not with certain geographic boundaries or self-consciously held political ideologies but with large cultural systems. As Homi Bhabha explains, "Nations, like narratives, lose their origins in the myths of time and only fully realise their horizons in the mind's eye" (1). Such an image of the nation may seem excessively metaphorical but we have to recognise that it is from agglomerations of political thought or religious sentiment or literary narrative or folk tradition that the nation emerges as a powerful historical idea; an idea whose cultural compulsion lies in the imaginative unity of the nation as a symbolic force. It is into these cultural formations that the agents of transnational interests seek to intercede. They do it effectively by systems of signification, like the Benetton advertisement, by representation of ideal modes of living. They create what we may call an 'electronic reality' through the media, suffused with images and symbols. These images and symbols obliterate any sense of objective reality, creating instead a world of make-believe. This is most clearly shown in the central role of advertising in contemporary culture. Within the frame of the advertisement our world becomes purely a world of simulation; the generation by models of a real without an original: the hyper-real. In hyper-reality, it is no longer possible to distinguish the imaginary from the real, the sign from its referent, the true from the false. The world of simulation is a world of simulacra, of images. But as I said, unlike conventional images, simulacra are copies that have no originals. In such a condition there can be no concept of ideology, no idea of the betrayal of reality by signs or images.

Frederick Jameson calls this instant myth-making 'image' or 'spectacle' building with the express intent of shaping the tastes and value systems of society. The emergence of such a society suggests a radically new relationship between culture and society. To Jameson it embodies the features of a late capitalist society where 'culture' has become the ordering principle; a veritable second nature. In such a context culture could hardly be regarded as the reflex and concomitant of society and the economic system as it had been earlier. In the late capitalist stage, culture itself is the prime determinant of social, economic, political and even psychological reality. To quote Jameson, "There has been a prodigious expansion of culture throughout the social realm, to the point at which everything in our social life—from economic value and state power to the very structure of the psyche itself—can be said to have become 'cultural' in some original and yet untheorised sense" (7). Culture in this specific connotation, we understand, is a product in its own right; the process of cultural consumption being no longer merely an adjunct but the very essence of capitalist functioning.

As I come to the final part of the paper I want to examine the import of this development to multicultural societies like India or Australia. As I see it, the ramifications are many. First, the different cultural spheres—the aesthetic or the ethical—lose their autonomy. Second, the cultural realm is no longer separated from the political, social or economic. Third and perhaps most important to our purposes, the hegemony of economic power comes to be replaced by the hegemony of cultural power as expounded by transnational interests. The inflation of culture becomes so marked that a kind of cultural imperialism asserts itself. Cultural theorists like Michel Foucault present illuminating accounts of how power, political, economic, sexual or cultural create themselves through representations and the uses that can be made of it (Foucault, 12). He examines, as a scholar, how dominant discourses to which power and knowledge are inextricably connected, are dispersed through the social and individual body. Foucault insists that one is never out of power relationships, that "power is always already there" and that there are no margins in which those in rupture with the system may gambol.

In conclusion, I wish to raise this question: where do multicultural societies stand in this game of power? Are they mere pawns totally trapped by omniscient binary power structures, the one side dominating and the other dominated? Is there no room for manoeuvre? The answer, as I see it, is both Yes and No. No, if we remain impervious to the workings of the late capitalist system which subtly but surely envelops differences into its master codes. Yes, if we are conscious and alert. But how? It is obvious that my paper refuses to admit any notion of authentic national identity insisting instead on the range of ways in which multicultural identities like the 'Indian' or the 'Australian' are discursively constructed. It is also obvious that it is this transference into the realm of discourse that lays us open to subversive influences from without. But does it mean that we should shut ourselves up? Close our windows to external influences whatsoever, taking refuge in a cocoon of essentialist fundamentalism? My answer is, the either/or isms of both acquiescence and resistance are inherent to, not outside of, power relations. Asserting a multicultural identity involves both. It calls for a consciousness of the multiple identities that together make our national cultural ethos, a resistance to invisibility and silencing by hegemonic powers. But more important, it calls for openness, tolerance and cosmopolitanism; a readiness to engage with other spheres of discourse.

WORKS CITED

Homi K. Bhabha, *Nation and Narration*. London: Routledge, 1990.

Michel Foucault, *Power/Knowledge: Selected Interviews and Writings 1972-1977*, ed. Colin Gordon. New York: Pantheon Books, 1980.

Frederick Jameson, *Postmodernism or The Cultural Logic of Late Capitalism*. London: Verso, 1992.

Negotiated Space: Cultural Crossings in Asian-Australian Women's Fiction

CARMEL KELLY
Australian Defence Force Academy

The emergence of numbers of anthologies, collections of poetry and novels by writers from ethnic minorities in the last ten years or so, has raised the question sharply and critically of what constitutes canonical writing in the Australian context.

The editors and critics, Sneja Gunew and Kateryna O. Longley have been in the forefront of criticism of what they perceive as the predominantly Anglo-Celtic nature of the Australian literary canon. One of their more radical suggestions is that publishers and editors should actively promote a proportion of writers from non-English speaking backgrounds. Until this becomes *pro forma* they believe that ethnic minority writing will continue to be viewed as peripheral. And they argue that by reason of this continuing bias and as a result of a proven policy of exclusion, we do not have a representative 'national' literature. (Gunew and Langley, xix)

The point at which the Australian community became 'multicultural' is subject to debate with critics such as John Docker challenging the view that this occurred after World War II. States Docker:

> I would argue . . . that the 1920s and 30s, with their Anglo-conformity, immigration mainly from Britain, and high percentage of Australian-born, were unusual in Australia history. Far more characteristic from 1788 and especially after the mid-century goldfield rushes in Eastern Australia was a high

> percentage of overseas born, with various 'colonies' of Europeans usually established at first near the goldfields (Danish, French), and a diversity of cultures. (17)

It could be argued that the perception of a continuous 'Anglo-Celtic' identity for the Australian population has been nurtured and used to maintain social hegemony and privilege. And within the literary arena many writers maintain this hegemony is being perpetuated by selective publishing.

Asian-Australian women writers can find themselves marginalised within the Australian community, as well as within their own primary cultures—a form of 'double colonisation'. Marginalisation can again take place within the literary arena. (Petersen and Rutherford, 9-10)

I will explore the work of two writers, Dewi Anggraeni, originally from Indonesia and Chitra Fernando, of Sri Lankan background. Both writers undermine first world feminist privileging of the West as being more liberated and as giving women more control over their lives. They show that the role of victim is not the sole preserve of third world women. The gap these authors reveal between the material reality of the lives of their characters and the representational discourse around greater freedom for women in Australia, challenges first world feminist assumptions.

Dewi Anggraeni, a writer born and raised in Indonesia, has produced an impressive body of work: two novels to date—*The Root of All Evil* and *Parallel Forces*; a collection of novellas entitled *Stories of Hindu Pacific* and several short stories, among them *Mal Tombee* and *Music for Libretto*. Her short stories and poetry are written in both English and Indonesian.

Born in Jakarta in 1945, she now lives in Melbourne with her husband and two children. In June 1994 she lost her job as a foreign correspondent with the Indonesian news and current affairs weekly, *Tempo*, when it was closed down by the Suharto government over a matter of censorship. She is now the Australian correspondent for *Forum*, a law news magazine published in Jakarta in Indonesian, and a feature writer for *Jakarta Post*, an English language daily.

The scope of her writing traverses many issues, involving race, class, gender, culture and political conflict in the Asia-Pacific region. Dewi represents an interesting phenomenon within the Australian literary milieu, writing about the Asia-Pacific from the perspective of a journalist working in both Indonesia and Australia. She has been in a unique position to become finely attuned to both cultures, and to return regularly to her former homeland and update herself on contemporary regional issues. She is no doubt the forerunner of what will become a body of Australian writers who have first-hand knowledge of several countries in the Asia-Pacific.

Her novel *The Root of All Evil*, was published by Indra Publications in Melbourne in 1987. The central character, Komala, married to an Australian, returns to Jakarta to visit her ailing father who has had a stroke. While there, she becomes aware of the plight of a bar hostess, Tati, mistress of nightclub owner Sonny Sudradjat. Tati has been disfigured for life through having acid thrown in her face by Sonny's jealous wife. Komala tries to persuade Tati to take legal action to win compensation and a large part of the novel concerns her search to find witnesses. This incident, according to the author, was based on an actual newspaper item published in Jakarta in 1983. (Kelly 1994)

The novel is an unashamed polemic, and succeeds in conveying the complexity of the difficulties which confront Indonesian women. Komala's clear gaze is used to expose the injustices women must face. The exclusive focus on gender and class issues reveals an almost indissoluble nexus between chauvinistic traditions, economic underdevelopment and Muslim religious influence.

The difficulties of being bicultural are explored through Komala's ambivalent relationship to her different experiences in both countries. The absence of social security benefits in Indonesia, for example, is brought home to her in a conversation with her father. Rural poverty keeps women pouring into Jakarta in search of work, and many women end as bar girls and servants, prey to sexual exploitation and poverty. It is in this economic climate that the options and choices for women are narrowed, and their personal freedom severely constrained.

At the opposite end of the spectrum we are given a glimpse into the lives of the Chinese middle-class in Jakarta. But even at this level of affluence, personal choice is absent in key areas. Komala's ex-boyfriend, Hanny Yo, entered into an arranged and loveless marriage. Again, Komala's close friend Narsih, a successful business woman, remains married to an unfaithful husband in order to retain business contacts and so as not to invite suspicion from fearful wives. It is suggested she would face sexual harassment as a divorcee. Even women who appear financially secure live in dread of poorer women beguiling their husbands.

It would seem that Komala's extreme distress at the plight of women, leaves her with a kind of cultural disjunction. Australia is not subjected to any critical comparisons, and emerges by default, surrounded by an unrealistically virtuous glow.

Komala sees that women are forced to engage with men through financial dependence. Yet when it comes to observing that her parents' household servants have become more assertive and less compliant, she finds it disconcerting. Living in Australia has not shifted some long standing expectations of social behaviour. Tati's disfigurement and the refusal of her lover to support her financially now strike her as intolerable: 'Was I becoming a foreigner in my own country? Had my values changed'? (RAE, 88) And again when she finds her direct questioning of people does not receive a welcome response: 'Probably I had become vulgar working and living in Australia. Western people never dream that their straightforward manner is regarded as vulgarity in refined Sundanese and Javanese society'. (RAE, 99)

These fluctuations in perception elude any simple formula. When the witnesses to the acid attack on Tati are uncooperative and Tati herself is reluctant to give evidence, Komala realises that the power structures confining Indonesian women are still too great to be challenged: 'So now I had to find the fine line between self-effacement and not achieving anything and being pushy, thus disconcerting the people assisting as well as those assisted'. (RAE, 127)

Komala is unable to allay her distress at abuses she once took for granted. Awareness of injustice cannot be translated into the complex web of Indonesian social relations. Komala becomes an expatriate experiencing the frustration and irrelevance of exile.

All the constrictions and restraints on human happiness eventually build to a forceful litany. The episodic structure of the novel provides gathering momentum for an intense vision of human suffering. The social realist approach places Dewi in the Australian tradition of writers such as Judah Waten and Katharine Susannah Prichard.

The idealistic vision of Australia which emerges in *The Root of All Evil*, is somewhat tarnished in Dewi's later work. The short story *Mal Tombee*, delineates the exploitative sexual behaviour of Australian men in Indonesia. Also in the novella *Uncertain Step*, Anyani, an Indonesian who has married an Australian, finds herself treated demeaningly as a Philippino 'mail order' bride by the local shopkeepers in her Adelaide suburb. Anyani arouses enormous fear in her husband when she decides to become a script writer. He feels threatened by her growing independence and later, she is almost raped by a film maker who sees her as sexual bait.

Anyani has married an Australian to escape becoming a spinster in an extended family where this is frowned upon. She gradually realises that in coming to Australia she has exchanged one set of social limitations for another. Her expectations of a more egalitarian society are gradually undermined. Anyani's life is defined in both countries relative to a male. Being linked to a male confines her in Australia, just as being unlinked to a male confined her in Bandung.

The Australian men are depicted as insecure and predatory, no less than their Indonesian counterparts. What is different is that women's relative financial independence gives them more dignity and capacity to bargain, augmented by greater recognition of the rights of the individual in civil law and religious institutions.

In her later work, Dewi has continued to pursue the theme of individual choice and liberty in sexual relationships. The short story *Music for Libretto* portrays an Indonesian musician who comes to Australia for a holiday and has an affair with an Australian man, her host, who is unhappily married. It would seem that the nascent theme of sexual freedom in *The Root of All Evil*, has found full expression in this story. When human happiness is at stake, her female characters are prepared to transgress convention, a far cry, it would seem, from the behaviour of middle-class Indonesian women in their own country.

In her novella *Parallel Forces*, we see a number of cultural influences on a family which moves easily in varied milieus—Singapore, Java, France and Australia. Claudine Dubois, a French artist is married to Hardoyo Kencoyo, an Indonesian poet-academic. The marriage between a 'lax Muslim and lax Catholic' becomes complicated when their daughter Amyrrha is told by a Javanese fortune teller that she is the reincarnation of the 13th century Hindu Queen, Ken Dedes, and fated to re-enact the Queen's life story.

Dewi Anggraeni achieves a degree of sophistication in her handling of these different settings and a diverse range of characters. The novel engages in a cosmopolitan world view. Whatever the setting, whether it be Bandung, Bordeaux or Melbourne, the tale of the Hindu kingdom of Majapahit still haunts Amyrra and her mother.

The fortune teller tells Amyrra that she will meet the reincarnation of Ken Dedes, 'According to the writings when East meets West, in a place where a fan opens and shuts'. This prediction is a metaphor for the essential dilemma of the family, who despite their overt capacity to live in Western settings, are still haunted by Hindu history.

Cultural narratives mesh and there seems to be no prevailing cultural centre to the novel. Feminist and political themes twist and turn as the author takes the opportunity to indulge in some polemical asides. Claudine's Dubois' friendships with younger men in Melbourne expose her to harsh judgements by her more conservative family and friends and she asserts her right, while married, to maintain these friendships and an artistic career independent of her husband.

When one culture is viewed through the gaze of another, the effect is one of overlay. Some parts of the picture will repeat, others will achieve a huge separation. It is clear that for these characters, western economies appear more desirable in terms of the financial and social independence which they offer, while at the same time subjecting Indonesian women to various kinds of stereotyping and harassment.

It is interesting that Dewi places herself within the Australian context as a multicultural writer, opposed to what she sees as the Anglo-Celtic mainstream. Says Dewi:

> Multicultural Australia will remain a myth for a long time

> if Australian literature does not give more recognition to multiculturalism by beginning to reflect it not only in published writing but also in the distribution and promotion of that writing. Non Anglo-Celtic writing can no longer be pushed to the side and labelled with names which mean anything but "real literature". (Gunew & Longley, 190)

In a recent interview, she said that she felt that multicultural writing was getting a higher exposure through anthologies specifically identifying multicultural themes. But that apart from these anthologies, mulitcultural writers were still being neglected by the prevailing canon. (Kelly, 1996)

Dewi's feminism further defines her within a group of women writers, whose sense of cultural nuance is augmented by the 'otherness' of gender. In some ways the novel *The Root of All Evil* is reminiscent of Indonesian puppet theatre based on the Hindu epics; crammed with incident, always bearing on some moral precept. There is a multitude of social experience never coalescing into a single event, rather a series, demonstating a philosophical position connected to endless change. No doubt, as multicultural writers examine more closely their cultural roots, including as Sneja Gunew and Kateryna O. Longley have recommended, Anglo-Celtic writers themselves, the concept of 'mainstream' will shift to include, justifiably, writers such as Dewi Anggraeni. (Gunew & Longley, xiii)

Chitra Fernando migrated to Australia twenty eight years ago from Sri Lanka and spent most of her working life in this country as a member of the academic community, teaching Linguistics at Macquarie University in Sydney since 1968.

She came from a middle-class Buddhist family (her father was a lawyer) and although her cultural roots are in Sri Lanka, now describes herslf as a cosmopolitan.

She also perceives herself as having made a positive adjustment to the Australian milieu, as academia has proved an intellectually tolerant and stimulating community. Her move to Australia increased her independence and social freedom as a woman—something that would have been constrained by social convention and family ties in Sri Lamka. At a recent reading and interview at ADFA library, she said, 'Sri Lanka gave me my soul, but Australia gave me my freedom'. (Fernando, 4 May 1995)

Chitra Fernando describes being bicultural as very much like being bilingual. As a linguist she says that there is always one language which will predominate. In her case it is the English of the Anglicised Sinhalese community of Sri Lanka. She does not see herself as comprising some kind of 'schizophrenic' entity in which there are 'two Chitras—one Sri Lankan and one Anglo-Celtic'. Rather, she says she experiences a 'synthesis' of these two main cultures. (Kelly, 5 May 1995)

Although her own experience of migration has been so productive, she is acutely aware that not all immigrants have been so fortunate and she has tried to address 'anomie', feelings of displacement in migrants in her writings. On the issue of being a 'feminist' writer, Chitra prefers not to label herself as such, although she writes mainly of women's issues. She wishes to retain her right to be critical of ideological movements by maintaining her intellectual independence.

Chitra's works include a novella, *Between Worlds* which is about the tensions caused by biculturalism and a collection of short stories entitled, *Women There and Here—Six Stories*. She has also co-edited (with Ranjani Obeyesekere) *An Anthology of Modern Writing in Sri Lanka*.

Chitra Fernando's collection of short stories, *Women There and Here—Six Stories*, is prefaced by two quotations. The first tells how Buddha's foster mother, Ananda, pleaded successfully with him to allow women *arahant* status, the potential for salvation. The second, from the Dhammapada, says, 'It is not plaited hair, nor birth, nor wealth that makes the Brahmana. He in whom truth and justice reside, he is happy, he is a Brahmana'.

These two extracts emphasize the possibilities within Buddhist belief for a kind of social justice which does not discriminate on the basis of gender, caste or wealth. And this underlying plea is the bedrock of all Chitra's stories against which the human failures to meet these ideals achieve various degrees of dissonance.

In the story *The Bird of Paradise*, Rupa Gomez returns to Sri Lanka to visit her family, unfortunately to find that her Uncle has died a few days before her arrival. "'He'd wanted," she thought, "some years away from the family, just as she had, to find a separate being'". (WTH, 43) Rupa yearns for her own private space apart from her extended family. Her parents begin to organise an arranged marriage involving dowry and she feels suffocated by the absence of choice. She plans her escape to Australia to a freer life.

The story resumes twenty years later when Rupa has married into an Australian family. She reflects that her Australian marriage is not much different from what a marriage in Sri Lanka would have been—moments of togetherness, shared celebrations and traditions settling into a familiar routine. The story concludes with Rupa daydreaming:

> And then out of the purple blaze of the bougainvillea flew out the shining bird. "It's you—you I've always wanted," she called out, jumping up from her chair. But the bird had vanished. She saw only the endless distances of the sky as she stood alone in the verandah of the silent house. (WTH, 51)

The bird appears at the end of the story almost as an apparition before death, a transmuted moment of exquisite beauty and realisation. Despite her atttempts at change and pursuit of freedom, something has evaded Rupa Gomez. The initial hope of Australia offering her freedom as a young girl has faded. Nothing has happened in her new setting that is in any way extraordinary. The yearning for something uniquely different hovers over her life unattainable in the ordinary moments she has lived: 'She'd been looking for something: a new being unconstrained by custom and tradition, a splendid freedom. Yet, she'd settled so easily for comfortable ordinariness.' (WTH, 51)

Rupa's desperate urge as a young girl to escape Sri Lanka, in later life turns to a yearning nostalgia for home and familiarity. Her early rebellion has been blurred by time and the knowledge that Australia has not released her from the social restraints that govern both societies. It would appear that middle-class comfort in Sri Lanka may even have been more desirable, bringing with it a richer cultural experience.

The short story *The Chasm*, set in Alice Springs in Northern Australia, provides another ironic comment. A group of Sri Lankan professionals decide to have a picnic at Standley Chasm, outside

Alice Springs. With them they take Manel, a woman from a lower caste who has attached herself to the group through loneliness. She is treated very much as a servant, and in the eyes of a visiting Sri Lankan, Vijay Ranawaka, with insufficient respect.

At one point Manel, finally humiliated beyond endurance, leaves the group and returns alone to Alice Springs. It is only then it is found out that she is engaged to a local doctor. Manel, by coming to Australia, has overcome the barrier operating against her in Sri Lanka on the basis of caste and she has exercised a certain initiative as a woman in moving outside this boundary.

It is clear that she has acquired a new power in Australia. She even dares to question the doctor in the group on his medical ethics. When she finally accepts that they do not like her, cannot see her outside the role of servant, she leaves. She has acquired strength and self-determination, something her compatriots cannot bear to witness. The balance of power has shifted irrevocably and for Manel, migration has proved highly rewarding.

But once again Chitra Fernando intrudes with a provocative comment, 'Vijay, thinking of the possible transformance of Manel into Mrs Roger Moore, felt a qualm. Would she in time become like these others? How could one really say?'

Chitra Fernando returns us to the exigencies of status seeking. It is debatable for the author that Manel's new found freedom will translate into a progessive positioning in her new home.

The novella *Between Worlds* examines the lives of three generations of Sri Lankan women. The structural design of the novella, with its sequence of present, past and future, mimics the triadic structure of the Wheel of Becoming in the Theravadic Buddhist beliefs of Sri Lanka. These three time sequences revolve in an endless wheel, 'becoming', death and rebirth, until human beings learn to cease unsatisfactory desiring. Only then is peace and tranquillity, *nirvana*, attainable. (Lester, 29-31)

For the three key women in the novella, Anula Piyasena, her sister Leila and Anula's granddaughter Mali, contemplating a universe where there are worlds beyond worlds in Buddhist teaching annuls pain, reduces suffering, and the grief they face in their lives and memory.

The title of the novella, *Between Worlds*, not only encapsulates the dilemma of women caught between East and West, but that of women caught between what is human and entails suffering, *dukha*, and the cessation of suffering, *nirvana*. When Anula Piyasena visits her daughter Srima in Australia she realises that Srima has slipped away from her. She is also now in another 'world'. Migration is a double-edged sword.

Part two of the novella is a concentrated narrative involving Anula's sister Leila who we learn retrospectively committed suicide in Sri Lanka in the 1950s as a result of becoming pregnant to a radical student, the son of a postal worker from the same town. It was the impossibility of crossing caste lines to marry him which led to her death. Leila was caught between Western notions of sexual freedom and the difficulty of implementing them within a Sri Lankan setting.

In part three of the novella, Anula Piyasena's granddaughter, Mali, pursues the quest for individual freedom and independence into the third generation. Mali's affair with a Japanese student in Sydney is unrewarding. Now it is emotional involvement which has become taboo, and Mali does not feel entitled to raise her emotional needs with her lover. The sexual freedom which Leila longed for has become another kind of tyranny. The subject position for women is once again passive. Mali does not participate in setting the terms for her love affair and her collusion in her own passivity seems even more dangerous than Leila's exclusion from decisions that entailed her survival.

But Mali's trials are not yet over. In Sri Lanka she commences an affair with a man who conceals that he is married and who rails against independent women. She meets the fiery feminist Anushka Pelpola, a Professor of Sociology in Colombo. But Anushka's failure to achieve equality with her male colleagues and within relationships has left her depressed, embittered, and on tranquillisers. Anushka has taken her rebellion to the point where she tells her lover, "a woman must cease to be the object of rival exchanges between two men". And, "You're a schizophrenic. . . . You talk of India's modernity—her space technology—and in the same breath you advocate a partriarchal phallocracy". (BW, 61) Like Leila, Anushka has taken her rebellion to the point where she is about to self-destruct. The society is not yet ready for the freedom she desires.

Mali returns to Australia with a replica of the goddess Tara, said to have been the spiritual consort of the Buddha Anoghasiddhi, relinquishing expectations of men and seeking spiritual verities. She finally decides that the spiritual path is the only safe road to liberation and that the power struggle involved in relations with men is too problematic to be dealt with.

Australia does not feature to any great depth in this novella. But it does offer a backdrop for visions of greater freedom. In Sri Lanka Mali boasts that Uluru is sixty million years old as a way of countering the hypnotic effect of Sri Lanka's 2000 years of Buddhist tradition. She had encountered something 'older' if not 'wiser'.

Chitra Fernando's women push themselves againt the limits of what is possible to achieve inner freedom, sometimes like Leila, paying an unbearable price. There is resignation at the end of *Between Worlds*, but Mali has achieved something closer to personal freedom that Leila could achieve in Sri Lanka in the '50s. And to some degree, Australia has provided the setting.

But the price of leaving familiar terrain is never wholly persuasive, the claims of Australian versions of freedom never without a barbed encounter. The powerful spiritual teachings of Buddhism are posited as a rich source of strength to deal with both worlds. The vast Australian landscape for both Dewi Anggraeni and Chitra Fernando, awe inspiring and overwhelming, is often underwritten by a paucity of cultural complexity.

Third world feminist critics have attacked Western feminists for prioritising gender issues and the project of the individual to the exclusion of class/caste race and cultural difference. But it is made patently clear in the writings of these two writers that the women in their stories desire the definition of self and identity that springs from subverting the social controls that accompany tradition and culture. The individualist project is often contrasted to the collective interests of the subaltern, the reality that disadvantage can only be combated by collective action. But this debate is in danger of becoming as polarised as the post-colonial binary distortions of 'colonised' and 'coloniser'. The view that gender issues should not be an exclusive focus for defining women's oppression can mean that they are neglected and critics slip into an apologia for patriarchal structures. Relative notions of freedom and independence will acknowledge that the oppression of women exists in regard to gender bias and in some cultures more than in others. Comparisons between cultures in this area need to be made more subtly, and at times more crudely, than current debate will allow.

WORKS CITED

Dewi Anggraeni in interview with Carmel Kelly, 14 September, 1994, unpublished.

______, *The Root of All Evil* (Indra Publishing, Briar Hill, 1987). Cited as RAE.

______, *Parallel Forces* (Indra Publishing, Briar Hill, 1988). Cited as PF.

______, in interview with Carmel Kelly, 30 October 1996, unpublished.

John Docker, *Dilemmas of Identity: The Desire for the Other in Colonial and Post Colonial Cultural History*, Working Papers in Australian Studies, Working Paper No. 74 (Sir Robert Menzies Institute of Commonwealth Studies, University of London, 1992).

Chitra Fernando, video interview, ADFA library, 4 May 1995.

______ in interview with Carmel Kelly, 5 May 1995.

______, *Foreword to Women There and Here—Six Stories* (Wordlink: Sydney, 1994). Cited as WTH.

______, *Between Worlds* (Calcutta: Chakraborty Enterprise Press, 1988). Cited as BW.

Sneja Gunew and O. Kateryna O. Longley (ed.), *Striking Chords—Multicultural Literary Interpretations* (North Sydney: Allen & Unwin, 1992).

Robert C. Lester, *Therevada Buddhism in Southeast Asia* (Ann Arbor: University of Michigan, 1973).

Kirsten Holst Petersen and Anna Rutherford, *Double Colonisation—Colonial and Post-Colonial Women's Writing* (London: Dangaroo Press, 1986).

Little Histories: Diasporan Family Narratives in Australia

KATERYNA OLIJNYK LONGLEY
Murdoch University

> A chronicler who recites events without distinguishing between major and minor ones acts in accordance with the following truth: nothing that has ever happened should be regarded as lost for history.
>
> Walter Benjamin

> It was precisely the partial nature of these memories, their fragmentation, that made them so evocative. . . . The shards of memory acquired greater status, greater resonance, because they were *remains.*
>
> Salman Rushdie*

Australia's sense of its national history and cultural identity is in turmoil. Hardly a day goes past without some kind of attention being drawn in newspapers, magazines and the other media to dilemmas of self-definition and self-description. This year, to mark Australia Day, which passed as usual with barely a ripple of recognition, let alone pride, in Australian households, the national and state newspapers rose to the occasion by presenting a mixed bag of consciousness-raising feature articles. A brief browse through some of those articles in *The Australian* of that day is sufficient to make the point that there is no solid and agreed sense of how Australian history and culture should be understood or promoted. This fluidity is nicely captured in the feature heading "Advance Australia Where?" and the half-page photograph, related to another feature article "A Nation Reborn", of six newly born babies at Melbourne's Royal Women's Hospital, their parents from all over the globe. (*The Weekend Australian*, 1997) Many factors are contributing to this situation where there is lack of common understanding and at the same time an urgent desire to find an agreed new vision of what it means to be Australian. One of the key factors is the rejection of the formal designation of Australia prior to European settlement as uninhabited, or "*terra nullius*", and the legal contests in relation to land rights which have followed. Another is the approaching centenary of Federation in 2001 and the related rising interest in the formation of an Australian republic. Yet another, is Australia's recent reorientation, in terms of trade and foreign affairs, away from Europe towards Asia. Less obvious than these, but playing a major role in the redefining process, is the more confident multiculturalism of contemporary Australia, a confidence which is both generated by and reflected in the writing of immigrants from both Europe and Asia. (Gunew and Longley, 1992)

In the context of the increasing influence of multicultural writing in this process, my particular focus here is on the genre of family history which, I want to suggest, is making an important and not yet sufficiently recognised contribution to Australia's rapidly changing sense of its post-settlement social history. It is doing this in two ways: first, family histories are providing new historical information in the form of recorded memories, which have in the past been considered irrelevant or peripheral to Australia's national self-image; and second, they are actively changing public understanding of the nature of the *genre* of national history in terms of its conventions, its ideologies and its principles of selection. This is because as more and more is written, family history as micro-history provides an ongoing and cumulative challenge to the authority of established forms of macro-history. By virtue of its difference in scale and focus, micro-history makes the structure of conventional history more visible to the critical eye, particularly its "neutral" viewpoint and its "natural" processes of selection. While I will only consider written texts here (or transcribed oral histories), film and television are equally important, for example, the current series on the SBS national multicultural channel, called "*Tales from a Suitcase: Stories from the Migrant Experience—1946-52*" and the popular life-story series called "*Australian Story*" on commercial television. Family history is only one of many related small-scale or alternative histories contributing to this new historical understanding which I believe is developing—amongst them autobiographies and biographies of people who have no special claim to fame, such as Albert Facey's *A Fortunate Life* (1987), the best known of a long list of titles produced by Fremantle Arts Centre Press, histories of towns, factories, buildings, ships, organisations, institutions, personal relationships. These minor histories can be pictured as points along the line of traditional major history, selected as though with a cursor on a screen and each clicked into visibility as a multi-dimensional world, which then offers potential further worlds at every point on every plane—via endless sequences of unopened doors or windows or websites. The fact that such histories are so infinitely available, at least potentially,—everyone has a collection of unwritten and perhaps unspoken stories from the past as does every place and object—does not seem to diminish the interest that written and published examples hold for readers. On the contrary, it appears that demand has never been so high in Australia for small scale histories which do not claim to be authoritative, nor even necessarily true. Indeed, in stories such as these, the personal recollection of events is unashamedly and seamlessly blended with pure fiction

This is, of course, nothing new. Since white settlement, there have always been personal and specialised written records of life in Australia, covering the whole spectrum, in terms of their claim to historical authenticity, from daily journals such as the early explorers kept, to highly fictionalised biographies such as that of Richard Mahony in Henry Handel Richardson's trilogy of novels (1929) based on her father's experience of early settlement in Victoria, and there is no doubt that all of them have contributed to the way that Australia is now imagined. (Paul Arthur, unpbld. research) However, what is new is the final crumbling of the long worn down wall between history and fiction, and the effect that this is having on the parallel even more resistant wall between major and minor histories. My argument is that "minor" family histories, a few of which will be discussed here, are contributing in a special way to this breaking down of old boundaries which in Australia amounts to a revolution of re-imagining and remapping of Australian cultural identity, past and present.

Theorists who have contributed to my understanding of this process of wearing down the distinction between fiction and the "grand narratives" of history are Robert Young, Hayden White, Mary Louise Pratt and Donna Haraway, besides Foucault, Abdul JanMohammed and David Lloyd, Deleuze and Guattari, whose works are referred to in this essay.

Interestingly it is the "otherness" of these histories, their status as different and "exotic", which makes them more effective in this critical role. (Longley, 1997) There is a highly ironic explanation for this. Initially, I believe, immigrant family histories/biographies were seen, unambiguously, as *not* belonging to Australia's cultural heritage. Because they were often about pre-immigration memories of another place and another time, they were safely distanced from standard Australian history and they could be read simply "for the story" as one would read fiction or the biography of a remote foreign figure. If anything, they initially helped to validate the standard image of anglo-Australia, by their difference and their outside position, just as the actual presence of immigrants (other than British) also did, by virtue of the low positions they occupied in the workplace and in the social scene. In fact, and this is where the irony lies, it is because these stories are both fascinatingly "other" and at the same time slight, highly individualised and "safe", posing no apparent cultural threat, that they are now having such a profound cultural effect. They have slipped unnoticed into Australia's line of historical vision. They are also having a generic effect. Their penetration into the Australian historical scene very effectively highlights the poverty of Australia's historical consciousness, a condition which can be seen to have been brought about precisely by the exclusion of all such minor histories (including those of British immigrants) from its national narratives which, until recently, have followed the inherited Western colonial tradition of grand historical narratives. The enormity of this exclusion is made so obvious that these Australian mega-narratives begin to look like parodies. The work of Ania Walwicz and Rosa Cappielo are important in this connection. Gunew and Longley's *Striking Chords* was devoted to the same project. They fit the pattern of Homi Bhabha's insight, which he applied in a very different colonial context, that transported or "out of place" colonial discourses tend to fall into the mode of mimicry which then emerges, he argues, "as one of the most elusive and effective strategies of colonial power and knowledge". (Bhabha, 1991: 234-41)

Family history exists outside of that powerful framework. Further, family history has traditionally been regarded as "safe" and inconsequential in another way. It has been considered to be a lightweight historical genre, one which is personal like autobiography but less first-hand and more anecdotal, closer to fiction. But in the arena of fiction, it tends to be seen as rather old-fashioned, naively realist, unselfconscious, and therefore backward in terms of postmodernist literary expression. Family history, then, it could be said, suffers doubly from its in-between position: generically, by being neither truly one thing nor the other and historically, by not quite belonging in this moment of literary postmodernism. On both counts I want to defend family history by arguing that its unclear pedigree as a genre is a strength rather than a weakness and also that far from being an anachronism it is very much a part of and a major contributor to the postmodern moment in many ways, but most significantly through the cumulative quiet challenge it is presenting to traditional histories of Australia. Diasporan family history is particularly effective because of its extra capacity, in an act of defamiliarisation, to expose the wheels and cogs of traditional settler culture and so to turn a critical focus on the Australian history machine and its products over two centuries. Aboriginal family history is equally effective but because Aboriginal writers dissociate themselves from the "multicultural" designation in Australia, their work is considered elsewhere. (Longley, 1992: 370-84) One could usefully apply Deleuze and Guattari's concept of deterritorialization as a model to explain this phenomenon, by which stories themselves, emerging at random from surprising and previously unnoticed worlds, are the variously camouflaged forces of guerilla warfare upon "mainstream" history. (Deleuze and Guattari, 1992: 139-271) Relevant, too, is Foucault's Nietzschean vision of "effective" history as opposed to historical tradition, as he describes it in his essay, "Nietzsche, Genealogy, History":

> An entire historical tradition aims at dissolving the singular event into an ideal continuity—as a teleological movement or a natural process. . . .
>
> [But] the world we know is not this ultimately simple configuration where events are reduced to accentuate their essential traits, their final meaning, or their initial and final value. On the contrary, it is a profusion of entangled events. If it appears as a 'marvelous motley, profound and totally meaningful,' this is because it began and continues its secret existence 'through a host of errors and phantasms.' We want historians to confirm our belief that the present rests upon profound intentions and immutable necessities. But the true historical sense confirms our existence among countless lost events, without a landmark of point of reference. (Nietzsche in Foucault, 1977: 154-55)

It is precisely family history's interest in delving amongst those countless lost events that gives it its disruptive power in relation to mainstream history. In fact, it is evidence of the success of the venture that "mainstream" is becoming a word of diminishing force in the contemporary literary scene. And if that word no longer sends out clearly understood signals, nor, at long last, does "marginal". Immigrant writing, Aboriginal writing, Gay and Lesbian writing—these are on the front shelves of every bookshop and on the reading lists of university courses. By being there, they are not *entering* the mainstream so much as jostling and dispersing the mainstream and, with it, literary canons.

This disturbance has resulted in a democratisation of literature in Australia. A barometer of change is the radically changing Year 12 School literature syllabus in all Australian states to include Aboriginal and multicultural texts and issues. How did this happen, and who were the main players in this spreading and flattening out of the literary? How has Australia changed so dramatically in a period of about two decades? Is it a local phenomenon or a global one? Will it last? Are there losses as well as gains? While I do not have the answers to all these questions, it seems to me that they need to be explored as we move towards the end of the century in which the last nails of semiotics were driven into the coffin of true meanings. Does all this expansion, fragmentation and dispersion mean that all the old landmarks have gone and we are therefore left drifting and wandering, having lost the old pride in national, cultural or ethnic belonging and instead valuing everything simply because it exists? (Considering such questions in India reminds me how differently they would be asked in this country with its millennia of written tradition and history in hundreds of languages and cultures.) My general answer in the Australian context is positive and optimistic. I would argue that having lost the big narratives with all their unquestioning certainties, people are looking for new meanings to depend on and link their lives to, and these are being made and found in an array of more personal and individual expressions of what could even be called *faith* in the significance of the small-scale, the local, the fragmentary, the inconclusive, the unverifiable and the fictional and it is no accident that these are precisely the problematic features which the big historical narratives could never escape but, to maintain their myth of authority, always sought to hide. The new configuration provides less security but there is no doubt that it is more inclusive and generous than the old and therefore more likely to welcome and provide for difference and a sense of national belonging at the same time. Further, the shift is, as I have already suggested, part of a global pattern of liberating postmodernist scepticism in relation to the monolithic narratives of nation which sustained the practice of colonial imperialism.

In Australia it took almost two centuries for Aboriginal cultures to be recognised and respected by the white settler culture and their own narratives have only recently begun to play a role in Australian cultural and historical self-definition. Even non-Aboriginal Australian writing has a very short history of acceptance as worthy of study in Universities and schools. Immigrant writing was unheard of even three decades ago unless, of course, all identifying marks of its ethnicity were either concealed or parodied.

It was only about fifteen years ago that my friend and research collaborator Sneja Gunew approached me to ask whether I knew of any immigrant writing which had been published in Australia, dealing with immigrant experience. At that stage, all we could think of was the book *They're a Weird Mob* (Culotta, 1951) with its crude stereotypes of Italian immigrants but that book was not even written by an Italian. Thirty years before that, when I first arrived in Australia with my Ukrainian refugee parents and my Russian grandmother, I lived day by day accepting as the norm, a feeling of embarrassment about my ethnic background, hiding it by not bringing friends home, not speaking my language in public, not letting anyone see how we lived—at that time in very primitive accommodation but already with a few foreign books, plenty of foreign food and one or two foreign decorations and trimmings, including an icon on the wall, draped with traditional embroidered *rushniki*. The British immigrant family in the big house on whose grounds we lived had children who let my brothers and me play with them in their garden but they openly laughed at signs of our foreignness and we learned quickly how to hide them. My memories at that time are full of feelings of shame at our difference from absolutely everyone else in the well-to-do beach-side suburb of Brighton where we found ourselves.

While we were living there, one night after we had all gone to bed, there was urgent banging on our door and we could hear the agitated voice of the oldest of the children, Marjorie Fletcher, who must have been about twelve years old at the time. My father got me out of bed to do the translating and we went to the door, worried, and expecting that there was some sort of emergency next door. She stood outside with tears in her eyes and distress in her voice, to tell us that something terrible had happened: the King was dead. It was an unforgettable moment for me because it underlined the shame of my foreignness more than ever. She was my friend and had done me and my family the honour of sharing the moment of this devastating news with us and I could not even rise to the most basic demands of the moment. Although I must have been only seven or eight years old, and had spent most of my life in displaced persons camps in Germany, I knew about the kings and queens of England because they were central to our history lessons at Brighton Primary School and we sang "God save the King" at Friday school assembly and at the Saturday matinee at the local Windsor Theatre Cinema. But, at that moment, I was so startled that, as I remember, I went blank and said, to my instant mortification, "What King?"

But returning to minor history and the question of literary democratisation, it seems to me that the revolution has been very real and far-reaching, notwithstanding evidence apparently to the contrary in the recent heated national debate on immigration and race, triggered by the maiden speech of the misinformed Queensland politician with racist views, Pauline Hanson. (Wear, 1996: 18-19; Kerry-Ann Walsh, 1996: 24-25) I attribute to minor history a major role in this process of change on similar structural grounds to those used by Deleuze and Guattari in their analysis of Kafka's writing in terms of "minor literature". As they define it, "minor literature" has three characteristics. The first is that it is "that which a minority constructs within a major language. . . . [But] in it language is affected by a high degree of deterritorialisation." The second is that minor literature is highly political. This is because "its cramped space forces each individual intrigue to connect immediately to politics. . . . The family triangle connects to other triangles—commercial, economic, bureaucratic, juridical". The third characteristic is that it "takes on a collective value", not so much in spite of the smallness of its community base but *because of it*, and so finds itself "positively charged with the role and function of collective, and even revolutionary, enunciation." (Deleuze and Guattari, 16-17) It is precisely this kind of movement from the individual case to the community experience which is repeatedly exhibited by immigrant family histories in Australia and it is also this which makes them political even when they appear to be conformist and docile in both their form and their content. The same is true of Aboriginal autobiographies and family histories such as those of Sally Morgan, Glenyse Ward, Alice Nannup or Ruby Langford.

Although it is beyond the scope of this essay to trace and identify the many contributors to the change that has occurred, I would like to clarify my own position by naming a few Australian writers and presses who have had an impact in the last decade or so on my own understanding of Australian history. (See Note) Mudrooroo's (then Colin Johnson) *Doctor Wooreddy's Prescription for Enduring the Ending of the World* used an Aboriginal point of view for the first time to recreate in fiction the experience of European invasion. His "Wildcat" series of novels, beginning with *Wildcat Falling* and ending with *Wildcat Screaming* has contributed greatly to understanding of urban Aboriginality and its special difficulties of representation. In 1996 there was wide publicity given to the fact that Mudrooroo was apparently born of a white Australian mother and a black American father, rather than an Aboriginal father as he had until recently, always believed. However, as he was brought up believing himself to be Aboriginal, with Aboriginal siblings and, further, was taken away from his family by the State as a child in the same way as part-Aboriginal children were, I do not believe that this changes the force of his writing on Aboriginal life and issues. A few years ago the first Aboriginal press, Magabala Books was founded in Broome and quickly produced more Aboriginal life stories, written by or in collaboration with Aboriginal people, than had ever been published before in Australia. In 1987, Paul Carter's *The Road to Botany Bay* provided an imaginative new model for reading history "spatially" rather than in terms of "imperial history's mythic lineage of heroes". On my home territory, Fremantle Arts Centre Press published Sally Morgan's *My Place* (1987) and became well known and respected for its support of high quality small-scale and alternative local histories and biographies. Throughout the decade Sneja Gunew's work focussed on immigrant writing and helped to give it new confidence and status and Rita Felski's *Beyond Feminist Aesthetics* proposed a situational feminist approach which always respects and takes into consideration the specific historical moment, the location and small-scale context of any event. Much more recently I have benefited from my colleague Vijay Mishra's work on diasporan theory, (Mishra, *Span,* 1992; *Ariel,* 1995) and from the Ph.D. research of my student Dai Yin who completed, in 1994 at Murdoch University, the first book length study of the representation of Chinese People in Australian Literature. But most of all I have gained from my parents' stories of the past, their sense of history and their complex relationship with their Ukrainian and Australian worlds.

Diasporan Family History

If, as I have argued, small-scale histories flatten and spread traditional histories which themselves are usually imagined as being vertical and linear, then family histories go one step further. From any point in the flattened historical plane, they send out, as it were, life-lines back in time to the imagined worlds of other generations or, to return to a cyberspace metaphor, they open sequences of sites, following random trails of family markers, and then *invent* as much as discover the world of each site. The special extra postmodern contribution of immigrant family history comes from its greater reach across the globe, or in other words, from its already dispersed diasporan mode of existence. Further, diasporan family narratives are always, of necessity, fragmentary and fictional, because whoever writes them obviously cannot fully know the other worlds—of the other places or of the other times or of the other people. And so, by their cumulative example, in a highly postmodern way, diasporan family narratives unravel *from the inside* the tenacious myth of traditional history's authority and impartiality. They infiltrate the established systems of historical accuracy, of cultural value and of narrative continuity by freely *using* them to tell their stories. In other words, by their double existence as both inside and outside the language, the culture and the systems of representation, they destabilise the genre of history. Even more importantly, in the current Australian scene, they expose the ignorance and stupidity of the recently revived old dream of a unified Australian national identity and history, linear, mono and pure.

History, as it is understood in this essay, is multi-directional and elastic, with an infinite capacity for expansion—or contraction. The history of every life lived in Australia is potentially part of the country's history as are all of those lives' connections with homelands elsewhere, but only if they are allowed in, allowed to be written and published. That is why the recent anti-immigration rumblings were dangerous not only to Australia's relations with Asia but also to its changing sense of itself and its history. Unfortunately the step is very small between the desire to restrict non-European immigration and the desire to elide or deny the newly emerging non-European component of Australian written history. Family histories, whether written or spoken—whether presented as fiction or biography, as diaries, letters, anecdotes or as any combination of these, provide a powerful defence against this threat.

The following examples, which can only be touched on here,

are selected to suggest the many ways in which they can do this.

Satendra Nandan, *The Wounded Sea* (1991)

In this account of life in Fiji, Nandan, from his current position as an established senior academic in Australia, mingles elements of his own biography with anecdotes of village life as it is experienced by a Fijian Indian family and its community. As the stories unfold, they are always framed by the pain of the moment of departure in 1987 from Fiji to Australia with which the book begins and ends—the pain of "a bleeding, unhealing wound." (Nandan, 1991: 168) In a very explicit way, this Fijian family story claims its Australian historical space but in the process, expands that space to connect with and include a web of Fijian history. However alien they may be to Australian experience the rhythms of life and speech in Fiji in the second half of the twentieth century, as they are represented here, flow into the expanding pool of Australian cultural memory and demand to be recognised as part of its moral history and therefore, part of its moral responsibility. The Fijian past erupts into the Canberra present of the narrative but the Canberra present, in the shadow of the 1987 military coup, reshapes recent Fijian history as a record of loss and betrayal, of a way of life irretrievably closed to the narrator and one which can therefore only exist now as an Australian story, reframed and repositioned and belonging in the new world. By the fact of its existence it extends this world's historical sweep and its historical responsibility. Such histories are now Australian histories and the more they are told, the clearer it becomes that they cannot be swept aside.

Emma Ciccocosto and Michal Bosworth, *Emma: A Translated Life* (1990)

This book records the story of Emma Ciccotosto and her family, as told to her friend Michal Bosworth, who acted as a translator, scribe, editor and shaper of the narrative. Like Nandan's book, this is an account of the experience of migration and of giving up one world for another, but in this case it is told from the point of view of an Italian woman who came to Australia with her husband and children, full of hope, on the eve of the second world to start a new life on the land in the southern Western Australian region of Waroona, later moving to Fremantle to work for thirty years in the Mills and Wares biscuit factory where "Arnott's" biscuits were made until only a few years ago. She still lives in Fremantle near her children and grandchildren. Through this story, which begins in Italy, we learn that the language and many of the traditions of the old world are carried through and maintained in Australia. There is not so much a sense of cultural loss or dispossession communicated here as of transplantation and nurturing in an environment which is, for the most part, indifferent rather than hostile, and which gradually allows the immigrant culture to develop its own thriving community life in Fremantle. This is a history which demonstrates precisely how individual family histories can contribute to the bigger picture of how a place in Australia came to develop its local character, in this case Fremantle, with its strong Italian cultural influence visible everywhere. In doing so the "little" history rebuilds the links and continuities with the histories of specific localities in Italy, and more broadly with the history of Europe—Europe not seen at all as the centre but as a collection of localities, many of which have embedded themselves permanently in Australia's memory in the lives of its immigrants and their descendants. In the Deleuzian sense, this gentle personal history becomes a highly politicised and collective history for the Italian community in Fremantle and throughout Australia. It becomes a social history of Australia's changing attitudes in relation to its European working class immigrants from the 1940s until the present. Through family histories such as this one, whether written or not, memories of other homelands will make their mark on the future of Australian identity far beyond the life-span of the original immigrants.

Yasmine Gooneratne, *Relative Merits* (1986) and *A Change of Skies* (1991)

Written in a mode which combines carefully researched historical information with memories, anecdotes and fictional recreations of scenes and conversations, *Relative Merits* is a family history of the politically powerful Bandaranaike clan in Sri Lanka, to which the writer belongs. Because the family was very close to the colonial rulers of Sri Lanka, the personal and the public are very obviously connected in her story and, for the same reason, the book offers a fascinatingly intimate viewing position for observing people who would qualify for and no doubt figure in "major" histories in Sri Lanka. By means of this positioning and through its highly parodic and iconoclastic approach to political power, the narrative draws the Sri Lankan history into the Australian historical arena and in the process weirdly skews and domesticates it. At the same time it is framed by an affectionate, comically expressed loyalty. Thus it feels free to put on display much that official histories prefer to leave out. Transported across the Indian ocean to Australia and across genres to family history, this Sri Lankan history of power and privilege becomes a comic exposure not just of the anecdotal underside of this family's history but of history itself. Its political force is primarily in that double exposure.

Gooneratne's multi-layered historical novel, *A Change of Skies*, moves further towards fiction, interweaving invented late nineteenth century diaries which record the circumstances of migration from Sri Lanka to Australia, with the story of the present day family descendants. By reading the diaries, the descendants piece together a story which becomes an important part of their own Australian history in the process. In this way the novel shows how contemporary Australian identities, both national and personal, are formed and reformed by an ongoing process of connection and negotiation with various histories, most of them, unlike the stories unfolded from the treasure-trove of letters, unknown and unreachable.

My last examples, from the many that are available, are from Greek Australian writing. Vasso Kalamaris is an immigrant writer who, in her book, *The Same Light* (1989), draws together stories of Greek immigrant life in Australia, based on the experiences of her family, with stories of return to Greece to visit the family village. She has written a number of books, plays and volumes of poetry, most of them on the same theme of migration, displacement and the double world of the immigrant in Australia. In her case, the stories are all written in Greek and self-translated into English with the help of various translators. Because her work is published in Greek and English, she has a large readership in Greece as well as Australia and it would be interesting to see how such stories of Australian Greek diasporan life are now filtering into and influencing contemporary understanding in Greece of their diasporan history.

In her novel, *The Mule's Foal* (1993), Fotini Epanomitis also writes about Greek family village origins, but in her case the family histories make no claim to historical accuracy. They are based instead on her personal vision of Greece as imagined, fantasised and projected from the point of view of a second generation Greek immigrant who is deeply influenced by a history which she has never lived.

Working from yet another point of connection with Greece, Beverley Farmer demonstrates in her book, *A Body of Water* (1990) how the history of another place can flow into an Australian personal history and keep on washing through it long after the original family tie, through marriage into a Greek family, is broken.

There are countless other written or screened family histories which are stretching the concept of Australian history, especially Aboriginal life narratives and those of recent immigrants from the Asian regions. The examples I have used can only begin to suggest the variety of approaches and forms that such histories can take. In that variety and unpredictability lies their subversive strength. In other words, it is precisely their individuality which is the key to their *collective* capacity to change the rules of the game of "big" history. In this way, diasporan family histories fit Deleuze and Guattari's "minor" model which they apply to languages and literatures but which works just as well for minor histories. The kernel of their argument is that "there is nothing that is major or revolutionary except the minor" (Deleuze and Guattari, 1992: 26). Further, "if the writer is on the margins or completely outside his or her fragile community," they argue, "this situation allows the writer all the more the possibility to express another possible community and to forge the means for another consciousness and another sensibility" (ibid: 17) This is precisely the situation of the diasporan writer.

In its random and multi-directional effort to attract attention in the shadow of "monumental history", little history performs another function, one which I have touched on in passing, but which carries perhaps its greatest potential cultural contribution. That is what Foucault, echoing Nietzsche, calls the "parodic and farcical" use of history. (160) In an age when "monumental history" takes itself so seriously, I would argue that this function can *only* be carried out by little histories. This is not to say that they all play an overtly parodic role in relation to big history. It is rather that by their very existence, proliferation and persistence they cannot avoid performing the carnival act of exposing the crumbling facade of the "monumental" backdrop against which they play their part. Whether they do so in a comic spirit or as a matter of life and death, the collective effect is the same. They show that history's traditional parade of heroes and high points, origins and identities, is itself a masquerade, and that therefore "'monumental history' is itself a parody". On the other hand, the purpose of new history, according to Foucault,

> is not to discover the roots of our identity but to commit itself to its dissipation. It does not seek to define our unique threshold of emergence, the homeland to which metaphysicians promise a return; it seeks to make visible all those discontinuities that cross us. (ibid: 160-62)

Family histories are written precisely from a situation where those discontinuites frame all experience in the new homeland. It may be, that in its desperate search for unified identity, Australia is looking for the wrong thing and in the wrong places. Perhaps its postmodern and postcolonial multicultural condition is best expressed through the motley carnival of its minor diasporan and Aboriginal family narratives.

WORKS CITED

Paul Arthur, unpublished research towards Ph.D. at The University of Western Australia on the way Australia was imagined and represented by Europeans in fiction prior to settlement 1997.

Homi Bhabha, "Of Mimicry and Man: The Ambivalence of Colonial Discourse" in Philip Rice and Patricia Waugh, ed., *Modern Literary Theory* (London: Edward Arnold, 1991).

Walter Benjamin, "Theses on the Philosophy of History" in *Illuminations*, trans. Harry Zohn (London: Collins/Fontana, 1968).

Paul Carter, *The Road to Botany Bay* (London: Faber and Faber, 1987).

Emma Ciccocosto and Michal Bosworth, *Emma: A Translated Life* (Fremantle: Fremantle Arts Centre Press, 1990). A later version of this book includes Italian recipes and traditions which have been maintained in Fremantle by the Ciccocosto family. It's called *Emma: A Recipe for Life* (1995).

Nino Culotta, *They're a Weird Mob* (Sydney: Ure Smith, 1957).

Gilles Deleuze and Felix Guattari, *Kafka: Toward a Minority Literature*, Trans. Dana Polan (Minneapolis and London: University of Minnesota Press, 1994).

______, *Anti-Oedipus: Capitalism and Schizophrenia*, trans. Robert Hurley, Mark Seem and Helen Lane (Minneapolis: University of Minnesota Press, 1992).

Fotini Epanomitis, *The Mule's Foal* (St. Leonards: Allen & Unwin, 1993).

Beverley Farmer, *A Body of Water* (St. Lucia: University of Queensland Press, 1990).

Albert Facey, *A Fortunate Life* (Fremantle: Fremantle Arts Centre Press, 1987).

Michel Faucault, "Nietzsche, Genealogy, History" in *Language, Counter-memory, Practice*, ed. Donald Bouchard, trans. Donald Bouchard and Sherry Simon (Ithaca: Cornell, 1977).

Yasmine Gooneratne, "Family Histories as Post-colonial Texts" in Anna Rutherford and Shirley Chew, ed., *Unbecoming Daughters of Empire* (London: Dangaroo Press, 1993). A pioneering work on the theory and practice of family history.

______, *Relative Merits: A Personal Memoir of the Bandaranaike Family of Sri Lanka* (London: C. Hurst and Co. 1986).

______, *A Change of Skies* (Sydney: Pan Macmillan, 1991).

Kate Grenville, *Joan Makes History* (St. Lucia: University of Queensland Press, 1988).

Sneja Gunew and Kateryna O. Longley, *Striking Chords: Multicultural Literary Interpretations* (Sydney: Allen & Unwin, 1992).

Sneja Gunew, *Displacements: Migrant Storytellers* (Geelong: Deakin University Press, 1981).

______. *Framing Marginality: Multicultural Literary Studies* (Carlton: Melbourne University Press, 1994).

Robin Hughes, ed. *Australian Lives: Stories of Twentieth Century Australians* (Sydney: Angus and Robertson, 1996).

Abdul R. JanMohammed and David Lloyd, *The Nature and Context of Minority Discourse* (New York and Oxford: Oxford University Press, 1990).

Vasso Kalamaris, *The Same Light* (Fremantle: Fremantle Arts Centre Press, 1989).

Ruby Langford, *Don't Take Your Love to Town* (Ringwood, Australia: Penguin, 1988).

Kateryna Olijnyk Longley, "Fabricating Otherness: Demidenko and Exoticism", forthcoming in *Westerly*, 1997.

______, "Autobiographical Storytelling by Australian Aboriginal Women" in Sidonie Smith and Julia Watson, ed., *De/Colonizing the Subject* (Minneapolis: University of Minnesota Press, 1992).

"Diaspora", special issue edited by Vijay Mishra of SPAN, Double volume (34-35), November 1992 and May 1993 and Vijay Mishra, "Postcolonial Differend: Diasporic Narratives of Salman Rushdie", *ARIEL*, 26:3, July 1995, 7-45.

Sally Morgan, *My Place* (Fremantle: Fremantle Art Centre Press, 1987).

Satendra Nandan, *The Wounded Sea* (East Roseville, Australia: Simon and Schuster, 1991).

Alice Nannup, *When the Pelican Laughed* (South Fremantle: Fremantle Arts Centre Press, 1992).

Henry Handel Richardson, *The Fortunes of Richard Mahony: Australia Felix, The Way Home, Ultima Thule* (London: Heinemann, 1917, 1925, 1929).

Salman Rushdie, *Imaginary Homeland: Essays and Criticism* (London: Penguin, 1992), 12.

Kerry-Anne Walsh, "The Power of One", *The Bulletin*, November 5, 1996, 24-25.

Glenyse Ward, *Wandering Girl* (Broome: Magabala Books, 1987).

Peter Wear, "High Wire and Hanson", *The Bulletin*, October 22, 1996, 18-19.

The Weekend Australian, January 25-26, 1997. The "Focus" section and the special supplement, "Australia Day 97", ed. Petra Rees.

NOTE

Many other writers and scholars, too numerous to mention here, from Australia and beyond, have also contributed to my understanding but I would particularly like to acknowledge my colleague Horst Ruthrof who, with the assistance of an Australian Research Council Grant in 1983, enabled me to work with him as a Research Associate on the project "The Negative Text in Australia". This allowed me to discover forgotten nineteenth century anthropological, historical and fictional material which led to my interest in the construction of national histories and identities. Publications based on this research include Kateryna Arthur (now Longley), "Katharine Susannah Prichard and the Negative Text" in John Hay and Brenda Walker, eds., *Katharine Susannah Prichard: Centenary Essays* (Perth: Centre for Australian Studies, 1984), Kateryna Arthur, "Pioneering Perceptions" in Reginald Berry and James Acheson, eds., *Regionalism and National Identity: Multi Disciplinary Essays on Canada, Australia and New Zealand* (Christchurch: University of Canterbury Press, 1985), Kateryna Arthur, "Fiction and the Rewriting of History: A Reading of Colin Johnson", *Westerly*, March 1985, No. 1, 55-60.

Towards Decolonising Australia

JOHN MCLAREN
Victoria University of Technology, Australia

I

It is a commonplace that former colonies remain tied to the imperial centre by their inherited institutions. Culturally, they remain tied both by language and by the forms in which their cultures express themselves. (Carter, 1987: 99-135)

The form of the novel remains tied to its origin in the early stage of imperialism, when the domestic freedom of the individual was purchased by subjugation of the peoples of empire—workers and peasants at home, slaves in the plantation colonies, whole peoples in the newly subject states, indigenes and convicts in the settler colonies. Even in independent postcolonial states, the novel continues to confine possibility within the same colonial and capitalist hierarchies of freedom and order. (Carter, 1992: 82) In his work, *The Great Indian Novel*, Shashi Tharoor has broken from this pattern by rewriting modern Indian history as a reprise of the *Mahabharata*. This paper will examine three options used by settler Australian novelists to escape the dominance of metropolitan order. The family chronicle takes possession of the colonial place but can only reproduce the imperial patterns within the new colonial space. The novel of migration frees its characters from this dominance but jeopardizes their possession of space. Finally, the novel of resistance reclaims its space by locating the place in the past. These forms will be examined in the work of Miles Franklin, Frank Hardy, Adib Khan, Janet Turner Hospital, Liam Davison and Rodney Hall.

Finally, the paper will suggest that Australia can become postcolonial only by coming to terms with the rewriting of national history from the perspective of the Aboriginal peoples whose displacement and marginalization provided the conditions for colonialism.

Although we may agree that nationalism is a nineteenth century invention, and that national traditions are based on mythological histories, nations are not free to adopt any mythology they choose. The two great Indian epics, the *Mahabharata* and the *Ramayana*, are not restricted in their provenance to India. They are deeply embedded in the folklore of Indonesia and Sri Lanka, and remain current in Fiji, where such writers as Subramana and Satendra Nandan have used them both as a touchstone of Indianness and a barrier to be transcended. Siva can no longer be returned to his home and ritually cleansed; he must learn to live as a native in his new homeland. But in India itself the epics provide a common basis for a national identity, a basis that Tharoor has exploited to satirize the failings of contemporary leaders and to suggest ideals that may offer guidance in an earthly future if they are able to turn their gaze from both the material prizes of this life and the spiritual promises of the next. Similarly, the United States has been able to use as a measure and a promise of its national history the foundation myths of western society. The quest epics of the *Odyssey* and the book of Exodus explain and justify its settlement, the battle myths of the *Iliad* and *Paradise Lost* provided exhortation and comfort for the wars it has engaged in during the twentieth century. Yet, although these myths may comfort individuals, the attempt to adapt them as national myths in Australia has generally failed.

The quest myths, with their image of the promised land, proved difficult to localise in colonies that were founded on convictism and expanded into, rather than away from, deserts. Like the explorer Thomas Mitchell, the novelist Henry Kingsley attempted to paint the land as "A new heaven and a new earth", but this vision was destroyed both by reality and by the sardonic humour of the settlers themselves, represented in the writing of Henry Lawson and his contemporaries. (McLaren, 1989: 354) The Aborigines were more commonly perceived as miserable or brutish than as noble savages, and thus the wars of settlement did not achieve the glamour of the American frontier wars. In history, Ned Kelly, and in fiction

Rolf Boldrewood attempted to supply the lack of a noble enemy by glorifying the bushrangers, but their attempts remain ambiguous.

While myths proved difficult to translate, forms did not. The two most common forms of Australian fiction were the yarn, which became extended into the discontinuous narrative, and the family saga, which of course is also known in India through work like Vikram Seth's *A Suitable Boy*, as well as Salman Rushdie's novels. The discontinuous narrative became a particularly important form for the expression of the fragmentary, disconnected experiences of migrants who failed to fulfil their expectations of mastering their new landscape. This failure similarly became central to the family saga in Australia, but behind it lies the paradox of the frontier. This paradox has been identified in American fiction by Leslie A. Fiedler, who recognizes that the frontiersman who escapes a corrupt civilization at the same time by his work tames the wilderness and so brings it into the domain of civilization. (Fiedler, 1967) In the same way, Frederick Jackson Turner's ideal of a democracy nurtured in the freedom not only fails when the frontier closes, but is fatally flawed by the dependence of the frontier on the capitalist centres from which the pioneers flee. (Smith, 1990: 524-36) The form of the family saga is shaped by historical continuity, and so emphasizes this dependence. The alternatives it offers are the replanting of the old civilization or the defeat of the family in the new land.

Although we might argue that the family saga goes back to the Orestean trilogy and the blood-soaked tales of Thebes, in its modern form its origins are synchronous with those of the bourgeois state. Taking a hint from Stephen Knight's discussion of Tennyson's Arthurian legends, we might say that the form gives shape to the worries of a bourgeois society where the sites of paid work have been separated from the domestic, and the concerns of fidelity, property and inheritance become a matter of intrigue and negotiation rather than of physical force and state power. (Knight, 1983: 160-63) When the objects of these concerns are translated into new lands, the saga becomes a form of the quest narrative. The hero, needing to maintain or establish his family, voyages to the colony, where his hopes and worries come to be projected on the land, that simultaneously removes the man and threatens the woman and the home that he first establishes and then abandons in search of further support or fortune. Kay Schaeffer argues that this construction is the product of the male insecurity, which sees the land as the woman threatening his security and identity. (Schaeffer, 1934 & 1936) However, the land functions similarly in the work of Barbara Baynton and Henry Lawson, as well as in the family sagas of Henry Handel Richardson and Miles Franklin, suggesting that its construction as enemy is the product of material rather than merely mental experience.

Typically, the family saga in Australia starts with the settlement of the land, and continues through the generations that either make it their home or are driven from it. It is thus inextricably involved in imperial history, originating in the home country and frequently returning there to finish. Unlike an American saga like *The Immigrants*, which emphasizes making of a new world, hiding its continuing dependence on the old world, the Australian saga is about transplanting the culture of the home country. In historical terms, Don Watson explains this in the desire of those who have been dispossessed to reproduce the known society in which they in turn will be the masters. This model appears as early as Henry Kingsley's *The Recollections of Geoffry Hamlyn*, where the main characters seek in Australia the wealth that will enable them to restore their fortunes at home. With variations, this model lies behind Henry Handel Richardson's *The Fortunes of Richard Mahony* and Martin Boyd's sagas of the Langtons and of Lucinda Brayford. In Richardson's work the land defeats Mahony's ambitions by first granting him and then taking away a fortune while at the same time alienating him from both his past and his present. In Boyd's novels, the first generation transplants a model of civilization that they eventually bring back to the home country, only to find that the source has itself become corrupted. In the sagas where the action remains in Australia, the first generation is either corrupted or destroyed, while later generations become absorbed in civilization and fail to maintain the alternative ideals planted by their forerunners. In Miles Franklin's *All That Swagger*, old Danny established his rural kingdom but loses his family. Brian Penton, in the trilogy beginning with *The Landtakers*, shows the innocent Derek Cabell corrupted by the land as he gains the vigour needed to tame it to his will. The later volumes show this vigour dissipated in later generations as it is subjected to the structures of urban society and wider political conflict (Buckridge, 1994: 196-98) More recently, Patrick White revived the genre in his *The Tree of Man*, yet while this novel contains all the elements of the saga it is concentrated within the lifespan of one man, who survives the conversion of the forest into his farm and then the absorption of the farm in the city, while his daughter declines into urban gentility and sterility and his son into criminality and death. Stan Parker, the questing hero, achieves his goal only in an ambiguous glimpse God granted to him just before his death. In his later work, White concentrates rather on this quest for spirituality than on the family elements of the saga.

The exception is, of course, *The Twyborn Affair*, where the family saga is the past that the central character, Eadie/Eddie Twyborn, spends his life in a quest to escape. The bomb that ends Eadie's life at the close of *The Twyborn Affair* can be read as the death of both the hopes of regeneration that the old world had invested in the new and of the illusions of true culture in which the new world had decked the old. Although Eadie/Eddie's change of identity and gender have enabled him to escape the restrictions of any particular society, and he has found a measure of satisfaction in each, ultimately his hopes in each are frustrated. The novel then can be taken as expressing White's disillusion with the possibilities of any modern civilization, and therefore as a valediction to the whole enterprise of imperialism that the quest form of the family saga at once celebrates and criticizes.

Yet several recent novels demonstrate that, if the family saga is dead, the quest novel retains its potency as a means of escaping from imperial origins to a postcolonial future. The link between the family saga and imperial history ties it to realist narrative in which the story of the family becomes a metonym for the process of settlement. Some recent novels, however, have presented the experience of settlement in mythical terms that, by escaping realism, also escape from the frontier trap of merely reproducing the culture of the home country. This is despite the fact that their mythology, necessarily, is itself European in its origin.

Rodney Hall, in his political fables *Just Relations* and *Kisses of the Enemy*, seeks to escape from realism into myths of nature, in the form of rainforests growing and whales singing, but the historical form of his narratives defeats him. The myths he creates function merely as symbols enriching but not supplanting the realistic story. In the trilogy that begins with *The Second Bridegroom*, (Hall, 1991) however, the myth structures the narrative, turning the realism of the setting into a metaphor of an eternal quest that is renewed in history but, like the contest of Krishna and Arjuna, lives forever outside it. The novel begins realistically enough, although with an element of the gothic, as the convict narrator is hauled onto deck still manacled to the body of the man he has just murdered. Even this moment, however, has mythical overtones of the doppelganger, the other self who is a constant reminder of what his companion is not. Once the narrator escapes from this self, plunging into the bush and being taken in by a mysterious tribe of Aborigines who at once capture him and give him succour, the narrative moves with the logic of myth rather than of reality.

Hall, like Patrick White in *A Fringe of Leaves*, presents the Aborigines from the outside, and therefore avoids the danger of either sentimentalizing or idealizing them. White, however, places his Aborigines within the frame of the tale of the lost white woman, and thus inevitably within the pattern of the natives as savages, primitives who threaten the cultural identity of the white intruder. Hall, in contrast, leaves them outside his narrative, disappearing at crucial moments, entering into no personal relationships with the narrator, keeping him not at the fringes but outside the boundaries of their lives. They thus perform a mythical role in the narrative, protecting the narrator within the alien landscape, discovering to him its intricacies while emphasizing his alienation from it.

The mythological weight of Hall's novel falls not on the Aborigines but on the narrator, who remains unnamed, although he is carefully placed within a Gaelic background of the Isle of Man. He does tell us that his brother's given name is Hall, so suggesting that he, as narrator, is a younger brother of the novelist, himself a migrant to Australia. Historically, he is a convict sentenced for forgery, but he meditates on the fact that his whole identity is a forgery, a work of art that owes its success to both the skill of the artisan who forges it and the originator whom he copies. In this particular case, the forgery is of a work that has never existed—Caxton's one hundredth book, a Commentary upon Twofold

Victims of Fate in the Thebaid of Statius, from the Press of William Caxton, Anno 1491. As a forger, the narrator is both master and slave of the supposed original. His narrative is offered as a love letter to the wife of his own Master, the settler who has purchased him. He dreams that she wants him to be both her master and her slave—the second bridegroom of the ancient earth mother who, in both Celtic and classic mythology, takes successive grooms for the summer and the winter: back to the most ancient of times before history there was a Goddess who took two bridegrooms each year—have you heard?—one for the winter and one for the summer. Each had the task of killing the husband who had lain with her for the six months before him.

While wandering through the forests of the new land, the narrator, the winter king, speculates about his rival, until eventually he is drawn back to the settlement which, partly at his bidding, is destroyed by fire. He kills the Master, only to find that his original double-ganger, comes back to life and once again draws him back to the settlement, where he imprisons him. Here he pours out his hopes and love to his lady, desperately seeking to become her second bridegroom. After the conclusion of his narrative, however, the novelist adds two letters that show that the lady herself was a forgery of the narrator's imagination, and that the regeneration he had hoped for had eluded him.

The labyrinthine wilderness through which the Aborigines conduct Hall's narrator is the counterpart of the woods through which mediaeval knights errant wandered in search of the lady of their imagination or, in the idealised narratives, the Holy Grail. For this wanderer, the Grail is the settlement, which he can possess only by killing the summer king and taking his place as groom the lady. Although he destroys the lady's Master, we are left in doubt about whether the Master was the true summer king, and the lady herself rejects the wanderer as his successor, or winter king. Her role is a metaphor for a process of settlement which imposes masculine will on an alien landscape rather than allowing its feminine. By rejecting the wanderer from the wilderness, and with him potential the wisdom of the land, embodied metaphorically in the figures of the Aborigines, the lady rejects the possibility of myth and imprisons herself and the settlement in history rather than finding for it the freedom and sanction of myth.

The mythology of Hall's novel is essentially pre-Christian, with mediaeval overtones. Its effect is to reject the whole enterprise of settlement as based on an incompatibility between the nature of the land and the motives of the settlers, an incompatibility that could be overcome only if the settlers were able to recover a pre-modern consciousness. Its emphasis falls not on the fact of settlement but on the resistance to it. It is thus similar to Liam Davison's *The White Woman* (1994), which tells the story of a party of settlers seeking to rescue a white woman who is rumoured to have been captured by Aboriginal tribes. As in Hall's novel, Davison emphasizes the unreality of the white men's experience as they wander through a bush that has the properties of myth rather than of history. Like Hall's narrator, they fail in the object of the search, but the woman herself takes on the properties of myth, becoming not a woman lost to civilization but a figure outside civilization and mocking the beliefs on which it is grounded. To the extent that she speaks at all, it is to tell us that we can possess the land only by renouncing everything we brought to it.

By contrast, Robert Drew's novel, *The Drowner* (1996), celebrates the engineer as the hero of a modernism that overcomes the deficiencies of nature. The culminating event of the novel is the completion of the pipeline that brings water to Kalgoorlie, but along the way its characters are absorbed in such modern miracles as photography, the scientific control of disease, and the construction of railways and harbours. Its central metaphor is water, which, in the most material sense, both sustains and extinguishes life. But while the technology of the engineer brings to Kalgoorlie the water that frees it from a hostile environment, the engineer's technology is rooted in the age-old art of the drowners, the men who nurtured the water-meadows of the Avon in Wiltshire. William Dance, the hero of the book, is an assistant to the historical Charles O'Connor, the man who designed the pipeline to Kalgoorlie and fought it through against the opposition of the petty-minded, only to be driven to despair and suicide before its successful completion. As a boy, Dance learns from his father the art of drowning, but takes up engineering to escape from his family as much as to continue its traditions. But water continues to shape his life. He meets his love, Angelica, in the pool at Bath, where his body recalled "that second's tensile softness in the bath. The beauty of her form and movement". (D, 39) He takes her with him over the seas, first to view the Victoria Falls and the prehistoric irrigation works nearby, then across a stormy Indian Ocean to a house by the Swan River in Perth. But the water that gives her to him also takes her away, first by the blackwater fever she contracts in Africa, then by her descent into alienation and madness on the bank of the Swan. Then, in the tank filling from the pipeline in Kalgoorlie, the water restores her to him. His combination of skill and art, of love and will, makes whole both the life of Kalgoorlie and his own life. On its way to this conclusion, the novel also provides realistic pictures of the traditional ways of Wiltshire and the hectic frontier life of Kalgoorlie and the variety of characters brought together by the lure of gold. Although set at the time of federation, the work presents Australia as a settler province, with Kalgoorlie as a metonymous image of its history. The writer gives us glimpses of the Aborigines, but they remain outside the chief action, victims rather than subjects. The burden of the novel however does not fall on its historical metonymy but on the metaphoric significance of the water as both a source of life and an object of technology. Through the person of William Dance, water is linked to the actual and mythological history of England, but through his actions it becomes a means by which the new settlement gains independence both from its past and from the heat of a land that, before the coming of the water, is both the source of its wealth and the agent of its imprisonment in a frenzy of heat, greed and disease. Hall and Davison both present the land as resistant to settlement, accessible only if it is realized in myth. Drew develops such a myth, but his novel uses it to implant and naturalize what remains an essentially alien civilization. Such writers as Thea Astley, in *Reaching Tin River*, or Janet Turner Hospital, in *Charades*, have tried to find most universal myths that lead the reader beyond the purely Australian experience. On the other hand, Aboriginal writers like Sam Watson or John Muk Muk Burke, suggest in their novels that Aboriginal myth contains both an explanation of the violence of settlement and a possible way beyond it. To this stage, however, few non-Aboriginal writers have been able to profit from this mythology without either sentimentalizing it or merely appropriating it. The escape from this dilemma may depend on settler society as a whole accepting the realities of their history and the myths they have been enacting. It also depends on extending Salman Rushdie's observation that we are all migrants now. If, as migrants, we are not to remain trapped in atrophied mythologies translated from our homelands, we must like mythologies also migrate, remaining always the same but always changing in response to historical circumstance. We may only be able to avoid the more virulent expressions of religious and nationalist sentiment by learning to separate myth from history, but we will only truly possess our own histories and the places we inhabit as we learn to recognize the myths that drive and frame our histories.

WORKS CITED

Paul Carter, *The Road to Botany Bay* (London and Boston: Faber, 1987).

______, *Living in a New Country* (London: Faber, 1992).

Liam Davison, *The White Woman* (St. Lucia: UQP, 1994).

Robert Drew, *The Drowner* (Sydney: Macmillan, 1996). Cited as D.

Leslie A. Fiedler, *Love and Death in the American Novel* (London: Cape, 1967)

Rodney Hall, *The Second Bridegroom* (Ringwood: McPhee Gribble, 1991).

See Stephen Knight, *Arthurian Literature and Society* (London: Macmillan, 1983).

John McLaren, *Australian Literature: An Historical Introduction* (Melbourne: Longman Cheshire, 1989).

Henry Nash Smith, 'The Myth of the Garden and Turner's Frontier Thesis', in James C. Work (ed.), *Prose & Poetry of the American West* (Lincoln and London: University of Nebraska Press, 1990).

Kay Schaeffer, *Women and the Bush*. Only the first two novels of the series—*The Landtakers* (1934) and *The Inheritors* (1936)—have been published. For the third, see Patrick Buckridge, *The Scandalous Penton: A Biography of Brian Penton* (St. Lucia: UQP, 1994), pp. 196-98. Although this third volume takes the characters back to England, Buckridge notes that its framework remains firmly based on the experience of Australia.

Women and the Is-ness of Empowerment

Lekkie Hopkins
Edith Cowan University, Western Australia

Women's Studies is an interdisciplinary field of academic endeavour established in Australia and other western nations as the academic expression of the women's movement which re-emerged during the 1960s. Many Australian Women's Studies programmes are highly theoretical and have strong affiliations with literature programmes, with history, politics, philosophy and psychology, as well as with that other hybrid, cultural studies. At Edith Cowan University the programme has a vocationally oriented, applied focus: a historical accident has located the Women's Studies programme not within the Arts Faculty with literature and the straight social sciences, but in the Faculty of Health and Human Sciences alongside vocationally oriented programmes in Children Studies, Youth Work, Human Services, Health Studies and Justice Studies. Graduates of the Women's Studies programme at Edith Cowan University, having studied a combination of feminist and community development subjects which are both theoretical and skills-based, are trained to work with women in the community, in women's refuges, sexual assault referral centres, women's learning centres, women's health centres and multicultural women's centres. A number of graduates also provide policy advice on women's issues to bureaucrats and politicians.

The various historical accounts of the struggles to establish Women's Studies within Australian universities during the last two-and-a-half decades all acknowledge that one of the strengths of the women's movement in Australia has been the constant dialogue between grassroots women's activists (whose campaigns have focussed on a range of issues including the recognition of women's health issues, the need to eradicate sexual violence and domestic violence, and many forms of discriminations against women in the public and private spheres), femocrats (those women who operate within the bureaucratic and political spheres to initiate legislative changes to implement gender equity in the public sphere), and feminist academics.

Whether the focus of the programme is theoretical or applied, or both, Women's Studies provides a critique of existing masculinist knowledge and ways of knowing, and concerns itself with the construction of new knowledges. A very real part of the agenda is to uncover the silences previously excluding women's experiences from being named, heard or recognised. Underlying all the women's movement endeavours is a preoccupation with access to power. A further preoccupation is with questions of difference. Within the universities, one of the great challenges to Women's Studies academics has been to convince funding bodies from the national Australian Research Council to the various internal Faculty research Committees of the need to accept a change in focus of research topic, as well as the value of a range of research methods, including, of course, qualitative research methods.

My paper provides an example of the kind of research into ways of reading power and its relation to subjectivity which fascinate me. It places as much emphasis on the research process as it does on research findings.

* * * * *

There is still in the feminist critique of power a predominant discourse of resistance to oppression, rather than a discourse which seeks to revise power as a construct and examine the ways in which marginalised groups (including women) can recreate and appropriate power for themselves.

Although such accounts of power and the way it is wielded are useful in identifying injustices and in creating ways to resist them, they worry me because they still accord a primary status, a legitimacy, to those persons and institutions who wield power—

over, and frequently position the oppressed, the victims, as Other, as supplicants, bravely arguing their entitlement to their share of the power cake. In order to try to start thinking about the impulse to power differently, I have tried here to investigate what being empowered feels like, or looks like, to non-dominant groups, in the hope that this can feed into a discourse which seeks to revise power as a construct, to see it *not only* in terms of resistance, *but also* as creative entitlement. To do this I have begun to read power as J.K. Gibson-Graham (in Caine and Pringle, 1995), suggests as an ubiquitous and fluid substance that is discursively as well as non-discursively constituted and is never absent from a social site or agent.

This paper, then, reports on an introductory study which has sought to give voice to a small number of WA women who perceive themselves to be acting powerfully in society. The study aimed to investigate the ways in which the women themselves discuss and interpret the power that they feel they have, and to trace their journeys towards what we all, inevitably, called empowerment.

My project in this paper concerns not so much an investigation of that *process* of *becoming* empowered, but rather, my project here is to look at the subjective experience of *being* empowered, the *is-ness* of empowerment, if you like: in other words, in this paper I'm seeking to explore the ways women imaginatively describe, view and locate their own power when they feel themselves to have arrived at this empowered space. Are they still in resistance to a dominant discourse, or is there something different happening in what may well be a fleeting moment? My decision to do this was inspired partly by Dorothy Smith's (1988) observation concerning discourse of power that "the ideological practices of our society provide women with forms of thought and knowledge that constrain us to treat ourselves as objects. We have learned to set aside as irrelevant, to deny, or to obliterate our own subjectivity and experience. We have learned to live inside a discourse that is not ours and that expresses and describes a landscape in which we are alienated and that preserves that alienation as integral to that practice." Dorothy Smith goes on to note that in one of Doris Lessing's short stories in *The Black Madonna* collection, Lessing describes a girl growing up in Africa whose consciousness has been wholly formed within traditional British literary culture. "Her landscape, her cosmology, her moral relations, her botany are those of the English novels and fairy tales. Her own landscape, its forms of life, her immediate everyday world do not fully penetrate and occupy her consciousness. They are not named. Doris Lessing's story", Dorothy Smith tells us, "is a parable of the situation of women in our society. Its general culture is not ours."

This passage from Dorothy Smith really sings to me, not least perhaps because my own disciplinary background is in literature and history, and my current doctoral work is with texts which cross and recross the fiction/reality boundaries.

In this study, then, I've been attempting to grapple with the issue of whether and how women who see themselves as acting powerfully come to recognise and operate from their own inner landscapes, rather than acting out of resistance to a dominant discursive landscape.

First I want to give you some information about the research process. The study sought stories of the journey towards empowerment of 13 women who considered themselves to be acting powerfully in society. Stories were gathered using an open-ended interview procedure. Participants were simply told that they were going to be invited to talk for an hour about what it is about their lives now that gives them a sense of empowerment, and about the journey they had undertaken to arrive at this place. Each interview was tape recorded, and lasted for about an hour. All tapes were subsequently transcribed. The interviewer, who was my research assistant, is an experienced facilitator of playback theatre workshops, and saw her role as facilitating the telling of the women's own stories of their journey towards empowerment.

I should say here that the whole notion of empowerment was not defined for the women, except that it's seen as being in a state of acting powerfully. Hence, each woman interpreted that term herself and gave her own journey in the light of her own notion of empowerment. As the paper will reveal, most women saw empowerment as the capacity to be truly yourself (or, in Doris Lessing's and Dorothy Smith's terms, to operate from your own inner landscape); frequently, the women saw their own power as enabling others, and stemming from their own imaginative self-conception;

their own concepts of self power and of the way empowerment operates in the society was mostly through creating positive self images in others, NOT in changing material conditions: and this, of course, reflects the material comfort and wealth entitlement that these women assume.

What has emerged, as all researchers using this method of data gathering seem to say, is a rich body of information. (My task, of course, is now to make sense of this information: to read between and beneath the threads of story, to locate common and eccentric patterns and pictures. My aim is to locate that magic wellspring from which self-recognised empowerment comes.)

Here is some of the demographic data on these women: they range in age from early 30s to late 60's. All are white middle-class profession women, though none considers herself to be a stereotypical middle-class woman: in other words, each considers herself to have chosen to live on the margins of middle-class Australia, but to be operating powerfully from there. (In relaying this I am aware of the relative nature of marginality and its difference from marginalisation.) In terms of professional occupation, two of these women describe themselves as storytellers; one is a human development consultant and storyteller; one is a singer and composer; one is an artist; one calls herself an actor/playwright/director; one is an unemployed architect and relationship counsellor; one calls herself a writer/consultant to organisations/playback theatre worker; one is an osteopath; one a social worker; one describes herself as a creative business woman; and one is a geologist turned mayor. Each of these women (except the social worker and currently the Mayor) works outside bureaucracies or large organisations. All describe themselves as heterosexual; just under half are single; all except one are mothers. Clearly then we are dealing with an elite group of sorts (although only one describes herself as materially wealthy); clearly, too, in terms of cultural background, class, and status, there seems to be a lot of cohesiveness here. (I want to point out here that this is an introductory study only: the plan is to do a much larger project with a much greater diversity of age, class, ethnicity, education and professional status.)

When I started work on this paper I wanted to unravel the stories of these women's lives and of their interpretations of what it is in their experience which is enabling, which allows them to feel powerful; and at the same time I wanted to draw together the common threads, to explore which experiences or attitudes are indeed seen to create the space for empowerment to occur. As my reading of the transcripts continued, however, my fascination with the ways in which each of these women imaginatively created her own inner landscape grew, because it seemed to me that this is what lay beneath each of the surface narratives: a capacity to construct an imagined landscape where the self was completely at home. These women frequently described themselves as empowered when they were most fully able to give creative expression to what they perceived as the self; frequently they spoke of this as finding a voice. Their stories indicate that the power that plays around this self, this empowered acting self, is not fixed or permanent, but is fluid, momentary, and able to be accessed more and more readily as each woman gains what she calls strength. All participants speak of the self as a subject capable of being self sufficient, or connected equally to other selves. Arguably, this means that their inner landscape is no longer resisting a dominant discourse, but is full, orgasmic, flying.

So rather than focussing on the experiences or attitudes which are enabling, which allow them to feel powerful, and rather than retelling the surface stories of these women, in the rest of this paper I want instead to look briefly at one of the common indicators of empowerment (i.e. the capacity to be creative, to find a voice); then to explore the tensions between the inner landscape which houses the creative self and what one could call the outer landscape, which is home to the dominant discourse; and finally, to see what wisdom or advice each woman would choose to leave for her daughters and their generation, because this too gives insight into those aspects of women's journeys which they consider most significant.

The transcripts of interview suggest strongly that finding a voice is very much tied up with giving expression to one's identity, and that this in turn is empowering. Participants spoke of joy, of strength, of love of self.

Hear this: *I am a practising artist and I feel that the work is strong. It satisfies me and says what I want it to say. I look at it and I like it.*

The actor/director tells of the joy she has in acting: she transforms through acting, taking on characters' stories and transforming her size, her shape, her voice and so on

The musician brings an incredible sense of joy to her music. She plays drums, uses voice, and composes on piano. Her singing and composing are rich sources of empowerment. She is delighted by her ability to use music to heal. She cites instances of using voice to work with Aboriginal street kids, and with alcoholics.

One of the storytellers, too, speaks of bringing together healing and story.

One participant was very clear about the feeling of disempowerment that accompanies attacks on her own notion of who she is: every time she is disempowered it is because the identity she is aware of is under attack e.g. as a new mother; as a wife being squashed; as a migrant woman who refuses to conform: and every time she is empowered it is because she feels well read and well heard e.g. by friends as a young woman exploring new age and hippy ideals; by her sons now: "I think the boys were worth every cent. They give me a lot of tenderness. They've turned into really great friends now. This empowers me and makes me a strong woman and gives me a sense of identity." Her narrative of empowerment is interesting because in spite of being unemployed after years of study, she says "I feel more content than ever with myself" and lists a series of actions: successfully carrying out an architecture project in Germany as a young professional woman; getting out of the marriage; raising children in a different country and having a good relationship with the children in the end; having a university degree from a foreign country and getting good marks; establishing a good network of friends in Germany. These are the things that nobody can take away really. What she would like to do is take up my creativity again which was crunched by my marriage and bringing up the children.

Another participant spoke of the class and family impediments to actualising, but stressed that the route to empowerment was through finding a niche, developing a sense of self, and feeling entitled to press on with that. This participant has literally found a voice: her niche is storytelling.

For some participants a sense of identity at odds with their surroundings became very evident very early in life. The tension between the inner landscape and another reality was so strong for two participants that they spoke clearly of feeling they were being reared by the wrong family: one says "I was always sure that I was a changeling and that the fairies had substituted me at birth because all the other people loved all the farm things and mucking about but not me, I was never more happy than sitting up in a tree reading a book." The other, who became an actor/playwright/ director, says "I was towards the arts and I used to have this feeling that I was born into the wrong house, that there was some mixup at my birth and they took me from the hospital and put me in the wrong family, except that I looked like my family and had the family nose." Now, she operates from a place of wholeness, developed after a lifetime of exploration, searching and risk-taking during which she found peace, created her inner landscape, by living for 6 months at an Indian ashram: the wholeness she speaks of now is used in her theatre work: of a recent women's production which she wrote and directed she says "We can explore death, explore looking in a mirror and seeing yourself truly, and then explore the ability to stand what one sees." She is very much aware of the value of her own empowerment in working with others: "to work closely with women, to see the faces of the women I worked with look at me with such love. There was such trust and all of them said there was no tyranny of power in the process. It was completely collaborative."

The notion that the inner landscape is not static or fixed comes through clearly in the interview with the musician. Her interview is fascinating because even in her music she sees herself not as resisting a dominant discourse but as powerfully *reframing* the whole notion of what it is to be a woman singer: she rejects the seductive sexy stereotype, and projects as an active, energetic drummer and magic-maker e.g. one performance series was self defence classes for women through song and clowning. That she operates out of a clear and strong inner landscape can be inferred from her discussion of power of voice: "When voice is used in an unconscious way and not in a cosmetic way, it is the most direct expression of the heart. When I am up there doing it, that is certainly when my spirit flies and people can see most clearly what I am

. . ." Still, for her there is the tension between inner landscape and dominant discourse: "there are certainly times when I think the world is just a big mess and nothing I can do will change it so what's the point? Those are the times when I doubt."

Grace, the business woman, is someone whose journey has been one of resistance to becoming "who you ought to be". Early family violence meant that a lot of the spirit got knocked out of her, but something essential didn't because "I knew I would always be good at something, that strength got left and I knew it was there." Hers was for a long time a journey of resistance: she has a clear perception of resisting the inaccurate diagnosis that she couldn't do maths and science; she resisted the notion that girls should prop men up; she resisted the notion that she was worthless, and even in her most suicidal teenage moments there was some powerful glimmer of resistance which kept her alive. Her resistance was to "a strong sense of shame, and a whirlpool of anger, rage, confused sexuality, fear and just sexual rage at having felt used and myself have abused myself and not knowing where the boundaries were and all that stuff." Her sense of self has come from superimposing a new landscape on her original damaged one: through following the meditation practice of Muktananda she has found beauty as a reference point.

The osteopath clearly articulates her own journey, and after a difficult beginning acknowledges that belonging with pride to an eccentric and courageously non mainstream family has given her the entitlement to journey counter to the mainstream without ever actually having to *resist* it.

The social worker, who grew up with a sense of entitlement to make choices, speaks eloquently of the struggle to develop and claim her inner landscape: discussion of the development of a spiritual dimension revealed that she got a message from her family that there was a certain way to be, and she used to struggle to be that, BUT an encounter group in her late 20s made her realize

> I was just me and that was OK. So that was a major liberation and felt like my head had burst out of the clouds and that I had touched on something very fundamental in myself. And I became interested in Oriental religions and so on that were

> able to give me a lot more ways of thinking to my spiritual pathway that my Christian upbringing had done, and I think in recent years I take various journeys into that side of my house through art, through my sexuality, through various cultural things, through nature, and that keeps reminding me that I have a soul, that I have a relationship with spirituality in a broad sense that helps me feel I fundamentally belong and I am part of something bigger and that is very empowering.

This connection with something bigger sustains her: "When I get lost from my inner world and the spiritual world below that then it is hard to feel empowered in my day-to-day life." She is also aware of the fluidity of power: "I feel moments when I am in touch with my Godliness if you like and that is inherently powerful." For her, imagination is liberating: "it makes me feel like a citizen of the world; my world is as big as the books I read and the radio programmes I listen to and the films I watch. If I were to draw my social network, I would have it in the radio and newspapers and things because they are very much a part of my daily life."

The Mayor, who of all participants was least ready to read her current work in terms of empowerment, had no sense of inner creation of her journey: it appears that this participant inhabits an inner landscape which is not of her own making: she is a survivor in alien territory: a great contrast to those women who do see themselves as personally empowered. For these women, acknowledging their own subjectivity and experience is transforming.

One participant whose journey has been fraught with obstacles phrased it this way: "I don't only survive now but I think I have changed into a different person. It is probably the true person who was always there and was on the edge of being crushed and really dying. Now, it has found its own spirit which was already there when I was a child really. It is the sense of freedom, passion and tribal identity, creative, spontaneous—it is coming through a lot again."

Finally, I want to give you a quick look at the advice participants said they would like to pass on to their daughters, since this gives us access to their own sense of the importance of acting out of a strong sense of self:

The musician: "Don't underestimate the power that there is in the combination of yourself with the music; never restrict yourself. Music is so broad. Don't let this culture restrict you: play with the edges."

The artist: "Never underestimate the chance encounter or the thing that you pick up on the street that suddenly makes you think, 'Ah yes, that's what it's all about.'; cultivate an openness for that sort of thing."

The social worker: "Befriend yourself so that you are able to enjoy your own company and value yourself. Develop curiosity about the world, and confidence to explore it and go for it so you'll be able to cope with change. Take pride in your femaleness."

The actor/director: "Know yourself, because if you know yourself then everything is known and people will accept you. Be outrageous because life isn't a dress rehearsal."

The business woman: "Most important is the ability to feel self love, and to come to a point where that is what the journey is."

Storyteller: "Be yourself. Follow your own dream."

The osteopath: "If you give someone a fish, you feed them for a day: if you teach them how to fish, you feed them for a lifetime. The gifts I want to give you are the skills to be self sufficient. Then you are much more likely to have a successful life at all levels because you will then be empowered."

The consultant: "Be loving and honoring of yourself: be how you are. Take your power: have a sense of your own power."

The development officer: "Know the importance of other people in your life."

The Mayor: "You have a right to be individuals, but at the same time you have to acknowledge you are part of a community. Be comfortable in yourself, and feel your responsibilities and a sense of sharing with others."

The other storyteller: "One thing I would like to give you is more ritual, more acknowledgement of the passing of different stages in life and the honoring of the fact that you are one among many—that you are not on your own. And I hope to give you a world of great women, not just me."

These, I would argue, are not women in a perpetual state of resisting someone else's power: these are women who conceptualise themselves as taking power for themselves, if fleetingly, using it to enable themselves, their daughters, their audiences, their Others.

What are the implications of all this then? I have chosen to interpret the information in these ways to help demystify some of the hype surrounding the notion of access to places of power in our society. Basically I want to argue that it is not enough for lawmakers to say, "OK we will change the selection processes so that you can have equal access to positions of power (via EEO and AA)," because that of course implies that you still have to alter your own inner landscape to adapt to the dominant organisational culture; rather, I want to argue that we need a paradigm shift in order for women to feel that their own landscapes are the ones they can operate out of. If my research indicates anything it is that once one is able to give voice to what one perceives as one's own self, true self, own inner being, or, as Dorothy Smith would have it, one's own inner landscape, then one is empowered and feels entitled to act powerfully in society: NOT resisting, but creating, taking and using power to initiate, to act, to change other lives.

I think we are living in exciting times, because I think the politics of difference, of multiculturalism and acceptance of multiplicity are precisely the politics which are going to be most enabling for those who do not imbibe the dominant discourse. As I am so fond of saying to my students, every woman is at the centre of her own story.

The danger, of course, is that running counter to the politics of difference, and maybe running faster, is the globalisation phenomenon, already hijacked by imperialist moneymakers without an ounce of social justice or respect for difference or appreciation of colonialism in their bodies or intellects; AND the economic rationalist phenomenon, hand-in-glove with globalisation, which overlays all interactions with an hierarchical, hegemonic dominant discourse which is anathema to the politics of difference.

So what then is the value of research such as this? I have come to see that I cannot do it all: all I am trying to do here is uncover, highlight, foreground the ways in which particular women understand the sources of their own empowerment. In particular, I hope that this identification of the value and nature of the inner landscape will play a useful role in legitimating that inner landscape as being a sunny space, an enabling space to act out of. I can use this knowledge to reinforce and endorse the enriching value of the politics of difference. Others can contribute their own research findings and skills to translate understandings of empowerment into social policy. I see the need for a strong public critique of economic rationalism to pervade the public sphere. I hope this in turn can feed into the debate about ways to interpret and deal with hegemonic power.

WORKS CITED

Barbara Caine and Rosemary Pringle (eds.), *Transitions: New Australian Feminisms* (Sydney: Allen & Unwin, 1995).

Dorothy Smith, *The Everyday World as Problematic* (Boston: Northeastern University Press, 1987).

All in a Good Cause: Australian Women's Experiences and Understandings of Menstruation, 1900-1960

SUELLEN MURRAY
Edith Cowan University, Western Australia

Menstruation is a recurring event of some significance in the lives of women. The onset of menstruation marks the commencement of potential child-bearing and for this reason, some would say that menstruation is 'all in a good cause'. Menstruation's association with child-bearing, however, is only one of a range of meanings that has existed during the early to middle decades of the twentieth century. Menstruation has material and practical implications in terms of the use of so-called 'sanitary protection' and restrictions on women's activities. It is also linked to the expression of women's sexuality and is a consideration in women's health. Hence, Australian feminist writer, Elizabeth Grosz has described menstruation as 'the archetypal "symptom" of women's unique biologies.' (1987, 14)

Medical knowledge is often the framework in which menstruation is understood in the latter decades of the twentieth century. Indeed, the major sources of documented understandings about menstruation throughout the twentieth century are found in medical texts and popular health manuals. Medical writers have exerted considerable influence through their constructions of femaleness and femininity, health and ill-health and normality and abnormality around menstruation. At the same time and particularly during the early to middle decades of this century, secrecy surrounded women's experiences of menstruation. Girls and young women grew up having been informed that menstruation was a private matter and that any evidence of menstruation should be concealed at all times. What medical writers said about menstruation, then, does not necessarily reflect women's experiences nor the meanings which women used to understand menstruation.

In my research, medical writers and women are accorded similar status regarding their knowledge claims concerned with menstruation. I challenge the idea that science and medicine create absolute forms of knowledge. Medical understandings of menstruation are particular conceptualisations located within masculinist frameworks of knowledge. These frameworks reflect existing gendered social relations where male bodies are perceived as the norm and where medical conceptualisations of menstruation were created in social contexts where women were expected to be wives and mothers. Rather, I argue that there is a range of ways of knowing including those understandings based in women's experiences. Whilst acknowledging that women's understandings and experiences of menstruation could have been informed by medical knowledge, my feminist research offers an alternative interpretation of a history of menstruation to those provided by other, primarily, medical discourses. Hence, my research has at least been partly concerned with documenting women's voices speaking about menstruation.

In this paper, I will consider the ways in which women understood menstruation and I will contrast these understandings with contemporary medical knowledge. I will question whether women understood menstruation physiologically and whether it was as closely associated with the feminine ideals of marriage and motherhood as promulgated by medical and popular health writers during these early to middle decades of the twentieth century. Firstly, then, I will provide examples of understandings of menarche, or the first menstruation, and, secondly, the ways in which menstruation was understood during adulthood. In particular, I will reflect upon these meanings in relation to understandings of femaleness and femininity.

Before I proceed. I think a brief note on methodology would be helpful. As I have noted there is little documented evidence of women's experiences and understandings of menstruation during the period 1900 to 1960. I interviewed a group of twenty Australian women from a range of social and ethnic backgrounds aged from their fifties to their eighties. It was not intended to be in any sense a representative sample of Australian women but rather the collection of memories of a particular group of Australian women regarding their individual experiences and understandings of menstruation. I would argue though, that their experiences may well be similar to many other Australian women. I also draw on other oral history collections, most notably a large life history project undertaken in New South Wales with older Australians which touched upon menstruation in some interviews. In addition, I examined a cross-section of medical texts used by medical students and practitioners and a selection of popular health manuals that were available in Australia.

The research of American anthropologist, Emily Martin, in particular, has informed my work. In her book, *The Woman in the Body: A Cultural Analysis of Reproduction*, Martin considered American women's responses to medical discourses about menstruation. She was concerned with women's experiences of menstruation and the ways in which they produced their understandings of it. (1987) Like Martin and others, I use a concept of 'experience' that assumes that it is not self-evident nor unproblematic. Nor is it authentic, natural, unmediated nor characteristic of a common womanhood, but rather something that is 'an interpretation and something that needs to be interpreted'. (Scott, 1991: 796-97) My research, then, is concerned with both women's experiences and their understandings of these experiences, as well as the production of this knowledge. Hence, I discuss women's experiences of menstruation in the context of changing medical knowledge, where it has increasing power and authority as the discourse of the body over the early and middle decades of this century, and where women were actively engaged in making sense of this and other knowledges.

When asked about their experiences of menarche, 'I thought I was going to die' is a response offered by several women who commenced menstruating in early twentieth century Australia. This comment reflects a range of ideas about menstruation. Firstly, it highlights the shock or surprise that these women experienced at seeing blood and the strong links between blood and death. It illustrates how these women had not been given alternative understandings about the loss of blood as being a part of normal and healthy female physiology. The shock or surprise itself suggests that they had not been told anything about menstruation prior to its commencement. And it highlights the way that silences operated and affected the lives of young women.

T.M., interviewed in the New South Wales oral history project, described her experiences of commencing menstruation in about 1906 and knowing nothing about it. She recalled that

> I thought I was going to die. It happened to me quite suddenly one afternoon and I rushed in where my mother and father were sitting and I said to them "I'm bleeding from between my legs" . . . My father got up and walked out and my mother turned round and started working on the sewing machine and after a while she said to me "this is going to happen to you every month" she said "wear these" and that's all she said. I was only twelve I think or only just twelve. (T.M., 1987)

T.M. was given no explanation about what had happened, either from her parents nor at school, nor did she discuss it with her sister, and found out physiological explanations for menstruation only when she studied zoology at university.

Similarly, Annetta Martin recalled her bewilderment at menarche. She commenced menstruating in about 1918.

> I knew nothing about it. I had two older sisters and I didn't know a thing about it. . . . I was eleven and a half and I remember waking up in the morning and there was blood on my nightie. I didn't know what on earth. I thought I'd cut my leg, but it wasn't. So I went out to Mother and I said "look there's blood on me" and she said "oh yes". And I said, "well how did it happen? I can't find a cut." And she said, "no, no every girl gets this". (Martin, 1994)

As a girl, Annetta recalled that when she commenced menstruating her mother did not discuss its physiology nor did she mention anything about its potential reproductive consequences.

More than three decades later, Elizabeth Douglas and Elly Overdijk recalled their own similar experiences during the 1950s. Neither were informed in advance and for both it was a shock. Elizabeth's older sister told her about it, and then they later informed their younger sisters. Elly was also responsible for informing her younger sister.

For some Aboriginal girls and young women, separated from their mothers and other female relatives on missions or in work situations away from their families, their access to women's knowledge about menstruation could have been severely limited and the impact of understandings of menstruation significantly changed. Isabelle Raymond was separated from her family and working on a station in the Western Australian Goldfields during the 1940s when menstruation commenced. Her mother had been brought up on the Moore River Mission and died when Isabelle was eleven. When she started menstruating, Isabelle recalled that it was a shock and she had known nothing about it.

By 1930, medical writers were insisting that girls should be prepared for menarche. They argued that mothers should provide knowledge to young women that was restricted to that of a scientific and medicalised nature and that emphasised morality and privacy. It is unclear whether it was due to medical writers' recommendations, especially as only the wealthiest women would have dealt with the medical profession in these earliest decades of the twentieth century, but amongst the women I interviewed who commenced menstruating after 1930, it was more likely that they were informed beforehand. However, it was not necessarily in the ways suggested by medical writers. Information which was provided to girls was likely to contain little contemporary medical knowledge. For Beryl James, informed in advance of her menarche in the 1940s, it was still a shock. Beryl recalled being told that she had 'to expect this and that it was a part of growing up.' She woke up one morning 'covered in blood'.

> It was an overnight thing. I woke up in the morning and back in those days, they didn't give you too many clues beforehand, just that you were expected to know and then they'd produce a knotted piece of elastic and a couple of rags and

> say you'll need these. (James, 1994)

For some girls, menarche was a positive event in their lives, albeit puzzling as well. For Julia Rathay, aged about fourteen years in the early 1940s, menarche was a positive experience even though she was away from home staying with family friends with her older sister. Julia had been informed in advance of menarche by her mother after a girl in her class at primary school had bled profusely and unexpectedly at menarche. After this incident in her class room, Julia recalled that

> I went home and I couldn't tell Mum fast enough . . . I told Mum what had happened and Mum explained to me. I remember standing near the window, looking out the window, and thinking "my goodness!" I said to her, "will I still have these periods when I am as old as Louise Bates?", who at that time was nineteen and Mum assured me I would. That was the bit that really got to me. . . . To think that it would go on forever. (Rathay, 1993)

Julia's recollections underline the concerns of adolescent girls. She was amazed that menstruation would 'go on forever', or at least until she was nineteen.

For those mothers who did not provide physiological explanations of menstruation to their daughters, it could well have been because they did not know themselves. Instead, girls may have simply been told that menstruation marked their transition to womanhood. But even when girls were told they were 'becoming a woman', they did not necessarily know what 'becoming a woman' meant. During these early teenage years, and younger, it might only have meant that it stopped them doing much-loved activities such as going swimming. It also meant dealing with the smell and mess of soaked menstrual rags in school situations where there were few allowances made for maturing girls.

Other girls may have been given explanations that were different from contemporary medical and scientific ideas. My interview with Elaine Turner, for example, suggested that she understood menstruation as a 'cleaning out process', an idea which she may have gained from her mother and one that was evident in popular health manuals during the early decades of the twentieth century. In Hartland Law and Herbert E. Law's popular health manual, *Viavi Hygiene for Women, Men, and Children*, they stated that menstruation was

> the greatest health preserver and life promoter that can be secured, the normal function throwing away diseased products and acting as a safety valve to the system. (Law and Law, 1903: 357)

Generally, girls were told something at menarche. If girls were told nothing else, they were informed about stemming the flow of blood. They were at least given some form of 'menstrual protection'. In the early decades of the twentieth century this menstrual protection was usually rags or some form of cloth, and later, from the middle decades, commercially available disposable pads. That they were at least told how to conceal evidence of it reinforces the secretive nature of menstruation at this time.

Girls were also sometimes given warnings at menarche. They were advised of acceptable behaviour during menstruation, such as not going swimming. There were also sometimes somewhat veiled references to the risks of sexual activity. Lillian Baxter, who commenced menstruation during the mid 1920s, recalled being told that she had to 'be careful' at menarche. However, other than knowing that menstruation was something that 'happened to girls' and that 'you got blood on your knickers', Lillian knew nothing of its potential consequences. It was not until she was in her twenties when work mates informed her of what it was that she had to be careful.

In contrast to these accounts by women, the medical literature emphasised the physiology of menstruation, its potential and desired consequences in terms of marriage and maternity and the potential disorders. I will now go on to consider specifically the ways in which medical and popular health writers understood the potential consequences of menstruation. What, then, were the medical understandings of menarche? At menarche, medical writers claimed that both physical and mental changes occurred. As well as the internal physical changes such as the development of the uterus and the ovaries and the commencement of ovulation, medical writers noted the visible external bodily changes such as 'roundness and plumpness' which, according to English gynaecologist and medical writer, W. Blair Bell, were 'features distinctly feminine and attractive'. (1910: 68)

According to the medical discourse of early twentieth century Australia, in addition to these physiological changes, young women at menarche also experienced mental changes that prepared them for their expected lives as wives and mothers. Bell remarked that 'the altered metabolism' which characterised the onset of menstruation, produced 'wonderful changes of character and disposition'. At menarche, a girl became 'more shy and reserved—the "Tomboy" disappears into the Juliet' and 'modesty takes the place of innocence'. Furthermore, 'the child becomes a woman'. (ibid, 68)

Both these physical and mental changes were explicitly linked with the goal of motherhood. American medical writer, E.C. Dudley, stated that

> the physiological features of puberty are the onset of menstruation and ovulation and notable psychic changes, all of which indicate that the reproductive organs and the sexual nervous organization are approaching maturity and that the girl is preparing for maternity. (Dudley, 1913: 23)

These ideas were also found in popular health literature such as Eulalia Richards' *Ladies' Handbook of Home Treatment*. Here Richards evoked an image of the blossoming of womanhood that occurred at menarche.

> The girl's form becomes more womanly; she grows taller, the chest broadens and the breasts become full and firm. There is also a broadening of the hips, while the limbs grow more round and graceful. The girl's face changes; new beauty is acquired, the lips grow more full and rosy, the eyes more bright . . . she is more womanly, having passed childhood and entered into the realm of womanhood with its increased capacity for joy and usefulness. (Richards, 192-(?): 584-85)

In the medical discourse of the early twentieth century, these changes in social characteristics of girls and young women were understood as biologically determined. The onset of menstruation, as a significant aspect of puberty, resulted in particular changes in the attitudes, behaviour and demeanour of young women. These biologically deterministic beliefs about understandings of femaleness and femininity are found consistently in the medical discourse across the decades of the early to middle decades of the twentieth century.

While the medical literature stressed the significance of the ways in which girls became women at menarche, women's own accounts were more ambivalent and uncertain about womanliness and potential motherhood. What, then, were the understandings of menstruation through women's adult lives? In this next section, I will again consider how women understood menstruation and then contrast these ideas with contemporary medical ideas.

Although menstruation was inconvenient and for some women it produced considerable pain and discomfort, for many women, including Julia Rathay, menstruation was 'all in a good cause'. Miriam Cohen, for example, expressed her pleasure at being female and the association of menstruation with motherhood.

> I was always pleased about having a body that could have children. Menstruation I always associated with childbirth, as a sort of natural thing. I never had any trouble getting pregnant, and having children to me, was all very fulfilling. I always tied it up one with the other. (Cohen, 1994)

For these women, at least some of the time, menstruation was understood in relation to reproduction and motherhood.

For other women, menstruation had mixed meanings related to motherhood. Alice Jackson believed that having children was very important to her. However, the ability to have children was also a burden. When I asked her what were the good things about menstruation, she replied, 'the only good thing was when it stopped and I couldn't have any more.' Some women also noted the relief they experienced when menstruation commenced each month when they were not wanting to be pregnant, or their disappointment when it came when they were hoping to be. Paradoxically, menstruation, although a sign of potential motherhood, was also a sign that conception had not occurred.

For other women again, menstruation had different meanings. For example, how did women who did not have children form understandings of menstruation? For Grace Atkins, who did not marry nor have children, menstruation was a normal part of being a woman. For her, womanhood was not necessarily linked to motherhood. For Lillian Baxter, menstruation was an intensely negative experience. Lillian had decided at a young age that she would not have children. And for her menstruation was not only an inconvenience, it was also very painful.

For some women, menstruation was integral to their conceptualisations about femaleness and womanliness. Here, women's understandings of menstruation are clearly embedded in their embodied experiences. Helen Blake explained that the changing nature of the menstrual cycle and menstruation itself were positive aspects of being a woman and were part of the richness of femaleness. Unlike medical writers who understood cyclicity as problematic and indicative of mental and physical instability, Helen interpreted the changing nature of the menstrual cycle as intensely meaningful and creative. Similarly, Joan Praed explained that menstruation

> is part of the magic of being a woman. It might be a very uncomfortable magic but that's part of the magic. It's very much a magical thing and part of the whole business of being able to create life which is very much women's business. (Praed, 1995)

Whilst by adulthood women were aware of the relationship between menstruation and reproduction, they did not necessarily have detailed physiological knowledge. Lillian Baxter, for example, recalled that menstruation was 'something to do with eggs and things'. Others admitted that they did not know the medical or scientific explanations for menstruation. Like Emily Martin, I found that the women I interviewed did not necessarily talk about it in relation to the physiology of reproduction but rather how they experienced it: what it looked like and how it felt. For example, I asked Alice Jackson how she would explain it to a young girl who knew nothing about menstruation. Alice explained that

> I'd just say what would happen. That she might be unlucky enough to have pains when she got her period, that she'd find blood, that she could feel unwell or she may not, that it was something you didn't go talking about in front of boys. I don't know what else I'd say. (Jackson, 1994)

Although Alice had worked as a nurse before her marriage, she could not recall if she had learnt about the physiology of menstruation then or at any other time in her life. If she had, Alice remarked, it was no longer important and she had forgotten.

Some women did have detailed medical knowledge of the physiology of menstruation. Some of these women worked in the health care area or else had had intensive exposure to medical treatment as a result of gynaecological ill-health. What then were these medical understandings of menstruation?

During the period from 1900 to 1960, there were significant changes in medical understandings of menstruation. As noted in the previous discussion of menarche, throughout the decades of the early twentieth century, medical understandings about menstruation were closely linked to beliefs about women's reproductive capacity. How, then, did the medical discourse explain the way in which menstruation occurred? During the early to middle decades of the twentieth century, several phases of knowledge concerning the physiology of menstruation can be discerned. Firstly, at the turn of the century, the physiology of menstruation was not clearly understood. At this time, medical writers believed that menstruation was greatly influenced by the nervous system and they commonly regarded menstruation to be the equivalent of the oestrus or heat of animals. During the second phase, roughly from the 1910s to 1920s, there was a period of confusion and change when new theories were being developed concerning the effects of 'internal secretions', later to be known as hormones, and at the same time, older ideas about the influence of the nervous system and models based on animal-like behaviour were maintained. In the third phase, by the 1930s, menstruation was firmly located within the menstrual cycle and it was attributed to the interaction of particular hormones. Endocrinology was then the primary medical framework in which menstruation was understood. Finally, by the 1950s, neurology, psychology and psychosomatic medicine were beginning to be explored in relation to the endocrinology of menstruation. Here I will briefly talk about medical understandings of menstruation within the menstrual cycle.

During the mid twentieth century, medical writers understood menstruation in the context of the menstrual cycle. They divided the menstrual cycle into phases which represented changes in the endometrium, or the wall of the uterus. Each phase was related to an aspect of the cyclic development of endometrial tissues and its loss at menstruation. Medical scientists believed that the interaction of changing levels of hormones were responsible for triggering these events. Menstruation was characteristically described as the destructive phase of the menstrual cycle and menstruation was compared to abortion, emphasising its relationship to potential motherhood. English gynaecologist and medical writer, T.N.A. Jeffcoate noted that menstruation was 'the weeping of a disappointed uterus' and in the popular health literature, Eulalia Richards stated that 'the womb ever lives in the hope that of fulfilling its high and noble purpose sheltering and nourishing a growing babe'. (Jeffcoate, 1957: 78; Richards, 1947: 705) These writers constructed ideas about menstruation that suggested that the most desirable outcome of the menstrual cycle was pregnancy. Emily Martin argues that medicine has used industrial metaphors to conceptualise menstruation as a failure of production. (1987) In contrast, women's experiences of menstruation clearly suggest that although some desired pregnancy and not menstruation some of the time, others had different meanings for menstruation in their lives. At times, women were pleased that menstruation came because it meant they were not pregnant. Others were relieved when menstruation ceased altogether, because it meant not only that they would no longer experience the inconvenience and discomfort of menstruation, but that they could also no longer become pregnant.

In conclusion, my paper has examined some contrasting understandings of menstruation according to a small group of Australian women and the medical and popular health literature of the decades from 1900 to 1960. The women had a diverse range of experiences of menstruation over their life times and they understood it in both positive and negative ways. For some girls and young women, understandings of menstruation were characterised by bewilderment and shock; for others it was a signpost to becoming a woman. As adults, their understandings were related to the desire for motherhood as well as the fear of pregnancy; and to their conceptualisations of femaleness. A number of the women I interviewed had acquired contemporary medical understandings of menstruation. Others had little or no understanding of the ways science explained it. Whether they understood menstruation from a medical point of view or not, the women also conceptualised menstruation in terms of what they saw and how they felt from the perspective of their embodied experience.

Acknowledgements

I would like to acknowledge the participation of those women who took part in my oral history project and to thank them for their contribution to my work.

WORKS CITED

Lillian Baxter, Interviewed by Suellen Murray. Private collection (March, 1995).

W. Blair Bell, *The Principles of Gynaecology* (London: Longmans, Green & Co, 1995).

Helen Blake, Interviewed by Suellen Murray. Private Collection (May, 1995).

Cohen, Miriam. Interviewed by Suellen Murray. Private collection, (March, 1994).

Elizabeth Douglas, Interviewed by Suellen Murray. Private collection (May, 1994).

E.C. Dudley, *The Principles and Practice of Gynaecology for Students and Practitioners*. 6th. Ed. (Philadelphia: Lea and Febiger, 1913).

Elizabeth Grosz, Notes towards a corporeal feminism. *Australian Feminist Studies* (1987) vol. 5, 1-16.

Alice Jackson, Interviewed by Suellen Murray. Private collection (December, 1994).

Beryl James, Interviewed by Suellen Murray. Private collection (April, 1994).

T.N.A. Jeffcoate, *Principles of Gynaecology* (London: Butterworth, 1957).

Hartland Law and Herbert E. Law, *Viavi Hygiene for Women, Men and Children* (Sydney: Australian Viavi Hygiene Co, 1903).

T.M. Interviewed by Bronwyn Hughes. *New South Wales Bicentennial Oral History Collection* (1987), Oral Trc. 2301. Int. 125.

Annetta Martin, Interviewed by Suellen Murray. Private collection (December, 1994).

Emily Martin, *The Woman in the Body, A Cultural Analysis of Reproduction* (Milton Keynes: Open University Press, 1987).

Elly Overdijk, Interviewed by Suellen Murray. Private collection (September, 1995).

Joan Praed, Interviewed by Suellen Murray. Private collection (December, 1995).

Julia Rathay, Interviewed by Suellen Murray. Private collection (January, 1993).

Isabelle Raymond, Interviewed by Suellen Murray. Private collection, (1994, April).

Eulalia S. Richards, *Ladies' Handbook of Home Treatment* (Melbourne: Signs Publishing Co.).

______. *Ladies' Handbook of Home Treatment*, Rev. Ed. (Warburton: Signs Publishing Co, 1947).

Joan W. Scott, The evidence of experience. *Critical Enquiry* (1991), vol. 17, 773-97.

Katharine Susannah Prichard: A Woman of Her Time or A Woman for Our Time?

GLEN PHILLIPS
Edith Cowan University, Western Australia

The question which the topic of this paper has posed is intended to provoke a re-evaluation of one of Australia's first internationally successful writers. Katharine Susannah Prichard was born in Levuka, Fiji in 1883 in the midst of a tropical hurricane. By all reports she was a tempestuous child, but storm and tempest were to follow her all through her long and distinguished life. Her father was a newspaper editor of ability, nevertheless an alcoholic and later a bankrupt. As a result of his suicide, Katherine was faced with the first of the tragic challenges to test the spirit of this 'child of the hurricane', as she had been named in Fijian by her childhood nurses (Throssell, 1975). Even before her father's suicide in 1907, Katharine had been challenged by two near deaths. An elderly admirer took poison when she rejected his proposal to accompany him back to Europe; her beloved elder brother, Allan, became critically ill and, for a time was not expected to live; her hopes of university studies were destroyed by the family's impecunious situation and she had to take whatever work would contribute to the collective Prichard income. But there were positive influences too. During her childhood in Tasmania and Victoria her life-long love of the Australian bush was established. A period as a governess in South Gippsland then gave her the background for her first international success, the prize winning novel, *Pioneers* (Prichard, 1915), which heralded her triumphant return to Australia towards the end of the First World War. There were other less auspicious but significantly morale boosting prizes for her work and early publication successes in her teenage years.

Perhaps the most important formative experience in her early life, however, was to work on an outback sheep station in the semi-desert of north-western New South Wales near Broken Hill. As opposed to the lush green of the rainforests of her earlier life, these harsh red landscapes prepared the way for her many later stories and works set in the dry spinifex Pilbara and Goldfields country of Western Australia, later to be her adopted State.

Much harder times were yet to come in her life. As related by her son Ric Throssell when she, by now a budding journalist, travelled overseas in 1911 to her greatly longed-for Europe, she was swept up into an 'affaire' with a much older man. This 'Preux Chevalier' certainly proved a great cultural ambassador to Europe for Katherine, but, since he a was middle aged friend of her father with three children of his own, the 'affaire' was doomed to ultimately become a setting for the older man's possessive jealousy, threats of suicide and ultimately her own bouts of corrosive guilt. Yet, she emerged from the experience to discover the important social issues of pre-war Britain—working class poverty, hunger marches, the Fabians, socialism and Mrs. Pankhurst's 'Women's Social and Political Union'. Then came the War itself and amidst the tragedies, particularly those of women widowed and children orphaned, she experienced the ultimate reality of the War, her own brother's death. As Throssell reports, the political resolve that lasted the rest of her life was distilled:

> I was consumed with desire to find some way of preventing the diabolical slaughter caused during the war. (Throssell, 25)

Ironically, by the War's end she was to become both a recognised novelist in Australia (by virtue of her success in winning the Australian sector of the Hodder and Stoughton All-Empire 1000 pound Novel Competition) and the passionate choice of Australia's newest war hero, the dashing young Hugo Throssell from Perth who had been awarded a Victoria Cross and then, wounded in the trenches, had been visited in a British Military hospital by Katharine prior to her departure. He pursued her back to Melbourne and they were married in January 1919. How could she have known that only 17 years later he would leave her life by the same violent and self-inflicted means her father had chosen?

There was one other vital influence, also one of mixed blessings, taking form in Katharine's life at this stage: her discovery of the Russian Revolution and the application of Marxist-Leninist theory which had brought about the birth of international communism. Katharine found an abiding cause in this new political credo and became a founding member of the Australian Communist Party. With the birth of her first and only child, Ric, in 1922 came the beginning of her 'other career' as a tireless and ultimately implacable 'old guard' figure of the local branch of the Communist Party in Perth, Western Australia. She had gone to live there with her husband Hugo (known to his friends as 'Jim'). The twin competing sources of joy in her life remained her family (both her husband and her only son) and her literary works.

What I have sought to establish in this briefest of summaries of the formative years of Katharine Susannah Prichard is the existence of a writer whose life was driven, on the one hand, by a great need to care for and to give love not only to those close to her but also to all disadvantaged people, but on the other by her personal tragedies of deaths and deprivations. The less personal challenges which she also identified with, such as the depressed status of women, the suffering of the Aboriginal people of Australia, oppression of manual workers and victims of war profiteers and fascists. All these also drove her not only to document the social problems but to propose what she thought were the unique and fail-safe social curatives inherent in Marxist-Leninist principles.

There is one more interesting nexus between Katharine the writer and the thirteen novels, five short story collections, two volumes of poetry, an autobiography and dozens of other books, pamphlets and individually published stories and articles which made up her life's work. It is the connection she herself had made with Australia, the continent itself. From 1920 until her death, the focus of her physical existence, the still point, if you like, about which her travels, her relationships and her work itself were all centred was a modest, if not diminutive, wooden cottage perched on the sun-baked slopes of the most westerly part of the Australian land-mass, the Darling Range. Number 11 Old York Road was, and still is a modest couple of acres. There's a southerly facing verandah with slightly pretentious square stone pillars, a corrugated iron roof which curls down the side to shade another verandah that protects the simple four roomed cottage with kitchen tacked on the back.

At the bottom of the house garden is another tiny weatherboard building—Katharine's writing studio. Beyond stretches an empty paddock enclosed by simple wire fences. Once this property had backed onto other bush blocks and to the nearby John Forrest National Park. This park is a vast wild area of tumbling ravines and huge granite boulders, of native jarrah and marri gum trees and masses of banksias, dryandras, acacias, hakeas, grass trees, zamia palms and (in season) profusions of wildflowers, including the State's emblem, the red and green 'kangaroo paw'. Here Katharine used to ride her favourite horse, Wynburn, and escape from the pressure of household and farmyard chores, the claims on her writing time of local and international visitors, the memories of those who had shared the intimacies of that cottage home. For it was here on the verandah her husband had committed suicide, influenced, she feared, by his reading (while she was overseas at a Peace Convention of her manuscript for the novel, *Intimate Strangers* (Prichard, 1937), in which a dispirited man leaves a suicide note to the wife he believes no longer wants to share his life. Also I, this house at 11 Old York Road, on the kitchen table she gave birth to her only son, Ric, who was to become a diplomat in foreign lands; and here, she withstood raid after raid by the Commonwealth Police seeking incriminating evidence of illicit political activities.

In this same small wooden house she breathed the last moments of her life and, respecting her last request, her ashes were scattered on the hill slopes of this place. The stories and poems that poured out of Katharine more often than not expressed her beloved connection with the landscape—her 1932 collection of poetry was entitled *The Earthlover*. The physical settings of those of her novels and stories which were not based in and around her Greenmount home (especially *Working Bullocks, Coonardoo* and the *Goldfields Trilogy*) do, however, reveal the same deeply felt attachment to the Australian natural environment which living for nearly fifty years in this locality had fostered in her. Whatever political and social doctrines she wove into her stories and whatever characters she brought to life in these narratives, she generally contextualised them in these Australian environments which influenced her so much. Perhaps it is not after all an accident that D.H. Lawrence, living in the same neighbourhood in 1922, was to develop the basis for his whole interpretation of the Australian environment on a fearful moonlight walk in the Western Australian forest:

> Richard Somers had never quite got over that glimpse of terror in the Westralian bush. Pure foolishness of course, but there's no telling where a foolishness may nip you. (Lawrence, 1922)

The vital identification of Red Burke, the hero of *Working Bullocks* (Prichard, 1926), with the karri country of the South-West rainforests, or the Aboriginal central character of *Coonardoo* (Prichard,1929), with the 'well in the shadows' in a creek-bed of the red country of the Pilbara are examples, set wider afield, of Katharine's own identification with what she believed was the essentially Australian character of the bush setting of her own Western Australian home in Greenmount. She prided herself on her Welsh heritage and perhaps some druidic collective memory had descended through her Celtic forbears!

Now to interrogate the basic question of whether Katharine was a woman of her time, or a woman for our time. In her first published novel, *The Pioneers*, she wove a somewhat romantic tale of a young wife, Norah Campbell, left alone on a pioneer property in Gippsland, south-eastern Victoria, and confronted by two desperate escaped convicts. Defying social conditioning and with some of the ingenuousness of Dickens's Pip in *Great Expectations*, Norah Campbell recognises that these men are redeemable and tries to help them in their plan for self-rehabilitation. Norah's faith in her convict escapees is borne out (one assumes) in the story when one of them returns years later with a young daughter and becomes the community schoolmaster. Optimism in a future for the downtrodden continues through the twists and turns of the plot of *The Pioneers* but is mixed with violence and tragedy which indeed had been comparatively recent characteristics of Australian colonial life. What Katharine Prichard was yet to consider deeply was that such violence and unhappiness was still a significant element in the lives of Aboriginal people and, though she eventually wrote passionately about this cause also, it must be acknowledged it still remains an unresolved issue for present-day Australian society and the subject of much of the finest writing of Australia's many contemporary indigenous authors.

Before she came to write her celebrated Aboriginal novel, *Coonardoo*, joint winner of *The Bulletin* newspaper's prize for an Australian novel in 1928, Katharine had other important causes to embody in short stories and the novel *Black Opals* and *Working Bullocks*. The second record of these, *Working Bullocks* (1926), and was the first which she set in the landscapes she had newly discovered in Western Australia as a result of her marriage to Hugo (Jim) Throssell, as previously mentioned. One of these landscapes was the WA rainforest.

On the back seat of her husband's motorcycle she first explored these unique rainforests of the south-west corner of Western Australia with their thriving sawmill towns cutting the karri and jarrah timber for export to India, east Asia and Britain. London street were often paved with jarrah hardwood blocks and many miles of Indian railroads rested on 'jarrah sleepers'. The wharves of countless of the world's ports were fashioned from this same giant eucalypt tree which Katharine saw being felled and hauled by bullock teams to the steam-driven sawmills of Manjimup and Pemberton. As a well-trained journalist, Katharine observed closely all facets of the industry, interviewed bosses, workers and families and made detailed records of the vernacular of the workers. But there was an added sharpness to her observation. She was now a 'card carrying' member of the new Australian Communist Party and anxious to note the interplay of social forces between the labouring classes who worked in the highly dangerous environment of the sawmills and the representatives of capitalism who owned the mills and the companies which sought to export the remains of the great forest trees, some more than 500 years old, for as great a profit to the shareholders as was possible. It is interesting that Prichard was criticised by her own party members because the one man in her novel who was capable of leading the workers into an organised opposition to the management could not persuade them it was time to do so. It was he, the proto-typical communist agitator, Mark Smith, who admits failure, and jeers at those destined to die or be maimed by the dangerous work.

> You look like men, but you're not. You're working bullocks. That's all you are. You'll go crawling back to work tomorrow when the whips are cracking. You'll let the boss do as he likes with you . . . smash you if he wants to . . .
>
> (WB, 247)

The author defended herself in a letter against all attempts to let her 'art' as she called it, become mere agit-prop:

> The indirect method, in my opinion should be the method of writers of fiction who use the novel or short stories to stir and convince their readers of real value in life. But in doing so, I believe that writers must remain faithful to their material, the stuff they present which must sway emotion and intelligence, not any preaching or obvious propaganda purpose. (Throssell, 158)

Her biographer son, Ric Throssell, records, "She could no more bring herself to invent a strike in the goldfields to give *Winged Seeds* a dramatic conclusion than she could ignore the historical truth of the abortive timber workers' strike in *Working Bullocks.*" (Throssell, 1975: 158)

Like many other Australian writers, Prichard held what we might call early conservationist attitudes toward the landscape, especially those which were exploited for timber-cutting. She would have met in Melbourne the immensely popular landscape painter, Arthur Streeton who was driven to such exasperation with the denuding of Victorian forests that he painted an imaginary landscape depicting the destruction of the forested Dandenongs, *Silvan Dam and Donna Buang, AD 2000.* In Katharine's novel, *Working Bullocks,* the early hero Red Burke, the bullock driver, is nearly destroyed by guilt when his co-worker is crushed by a huge karri log. Red takes refuge from the accident scene by walking blindly into the forest:

> He tramped through the wilderness of trees, miles on miles of them. Great bodies thronged, gleaming, in warm light beneath their high leafage . . . They looked like moss in the distance, a wan grey lichen, though each tree was a giant; there were trees beside which a man was the merest speck of living dust. (WB, 28)

Yet later when he glimpses a wild brumby stallion dominating its mob of mares and foals, his sudden admiration re-awakens his normal responses to the almost Arcadian forest landscape:

> He began to see lights in the forest, the luminous green of the budding saplings. A wild-fire passion of admiration, a lust for possession, took hold of him. (WB, 29)

Later in the novel the focus has shifted from the character of Red to Deb Colburn, a bush girl who becomes his bride, and she too is sensitised to the 'unspoilt' forest:

> Deb knew nothing of ancient philosophies but she had a sense of being close to the life about her, a knowledge of one-ness with it, profound and serene. She could not have put it into words; but the feeling hovered. The great trees with their power, the flame of their lives, the fate they were moving towards, she was akin to them; and to the earth, sombre and fecund, thrusting forests from her deep soil, holding them in the air through all the years. (WB, 312)

It would be easy to dismiss such writing as that of an author still in the first flush of a fulfilling marriage, with her new baby son, living on the fringe of a national park near Perth and overheated in the mind with recollections in tranquillity of a whole line of romantic writers she had sampled from the English and French Classics.

There are two reasons I don't want to do that. First, that we find in her next major novel, *Coonardoo*, a remarkable transition in the landscape setting that is the backdrop for a decidedly unhappy Australian story; and in the second place it invites contemporary revaluation in the light of much new writing about landscape in general and the Australian landscape in particular. For example, Simon Schama's interesting attempt at a history of Western conception of landscape in *Landscape and Memory* (1996), puts forward the view that modern environmentalism is a chapter in environmental history which rather than being a 'sad history' of self destruction is a potential starting point; "a way of looking, of rediscovering what we already know, but which somehow eludes our recognition and appreciation." (Schama, 1996) We might conclude that we have, in texts like *Working Bullocks*, amongst many other things, of course, is a way of looking at our environment which stands like an island in the stream of despoliation of landscape. That is, if Schama is to be believed. It could well be profitable to read, *Working Bullocks*, from such points of view as have been expressed on Australian landscape as those of Paul Carter, Kaye Schaffer, Josephine Flood, Brian Elliott or George Seddon. Better still would be the texts of Australian Aboriginal authors: Kim Scott, Alice Nannup, Sally Morgan or Kath Walker (Oogeroo Noonuccal).

Turning then, to *Coonardoo*, a novel of remarkable success since its publication in 1929 and still in print, still set for study in my course and still the subject of many post-graduate studies, particularly students from Australian Studies Centres overseas. I have read papers by students in Italy and in China, from my own university, and from persons-of-letters as diverse as Dame Mary Durack and Dr. Dale Spender. This critical industry began at least twenty years before Prichard's death and no doubt will continue for many a long academic year. But the point of interest is really the selection by Katharine of the hot, dry semi-desert landscapes of the Pilbara, a contrast of enormous degree with those lusher setting of *The Pioneers*, *The Wild Oats of Han* and *Working Bullocks*. She had set *Black Opals* in the equally dry Coober Pedy region of central Australia and perhaps her youthful experience of the 'backblocks' of NSW as a governess was extended by the much later research trip she took to a cattle station in the Pilbara, accompanied by her young son. She wanted to get to know at first hand the nature of life in this seemingly hostile country and the relationships existing between the original tribal Aborigines and the dispossessing white settlers. Actually, there are three other very important texts which Prichard wrote from this experience of the Pilbara. The award winning stories *The Cooboo* and *Happiness*, depict contrasting bleak and positive versions of aspects of Aborigine/White settler life on North-West cattle stations, just as the cycle of life related in *Coonardoo* has some good and some bad times. Yet in each, the intrusion of Europeans is the unsettling influence, forcing adjustments both to the way of life of indigenous people and to the landscape itself. Another prize-winning text, the remarkable play *Brumby Innes* (Prichard, 1929), although rarely performed, partly for technical reasons, partly because of the controversial and challenging content of the play, is in many ways a significant supplement to the side-issue in *Coonardoo*: the 'combo' or white man who has 'gone native' to the extent of turning from white culture to the indigenous, to establish a polygamous household but ultimately an exploitative one.

Coonardoo, as mentioned already, is subtitled 'The Well in the Shadow' and has been the subject of so much theorising that it is difficult for the contemporary reader to make a fresh start with the book. A very recent and interesting attempt was Cath Ellis's "A Tragic Convergence: A Reading of Katharine Susannah Prichard's *Coonardoo*" (*Westerly*, 1995) which looks at the novel from an Engelian point of view. Ellis argues that the book is an exposition of Engel's *The Origin of the Family, Private Property and the State*. Thus Miss Bessie protects 'her' black woman against Sam Geary because, according to the Engelian theory she has hybridised the original tribespeople into 'property' in her attempt to frustrate the 'tragic power of convergence which is beyond the scope of any of the characters, even the strongest, Miss Bessie, to escape. (Ellis, 1995: 71)

Other critics have reached out to Greek tragedy for convenient parallels to categorise *Coonardoo's* narrative structure and intent. It would be easy to misinterpret such an early 'sympathetic' portrait of an Aboriginal woman's 'fatal encounter' with white culture as merely another self fulfilling white prophecy of 'the dying race' as so often presented by the pre-Jindy-worobak writers such as

Mary Gilmore. But, like *The Cooboo* which Prichard explained was deliberately open-ended and not a simplistic depiction of the results of cattle station exploitation of Aboriginal labour, (Throssell, 103) the story of *Coonardoo* offers a rich texture of themes and relationships re-inforced by an authentically presented yet symbolic landscape quite outside of the Arcadian traditions of Western landscape concepts, but which the more southern Australian climes permitted Australian artists to go on using in visual or literary art works. It is to be expected that Katharine herself would have rejected the notion that she had invented Coonardoo, the black woman, as a comment on a white woman's then socially taboo psychological and sexual behaviours. Yet it is difficult to deny that in their grappling with the challenges of the desert life and the artificiality of the relations produced in the running of an isolated cattle station, the characters of both races and both sexes often merge and exchange personae with different critical readings of the book.

An interesting sidelight on the interpretation of *Coonardoo* was a video interview conducted a few years ago by some of my students and an Aboriginal lecturer from the Department of Aboriginal Studies at Edith Cowan University. Although sympathetic to the historical contribution to enlightenment about the problem of the cultural confrontations occurring in the early part of this century which Prichard had provided, the speaker, Jan Herring, expressed significant concerns about the artistic appropriation of Aboriginal culture which was inevitable in such a work. She also stressed that no amount of good-will and empathy on the part of an author, even of Prichard's undoubted ability and reputation, would overcome the impossibility of a credible representation of an Aboriginal character's point-of-view, or inner life, by a white author.

I conclude my investigation of the original question posed by this paper by a fleeting mention of some of Katharine Susannah Prichard's subsequent major works. *Haxby's Circus* (Prichard, 1930) was also a popular novel which took up the dual issues of the status of women as exemplified in the circus bareback rider, Gina, in the microcosmic tribal word of a company of circus performers, and the contemporary challenge of seeing beyond the disability of such victims of accidents as paraplegics. *Intimate Strang-*

ers (1939) is in some ways an extension of the study of human relationships in and out of marriage which Prichard had initiated in the 'special' setting of *Coonardoo*, but which was now transferred with perhaps unconscious irony, to the bourgeois suburban beach side environment familiar to the majority of Australians, whether Communist Party members or not. For some critics this novel was more satisfying than *Coonardoo* but the tragic circumstances of Katharine's husband's suicide, which, as noted previously, she thought might have been provoked by a reading of the manuscript while she was attending a convention in Moscow, caused her to re-write the ending. To some the result is less credible, less moving and opened the way to a disappointingly doctrinaire conclusion. Subsequently, when she set out to write a trilogy based around the goldmining industry in Western Australia covering some sixty years, the doctrinaire element again loomed large.

Nearly all critics do agree that the Goldfields Trilogy, *The Roaring Nineties* (1946), *Golden Mile* (1948) and *Winged Seed* (1950), begins strongly, contains much authentic material, but increasingly betrays the bony structure of Katharine's ideological principles. Yet it cannot be denied that the subject, the mining industry, not often the choice of Australia's leading novelists, is nevertheless today one of the most characteristic workplaces as well as the dominant source of Australia's income. But I was born in one of the gold-mining towns which feature in the trilogy, so I must declare my bias.

Katharine's final novel, completed when she was over 80 years of age and so paralysed by a stroke she had to learn to handwrite again, was a remarkable act of social confrontation in the 1960s in Australia. It drew upon two issues which were almost taboo subject: nuclear disarmament and drugs. Since the time when this final book, *Subtle Flame* (1967) was published, the first of these subjects became one of the most important rallying points of the post-modernist social revolution in the West. The second topic is very much a contemporary unresolved problem of continuing seriousness. The novel itself, written under enormous physical difficulty by a woman whose stubborn persistence was exemplified in her personal symbol of survival against the greatest odds—Daudet's parable of the mother goat defending her young against the wolves until dawn come. (Ferrier, 1992: 87) Nevertheless, during this time she maintained full contact with family, political comrades and the world-wide fellowship of writers who were her respected and respecting friends. Strangely enough, among those friends was the son of an immigrant Jewish family, one David Helfgott, a musical genius who came up to the Greenmount cottage to entertain her life-long passion for classical composers by playing the most elaborate piano pieces for her on the ailing ancient piano in her Greenmount home. In the 1996 film Shine, Katharine, in a somewhat freely interpreted depiction by the Director, lives in a home of mansion-like proportions transferred to the Adelaide Hills. Perhaps this had immortalised the old piano as well as David Helfgott.

The answer to my original question now seems quite easy to reach: Katharine Susannah Prichard was very much a woman of her time and equally a woman for our time.

WORKS CITED

Cath Ellis, "A Tragic Convergence: A Reading of Katharine Susannah Prichard's *Coonardoo*". *Westerly* (1995), vol. 40, no. 2.

Carole Ferrier, (ed) *Good as a Yarn with You* (Cambridge: Cambridge University Press, 1992).

D.H. Lawrence, *Kangaroo* (London: Heinemann, 1923).

K.S. Prichard, *The Pioneers* (London: Hodder and Stoughton, 1915).

______, *Working Bullocks* (London: Cape, 1926). Cited as WB.

______, *Coonardoo* (London: Cape, 1929).

______, *Haxby's Circus* (London: Cape, 1930).

______, *Intimate Strangers* (London: Cape, 1937).

______, *The Roaring Nineties* (London: Cape, 1946).

______, *Golden Miles* (London: Cape, 1948).

______, *Winged Seed* (London: Cape, 1950).

______, *Subtle Flame* (Sydney: Australasian Book Society, 1967).

S. Schama, *Landscape and Memory* (London: Fontana, 1996).

R. Throssell, *Wild Weeds and Wind Flowers* (Sydney: Angus and Robertson, 1975).

The Feminist Poetry of Australia: A New Creative Configuration

Subhas Chandra Saha
Silchar, Assam

The Australian experience may be defined as the human experience gained and gathered from within the perimeters of Australia as a country, and from within the context of the Australian culture that has evolved within the bounds of the history of the country. The expanding horizon of the Australian experience, thus defined, is mirrored in the graphics of a growing Australian literature.

The creative configurations of Australian literature are expanding with the passage of time. Where once no tradition existed, with the passage of time a tradition has evolved. But with the expansion of the horizon of the Australian experience in the context of the Australian culture, the creative configurations of Australian literature are not only built but rebuilt again and again in reflexive responses to the chain of reactions and revolt against the monoliths of Australian tradition. The traditional culture of Australia that developed through the span of two centuries betrays predominant traces of masculine hegemony through the concept and cultivation of historic mateship. But the creative configurations are shifting and acquiring new patterns under the impact of new ideologies and iconoclastic forces operating at multiple levels with the speed and momentum of the ever-changing cultural scenario within the country.

The masculine hegemony has been critiqued, questioned and deconstructed by women writers of Australia in successive years. Woman's voice was mute and almost nullified during the nineteenth century. But, however mute and nullified they might have been, the women's voices were nevertheless clear, if not loud. Hence an attempt to rewrite the history of Australian literature providing enough room for the writings of the neglected women writers of the past has been made in 1980s by feminist literary historians and critics like Dale Spender, Debra Adelaide, Lynn Spender, Susan Hampton and Kate Llewellyn, to mention only a handful of the many feminist writers of Australia.

In 1960s, '70s and '80s, the wave of feminism that effected a cultural reorientation throughout Europe and America also reached the shores of Australia. With the reprints of women's literary works, the rewriting of Australian literary history in perspective has become a critical inevitability. Within the short span of this paper, it is not possible to analyse in depth the whole gamut of this new creative configuration in Australian literature. I will take up for close comment the aspect of Australian women's poetry that has added a new dimension to the expanding horizon of the Australian literary perspective.

The need to develop a distinctive female identity within the larger framework of the social, cultural and literary configurations of Australia was felt time and again by the women who migrated, settled and grew in Australia. Ania Walwicz articulates this need in an interview:

> The woman has to establish an identity for herself other than the one she is offered. . . . I have to state my identity. I have to reconstruct the world. My writing deals with stress, chaos, and the need to express this and thus reconstruct my world, through the record of my personal experience. (*Mattoid* no. 13)

The paradox regarding the need to articulate the distinctive female identity within the verbal structure of Australian poetry has persisted since the first days of white settlement in Australia, but the country waited for two centuries before according any recognition to this extremely dynamic strand in the evolution of Australian literary culture. We will find from our analysis of the phenomenon in this paper that this distinctive strand in Australian poetic culture has lent Australian poetry new vigour and vivacity of an extraordinary kind. In addition, the Australian poetic idiom evolved by the women poets of Australia has not only made Australian poetry richer and more vibrant but also has served the purpose of voicing the agony of oppressed femininity in Australian culture.

Male mateship and masculine hegemony endowed Australian poetry with dry intellectualism and cultural dependency on the traditional verbal structures of British and American poetry. Whether in the poetry of Charles Harpur, Henry Kendall, Adam Lindsay Gordon, Banjo Paterson, Henry Lawson and Christopher Brennan or Kenneth Slessor, A.D. Hope and James McAuley, the echoes of Milton, Dryden, Pope or Mallarme are too obvious a resonance. Of course, it is not a phenomenon of direct imitation but a phenomenon of linkages between the male poets of Europe and Australia.

Against this robust echoing poetry of the male Australian poets, a new original mode of expression was developing through the poetry of the women poets. The women poets are subjective, and sometimes even hysterical. The straitjacket of heroic couplet or iambic pentameter were thrown overboard by the women poets as they found those configurations too limiting and inadequate for expressing their strong passions and for verbalising their aggression against the male dominance and oppression. Vicki Vidikas writes:

> Each moment, each experience is unique, as therefore each poem is. . . . If a poem is emotional, subjective, hysterical even, then chances are the form will be scattered over the page as randomly as the emotions which motivate it. I want a poetry of the spirit / of the body / of the emotions.
>
> (Viidikas, 1973: back cover)

The novelty in the verbal idiom and phrasal structures of the poetry composed by women poets originates to a large extent from their urge to break down shackles, and create a new sense of freedom. Subjectivity in this respect sometimes leads to hysterical expressions. Juliet Mitchell's comment is enlightening:

> Hysteria is the woman's simultaneous acceptance and refusal of the organization of sexuality under patriarchal capitalism.

> It is simultaneously what a woman can do, both to be feminine and to refuse femininity, within patriarchal discourse. Women poets of Australia have contributed this hysteric subjectivity both as theme and idiom to the creative configurations of expanding Australian experience. (Mitchell, 1984)

Hysterical subjectivity has widened the horizon of Australian poetry both in terms of themes and mode of expression. This has led the poetry to be, in the words of Jennifer Maiden, "ambivalent, ambidextrous, ambiguous, androgynous, amorous, ironic" (Maiden, 1977). Stylistically, the women poets exhibit a propensity towards "breaking the old forms, multiplying the meanings, inviting new juxtapositions" (Hampton and Llewellyn, 1986: 3), to project the world of their life against the background of the male representation and dominance in the evolution of Australian poetry.

The poetic idiom developed by poets like Harpur, Kendall, Gordon and their male followers appears dry and tame beside the poems composed by women in the nineteenth century. In 1887 Ada Cambridge (1844-1926) published anonymously the significantly titled volume of her poems, *The Unspoken Thoughts*, from London but she was forced to withdraw it from circulation as her unspoken thoughts might have jeopardised her clergyman husband's career. Her poems turn out to be subversive in the dominant context of the time of male-centred sexual decorum. Her poetry challenges the conservatism of orthodox male-dominated society. In her poem "Desire", she not only openly celebrates carnal desire but also ceremonially articulates her love for women in contrast to the accepted form of man-woman relationship:

> I kiss; I feast; but I am hungry still.
> O woman, woman, passionate but strong!
> True to thy love as needle to the pole—
> True to the truth, and not alone to me—
> O mate and friend, elusive in the throng,
> With thy clear brows, thy straight and upright soul,
> Nameless—unknown—my hunger is for thee.
>
> (Hampton and Llewellyn, 23)

All the poems in the volume *The Unspoken Thoughts* betray the poet's irresistible desire for woman's love:

> I feast; but I am hungry still,
> That only hungers for a woman's kiss
> And asks no life that is not one with hers.
> Not such hereafter an I wish to see;
> Not this pale hope my sinking soul exalts;
> I want no sexless angel—only thee,
> My human love, with all thy human faults.
> ("The Shadow", Bradstock and Wakeling, 1991: 96)

Is it not indicative of lesbian love? Lesbian love is the theme of many a poem by the women poets of Australia. They not only lend variety to the thematic content of Australian poetry but also evolve a new idiom for the expression of love.

The last poem in the volume entitled "An Answer" eloquently expresses Cambridge's vehement questioning of conventional wedlock:

> Thy love I am. Thy wife I cannot be,
> To wear the yoke of servitude—to take
> Strange, unknown fetters that I cannot break
> On soul and flesh that should be mine, and free.
> (Bradstock and Wakeling, 1991: 105)

The stringency of marital wedlock within the framework of the conventions of male-dominated society is doubted and disparaged by those women poets who have sought freedom from male domination through the love of women. Lesbia Harford (1891-1927) articulates this love of women in a forthright manner:

> If I should once kiss her,
> I would never rest
> Till I had lain hour long
> Pillowed on her breast.
>
> Lying so I'd tell her

Many of secret thing
God has whispered to me
Then my soul took wing.

Would that I were Sappho,
Greece my land, not this!
There the noblest women,
Then they loved, would kiss.
(Poem Untitled, Hampton and Llewellyn, 1986)

In the same volume, Harford makes woman's menstrual pain the theme of her poem 'Periodicity':

Meaning must lie,
Some beauty surely dwell
In the fierce depths and uttermost pits of hell. (p. 45)

Thus women poets extend the thematic range of Australian poetry by the inclusion of topics relating to women's intimate experiences.

Judith Wright (b.1915) delves deep into the psychic experiences of the expecting mother. She verbalises the mental state of the mother who experiences the movement of the embryo within her womb:

This is the strength that your arm knows,
the arc of flesh that is my breast,
the precise crystals of our eyes.
This is the blood's mild tree that grows
the intricate and folded rose.

This is the maker and the made;
this is the question and reply;
the blind head butting at the dark,
the blaze of light along the blade.
Oh hold me, for I am afraid.
(Wright, "Woman to Man", 29)

Helene Cixous writes about the woman writer's use of the language of the woman's body:

> Women must write through their bodies, they must invent the impregnable language that will wreck partitions, classes, and rhetorics, regulations and codes, they must submerge, cut through, get beyond the ultimate reserve—discourse. (Cixous, 1976: 256)

The French feminist's espousal of the language of the woman's body finds a poetic representation in the poetry by Australian women. This widens the boundaries of Australian poetic idiom. The language of masculine mateship is given a jolt: the Australian woman writes not only about her soul but also about her body in a new defiant linguistic configuration.

Gwen Harwood (b.1920) sheds all conventional squeamishness when she writes "Night Thoughts: Baby and Demon":

> Baby I'm sick. I need
> nursing. Give me your breast,
> My orifices bleed. I cannot sleep. My chest
> shakes like a window. Light
> guts me. My head's not right.
> Demon, we're old, old chap.
> Born under the same sign
> after some classic rape.
> Gemini. Yours is mine.
> Sickness and health. We'll share
> the end of this affair. (Hampton and Llewellyn, 96)

Woman's physiological items are put to poetic use: they acquire a novel subjective nuance, and make the Australian poetic idiom vibrant. The gender bias in Australian poetic style is thus liquidated by the women poets who incorporate woman's body language into the poetic syntax of Australia.

Dorothy Hewett (b.1923) transfigures Australian poetic idiom into a more comprehensive form. She states:

> In the last five years I've been working towards a plainer,

> more colloquial, clipped short line, a dramatic, uncluttered utterance . . . Behind it all is the sound of the human voice talking and the jagged inconsequential nature of thought . . . . I try to use myth and symbol interrelated with the tough and 'unpoetic' stuff of modern life. (Hampton and Llewellyn, 6)

Her poetry discards all inhibitions while portraying the cameos of woman's life:

> I have seen her, wonderful!
> A waterfall of hair, body like glass,
> Wading through the goldfish pools in winter,
> Her white shark-skin dress dark-wet above her thighs,
> The very shape and effigy of love: Or
> turbanned, earringed, lying on the lawn
> Among the clover burrs, her bangles clacking,
> reading Ern Malley.
> Oh! her nipples under her black lace bras
> And flimsy blouses . . .
> ("This Version of Love", Tranter and Mead, 121)

Hewett does not try to idolize love, rather she presents it at the earthy human level:

> Hands touch, eyes falter, tremble, fix and cling,
> the heart leans up, the blood beneath the skin
> tingles like frost, then all disguise is shed,
> until he husks me naked in my bed.
> ("You Gave Me Hyacinths First A Year Ago", Tranter and Mead, 122)

Gig Ryan (b.1956) invents a language that upsets the Australian masculine idiom: she shocks readers through her poetic style only to sharpen their awareness of woman's status in society. Both in her themes and style, she registers her revolt against male domination:

> She spreads her pale legs

> out across the table
> and the beer
> while he, the last car accident
> red and tight across his eyes,
> sucks her off, ungracefully.
> But is she happy? . . .
> She kisses the man, his mouth smells
> of another woman's cunt.
> But nothing gets to you.
>
> How well we cope.
>
> ("In the Purple Bar", Tranter and Mead, 1991: 438)

Ryan deals with male hegemony in a devastatingly sarcastic manner: she manufactures her style into a verbal hammer for shattering into pieces the male social and cultural shackles with utmost defiance. Man's domination over woman is lambasted with scathing effect.

Ryan creates a dynamic poetic idiom of protest and self-assertion establishing paramountly her identity as a woman who defies and challenges man's arrogance. The following lines are illustrative of her defiant style:

> I'd shoot the man who can't look me in the eye who stares at my boobs when we're talking who rips me off in the milk-bar and smiles his wet purple smile who comments on my clothes. I'm not a fucking painting that needs to be told what it looks like.
>
> ("If I Had a Gun", Tranter and Mead, 1991: 440)

Kate Llewellyn (b. 1940) treats her female physiology as a theme in her poem entitled 'Breasts':

> As I lean over to write
> one breast warm as a breast from the sun
> hangs over as if to read what I'm writing
> these breasts always want to know everything
> sometimes exploring the inside curve of my elbow

sometimes measuring a man's hand
lying still as a pond
until he cannot feel he is holding anything
but water
then he dreams he is floating
in the morning my breast is refreshed
and wants to know something new
although it is soft
it is also ambitious
we never speak
but I know my breast knows me more than I do
prying hanging over fences
observant as a neighbour
or eager as a woman wanting to gossip
they tell me nothing
but they say quite a lot about me
when I lie
these breasts spread like spilt milk
and standing naked in the sea
float like figs as you will realise
these are my body's curious fruit
wanting to know everything
always getting there first
strange as white beetroot
exotic as unicorns. (Hampton and Llewellyn, 1986: 158)

Llewellyn translates Cixous's theory about writing the body into poetic reality in Australia. She demonstrates the Australian woman's proclivity towards freedom of expression. She exemplifies in her poetry the defiant subversive style of articulation that the Australian woman adopts in order to project her mind that "will be free to write what it likes", to use Virginia Woolf's phrase.

Women poets of Australia have not only deconstructed the stereotype images of womanhood in male Australian poetry but also challenged the rhythmic and syntactic structures of Australian male poetry. Vicki Viidikas is an outstanding experimenter with poetic language as illustrated by the following extract from her poem "Going Down. With No Permanence":

> I'm finding it impossible to begin, as you've ended so little. Last night my heart was a cheap flag waving to the nearest mirror in sight. I couldn't believe anything, seeing you drive away into others' arms. I'm no sweet virgin sock-washer either. So it's a matter of priorities I guess, just who wants to gamble. Talk of loving when there is no goal. Of belief when there is no road. My shoes are off and I'm walking barefoot. Down a long avenue of arms and kisses like knots. I'm getting tired and angry and thinking hell, I'm no sock-washer but there must be some other venue. I say my heart's big enough, it is. Every time it's eaten and collapses like a cough. (Hampton and Llewellyn, 202)

Women poets of Australia have endowed Australian poetry with a new freedom from the stereotypes of the colonial cringe. Women's poetry in Australia is a post-colonial phenomenon both in theory and reality. It must, however, be admitted that even during the colonial period women's poetry appeared albeit under the disguise of male authorship. Still, it must be conceded that only during the later decades of the twentieth century, has Australian women's poetry made its appearance with open defiance and denial of colonial conservatism. And it gains in both momentum and recognition as the years pass by. Women's poetry has now become an effective instrument of social and political transformation leading to the gradual removal of the gender bias of the colonial period. It has opened a new chapter to record a new poetic document of Australia's movement towards gender equality in all walks of life, in an emancipated society with multicultural values.

It will be appropriate to conclude this brief paper with two quotations: one from the concluding lines of Pamela Brown's (b.1948) poem "The Dear John Letter":

> I would rather kick and shout
> than grieve like that (Hampton and Llewellyn, 207)

and another from Dale Spender's introduction to the *Penguin Anthology of Australian Women's Writing*:

> In any appraisal of the Australian continent, its people, its place, an appreciation of the writing of its women is essential.
> (Spender, xxxiii)

Hence we must conclude that the history of Australian poetry has to be rewritten not only to encompass but also to give proper recognition and position to this new creative configuration in women's poetry in Australia.

WORKS CITED

Margaret Bradstock and Louise Wakeling, *Battling the Orthodoxies: A Life of Ada Cambridge* (Ringwood: Penguin, 1991).

Helene Cixous, "The Laugh of Medusa" (1976), in *New French Feminisms*, ed. Elaine Marks and Isabelle de Courtivron (Brighton: Harvester Press, 1981).

Susan Hampton and Kate Llewellyn, ed., *The Penguin Book of Australian Women Poets* (Ringwood: Penguin, 1986).

Jennifer Maiden, "Questionnaires on Poetry", *Australian Literary Studies*, Vol. 8, no. 2, 1977.

Juliet Mitchell, *Women: The Longest Revolution* (London: Virago, 1984).

Dale Spender, ed., *The Penguin Anthology of Australian Women's Writing* (Ringwood: Penguin, 1988).

John Tranter and Philip Mead, eds., *The Penguin Book of Modern Australian Poetry* (Ringwood: Penguin, 1991).

Vicki Viidikas, *Condition Red* (St. Lucia: University of Queensland Press, 1973).

Ania Walwicz, *Mattoid*, No. 13.

Virginia Woolf, *A Room of One's Own* (London: Hogarth Press, 1929).

Judith Wright, *Collected Poems* (Sydney: Angus and Robertson, 1985).

'A' is for . . . ? Representations of Asia in the Poetry of Bruce Dawe

DENNIS HASKELL
University of Western Australia

Reviews of Bruce Dawe's work often begin by noting that he is Australia's "most popular poet","an ordinary bloke with a difference", (MacGregor, 1982: 19) the "sage of Sao biscuits". (Coleman, 1996: 20) A distinctively masculine voice and renowned as the most outstanding exponent of Australian vernacular amongst writers, it is hardly surprising that he is not known for his concern with Asia. Born in 1930, he is of the Australian generations that took little notice of Asia. By temperament not a traveller, to make matters worse, Dawe has lived for many years in Queensland, the most conservative of Australian states, in fact perilously close to Ipswich, home of Australia's most infamous fish and chips shop.

However, anyone who has had any contact with Dawe's work will know that he is a very independent thinker. His consideration of Asia in fact goes back many years, and it covers a number of different countries in the region. Dawe's poems concerned with Asia include rhymed poems, stanza forms and free verse; Dawe has also written poems not concerned with Asia in the Japanese forms of senryu and tanka, (*SG*, 1993: 189, 242) despite his feeling that "our more abstract alphabet" and "cultural and philosophical assumptions" put us "at a great disadvantage" compared with the Japanese and Chinese with their "ideographic" languages. The only well-known Dawe poems on Asia are "Homecoming" (*SG* 85), concerned with Vietnam, and "The Not-so-good Earth" (*SG* 62), concerned with the depiction of Chinese peasants in a television screening of the film *The Good Earth*, based on Pearl Buck's novel. In "The Not-so-good Earth" six hundred million peasants vanish "without a trace" from the family's consciousness when Dad trips over the electrical cord, dramatising the statement made by Dawe at a 1970 conference on the Arts and Communication: "Television could cause viewers to accept the sight of human suffering in the same way as they accepted commercial advertising—almost as a matter of course". (Rowbotham, FL Box 12) To the family the film is just a fiction about which "We never did find out how it finished up" rather than a representation linked to actual human suffering. This anti-Baudrillardian poem highlights Australian inattention and lack of compassion, two of the key themes of all Dawe's work.

Something similar is true of "'A' is for Asia", published in Dawe's second book, *A Need of Similar Name* (1965). White Australia has always been prone to depicting itself as young and innocent, as in "Advance Australia Fair" or the symbol of the boy from Manly. In "'A' is for Asia" Australian innocence, represented as a child at the beach, is castigated as synonymous with ignorance and sentimentality, an escape from facing up to responsibilities. The Asia allegorically depicted is one of nations collapsing, presumably politically or economically, and Australia is seen as unquestionably implicated in the region.

Dawe is best known as a poet of protest and social commentary, and he is no respecter of official authority. An unpublished poem written many years ago takes on R.G. Menzies, the longest serving Prime Minister of Australia, for his neglect of Asia:

> How to Win Friends
> Thinking it over—rather than resent
> The implications of the simple fact,
> You should look upon that lack of tact
> As a proportionate mercy, quite unmeant . . .
>
> Thus, brother Asians, you've small cause for tears
> That our globe-trotting leader should have never
> Got around to visiting one of you (weak or clever)
> —Not once, in sixteen years. (FL, Box 9)

Dismissal from Australian consciousness, not of a PM but of a representative Australian, is explicitly the subject-matter of another unknown Dawe poem, "After the Battle", published to the best of my knowledge only in the *Catholic Worker* in May 1967 (p. 374). It is a poem in two parts, "Peasant to Digger" and "Digger to Peasant", and clearly owes a great debt to Wilfred Owen's "Strange Meeting". In the first part the peasant asks the Australian soldier,

> . . . In which
> Place would you have me buried — in this rice
> Padi where in my life-time I died twice,
> Or in the muddy ditch of your own thought
> Where I did not exist until I fought
> My way to bloody consciousness? . . .
> ... I and thousands like me died to prove
> That we existed and were worth your love . . .

The dead digger observes that

> —A man seems suddenly smaller when he dies,
> Shrinks from the mythic target in the mind
> To something stranger, more like humankind . . .
> Our common fate unites us now, alone,
> Side by side, we know, as we are known.

"After the Battle" is one of many Dawe poems that emerged from the Vietnam War, "that long dishonoured honourable cause" as Dawe described it in the poem, "Vietnam Postscript, 1975" (*SG* 154). Dawe's interest in Vietnam goes back to the 1950s and the French colonial period, but his many poems on Vietnam all concern the war that incorporated American and Australian foreign policy. These poems include the ironies of B 52s and helicopter gunships "liberating endlessly" (*SG* 146) in the name of "democracy, / that aphrodisiac to the powers-that-be, / just beyond the next turn of the screw". To Dawe's mind the Vietnam War represents an anti-communist ideal that deteriorated into a matter of mere economics:

"the American presence became an ever-vaster emptiness, / became only the sour rain of money". (*SG* 154) "The Saigon-Dalat Night-train Runs Infrequently . . ." (*SG* 55) opens with the ironic declaration that "These things all happen in a world apart" but concludes with comfortable people in the west having to "raise a hand to brush the blood away." The link between Australia, America and Vietnam is concrete, intimate, undeniable.

Less well-known, partly because fewer in number, are Dawe's poems about political events in Tibet, Timor and China. In "A Party Official Considers Tiananmen Square" a member of the Chinese Government parentally dismisses the student protesters as "children" and refers to their murder as "a little chastisement" (*SG* 235), proving himself equal to the "squads of politicians" who in the Vietnam poem "The Gift of the Gods", ominously "advance / with the wreaths of their breath" (*SG* 146). Egocentricity and authoritarianism know no national or ethnic boundaries. In "Santa Cruz" Australia tries to maintain the sense of separation between Australia and Asia which "The Saigon-Dalat Night-train Runs Infrequently" denies, and pursues that *bête noire* of all *bête noires* in Dawe's poetry, allegiance to money. A sub-title tells us that the poem's concern is "*the Indonesian oppression of East Timor as seen from a southern continent*" and Dawe, characteristically, adopts the technique of speaking from the point of view of his opponents:

> In a small place
> what foreign soldiers do
> will not make headlines here
> for very long . . .
> trade casts out all fear
> and rights all wrong. (*SG* 247)

Dawe's sympathy for the politically oppressed of Asia in these poems is clear, and intrinsic to his statements is a "universal interest in other human beings" (St. John's College, Oration, FL Box 12) and an equal valuing of Asians and Australians as people. More controversial are Dawe's poems about Australian attitudes to the Japanese and about the increasingly strong influence of Asia on

Australia. The poems present a complex of attitudes but behind many of them is a belief that Australian governments are interested in Asia only because of money and will sell out history, pride and anything else in order to get it. When Emperor Hirohito died the Australian government debated whether senior members of the government should attend the funeral. Dawe wrote:

> It's *Sayonara* to our pride,
> And an end to memory
> —A government's love of the mighty yen
> Has crooked the official knee.
> ('On the Funeral of the Emperor Hirohito', 1989)

To Dawe, the government's consideration of displaying respect to the wartime emperor represented a betrayal of all those Australians who died fighting the Japanese in World War II, as well as a lack of "ongoing respect for the past", which he has said "is the necessary tribute we pay in the present". (FL Box 12) The same attitudes are expressed in the provocatively titled "All Aboard for Changi", (TSS 48) which disdains "the government policy of perpetual/ crouching" and whose speaker declares: "the rising sun/ that shone on digger hats can't hold a candle to/ the incandescent omnipotence of the yen". When in 1979, controversy erupted over a Japanese businessman's plans to develop a tourist resort at Yeppoon in Queensland, Dawe, envisioning Queensland as "Aussieland's first Shogunate", wrote a mock-prayer:

> Lord of the sacred money trees,
> Preserve us from your frown!
> Confer on us your tourist breeze,
> Breathe over our poor town
> The kamikaze of your cash. ('Circus Minimus' 1979: 14)

Lest these poems seem racist, it is worth noting other Dawe poems on Asia or on cash. In the same "Circus Minimus" series as the Yeppoon poem, Dawe criticised the then Prime Minister, Malcolm Fraser's proposals to encourage American investment ("Give us your Yankee dollars, your spare '*hoot*'") and to get tougher with

Vietnamese refugees "Fleeing the self-same Reds our diggers fought". ('Circus Minimus', 27) Compassion towards the Japanese is shown in "On the Shadow of a Japanese Child Blasted upon a Wall after the Dropping of an Atomic Bomb in 1945", which is spoken by her parents. In muted tones "this stencilled outline on the wall/ haunts us all with its unending play" (*SG* 233); the word "play" is charged with painful irony for the child is never allowed to grow away from that unworried state. In another poem, one that employs the potent symbol of bread, the basic food of most western societies, Japanese suffering at Hiroshima is equated with suffering at Dresden and Auschwitz:

> The bread I eat was broken at Hiroshima,
> In Dresden's monstrous furnace it was baked,
> The dough was ably kneaded at black Auschwitz
> Where flesh and blood was pounded into paste.
> ('Circus Minimus', 27)

Dawe has written explicitly anti-racist poems such as "Austral-Aryan": "He watches from his righteous bed the morning light take hold, / ... Red! Red! The very landscape seems in league against the whites." (NSN 39) Dawe has even written one poem which warns against easy accusations of racism, titled "Ornithology":

A "racist"
can be anyone
who dares to disagree
with you . . .

So what's the point
of trying to think
a single issue through
— when it's
more fun
to flap and screech
like a gang-gang cockatoo? (Sent to author, 1996)

It is true that Dawe would like to "slow down the process of the

Asianisation of Australia" but this is largely because the process has reflected "the infinite capacity of Australian politicians to adopt a swimming stroke you could call 'the Australian crawl'" (Author, personal interview: 15 July 1995) and the motivation of money values. In the poem "Asianisation" Dawe laments "our present eagerness to bow down before that land-mass with its vastly profitable islands and appendages/ as before some uncomplicated god". (Sent to author, 1995) The stance is at one with that expressed in the non-Asian poem, "The Return of the Magi", in which the Magi come back to find in the manger not Jesus but Santa Claus: "where once the love of God shone forth,/ now glowed the dollar-sign." (FL Box 10) It is this "blow-you-Jack principle" which enables human rights abuses in East Timor to be tolerated and which means that in Australia "too many people are being hopelessly crushed —small businesses, secondary industries, honest talents, people who set a value on their self-esteem which is not negotiable". (Against the Tide, FL Box 12) Dawe is also strongly against all forms of politically correct government manipulation and "salvation socially engineered". ('The New Race Vilification Law', *The Australian*, 1994) Ever alert to the hypocrisy of the powerful, Dawe does not hesitate to satirise Asian leaders as much as Australian. At an APEC meeting of regional leaders in Bogor:

> Javans [sic] struggling for a minimum wage
> and the right to strike are nowhere to be seen,
> nor are Timorese students' rowdy rage
> —like the hands of Pilate, all the streets are clean.
> ('The Apec Meeting at Noger', poem sent to author 1996)

The Christian simile remains powerful in this non-Christian context because of its imaginative yoking of unlike things and the sense that governmental manipulation has an awful universality.

While serving in the Air Force, Bruce Dawe was stationed at Butterworth Air Base in Malaysia for most of 1966 and there wrote a number of poems, some published and some not. At Butterworth he was "dismayed by the racism of Australian servicemen". (Personal response to author, also Goodwin, 1988: 61) In the poem "Butterworth Road" "Aussies" and "Poms" name all Malaysians

"'Noggies'", an "all-inclusive word/ Which spares us from the more absurd/ Necessity to think at all". The Malaysians are "not impressed" as the westerners' "buses pass/ Like magnified bugs beneath a glass" (*SG* 67). Dawe and his wife felt an Australian uncomfortableness about having servants, and he was horrified by other people's treatment of their *amahs*. One beautifully delicate poem portrays the *amahs* as "Smoke-people" who

> Flatter their big-nosed Masters,
>   Eat their meals alone,
> Efface themselves until they seem
>   Impersonal as bone. (*SG* 65)

The amahs are dehumanised into mere roles, but the total force of this attitude is only realised when you remember Vietnam poems such as "Revenants" and "After the Battle". It is the reduction of individual humans to undifferentiated "gooks, slants, slope-heads, dinks" ('Revenants' SG 199) that facilitates atrocities and their consequent "spider grief". ('Homecoming' SG 85) Racism is a serious topic on which many people are inclined to be self-righteous, so it seems worth noting the sense of fun involved in the, I think unpublished, poem "Malais-ia" about an Australian air-man who took a holiday in Thailand:

> Malais-ia
> a Butterworth incident
>
> A gluttonous fellow-airman, taking stock
> of his annual leave experience in Bangkok
> (where on high-spiced local tucker he had dined
> widely if not well), now chock-a-block
> with abdominal remorse, raised up his head
> and, remembering that country of the kind,
> paid tribute to them in a voice of dread:
> "Terrific people—and the *food*! But oh," he whined,
> "my God, the *constipation* . . . !"
>   "Ah," I said,
> "So that is what is meant by the Thais that bind!?"

Dawe's poems concerning Asia are all written from a western perspective, and cover western, especially Australian, attitudes to Asians. The values he brings to bear are those he brings to bear in his poetry generally. Dawe has said of himself, "Like most I suspect, I find myself by the light of other lives" and, more generally, "I hold all human life to be sacred, and *all* life to be *considered.*" As such, compassion is a prime value. While Dawe is sometimes seen to be a pessimistic poet, in one poem, "The Weak Sister", he insists on the durability of compassion: "Compassion, the sickly thing,/ will outlast them all". (*SG* 32) Compassion is an ongoing value. Dawe's goal in his poems dealing with Asia, as with his other poems, is that which he notes "Patrick White proposed for us in his Nobel Prize acceptance speech: that we should become a people possessed at last of understanding". Accompanying that value is an awareness that:

> Whatever is to be
> these things yet abide:
> tyranny, grief unseen,
> courage, blood, and flowers. ("Santa Cruz", *SG* 247)

Poems included in *Sometimes Gladness*, are referenced to their individual volumes or, in the case of poems never collected, to their place of original publication or their archival sources.

WORKS CITED

"Circus Minimus", *The National Times*, 7 July 1979.
John Coleman, *Australian Catholics*, Winter 1996.
Bruce Dawe, *An Eye for a Tooth* (Melbourne: Cheshire, 1968). Cited as ET.
______, *Sometimes Gladness: Collected Poems 1954-1992* (Melbourne: Longman Cheshire, 1993). Cited as SG.
______, *This Side of Silence: Poems 1987-1990* (Melbourne: Longman Cheshire, 1990). Cited as TSS.
______, *A Need of Similar Name*. Cited as NSN.

FL, Box 9, "A Leavened Bread", written for Verve, a literary magazine at the University of Adelaide.

FL, Box 12, "Against the Tide", written for *Social Alternatives in the 1980s*.

FL, Box 12, Notes for a creative writing class.

FL, Box 12, "Other People's Lives", The 1984 St. John's College Oration, delivered 4 October 1984.

Fryer Library archive, University of Queensland, Box 8. The Fryer Library archive is hereafter cited as FL.

Letter to Gary Maller, 1 December 1988.

Craig McGregor, "Australia's Most Popular Poet", *The National Times*, 4 September 1982, p. 19.

"On the Funeral of the Emperor Hirohito", published *Sydney Morning Herald*, 25 February 1989.

David Rowbotham report on a conference at the University of New England, FL, Box 12.

Heroic Inventions: Christopher J. Koch's *Highways to a War* and Australian Fiction

ADRIAN MITCHELL
University of Sydney, Australia

There have been a number of memorable acceptance speeches on the evening of the Miles Franklin Award. Some I recall more clearly than others, and sometimes I recall more particularly the effect: for example, a wry and witty speech from Alex Miller, who had been writing for a lifetime and had not until then ever had any recognition. Everyone was delighted for him to have his moment; but then he went on and on and on again, and the universal pleasure, I have to admit, dispersed. Besides, those gathered together for the occasion had entertaining things of their own to say to each other, and wit does not wait. Then there was that speech by what's her name, absolutely unconscionable as it turned out, claiming the award for multi-cultural writing. Well that is how she saw it at the time.

So when Christopher Koch fired off his salvo last year, he was standing in the middle of a well-established site of contestation, the literary equivalent of one of those ancient Aztec ball-courts, and where the outcome was likely to be just as bloody. It is still not exactly clear why he chose that evening to make his stand. He had already had one substantial tilt at the practitioners of modern critical theory when he gave the Blaiklock Memorial Lecture some five or six years ago—contrary to custom, this was never published in *Southerly*. There is no doubt that he feels strongly about matters of critical fashion, and likewise that he felt it important to make his point on an important public occasion; but it is not as though he had a speech lying around either in his drawer or in his mind, just in case that should come in handy. The prize winners have at most 48 hours' notice to gather their thoughts and their toothbrush and head for Sydney and the media. And that year, last year, the media were already revved up, much more so than on previous occasions, circling like sharks as feeding time approached, creating the buzz ahead of time as the press in particular is wont to do. In other words, context was already determining significance, and the text—his text—was as far as the media were concerned, irrelevant. And no doubt if you had spent some years putting together a substantial novel, it is highly probable in those circumstances that you could feel, well, nettled. It would confirm your darkest suspicions about the self-importance of the popular opinion-makers, but this was also a classic example of the altered state of things, the re-alignment of values and priorities.

It seems to me that what Koch particularly adheres to is a standing, enduring set of values, indeed to a concept of value itself towards which each writer and each text aspires, as though that can exist independently in some domain beyond the text. There is no relativity about this. Good is good, bad is bad, beauty is beauty and occasionally truth. These are by his lights universal principles. He is however not really talking about metaphysics, and he is not being a neo-Platonist, though no doubt aspects of these apply. At the time of writing this paper I was also busy writing a piece on Christopher Koch for *Australian Literary Studies*, for which Laurie Hergenhan asked me to do an interview as well. In that interview, Koch spoke of "permanent artistic worth", the sort of proposition that could reduce many, and possibly some here today, to nervous disorder. He spoke of the mystery, the beauty and the real worth of great artistic achievement, and especially of the mystery of a great work of art.

As you might expect from someone not only endorsing those values, but attempting them himself in his own writing, he has very little time for mere popularist literature, especially grunge literature: his objection to that is not prudish but a reaction to the facile vulgarity of it, and more importantly its manifest nihilism. That is a literature without standards, and furthermore it decries, belittles, standards of value. It is a puerile, cheaply sensationalist literature, it despoils the mystery inherent in personality, in life, in things. It is certainly not high culture, not a literature you can, or even are meant to love. I haven't been using Koch's own words here but I believe I have summarised the line of his thinking accurately enough.

All great literature, he would maintain, is informed by passionate feeling, and you cannot get passionate feeling without passionate adherence to values. When Dostoevsky proposed in *The Possessed* that there are no values, he was expressing a form of value in itself, whereas the nihilists who maintain that there is no particular value in anything, that everyone determines their own set of values, are doing something quite different. At the very least theirs is an extremely trivial and minor art form: for to repeat his axiom, you cannot have major art from nihilistic values. And similarly with the critical theory which underwrites it. Postmodernists, poststructuralists, any kind of -ists, are in his view people who do not love literature, have no passionate attachment to it because they do not believe in it; they cannot recognise and therefore appreciate the *mystery*. Two things to say here, in passing, to those who feel challenged, even intellectually challenged, by his line of argument: first, while he feels called to air his views, the important consideration is their relation to his own practice; and second, to deny him his position is to invoke notions like the thought police and critico-political correctness. Koch isn't debating specific aspects of modern theoretical positions—I doubt whether he would be interested. He is examining what he sees as the underlying impetus; that is what he works with best, and what he objects to is consistent with what he affirms; by which clumsy phrase I mean his position is self-consistent. He does maintain a position.

So it seems to me that those who were hissing in the back row at the Miles Franklin Award presentation, and those who have conducted their hissing more up front, in the columns of the papers and journals, have largely missed the point. They epitomise for him precisely the absence of the imaginative, and that's too bad. His criticism is not of those persons, or of the values they do or do not hold—though clearly such persons are not for him on the side of the angels. Rather, they are accessories to a larger historical current, a large and, for him, murky cultural movement; they are insignificant in themselves.

Much the same criticism emerged in a review he wrote recently, where in commenting on two biographies of Lewis Carroll, he regretted the miscue of the authors, two literary academics who, typically in his view, had embedded their books "in the social, never in the imaginative—so that those who go to them for an insight into the genius that produced the Alice books will be disappointed . . . " To understand the nature of magic in that kind of writing, he goes on—citing an older and in his view more honourable kind of academic critic—one has to look at the style. Writing in *The Australian Review of Books*, Koch describes how everything in Carroll happens with deceptive speed, and in much the same easy, insinuating way as our dreams bring us truths from the *autre monde*, (and he went on to applaud Carroll's mastery of "the utterable sentence" (October 1996). You see the distance between these kinds of interest and that which he summarises as "sociologically based". That kind of criticism has nothing to offer him or any other serious writer. What he wants from criticism is an insight into the creative genius of the accomplished writer. He can make nothing of unhelpful and unappreciative criticism as he hears it. More than that, its effect is blighting. And if the criticism is debilitating for writers and sensitive and appreciative readers, then the question that is left is—who is it good for? So far, the only acid answer he has allowed is that it may be good for the career of those who write it.

I don't wish here to pursue the polemical side of these reflections. I'm more interested in the other set of echoes. There's the question of style itself, and his own mastery of the deceptively easy style—the Graham Greene style perhaps, but in his case a vehicle to permit access to the truths from the *autre monde*, the Otherworld. And that is so as to discover the magic, or in his preferred term, the mystery, which lies available at the heart of our experience. It is a mystery he finds in many ways and in many places—in the personality of his protagonists, in the places they come from and the places they seek, in the actions they undertake. And that mystery is also a zone or site of persisting and potentially disturbing values.

For example, in his volume of essays *Crossing the Gap* (1987), he wrote in various passages of the essential mystery in the landscape of Tasmania—and that is also written throughout *The Boys in the Island, The Doubleman* and the early section of *Highways to a War*, and no doubt it will form a considerable part of the imaginative fabric of his forthcoming novel, the 'prequel' to *Highways*, to be called *Out of Ireland*. It is a particular application of a larger principle, that there is in fact an essential quality, an "essence", in landscape and climate that affects and to some extent shapes us all, and artists in particular. That is apparently for him more than a figure of speech. And it is worth noting how he lays down this premise. There is something other than ourselves which determines how we are—and it is not sociology. It is another force altogether, some kind of drive from or toward the *autre monde*, the world beside, adjacent to, possibly within this one. Each of his novels taps into this other—the longing for and certainty of a 'yonder' in *The Boys in the Island*, the realisation of potent Hindu mythological types in *Across the Sea Wall*, the convergence of recent political history and ancient cosmic mythology in *The Year of Living Dangerously*, the unhealthy proximity in *The Doubleman* of the Otherworld and the temptation to surrender the individual will through drugs, pop cults of one kind or another and other acts of occasional conformity posturing as radical challenge—not to mention the exotic mishmash of New Age arcana, of gnostic, folk and faery lore. In *Highways to a War* he locates this Other in ancient Cambodia, the country sealed off from time, and where once was a kingdom stretching all the way to Malaya. It is for Mike Langford, the hero of the novel, an enchanted land, persisting on the edge of a precipice, and for much of the novel's action it lies outside all the other forces that are in play just as was the case in the unfolding of the Indochinese political scene.

Now it has to be noted that it is Mike Langford who romanticises Cambodia, and another character, the journalist Harvey Drummond, who interprets that romanticism. It would be much too simplistic to propose that Koch himself is flying in the face of say Said's Orientalism here. What we can say, what we can find in the sequence of his novels is the opportunity taken to locate a substantial set of values in some schema outside the characters themselves, in the Hindu pantheon, the *wayang kulit* puppet plays and behind that the *Ramayana*; in an enduring half-awareness of faery lore, even in what from a Tasmanian point of view the Australian mainland must know and have. In his most recent novel one can find any number of examples; a useful example is Mike Langford's perception of old Singapore. He comments on the little roadside stalls that they stir "memories from another existence: a life of medieval simplicity, always known about, yet forgotten until now" (68). The allure of Singapore, his point of entry into old colonial Asia, is not the particular fact of its residual medievalism; nor is it that because he has as a young man heard so many stories about it that it has for him a "private and occult meaning". Its significance lies close to the edge of the inexpressible: here Mike enters into a place characterised by curious hybridity, blurring the known and established categorical distinctions, and tantalising because it promises access to old and ancient ways and yet is itself undergoing change, entering into the race with time. Koch is not unique nor hopelessly traditional in this; Gaston Bachelard is another to propose comparably that "Only those scenes that have already appeared in dreams can be viewed with aesthetic passion."

Mike's role as war photographer in some sense replicates this curious circumstance, in that he must report on what is most up to date from the war zone, yet his photographs freeze time and action. For him, what is inside the lens is most real. The corollary is that while he is looking through his camera lens (update of Lewis Carroll), it is as though only the imaged object exists; and he has to learn early that just because as agent he is out of the picture, he is not invulnerable to Viet Cong bullets. In Singapore, his romantic fascination with the new order of reality comes at a personal cost. He falls seriously ill: his feverish hallucinations as it were act out for him some transition, serve as a rite de passage. And you begin to see what is happening here. Koch has already warned us in *The Doubleman* that these encounters with the Other come at personal cost, that they are dangerous; and that was also the point of *Across the Sea Wall*. What the hero does if he is lucky is to go home, knowing now where his proper place is and what its value is. Mike Langford chooses to step over the threshold, over the border; and there can be no return. It's like a grim rewriting of *Lord Jim*. Asia represents some kind of Other to the Westerner, but that otherness is very often to be measured in terms of time—

for Asia endures something now forgotten by the West, something once known and now lost. And if *Highways to a War* carries a single moral motto, it is that you always lose the thing you love.

Furthermore, it's curious that the hero keeps on disappearing, to appear instead as the invention of the subordinate characters. The novel is *about* Mike, but he escapes the centre. If as some have claimed this is a conventional novel, then the hero is unconventional—though as I shall suggest, recognisably Australian in this. If he is a version of the warrior hero, he is unarmed; and in classical terms, the unarmed, or disarmed hero ceases to be agon, protagonist or antagonist. He becomes a hero in waiting, a hero waiting to be made; and that invention is by others. It's a bit like waiting for Achilles, for so long the do-nothing hero; in the meantime everyone keeps him as it were alive by talking about him. And this absence of centrality or active involvement in one's own narrative is a persistent feature in Australian fiction—a hero at a remove, not displaced but unselfregarding, perhaps unaware.

That throwaway reference to Conrad is apt, for it is Koch's practice to enclose the action in a set of narrative or situational frameworks—the story is 'told' in some form or other through a variety of intermediaries: through mythic reference, the puppet show, various narrators. Here an amateur historian, Ray Barton, patches together the testimony of people he interviews as well as notes from the hero's audiotapes. And those he interviews each have a slightly different orientation, so that Marlow-like, Ray offers a best-fit account of the mystery of Langford's character. In fact he tells two different stories, or the one story from two different orientations: the history of Mike Langford, and the estimation of Mike Langford by his colleagues. In so doing, I would like to argue, Koch has re-inscribed certain recurrent features of Australian fiction. Mike Langford is the very type of the Australian hero, a country boy, good-looking, tallish, a natural athlete, immediately likable. A generation ago he looked like My Brother Jack; and interestingly, it's agreed that both of them are also a bit boring, as well as a bit secretive (quintessentially Australian?). The details of the type are only of incidental interest, however; to me it is the resort to a type inside a novel careful in point of constructed detail, true to matters of fact, that becomes interesting. Koch had done the same thing with his hero in *The Year of Living Dangerously*, and to a lesser extent with Brian Brady, the alternate hero inside Richard Miller's story in *The Doubleman*. If it is a point of professional pride with Koch to get the details right, why then this recourse to a standard figure?

Again I suggest it reflects an interest in that which is permanent or recurrent, pre-existing; and one possible source for this interest is hinted at in an essay in *Crossing the Gap*, where Koch acknowledges he was particularly influenced in his preparation for writing *Across the Sea Wall* by his reading of Heinrich Zimmer—whose ideas we might more familiarly recognise in the work of Zimmer's protege, Joseph Campbell. What they contribute is a consideration of how myth works, what kind of truths it reveals; and specifically here how figures such as the hero (with a thousand faces more or less) represent available truths for those who consider the stories, not for what is revealed about the psychology of the figure—the hero—himself or herself. They encourage the use of large propositions, talking confidently about Eastern and Western myth, proposing for example that Western mythology masks its true Eastern nature, etc. This is commentary on such a vast scale that most of us would, I imagine, feel very uncomfortable about taking it up. Yet it is the kind of universalist reach that you can find informing aspects of Koch's novels. They are not meant to be taken as prescriptive, they are instead the digest of observed tendencies; and at times they lead into the arcane, into mysteries.

Certain assumptions follow from such an approach. One is that all mankind is pretty much the same, and constant in its make-up. Whereas functionalists like Malinowski read mankind not as a species but as infinitely variable, the Zimmer/Campbell school are more like essentialists. They do something different, they reach after a kind of residual knowledge encoded in myth, rather than reading the anthropology (and sociology?) of different groups of people. Their goal is a higher unity, not diversity; and that is what Campbell for example sees as the end of all myths, that kind of reconciliation and attainment. Myths symbolise for us both metaphysical and psychological truths; and to me that kind of reading argues a notion of permanent truth or value, for myths repeat recognisable patterns.

I do not propose to summarise Joseph Campbell's theories for you—you can read the very useful digest by Robert A. Segal [*Joseph Campbell: An Introduction*, Garland 1987] if you are interested. But their application to the work of Christopher Koch is arresting. Chief among these is his version of the hero. All hero myths are the same, according to Campbell; and the true subject of the hero myths is the mind. There are recurrent features—for example the separation from the father/begetter (and keep in mind that the hero in our case is an Australian hero). There is rescue and nurture from the natural world and from commoners, among which and whom the hero spends his formative years; then comes the occasion of proving the self, in adventures and contests. For Campbell the myth is completed by the triumph of the hero, the return home, the freeing of his mother, the founding of new cities and death while still young. Patently, not all of that applies in Koch's novel, but the first part does. There is an available ur-pattern in which the meaning of the hero is revealed, his mystery discovered. In modern narrative terms, there is a story within the story; in Koch's instance, there is the originating question—what was it about Neil Davis, Tim Page, Sean Flynn, the acknowledged models for Mike Langford, that made them so attractive, and established them as legends in their own time? What was the basis of their allure, their glamour? How were they invented into heroes? The significant point is that by definition, they come to mean more than themselves; and so Koch's hero must undergo an apotheosis. Yet being a—the—good Aussie bloke, he has to be guarded against too much elevation. That is part of the necessary image.

But further than this, Koch's strategy is, wherever it becomes possible for him to hint at the traditional patterns of the heroic quest, both to achieve this necessary 'heroic' significance, this meaning beyond the self, and to inscribe in yet another way the connection with pre-existing meaning. In plain terms, there are both archetypal resonances and narrative echoes; and there are echoes within the narrative structure that he has invented too, so that his story discovers as well as creates its own archetypes. Think for example of the sequence of love affairs, all of them disappointed, all confirming the pattern that you lose what you love. But think also of the matter of the narrative, a large ranging narrative of love and war, and a warrior-hero; this is the matter of epic, and the taking up of arms for love, and the laying down of the self. At the heart of the war, when Mike and his friends are prisoners of the North Vietnamese, and they are all eating from the common pot—a charged image Les Murray would no doubt endorse—Mike sets out his own astonishingly simple, astonishingly important philosophy: "I think we have to care for one another." When war comes down to individual cases, as ultimately it must, there seem to be no grounds for it. What is at issue is ideology, points of view and beliefs held to the extremes of fanaticism. The ideologues are the villains, whether the soldier nick-named Lenin, or the tired old spymaster left over from the cold war, and who for petty vanity is responsible ultimately for Mike's betrayal.

If we were to entertain for a moment the hint of epic then it is immediately apparent that Mike is not the customary epic hero. He resists that kind of elevation. If one can speak of the matter of Australia as one speaks of the matter of Troy or the matter of Britain, then the evidence suggests that Koch is quite right in this: we like absolutely ordinary heroes. The large scale Australian novels have all done this: Patrick White's Stan Parker is another epic of the ordinary man, Ted Tice the hero in the wings of Shirley Hazzard's *Transit of Venus*; Henry Handel Richardson's provincial heroes, Christina Stead's—we distrust the grand gestures.

Yet there *is* elevation in this novel too, but it comes from the testimony of the friends. They keep coming back to Mike's allure, his charm, his magnetism, his *essential mystery*. Maybe Mike has been crucified—there's an elevation of a kind. It takes place by report though, it has not been witnessed as other events have been witnessed; and that also means Koch hasn't to confront the embarrassment of having his hero get down off a jacaranda tree. Mike carrying his weakened friend into the safety of the jungle is performing a huge and moving action, profoundly caring and disturbing as the Deposition or as Lear. These resonances don't strike you as literary artifice; they are natural to what Mike is doing. But they are resonant with comparable actions; they loom large in their own right, and they endorse the continuity of deep human concern. One of the characters remarks that it was Mike's gift that he made each person feel he cared for them individually. I stop short of saying this is Christ-like; but you might recall Campbell's summary and see how that also includes the Christian story.

There is a key passage in the novel, where the journalist Harvey Drummond tries to articulate what that mystery in Mike Langford was. He concentrates on the kind of beauty that could express itself in Mike's face—"It was a face that tended to change a lot. . . He could appear plain or good looking; tough or sensitive: sensitive to the point of being feminine." (HTW 179-80) Mike carries the extraordinary within his ordinariness; he carries a sense of *exemption* which lets those who look on him forget about mortality for a while—and in war zones there is a fearful lot of mortality. And Harvey makes a bunch of interesting propositions about this kind of face: it is associated with youth, as Mike is throughout the novel, until he abandons his professional neutrality at the end, and takes up arms—and then his face grows sterner, traces of tiredness and time appear. Until then, he has been untouched: and that was one mark of his distinction. Second, his face was both tough and sensitive, masculine and feminine—and one can think of a number of the Arthurian knights for whom this also was true, or even of classical heroes. Koch found confirmation of his own intuition in Camille Paglia's *Sexual Personae* where she writes of the persistent recurrence in great literature of the Beautiful Boy, Apollonian beyond nature, and asexual, impossibly if not intolerably perfect.

The hero then is constructed by how others read him. The Australian hero has to keep his connection with his fellows, he cannot afford to become remote from them. The problem for the writer is how to contrive the revelation of that special status. And here it is interesting to compare what Koch has done with what happens in some other Australian novels. I mentioned in passing George Johnston's *My Brother Jack*: Johnston contrived a division of the central figure, into the mythic and the revised version. It worked admirably. Another manoeuvre is epitomised in Paterson's Saltbush Bill, who calculates defeat to achieve a greater good. In Walter Scott heroism is not the only option available, and it is of interest to note how frequently it is the case in Australian fiction that a narrator or central figure is unaware that he/she is the real centre of interest. This can be seen as early as in *Robbery Under Arms*, where it never occurs to Dick Marston tha he is the hero of his own story. He assumes that Starlight is the hero. That is only true if you fail to recognise there can be a colonial hero. A comparable circumstance emerges in Catherine Helen Spence's *Clara Morrison*, and arguably in a good many women's novels, where it is assumed that the centre of attention is of course going to be a man. Tom Collins is no other than the first inversion that proves the premise. It's a configuration that begins early in our writing and possibly in our culture and continues—think of Martin Boyd's travesty of himself, Guy Langton; think of David Malouf's *Johnno*, or *The Great World*; think of just about any fiction and even of the non-fiction: Sally Morgan's *My Place* and Bert Facey's *A Fortunate Life*, for example. The participating narrator is of an interest to us that he or she does not appear to recognise. If it is "recognised" then that narrator is very likely to get in our way. With us, obliqueness is ingrained—so that of course there is a habit of irony.

What in an Australian narrative makes a hero? In his own way Koch has been exploring this curious aspect of our story-telling in each of his books. Each of his major protagonists is in some way limited, and this is so persistent a pattern it has to be by his design. In *Highways to a War* he modifies the Campbell prescription: his hero fails to return. That's of interest: if heroic narrative is of a realm where the hero takes a step beyond the necessary (can there be a minimalist hero? can there be military intelligence, civil service and standard deviation, I ask myself), then what if the hero fails to return? Is this the failure of the over-reacher? *Voss* as absurd epic? What happens in such cases to the grand heroic gesture? Yet the Mike Langford who exists as the object of attention, and invested belief, in the narratives of all those participating narrators does return, as a story. He is *their* heroic invention. And that means we have the story within the story, and each is defined by access to a set of determining values outside the frame of the sustaining narrative itself.

Koch's narrative structure is much more complex and subtle than I think has been recognised; and it is little wonder that he has shown himself vexed by those who, in his view, cannot use their critical predispositions to read what he has put in front of them. It has to be irresistibly tempting for him to say that critical ideology, as he sees it, has obscured the tale. And yet it is equally irresistible to find in his narrative enticements to the sorts of questions that engage the interest of contemporary critical practice: questions about alterity and hybridity, about the heightening awareness of the Other, however this is represented; about the problematic nature of the hero and the persistent practice in Australian writing of decentering that hero; and so on. So, as is nearly always the case at the end of these condensed conference papers, there is plenty more left to say.

WORKS CITED

Rolf Boldrewood, *Robbery Under Arms* (London: Macmillan, 1937).
Joseph Campbell, *The Hero with a Thousand Faces* (Cleveland: World Publ. Corp., 1956).
Joseph Conrad, *Lord Jim* (London: J.M. Dent, 1935).
Albert Facey, *A Fortunate Life* (Perth: Fremantle Arts Centre Press, 1987).
George Johnston, *My Brother Jack* (London: Collins, 1964).
Christopher Koch, *Across the Sea Wall* (London: Heinemann, 1965).
______, *The Boys in the Island* (London: Hamish Hamilton, 1958).
______, *The Doubleman* (Pymble NSW: Angus and Robertson, 1985).
______, *The Year of Living Dangerously* (Sydney: T. Nelson, 1979).
______, *Crossing the Gap* (Pymble NSW: Angus and Robertson, 1993).
______, *Highways to a War* (Melbourne: Heinemann, 1995). Cited as HTW.
Sally Morgan, *My Place* (Perth: Fremantle Arts Centre Press, 1987).
Alex Miller, *The Ancestor Game* (Ringwood, Vic.: Penguin, 1992).

The Expanding Australian Experience: The Hindu Doctrine of Transmigration of Souls in Rodney Hall's *The Law of Karma: A Progression of Poems*

K. RADHA
University of Kerala

Rodney Hall, born in England in 1935, came to Australia after the Second World War. He is now a well-known novelist, poet, editor, critic, biographer and non-fiction writer.

In his poetical works Hall used a different kind of art which he calls a "progression of poems," a sequence of short poems on a single theme. Hall published *The Law of Karma: A Progression of Poems* in 1968. The author in his note says that the Law of Karma is the Hindu doctrine of the transmigration of souls. He adds:

> In outline, it teaches that each life is rewarded, or punished, in the next. An evil life leads to rebirth as an inferior person or animal and sets back the progress of the soul. The ultimate aim of every good man is to escape this cycle, to become a saint who, after living righteously, may be received into the Divine Essence. (n.p.)

However, Hall remarks that in his progression of poems a variant on the Law of Karma is presented: without ever becoming animal the original soul degenerates by one stage of dehumanisation.

The long poem is based upon the Hindu doctrine of transmigratory souls and follows five hundred years of violent betrayal in several different countries before culminating with the World War II horrors at the Auschwitz death camp. At the centre is a holy man of India who despite all his faith in God and his philosophy, looks down upon the people around him. Like Scobie in Graham Greene's *Heart of the Matter* he is privileged to see his fellow men "with pity." He tells his admirers that before long he will ultimately be accepted into the Paradise of Fathers and that for such a life of dedication the Gods will grant "a time of rapture" and that they will take him to the moon, "from there through all the emptiness beyond." When people ask the holy man, "What of your body, Master?" he replies, "By then I'll be no more substantial. . ." (4). He goes from village to village and everywhere he is treated like a saint. At the age of 83, the saint "achieved his final pilgrimage" and became "a holy shrine himself," which many pilgrims visit. The time for his death comes but his favourite, i.e. God, says:

> You've played the part of God, brave
> with promising yourself divine reprieve,
> but you rejected people—such a sin
> the Law of Karma punishes by birth again. (8)

In the words of the *Chandogya Upanishad,* "Those whose conduct has been good will attain good birth; but those whose conduct is evil will verily attain evil birth." (Prabhavananda, 1957:89) Not Karma, mere action but Karma Yoga, union with God through action, is the essence of the teaching of the *Gita* on this score.

The holy man dies in fear. This is the gist of the first part, "The Exposition: Holy Man 1344-1435 India." By the poem's end the soul has reached Auschwitz (1944). The 500 years' fall from Hindu grace takes the soul from India to Persia, then to Turkey, Malta, Venice, Trieste, Austria, Moscow, Guinea, France and finally to Poland.

The word *Karma* is derived from the Sanskrit *Kri,* "to do." According to Swami Vivekananda:

> Our Karma determines what we deserve and what we can as-

> similate. We are responsible for what we are; and whatever we wish ourselves to be, we have the power to make ourselves. If what we are now has been the result of our own past actions, it certainly follows that whatever we wish to be in future can be produced by our present actions, so we have to know how to act. (Vivekananda, 1989: 31)

Rodney Hall visited India years ago and for him Cochin in Kerala was one of the world's great intersections. *The Law of Karma* is a result of his travels in India and his knowledge of Hindu and Buddhist teaching about the transmigration of souls.

The second part of the poem is titled "The First Decline Prince 1435-1465, Persia." The Indian saint's soul transmigrates into a Persian prince. Hall describes the death of the Shah of Persia and refers to the indifference and arrogance of his son.

> Let me prove a pattern for mankind,
> a ruler to be sung in anthems
> held as paragon by coming generations.
> I pray my destiny, divinely authorised
> atones for all my father's.

While the body of his father lies in the palace "Gripping the insignia of power, / he faced the right and hurried out, trembling with the weight of his resolve". The Persian atmosphere is vividly recaptured by Hall:

> He crowned her head with jewels of love,
> an ornament of pearls
> Countless as the moons in all their phases
> that glimmer . . . (LK 12)

In the rocking boat the Prince makes love to his beloved:

> Pearls for hair! in brittle sequences
> in stiff progressions, on wires
> in orient curls
> fantastic for their independence,

graded gems that taped finely
as arabesques of incense.

Hall adds:

And still the cruel pearls play on
developing a dance from every quiver—
tusks of the fabulous Medusa
the skeletons of snakes for hair—
Chill as lights from static water
blinding the man transfixed in air. (LK 14)

"The moon is my hope," the lady says, "The moon shall be a sign of tenderness you offer me" and her eyes are moon-dark (15). (The moon is frequently mentioned in the work.)

Past the pavilion is embroidery
where prince and Princess thrash
on golden carpets for their child,
there the new palace rises, overtopping trees,
too high for snakes, and too exposed for birds.
They say the dome will be completed soon.
But cranes are leaving; to their plumbline sight
the artisans are lice in festival
upon the surface of a shattered moon. (LK 16)

Thus the poet describes the Indian saint in his first decline as a naughty prince of Persia.

His next decline is described in the second part "Janissary 1465-1565, Turkey." This part opens with the following words:

I am now so old. When all the court were children
I was just as old. And yet I feel the ghost of beauty
in me. I, who was an Ajam-oghlan, 'foreign youth,'
star of the Ottoman Empire, more than human.

This man is cruel, strong, and violent. He dictates the following words to his clerk:

> Who knows but I'm a hundred?
> And last made love eight years ago. The woman
> trembled at my violence and groaned beneath my weight.
> I told her: Once upon a time
> I broke a man in two. And she believed
> because she was afraid. I did no wrong,
> he was an infidel; almost like love itself, that was,
> so sweet the blood-flow round my bones. I laugh. (LK 19)

He is so arrogant that he tells the clerk,

> Clerk, I trust you, you are such an insect
> how would you have courage to betray me! Write
> my little insect. I was born
> to the south a hundred marching days from here
> At fourteen came the time to be divinely chosen (LK 20)

and he adds haughtily that the soldiers who were weak were "left to wail and rot in villages at home" while the strong among them "hopped away proud of the leather thongs about our necks; / leaping like randy horses, at the sting of whips" (LK 20). "'Let the body be your God,' the Captain told us / and that has been our faith." The old man is so insolent that he remarks,

> I've lived to know the truth of it,
> For how can there be Gods outside ourselves
> if we have strength to conquer any man?
> For thirty years the Sultan, even,
> prayed to me in secret

and he boasts that even after a hundred years

> you still may feel the eagle wings
> folded flat beneath my shoulder blades (LK 21)

He also refers proudly to the jewel he wears, a gift from Suleiman and he quotes the words of Suleiman when he honoured him with the jewel. The old man wants his clerk to write the words of Suleiman secretly and bury them in his tomb "in place of me; for *I shall never die, I know that now.*" And he concludes that the clerk will be remembered for writing neatly what he had been dictating! At the end of the dictation the cruel man strangles his clerk:

> You'll hardly feel a thing
> just the moment of my hands about your neck. (LK 24)

This callous man—this time as a lady—is born again. In the Third Decline "Lady 1565-1581, Malta," we find the Janissary being born in Malta as a lady who falls in love with a Turk. In the first few lines of this section we find the Turk walking with the lady. She tells him about her uncle Don Francisco de Sanoguera, most beloved of all the Red Cross Knights. They see a church with a Venetian tower and he thinks of the bloody siege, the knights all holding out against bombardment, "cut to pieces / by the Turkish hordes, striking back long after any effort seemed impossible." In beautiful language the poet describes the Church and also the love-making between the Turk and the lady of Malta (LK 28-29). He tells her:

> Think—of the Turkish fleet—
> Keels in this water—
> Thousand galleys—crowded in the harbour
> waiting for a signal
> From Admiral Piali Pasha—
> senile fool—rotten with disease—and lice
> mad with jealousy against his equals—
> who gave no signal.

When the lady looks at him with a questioning glance, the Turk replies, 'A relative of mine was in that fleet'. But he cannot stop, he adds, 'My blood is Saracen' (LK 29). She takes him to an empty house and they make love. When they leave

> Already
> night had rolled the moon on black saliva.
> Down below St Michael's parapet

we strolled, down the maw of that ravine
depths ahead and granite teeth above

Her words frighten him: "On the day when I was born, the giant died, the Master Janissary of all the Turks / our people feared that giant most. By morning Don Garcia's galleys rowed in sight / flocking round the head land—Christ had won!" (LK 31). The enmity between the Christians and the Saracens is very well brought out in the poem. The poet says,

We stopped and did not kiss. The sky clamped shut
above us. I've paid my love
I'll never be the bride of any Turk (LK 31)

In the morning she betrays him to the mob and he is dragged to the Christian square and he hears their shriek KILL KILL KILL and he is killed. It is a fact that in 1565 the knights under La Valette withstood a tremendous siege at the hands of the Turks.

In the Fourth Decline, "Envoy 1581-1618 Venice" we have the Hindu saint born in Venice as Gonzalez Martello, son of a Spanish Knight trusted envoy of Spain to Venice. Martello says: "I dreamt I'd lived another life—as a girl so great in bravery and pride she watched her lover die, then like a man / faced the crowd and committed suicide" (LK 35). The atmosphere of Venice is recreated in this part of the poem with the gondolier winging his easy craft away, curving out towards Guidecca. "St Mark's own lion, high upon its plinth glistening wet as a creature newly born, shook off the tunnelled chrysalis of night and spread its wings" (LK 36). As far as Martello is concerned "Kill" was the love he preached,

Kill. Kill.
Somebody must die at my command
(if not the enemy, why then the friend). . . .
  My words like kestrels hover at your head
terror ravishes the virgin blood, tugs at the
  scalp, the face in a grip of skin and now,
  Blind in his execution:
Once blind with arrogance, now blind with fear. (LK 39)

"The Fifth Decline Countess (1618-1710) Trieste" opens with a description of a Countess and her lover, "a small soft" man, bald and ridiculous without his wig "sleeping beside her." We are reminded of the cold love-making in *The Waste Land* by the lady typist and others. The ridiculous man rolls aside murmuring the fashionable cliches—"she gaped a silent laugh—believing what they meant" (LK 45). Only the cruel Bosnian, the perfect diplomat, had struck her heart to sudden life when he had raped her. This Bosnian wants her to sleep with adventurers and noblemen—"whoever he might nominate she had to win" (LK 47). So it went on, her bargaining for love, night after night the same:

> the candles clustered
> in her rich unfashionable house,
> the visitor at ease, wins
> in moderation, a smile, a touch,
> and the ceremonial of bed.

And

> Into the keeping of her secrecy
> they poured confessions that could earn them
> ruin, exile, death. While she
> so honoured, lay reliving moments of her passion (LK 48)

"The Sixth Decline Woodman 1710-1768 Austria," which is perhaps the weakest part in the whole poem, describes the rebirth of the saint in Austria at a time when people lived in terror. Here is again a betrayal: the woodman leaves his family and steals towards the cliff, mountains, forest track, and slips away with a gentle sigh—"A great age lies before him" and in his heart he sings, "I live" (LK 56).

The locale of the next part of the poem is Moscow, "The Seventh Decline Doctor 1768-1813 Moscow." It was during this period that Napoleon's Russian campaign was launched and his army retreated from Moscow in 1812 after suffering a big defeat. This part of *The Law of Karma* has a different technique of narration. It is in the form of an epistle in verse to his friend Maxim Maximich, written by a Russian doctor who derives great pleasure in trying various methods of torture on a French soldier, three weeks after the Bonaparte's withdrawal. The Hindu saint reborn as the Russian doctor keeps the French soldier secretly in his upstairs surgery. He requests Maxim Maximich to join him "before the silly fellow dies". The letters are dated Sunday 7th, Tuesday 9th, Wednesday 10th and three letters, Thursday 11th. On Wednesday 10th, the doctor writes to his friend,

> Today I tried the Chinese torture,
> beating a gong ten centimetres from his ear.
> At every stage you'd see him titch: . . .
> Do you realise what you're missing? (LK 61)

On Thursday 11th, the doctor informs his friend about the kvass Maxim's wife had sent him. Even though it is winter "I felt like something cool". He writes thus to his friend, impatiently,

> How foolish of you not to come
> and join me in my ecstasy . . .
> I didn't want to spoil his looks
> because I know you'd like your pleasure too.
> But now I cannot wait,
> I'm going to try some surgery (LK 64)

It is not at all surprising that the cruel Hindu saint—the Russian Doctor of this section—has his eighth Decline as Slave-trader (1813-1881) in Guinea. This part of the poem begins thus:

> Like a wave that sweeps back down the beach
> Napoleon's armies bled away, leaving
> among the pools of grief
> castles broken as if built of shingles . . .
> and somewhere, helpless in the flow, a child

The child "passed with his camp-girl mother / from the French to the English lines" till finally the wave of battle drops him jetsam in a shack near Liverpool. Later we see the child as skipper of

The Moghul which reaches "Africa's amber beaches / and vivid jungle fringe" to take a chain of slaves. There is a beautiful account of flamingoes:

> Flamingoes break to air
> like human instinct, human panic,
> flutter helpless wings
> against the bars of light (LK 69)

The poet tells us that on the fifteenth day at sea again the men are waiting for the skipper's afternoon inspection.

> The door bangs open, deckhands carry him upon a stretcher
> Crippled, hollowed out of so
> thus he begins his circuit of the vessel,
> leaning over, desperate for his day's enjoyment
> he swipes whoever passes near
> tearing the seamen's faces with his uncut finger nails.
> The day before, he killed a cook who burnt the roast
> today he has the bosun's teeth knocked out
> for being found at sunrise licking dew from his private hencoop.
> (LK 70)

The skipper does not want to miss any detail of the pain he inflicts on others. The bosun in a letter to his "darling Mary" describes the slaves as "Black leather / covering a bunch of sticks" (LK 71). An old man remembers while he dies alone in an English slum how in big ships slaves were taken to Brazil, a thousand slaves a week:

> Who cared for Palmerston!
> Times often bad—
> one day counted thirty corpses
> dragged on deck.
> Dysentery. Were mainly women. (LK 72)

The ninth decline of the Hindu saint is in his rebirth as a Cavalry Officer (1881-1915) in France. This section opens with the date,

May 4th, Paris. The people of France hear with deep regret of the death of one of her most gallant soldiers, Captain Andre Paul Regnard, who had led his cavalry squadron in their final heroic defiance of the enemy in October. His fame had spread with the cavalry changes in the Battle of Chavannet. The speaker of the poem, Captain Regnard's aide, has been a great admirer of the Captain. However, in a letter which the Captain gives his aide just before his death he confesses how in order to save his reputation he had betrayed every man in his command and caused their deaths. The aide as requested by the Captain breaks the seal of the letter on his death and hands it over to the press to inform the public. Thus the protagonist has another birth.

The tenth decline is as Reichs-Kommissar (1915-1944) in Poland during one of the most crucial periods of world history. The Reichs-Kommissar whose duty is to torture Jews, declares:

> Depopulation is a great and necessary task.

In the last part of *The Law of Karma* we have the French captain's words

> We live by principle.
> And this is also how I die, (81)

The Reichs-Kommissar also says,

> We live by principle, such principle
> shall be our life through all posterity. (85)

According to the Fuhrer (Hitler) "the role of Jews in Europe / now has reached its end" and therefore, the obedient Kommissar also feels that "it has reached / its end" (85). Various methods of torturing the Jews are mentioned.

> The rifles crackled . . .
> a pestilential stench floated in the air.
> The great man swore and wound his window up,
> took out a perfumed handkerchief

> and clapped it to his face,
> gulping the sweetness of cologne. He flicked
> some ash that settled on his uniform. (88)

The poet also describes the torture of the Jews in the chamber. The commandant explains:

> We tell them this will be their showering room

and in the chamber there is no water, but only gas. Thousands of Jews are killed. Their gold teeth are knocked out. The callous Reichs-Kommissar smiles and visits the furnaces, and is later ushered to his limousine, and handkerchief to nose, proceeds into the emptiness beyond.

> Tired, he wished this new creation of a race were done,
> longed for the kisses of his wife and children (90)

The land is dead, "miles of it on miles. . . . Not a living person left in sight. . . ." (91)

The long poem ends perhaps rather abruptly. The character of the protagonist deteriorates in every scene. Each rebirth reveals only further degeneration and the poet has to stop at some stage. Each part in the progression of poems can be read and understood as an independent poem but at the same time all the parts interact to form a total unity.

Robert Ward describes *The Law of Karma* as "neat, controlled and tasteful." However, he adds that it is a "gigantic conceit." According to him, the Hindu Saint's distaste for the mob leads his soul in a degenerating spiral that five hundred years and ten lives later reaches Auschwitz as "Reichs-Kommissar 1915-1944." He continues:

> This is not a very profound thought, in fact it's nonsense, but it does make a good foundation for the poem. What is more interesting is the carefully detailed historical, social and geological contexts each life cycle is given. These are handled very neatly with cross-referring imagery adding texture and

> binding the poem together.
>
> To my mind *The Law of Karma* contains the best, the most accomplished and polished poetry Rodney Hall has written. In evoking mood and place he is quite excellent. (Ward: 44)

Hall is credited with having helped to expand the styles, forms and concerns of Australian poetry. Porter thinks that Hall has been an important influence along with Tom Shapcott, in the change which has come over Australian poetry since the 1950s. (Porter, 1976: 431-32) Hall's verse in *The Law of Karma* is suffused with witty observations and examines themes relating to love, death, violence, history, etc., but the main doctrine behind the poem is the Hindu law of Karma.

WORKS CITED

The Complete Works of Swami Vivekananda Vol. I (Calcutta: Advaita Ashrama, 1989).

Rodney Hall, *The Law of Karma: A Progression of Poems* (Canberra: Australian Nation UP, 1968). Cited as LK.

Peter Porter, "Breaking the Tribal Bounds," *The Times Literary Supplement*, No. 3865, 9 Apr. 1976.

Swami Prabhavananda, *Vedic Religion and Philosophy* (Mylapore: Sri Ramakrishna Math, 1957).

Robert Ward, rev. of *The Law of Karma in Australian Book Review*, Vol. 8, Nos. 2 & 3, December 1968 and January 1969.

"Salabhanjika"—A Cultural Option

C.P. Ravichandra
University of Mysore

Salabhanjika

Salabhanjika, inmate of my house,
You have hung for years over the kitchen sink,
Cut from some brochure about Indian art.
My wife, my niece, to fortify their vows
Against the insidious lures of meat and drink
Pinned you, voluptuous, by their diet chart.

My own response to your delightful frame,
Those generous breasts, the bold haunch, the full thighs,
And rapt face—did it seem to dream or brood?

Symbols of plenty to my masculine eyes,
Abundance and promise, grace and plenitude,

And mystery: India, from which you sprung,
Its arts, its past and its unnumbered gods
Was at that time to me almost unknown.
I saw you as a woman, enchanting, young,
And did not know by what improbable odds
My kitchen harboured your smile of ageless tone.

I used to think you, in my ignorance,
One of those lovers who endlessly embrace
At Konark on its Temple of the Sun,

In every erotic posture known to man's
Power to create supple and sensual grace;
At other times I saw you as a lone

Dancer at some maharajah's court.
The nizam, with a connoisseur's cool glance
Followed the fluid ecstasy of the nautch,
Appraising the pearl his boundless wealth had bought,
Ignoring the exquisite artistry of the dance
In contemplation of his coming debauch.

Mere fancies: Now I have visited your land,
Viewed you and your voluptuous sisterhood
And know you for a goddess of the trees.
Yours is no dancer's pose. As the trees stand
True to the zenith and draw up their green blood,
The classic stance of Hindu dryades,

But older than all Hindu gods, as old
As the first worshippers on that continent,
You stand, straight torso, weight upon one foot,
The other drawn back and poising to withhold
Its touch, the arms uplifted, the knee bent
The legend was: one kick against the root

Made the tree blossom from contact with the heel
Of any beautiful woman, but blossom more
Caressed by such a spirit of the wood,
Since all trees have a deep desire to feel
A woman's touch and will give all their store
Of nectar, colour, fragrance if they should.

The legend charms me, I do not think it true;
And yet I long to put it to the test.
Now I am old and, in my season of fruit,
Shrivelled by drought, I too would turn to you,
If by contact with foot or lip or breast
My buds might burst or water drench my root.

Bring me, Salabhanjika, what your smile
Portends, that miracle of late blossoming.
But, till that moment comes which sets all free,
Pause, let me feel my new sap rise awhile;
Then, flood me with the providential spring,
Touch, tend and make me flower, I am that tree.

A.D. Hope

The one accepted mode of Comparative Literature Study is to single out two works, preferably different in cultural ethos, and to present those assonances and dissonances which the mind may distinguish. Such an exercise makes the scholar, the critic, firstly grow aware of what constitutes the *difference* in literatures. Secondly, it demands that the critic equip himself or herself with a broad spectrum of analytical prowess. For to contextualise a new material calls for the patience and purposiveness of a discoverer.

Having stated, at the outset, the importance of having before us two works for study, I hasten to admit that my paper does not. Yet I believe that this essay of mine is not entirely indifferent to the seminal questions that this seminar raises. For it is based on the assumption that Comparative Literature is also a discipline which prods the critic to assay the contributive factor which originates from a writer's conspiracy with a second culture, indulged in for whatever purposes.

My paper takes up but one poem for study. But I wish to show how the poet, A.D. Hope, who is aware of the entire western tradition—from the healthy Greco-Roman landscape to the Eliotian wasteland—finds it requisite to turn to India for an answer. The paper will be relevant insofar as it attempts to point out how well the myths thrown up in our ancient legends have once again been used successfully by someone who is not born to our culture, revitalised in a novel manner. Hope's "Salabhanjika" is an act of discovery. If I can successfully read it thus then I am sure that this intrusion of mine is justified.

In "Salabhanjika", Hope reaches the state of mind of a devotee of love. Love becomes almost a religion with the attendant myth. In virtually a medieval frame of mind, Hope turns not to Europe but to India. The poetic image of the Salabhanjika is taken from Sanskrit myths. In fact the idea, the culminating experience of the poem, has its parallel in Kalidasa's *Malavikagnimitra*. For example, King Agnimitra's aside with which the Fourth Act of *Malavikagnimitra* begins indicates beyond doubt that it is India, and more exactly the past of India, which provides whatever consolation there can be to yet another poet caught up in the circumstance of the decay of the soul:

> King—(to himself): May the tree of love, which took root with regard to her coming within the range of (my) ears, through (my) interest (for her); which put forth the form of attachment, when she came within the range of (my) eyes; which has as though put forth buds owing to the horripilation being manifest at the touches of (her) hand; make me who am pining (or languid) conversant with the taste of (its) fruit. (Karmarkar, 1950: 65)

Salabhanjika could well be the "tree spirit" or "a female figure from Gyraspur, Madhya Pradesh" as Hope tells us in his notes to the poem (Hope, 1981: 108). But as we go through his poem we do grow aware of the kind of spirit Salabhanjika is. Salabhanjika is the personified spirit of Eros as the procreative impulse of life.

Hope has lifted Salabhanjika not only out of the Archaeological Museum of Gwalior (Hope, 1981: 108) but he has, like Ovid's Pygmalion (the consummate artist), given the work a vitality whose force appears to us at this moment to contend with Time itself.

The poem also testifies to Erich Fromm's indestructible belief in humankind:

> The human passions transform man from a mere thing into a hero, into a being that in spite of tremendous handicaps tries to make sense of life. (Fromm, 1974: 8)

Hope's "Salabhanjika" is such an attempt—an attempt "to make sense of life". Salabhanjika is a metaphor which has grown both necessary and useful for the poet. For Hope, woman is both the destroyer and the creative principle. "Salabhanjika" is a poem which turns Hope away from the Freudian, psychoanalytical mode of approach to sex and love characteristic of a number of his other poems, towards a study of love as an attempt at sanity. The poem is at once a revelation of an aesthetically and morally decrepit society and an invocation addressed to Woman as the Recreating Force. Woman is Prakriti, the kinetic force of life, divorced from which there can only be an unalterable passivity in the condition of male, the Purusha.

In "Salabhanjika" Hope is at one remove from the thematic exploration of the legend of Daphne as seen in his "Apollo and Daphne, I" (Hope, 195: 17). If in Daphne's act of self- preservation and in her prudery is seen an inexcusable transgression of trust which condemns not only the transgressing Daphne but also her lover Apollo to an irrevocable fate of non-union, the poet sees in "Salabhanjika" the woman turned into an artefact as the very source of the solution to the malady of modern times: the strife in love.

Pandit Kokkoka in verse six of *Rati Rahasya* defines the aim of the art of love:

> The object of the art of Love is, in the first place, to win the affection of unattached woman; having won it, then to enjoy it, and having enjoyed it, to perpetuate and enhance the enjoyment. (Kokkoka, 1965: 20)

This Apollo fails to achieve in "Apollo and Daphne, I", and the result is the frightening metamorphosis of Daphne. The touch of man, rather the male god—deified male—results in the living flesh of woman turning into the hard "woody rind". But contradicting this attitude we have the poet offering to make the male, a dried up tree, blossom.

> The Salabhanjika is a common enough image among our temple treasures. It is said poets go in search of material. But here was material waiting, according to traditional belief, for that propitious moment when a woman of radiant beauty, frozen in stone, has cast her spell on the great lover, a revelation to the seer in him. Critics talk of Mr. Hope's sexual

> preoccupation but fail to see what sex is doing in his poems: it is not there for its own sake: he is far too distinguished for it. Woman here touches the poet at more than one level and at every level each liberates the other. We are here in the debt of a great poet who gave us eyes to see and brought inert stone to life, and in the process made a dull pulse beat—one of those evanescent moments which had glimpsed eternity itself. At such a touch of the foot it was that the Asoka tree blossomed into a glory, and in this case, poetry into pure flame. (Narasimhaiah, 1980: xvi-xvii)

Such is the accolade the poem received even before it was published.

Salabhanjika has crossed the Pacific and has now found room in a new climate. From the socio-cultural and religious centre of the Indian temples she has been transplanted to the wall above the sink in the poet's kitchen. She is no more the mythified woman, but is serving a merely functional purpose, reduced to a model:

> My wife, my niece, to fortify their vows
> Against the insidious lures of meat and drink
> Pinned you, voluptuous, by their diet chart.

This corruption of taste and failure of imagination is not a peculiar phenomenon applicable only to the poet's wife or his niece. He himself has been afflicted by it— of course, not without some help in this direction lent by other images of woman in India that he has glimpsed. In the past, she has been a mere nautchwali (dancer) of some Nizam's court; the Mohgul splendour subjecting the Salabhanjika to a "connoisseur's cool glance". But this "connoisseur", we see, is in no way different from the patron of the cabaret of modern times:

> Appraising the pearl his boundless wealth has bought,
> Ignoring the exquisite artistry of the dance
> In contemplation of his coming debauch.

She has also been (as the poet tries to remember his perception of Salabhanjika before) a bold expression of sexual procreation on the walls of the Sun Temple. That is the result of demythification. Salabhanjika of the brochures could only evoke such images, at best, removed as it is from its native climate. But the realisation that the Salabhanjika is a "goddess of the trees" comes home to the poet once he visits India. It is then that he understands the divinity of the dancer. Here is the "classic stance of Hindu dryades". The Augustan in Hope surfaces for a moment to voice a weak protest: "The legend charms me, I do not think it true". But then an awareness of his own poor condition makes him long to test the legend:

> Now I am old and, in my season of fruit
> Shrivelled by drought, I too would turn to you,
> If by contact with foot or lip or breast
> My buds might burst or water drench my root.

He is Purusha segregated from Prakriti. Hence the cry of the last stanza of the poem which reminds us at once of Agnimitra's longing for Malavika:

> Bring me, Salabhanjika, what your smile
> Portends, that miracle of late blossoming.
> But, till that moment comes which sets all free,
> Pause, let me feel my new sap rise awhile;
> Then, flood me with that providential spring,
> Touch, tend and make me flower, I am that tree.

Here Hope is going to the very roots of Sankhya philosophy in his attempt at unravelling the Gordian knot which love and sex have grown to be in recent times. The "Salabhanjika" is the final answer "which sets all free". Here is an unequivocal assertion, in poetry, of what Thomas points out in the Sankhya vision of the universe:

> The most ancient philosophy that explains the dual conception of the Universe is Sankhya. The Sankhya does not support a belief in a Supreme being or God. It teaches the existence

> of numerous Purushas or male Purushas or male entities which are pure and quiescent in themselves and of Prakriti (the female principle) the vast mainstay of the universe. The Purushas, independent of Prakriti, are passive, but they come into constant contact with Prakriti and give rise to the phenomenal world. Prakriti, the female, is essentially active and since all activity is conditioned by Time, Space and Causation, the Purusha that gets caught by Prakriti necessarily becomes bond. Every living being is thus a combination of Purusha and Prakriti, and the object of life is the liberation of Purusha from Prakriti. (Thomas, 1963: 112)

The Salabhanjika thus takes on once again the nuances of a metaphor, this time in the hands of an Australian poet. For a poet like Hope who sees around him the reign of carnality as in "Imperial Adam", "Sportsfield", "The Dinner", the West fails to throw up an image that would offer a way out. His troubled search for a metaphor that would sustain him has led him ultimately to Salabhanjika. For Mr. Hope the West is demythified because of the decay of civilisation. As a man without a mythical past he can only think of himself (and his woman) as "Two recent mammals, perhaps the least of all" (Hope, 1981: 21). And the trauma of not having a valid archetypal image for the progression of life is not unfamiliar to us even in India. It is a search for such an archetype that leads the Australian poet to the Museum of Gyraspur.

In this poem, Hope has turned away from traditional European myths and legends. The Sleeping Beauties, the Red Riding Hoods, the Nicolettes, the Isoldes, the Daphnes, the Psyches no longer have a positive suggestion for him. In his search for a new myth, a new creative principle, he has chanced upon the image of Salabhanjika. And how immediate the meaning of *kavisamaya* grows on us. That is the essential function of poetry. Now the Australian imagination has added to its mythical consciousness a new turn, the echoes of which will surely be heard again and again.

"Salabhanjika", with its power to civilise the reader, is one of those rare human events that provide an inner conviction which bolsters up a lagging spirit. The poem is a fine example of how in a situation of cultural cross-contact (which can only take place in the care of a sensitive mind) a reflective attitude unifies the sensibility of the creative writer and leads him on to what is ethical. This poem reveals an act that penetrates the superfluity of the world at large. It is an act of emerging from the man.

WORKS CITED

Erich Fromm, *The Anatomy of Human Destructiveness* (London: Jonathan Cape, 1974).

A.D. Hope, *A Late Picking: Poems 1965-1974* (London: Angus & Robertson, 1975).

______, *Antechinus: Poems 1975-1980* (London: Angus & Robertson, 1981).

R.D. Karmarkar, trans. and ed., *Malavikagnimitra of Kalidasa* (4th ed. revised, Poona: R.D. Karmarkar, 1950).

Pandit Kokkoka, *Rati Rahasya*, trans. S.C. Upadhyaya (Bombay: D.B. Taraporevala & Sons, 1965).

C.D. Narasimhaiah (ed.), "Introduction", *The Literary Criterion* (*The Flowering of Australian Literature*) (Mysore), XV, Nos. 3 & 4, 1980.

P. Thomas, *Kama Kalpa* (13th ed; Bombay: D.B. Taraporewala & Co., 1963).

James Weiland as a Critic of Nissim Ezekiel

A. RAGHU
T.K.M. College of Arts and Science
Quilon

In his well-known essay, "Naipaul's India and Mine," Nissim Ezekiel relates that when he was a young man of eighteen a friend asked him what his ambition was and that Ezekiel replied that his ambition was to do something for India. (1974:88) There is no doubt that he has been able to amply fulfil his youthful ambition. Ezekiel has contributed to Indian literature as a poet, as a playwright, as a critic, as a translator, as an editor and as a writer of books for children. If Indian poetry in English is what it is today, the credit goes to Ezekiel to the extent that it can go to one man. For one thing, Ezekiel's corpus is a significant element in post-Independence Indian poetry in English. For another, the publication of Ezekiel's first collection, aptly titled *A Time to Change*, in 1952 set in motion a revolution which remarkably altered the contours of the landscape of Indian poetry in English. This paper is an attempt to study the interaction between the poetry of Ezekiel and the critical intelligence of James Weiland, the Australian critic. Weiland is himself a poet, besides being an academic, reviewer and editor.

In my paper, "Nissim Ezekiel: The Making of a Natural Outsider," (1994: 56-59) I have traced the development of Ezekiel into what he himself calls a "natural outsider," the starting point of the process being his birth into the Bene-Israel community in India. The strongly academic atmosphere in his parental home, the influence of the later philosophy of M.N. Roy and his sojourn in England between 1948 and 1952 were the other factors responsible for this evolution. Ezekiel's position as an outsider denies him access to the vast and richly complex history of India which he neither accepts nor rejects. Being an outsider he is unable to accept it. He refuses to reject it because he feels that it is not his to reject. He believes that contempt for background is as distorting as pride in background. Weiland observes that Ezekiel is a poet who is no inheritor of the comprehensive history of his country, a poet who nevertheless understands that the past significantly influences the present and above all a poet who thinks the present and the future are more important than the past. Weiland says,

> Ezekiel feels that he cannot open the trap-door into the past because of his outsider status, and while he recognizes that the past impinges on the present, he feels himself to be on the brink of the future. (1988: 4)

To see Ezekiel as a Jew living in India would not be accurate enough. He is no mere Jew but a lapsed Jew. He is a Maharashtrian Jew who speaks almost no Marathi. He is a Jew living in a predominantly Hindu India but in a Muslim neighbourhood of her most cosmopolitan city. No critical dragnet used to scour the corpus of Ezekiel can catch the specific attitude to history embedded in his poetry for the simple reason that Ezekiel has no one stance in the matter. His attitude to history is complex and Weiland uses two key phrases, "long perspectives" and "present tense," both borrowed from Ezekiel in his attempt to map this difficult terrain. Weiland explains that on the one hand the phrases suggest a preoccupation with the past, the present and the future, with a utopia and with the complexity, dynamism and transitoriness of the moment. On the other hand, the phrases point to a psychological realm, to bliss and harmony, to an imaginative engagement with the immediate which leads to an insight into the self as well as into the universals.

It is illuminating to contrast this very sympathetic attempt of Weiland to analyse and understand Ezekiel's approach to history with R. Parthasarathy's observations on the matter. Parthasarathy is the archetypal insider in post-Independence Indian poetry in English and to say that for him the past is sacred almost simply because it is the past is only the exaggeration of a vital truth. The status of Ezekiel as an outsider cuts him off from the comprehensive history of India and Parthasarathy feels that this places Ezekiel in an unenviable position. Ezekiel has expressed amusement at Parthasarathy's remark. (1989: 75)

The past is the soil out of which myth springs and into which its roots go deep. All poets being word-smiths are concerned with the essential meaning of myth. Weiland explains that a myth is a direct metaphysical statement beyond science. It embodies in an articulated structure of symbol or narrative, a vision of reality. Its origin, let alone its originator, is unknown. It is a public repository of truth which is absolute and constant through time. Weiland quotes from *The Klein Papers* to show that a myth deals with the fundamentals of existence. (1988: 5) It does not explain, it simply relates and its assumptions are unquestioned.

As an outsider who is unable to identify himself with the comprehensive history of the country, Ezekiel does not have access to the traditional myths of India. Even if such an access had been available to Ezekiel, Weiland believes that it is doubtful whether it would have made much difference. The creative mind of Ezekiel is too logical and too analytical for that. There is something unchangeable about the myth. This absolute quality, suggests Weiland, makes Ezekiel turn away from it for Ezekiel generally insists on change and transience.

Under these circumstances, it is only natural that Ezekiel makes use of what Weiland calls "fictions." Weiland sees fictions as manifestations of the urge to rename and to remake. Fictions are private and open-ended and directed towards making sense of here and now. The concept of change is central to them. They are constructs of the individual imagination which easily allow us to identify the hand of their maker.

Weiland points out that an acute awareness of the need to return to India is present in the title poem of Ezekiel's first collection *A Time to Change* and also throughout the volume. He has been marking time on unknown ground for too long. He wants to return home and make a commitment to life. Weiland comments on Ezekiel's concern with love, especially physical love. He observes that the pilgrim motif constantly occurs in Ezekiel's verse. The poet is in a way himself a pilgrim engaged in a search for poetry, for a fulfilling love, for a sense of moral and spiritual balance. Weiland mentions V.S. Naipaul's contention in *India: A Wounded Civilization* that the racial sense is alien to Indians (qtd. Weiland 246) and argues that it is not valid in the case of Ezekiel. In Ezekiel, especially the late Ezekiel, we find repeated assertions of the Indianness of India. India, especially urban India, is where he belongs. Weiland says that we sense that Ezekiel is trying to construct and convey a dynamic continuum.

The poetry of Ezekiel is the poetry of a highly westernized English-speaking Indian. Weiland, probably because he views more, finds a very palpable India in the work of Ezekiel. He sees Ezekiel's view of history as almost ahistorical. What in many non-Indian poets has been a reaching back into history for a sense of continuity is converted in Ezekiel in a very Indian manner into a deeply philosophical concern with a perception that intuits the primal landscape in which God's mills furiously turn and myths meander like rivers through a topography of pain. Weiland quotes Raja Rao who says something to this effect in "The Meaning of India": India is not a *desa* (country) but a *darsana* (perspective) not a *kala* (climate) but a *rasa* (mood) in the play of the Lord. It is not the Indian who makes India but India which makes the Indian. (qtd. Weiland, 1988 80)

Perhaps the most significant contribution of Weiland is his attempt in his book *The Ensphering Mind*, to place the poetry of Ezekiel by the side of the work of five other Commonwealth poets: A.D. Hope of Australia, A.M. Klein of Canada, Allen Curnow of New Zealand, Derek Walcott of the Caribbean and Christopher Okigbo of Nigeria. In the preface to the book, Weiland explains the choice of Ezekiel and the five other poets. They are six very good poets whose work is worthy of concentrated study. Each of them has a significant body of poetry behind him. All of them share the same language and are from countries where the residues of the British empire have lingered far into the twentieth century. The quarrels with history conducted by the six poets lead them to seek in myth and fictions, the order and coherence missing from the dislocations of history. Hope seeks to re-establish Australia's links to an European heritage. Curnow in contrast fears New Zealand's tendency to import her myths. Klein tries to draw on his Judaic heritage. Weiland sees Walcott as a New World Adam-Crusoe-Odysseus figure cast out of Eden to a life of endless journeying into unknown seas. Okigbo and Ezekiel writing out of the Old World meld the old with the new and seek new visions of life. Weiland admits that there is great diversity in the work of these poets. However, two unifying experiences throughout the Commonwealth are a shared history and a common language. All the six poets write in English. For each it is his first language and the language of his education.

Every one of them is deeply read in English literature but it is not true that the sources of their inspiration are exclusively within the English tradition. Weiland observes that for all of them there is a rich heritage in other languages. Hope, Klein, Okigbo and Walcott have the Classics behind them. Okigbo spoke Igbo and majored in the Classics. Klein attended a French-speaking university in Montreal to read law, speaks Yiddish and reads Hebrew. Walcott speaks French and has written poems in Creole. Curnow has studied the interaction between Polynesian and European cultures in New Zealand. Ezekiel has translated Marathi poetry into English. Weiland establishes a special comparative equation between Ezekiel and Klein because of the vast Judaic tradition that lies behind them both, a tradition which has probably dwarfed their interest in local literatures. Ezekiel started taking an interest in Marathi literature rather late in his career as a poet and the same can be said of Klein's interest in Canadian literature.

Anisur Rahman has focussed attention on form and value in the poetry of Ezekiel. Chetan Karnani has published a monograph on Ezekiel. In my book *Nissim Ezekiel's Poetry: A Study of Themes and Styles* which is in the press, I have attempted to see the poetry of Ezekiel as a bridge between pre-Independence Indian poetry in English and its post-Independence counterpart. Weiland tries to view the poetry of Ezekiel from a very fresh perspective by placing it by the side of five other Commonwealth poets, thus imparting a Commonwealth identity to Ezekiel.

In the epigraph to *The Ensphering Mind*, Walcott says, "The mind enspheres all circumstance." (1) There is no doubt that the critical mind of Weiland has ensphered the poetry of Ezekiel and interacted with it with sympathy, profundity and precision and made the poetry of Ezekiel part of the expanding Australian critical experience.

WORKS CITED

Nissim Ezekiel, "Naipaul's India and Mine," *New Writing in India,* ed. Adil Jussawala (Harmondsworth: Penguin, 1974).

_____. Interviews with four Indian English Poets by Eunice de Souza, *The Bombay Literary Review* (1989).

A. Raghu, "Nissim Ezekiel: The Making of a Natural Outsider," *Littcrit* 20.1 (1994).

Derek Walcott, *In a Green Night*, qtd. by Weiland.

James Weiland, *The Ensphering Mind* (Washington D.C.: Three Continents Press, 1988).

INDIAN SKETCHPAD:
Poems Written and Presented during the AASA Conference in Kerala

Annalisa Orselli-Dickson
Edith Cowan University

The Rungs of Poesies

or

"to find the l o d e"

or-perhaps-our poetry is like	eternal bubbles of Creation
descending the ladders of mind	extracting inkdrops of eternity
down those rungs of memories	timefolds of depth and summit
selected by filters of years	prospecting the layers of time
fastened by pegs of imagination	paper-tracks of perspection
onto these wooden frameworks	of sounds tracing on papers
of our consciousness and being:	the levels of meaning in sound,
to reach the ground of poesies	and then ascending the levels

to find the l o d e

or-perhaps-our poetry is like eternal bubbles of Creation descending the ladders of mind extracting inkdrops of eternity down those rungs of memories timefolds of depth and summit selected by filters of years prospecting the layers of time

fastened by pegs of imagination paper-tracks of perspection onto these wooden frameworks of sounds tracing on papers

of our consciousness and being: the levels of meaning in sound, to reach the ground of poesies and then ascending the levels

to find the l o d e

The poem can be read in 3 different ways, or all these 3 as a continuum:
From top to bottom (left) and then bottom to top (right) and also right to left, top to bottom ad infinitum

DAWN AT COCHIN FORT

Gentle ripples on the face of the lagoon
azure and ochre paintstrokes
an unknown Venetian master
trembling flotsam of spent weeds
dancing on the surface
as the words of poets
on a pond of
luminous
paper.
Counter - balanced
nets rhythmically
dipping in
and emerging
from the quiet waters
of imagination search
the bay of mind
for some treasured

reflexion
reflection
of meaning

ashore
on broken black rock
bundles of netting like fairy floss
are being spun by patient coolies
waiting
for the day catch
on the pier of verse . . .

and the poet with a painter' s mind
indulges in the Chinese game
of making syllables shine
as a rainbow
fish.

KANYAKUMARI

Swami Vivekananda Rock Memorial

Be my
illumination
as a temple on the rock
of my inner heart:
where the three oceans meet,
Love, Wisdom and Being merge
with the wind of self and the
noise of unreality
falls away into
nothing
ness. . .

"And the Spirit of God
blew upon the face of waters
and it was Light"

Trivandrum 18-1-97

COCHIN SYNAGOGUE

Pillars of polished brass
standing strong and still

as men in silent prayer

Behind the women balcony
a line of ancient oil lamps
offering their mystic hearts
to the light of God

In its canopy of gilded wood
and red silks
the Word *Keter Torah*
is held veiled,
a thing too sacred to be seen

while
this pilgrim
pauses to rest and sip
the shade and stillness
of holiness

Sunset at Trivandrum

Abode
of Anantha,
the white cosmic snake
gently holding in its spires of milky spacetime
an ancient-young Vishnu dreaming
a dream of Brahma.

The layers of the great temple
darken at the fall of light but in the sky
another golden temple of clouds
is pierced by
the setting
glory of
sun

and all our gods fade
in the shadows of this night.

To Lord Nataraja as god of poetic utterance

G o
D
bal anc ing
ing
on
the thin hedge
of a single breath
suspended between
the two universes:
in-spiration and ex-piration,
life and destruction,
vision and sacrifice,
sacred fire, deadly pyre,
gracious and terrifying,
bestower and denier
of the power
of Word,
you
hold
for ever

your cosmic step in rhythm
weaving tones and patterns
from the tear of the first
universal seed of Sound

Bija
inventor
of rhyme,
a tantric ritual
of love, releasing
into the jungle of minds
your growling golden tiger
with glowing stripes of the Pen,
wild me(n)s-merising Creativity itSelf!
by which all poems
unfold or
die

The Tribal Story Lost in an Alien Tale: A Search for the Enigmatic Dimension of History in Judith Wright's Poetry

ANNAMMA JOSEPH
College for Women
Thiruvananthapuram

My paper is an attempt to identify an aspect of the reality Judith Wright unfolds through a grand creative act of perceiving which has recently taken up considerable space within the expanding Australian experience. In other words, it concerns itself with the attempt by Judith Wright, in her poetry, to come to grips with that enigmatic dimension of the Australian experience which has its roots in the Aboriginal experience of some 100,000 years and its strong spiritual bond with the land. The space provided by the absence of this mysterious "other" makes history a field of infinite possibilities for the poet. Her attempt to identify and retrieve it, so that it reoccupies that space, is supported on the one hand by a questioning of the apparent reality of the social experience, and on the other, by an imaginative return to a pre-symbolic world, whose raw violent beauty is something to be endured, and not restrained by reason.

The Australian settler has always sensed in the land an undefinable something which demands the sacrifice of a part of the European consciousness, leaving behind a void. It has been present in the unwilling exile and the dedicated seeker, the two stereotypical figures of the literature of the settler. It rears its head at the most unguarded moments throughout Australian literature. It is there in the works of the greatest, in Henry Handel Richardson's trilogy, and in Patrick White's *Voss*. At the same time, in all such contexts, one is struck by its resistance to definition, its identification in literature being limited to its impact on the psyche of the settler, and its outer equivalent, a landscape hostile to its human inhabitants, pressing them relentlessly on to their doom.

It is a situation in which a part of history goes unnoticed by, or even absents itself from, the exile consciousness which is busy grappling with its own tensions and traumas in an alien environment. A recognition of this led to the seeking for, and arriving at the hitherto unidentified dimension of the peculiarly Australian inner reality. Judith Wright named it "the scar left by the struggle to conquer and weaken, for our own purpose, a landscape that has survived on its own terms until the world's late days" (Wright, 1965: xvii). She makes no mistake about the inalienable relationship between this land and its people, and elaborates: "Its only human inhabitants were the Aborigines whom we dispossessed—who were bound to the land we took from them, by the indissoluble link of religion and totemic kinship, so that our intrusion on the land itself became a kind of bloodless murder, even where no actual murder took place" (ibid.: xvii).

The Aborigine as subject matter is found as early as 1863 in Henry Kendall's "The Last of his Tribe". With Katharine Susannah Prichard's major novel *Coonardoo* (1929) and Xavier Herbert's seminal novel *Capricornia* (1938), perspectives on the thematic use of the Aborigine expanded. But it was with Judith Wright's poem "The Moving Image" (1946), the title poem of her first volume, with its lament

> The song is gone; the dance
> is secret with the dancers in the earth,
> the ritual useless, and the tribal story
> lost in an alien tale. (*CP* 8)

that the Aboriginal theme acquired a moral dimension and became a symbolic interrogation of exploitation and dispossession. It was one of the earliest attempts, to apply language to a pre-verbal, incompletely articulated awareness, to fill in the gaps of absences and silences.

The pioneering quality of this work can be realised only if we measure the distance literature has travelled since then, so as to be able to speak authoritatively of the 'breakdown of meaning' in modern culture and of the fact that it is a philosophical illusion that language relates to an apprehension of the nature of reality. Ken Goodwin, in his essay on Australian national identity (Goodwin, 1955: 5-6) traces how it was only in the late seventies that a canon of major Australian writers, strongly represented by male writers and controlled by European notions of literary decorum and political values, was displaced by an interest in absences, in under-represented social groupings and invisible historical areas. Michael Wilding in his overview of the Australian novel since the sixties comments, "This is one narrative of Australian fiction from the sixties through the eighties, you begin with rejecting the Australian legend and end up with American lies. But there are other narratives, other narrators well worthy of attention" (Quoted in King, 1991: 31).

Hence Wright started without precursors. The promptings came from inside. In her essays on the Australian artist, dropped from Europe into "a pocket of silence and space", Wright records her own primal awareness of an alien fallen world. Her landscape is a wasteland of bones, rock, fire and flood, haunted by the Aborigine and the swagman. It was something she was born into and grew up with. She described Australia as

> my blood's country
> full of old stories that still go walking in my sleep.
> ("South of My Days")

Wright had no tradition to model on. There was no strategic location; the authorial position with regard to her material could only be precarious at best. She had to invent a new narrative voice and manipulate images, themes, and motifs to bring into being the unknown dimension of experience she was trying to grapple with and tame. She had the additional job of tackling the new myths, deconstructing them, or ignoring them altogether and going round them to reach her preferred field of activity. She was moreover risking the sanity of a sensitive mind and of its desires and dreams by pitting them against a powerful political process controlling social, cultural and linguistic values. This philosophical dispute between the mechanical and the magical other which lies behind so much of contemporary post-colonial writings finds expression in one of her early poems "The Trains" (*CP* 12), where she opposes the trains with their animal cry, going north carrying guns, with the tiger whom she addresses:

> Tiger, you walk through all our past and future,
> troubling the children's sleep; laying
> a reeking trail across our dream of orchards.

Wright is like the old woman of her poem of that name, who carries home

> this branch of pear
> that makes such obstinate tokens still
> of fruit it cannot bear

by putting out some blossoms even after having fallen in a storm (*CP* 197). It is a project where literature struggles against the limits of social reality, yet remains within human reality. It traces the unsaid and the unseen in a given culture, that which has been silenced, covered over, and made absent. It shares many features with the fantastic, yet it stops short of its non-signifying nature, and uses conceptualisations and metaphorical structures to retrieve what has been evicted. Its movement is metaphorical rather than metonymical. Its basic relation to the presences is a conceptual one, a linking through ideas and ideals. And for this project to succeed, it is imperative that the invisible should be brought within the range of the visible, because 'reality' is related to an epistemological and metaphysical system which makes "I see" synonymous with "I understand", in which knowledge, comprehension, and reason are established through the power of the 'look' and the human subject whose relation to objects is structured through his field of vision. In her poem "The Morning of the Dead" we find the appeal to this 'look':

> . . . So take life further,

> let the thin bubble of blown glass, the passion
> of vision that is art, refine, reflect and gather
> the moving pattern of all things in consummation
> and their rejoicing. . . .
> Burn with a fire of sight the substance of my sorrow.

Such a project, inspired by the conviction that truth is complex and mysterious starts with an interrogation of the apparent, deficient, and distorted reality. It naturally gives rise to a situation of confrontation with two opposing categories, one of which, namely the suppressed and the dispossessed interrogates the dominant, using its difference as its weapon. "Reason and Unreason" (*CP* 203-4) is a poem which spells out this conflict of opposites. It begins thus:

> When I began to test my heart,
> Its laws and fantasies against the world,
> The pain of impact made me sad.

Exploiting difference, Judith Wright's choice of the remnants of a prescientific Australian world, represented by its landscape and animals, to counter the settler's human world with its competing political and economic interests, is thus a brilliant stroke.

The world of her poetry is inhabited by animals of a great variety. The wolf, the lion, the bull and the tiger, sparrow, hawk, wren, finches, move among shallow creeks, or uninhabited mountains which

> stand up green,
> naked with rock, or clothed with an old forest
> where vines and thorns tangle in damp and dark
> among the trunks and boulders.

It is a world throbbing with life, vital to its fingertips, yet remarkably devoid of human presence. While whatever human beings there are, are often lifeless caricatures, we are surprised by inanimate features of landscape which live and breathe causing the fluid boundaries between the living and non-living almost to disappear.

The opening lines of "Camping at Split Rock" confront us with such an extraordinary situation:

> Red mounting scales of cliff lead the eye up;
> but here the rock has spaces of tenderness
> where light and water open its heart. A lip
> of narrow green shows where the creek-banks bless
> a niche for trees and birds. (*CP* 245)

As far as nature is concerned, it provides a veritable feast to the eye and the ear. Yet the gaze goes beyond nature's external beauties; the enjoyment or the response is not of the senses. The sights, sounds, and smells of nature stimulate the poet's imagination and the resulting vision goes beyond them to a pervasive sense of the spiritual and the philosophic:

> The finger of age-old water splits the rock
> and makes us room to live; the age-old word
> runs on in language and from obstinate dark
> hollows us room in seeing. The birds go by;
> but we can name and hold them, each a word
> that crystals round a more than mortal bird. (*CP* 245)

Wright's strategy of projecting the animal world (as opposed to the human) to identify the 'other', is reinforced by the well represented hostility of the land to its people in Australian literature. Thus the animal world and the land they inhabit become for the poet powerful tools to reach after the invisible other. By being outside the field of power constructed by human beings, they provide a metaphor for the presymbolic world or suggest the possibility of another order of reality, a reality which suggests the intransigent nature of experience which is raw, violent and beautiful. This world that sits astride the imaginary as well as the real readily permits a critique of human culture which is invariably constructed around the viewpoint of a specific class or race of people. It allows the history of the other by preserving recorded events of a past hitherto unrecognised by the history of the dominant race. Moreover, it is a discourse with the ability to subvert the tradition of writing tied to a political discourse of domination even as it conceals itself in natural metaphors that resist violence. It suggests further the possibility of alternative literacies which would allow alternative political viewpoints. Thus the author's success in exploiting the subversive potential of the animal world and the strange environment it inhabits, is near total.

The location of this world within the unoccupied spaces within history keeps it free from many of the conventions and restraints of the more realistic texts. So does its business, which is soul-making through the quintessential activity of new ways of inscribing reality. Poems do not merely reconstruct events, but recreate the enigma of their origins and the motives that provoked them. Traditional reconstruction of events and experiences gives way to an emphasis on a spiritual dimension. This involves the doing away with chronology, the "trap of time" as Wright calls it in "Clock and Heart" (*CP* 232), with three dimensionality and with rigid distinctions between animate and inanimate objects. A typical example is the poem "Bullocky" (*CP* 17), which projects the archetypal figure of an Australian bullocky, striding like Moses over time and space, and gathering into his future the possibilities of several dimensions of personal and spiritual fruition. Several images throughout the body of this poetry are characterised by similar associative leaps and disrespect for conventions. In them the arbitrariness of the space/time coordinates reinforces metaphoric and symbolic associations to dislocate history so that the past becomes immanent in the present. The fluidity of time and the deliberate blurring of geographical boundaries demonstrate the illusion of progression and the futility of the aspiration for a concentric universe.

Language is an extension of nature. The conceptual terminology used by the poet lives in the gestures, the sounds, the smells, and the emotional disturbances within nature. Telling implies using the language of the dominant order and so accepting its norms and recovering the dark areas. Hence creation is affected not so much through words as through gaps. Rather, they, words and gaps, together function to capture an extralinguistic, preverbal dimension of human existence. Language here assumes a potency as solidly meaningful as physical fact. It becomes for the writer the most powerful tool to subvert the oppressive status quo, to deconstruct and denounce myths and to rewrite and reclaim them, to reinscribe irrationality and disorder into a different version of culture which would invest them with alternative powers, and to revalue the powers of magic, the supernatural, and the spiritual.

Violence is an essential element in such a project which has at its core the relationship of power between the coloniser and the colonised. Violence is involved when something or someone is suppressed, silenced, and humiliated. This violence causes further violence when an attempt is made to retrieve what has been silenced. The consequent disturbance will have greater intensity if it is larger than its container, more eloquent than the people who presume to speak for it. While the first is metaphorically represented through individual figures and situations, the second courses through every vein of the colonised world which wakes up to the reality of freedom and visibility. The former violence is represented while the latter is committed through representation.

A sharp note of anger accompanies every representation by Wright of an animal or a form of nature as a victim of the violence committed by the coloniser. "The Bull" (*CP* 40) is described by McAuley as "a splendid celebration of organic life—in particular of fulfilled sexuality" (McAuley, 1968: 206). However, the bull, the central image of sensual magnificence, ends up being "driven by dogs and humiliated, unable to cope with the harrying forces of the outer world". The poem ends on a note of interrogation:

> What enemy steals his strength—what rival steals
> his mastered cows?

Similar victims of the politics of power are strewn throughout this world and become landmarks of the poet's protest against the despoiling of a remarkable culture and a nascent land. In "Eroded Hills" (*CP* 83) the victim is nature:

> These hills my father's father stripped,
> and beggars to the winter wind
> they crouch like shoulders naked and whipped—
> humbled, abandoned, out of mind.

> I dream of hills bandaged in snow,
> their eyelids clenched to keep out fear.
> When the last leaf and bird go
> let my thoughts stand like trees here.

In such a history, however, the stress is on the creative forms of violence, that which is committed by the writer to right the wrongs committed by the oppressor. Violence of representation erupts when the attempt is made to suppress difference and retrieve the past. The author, the author also of this violence, takes a position outside the field of power, or at least writes about it as if it were "out there". In other words, she situates herself in a female position relative to the discourses of the dominant culture, so that she may presume to speak for the excluded. She manipulates every aspect of language and expression to fulfil her mission, including phonic structure, image, grammar, the play of meaning and association, etc. And the violence is often represented by a disturbance, a kind of menace lurking behind the landscape, angry at and refusing to accept a power relationship, and attempting to destroy it in favour of a new way of being devoid of exploitation. It is something to be experienced and read about, conveyed through the mood and atmosphere surrounding each poem and connecting them all into a single whole. "Bora Ring" (*CP* 8) which is a lament for the bygone days ends with the lines,

> Only the rider's heart
> halts at a slightest shadow, an unsaid word
> that fastens in the blood the ancient curse,
> the fear as old as Cain.

"Australia 1970" (*CP* 292) reverses the roles of the victim and the victimiser, sending a shiver through the latter:

> For we are conquerors and self-poisoners more than scorpion or snake and dying of the venoms that we make even while you die of us.

This violence is not, however, without an end. On the other hand it is creative in that it results in a violent birth. This brings us to the anagogic function of Judith Wright's poetry. It is distinct from most allegorical quests for a return to Eden. If it had been such a one it would have been self-defeating because the one who pursues it is trapped in history. It can be understood on the other hand, in terms of a process of conception, gestation and birth. The poem "Woman to Man" (*CP* 29) gives a visionary flash into this poetic mission. Its first three stanzas are a meditation upon the mystery of conception and gestation. The first stanza expresses the poet's delight at the mysterious activities within:

> The eyeless labourer in the night
> the selfless, shapeless seed I hold,
> builds for its resurrection day—
> silent and swift and deep from sight
> forces the imagined light.

From there the poem moves forward with increasing urgency to the climax in the last stanza, of an anticipation of the moment of birth:

> This is the maker and the made,
> this is the question and reply,
> the blind head butting at the dark,
> the blaze of light along the blade.
> Oh hold me, for I am afraid.

"The blaze of light" which literally refers to the knife cutting the cord, symbolises, according to McAuley, "the first flash of light and consciousness" (McAuley, 1968: 205). It also represents the moment of fulfilment for the poet, which parallels in its delight over the successful outcome of her efforts, the turning of the woman from her meditations over the mystery of the growth of the 'seed' within her to utter a direct personal cry to the man. The word "Resurrection" is the key which opens up another world within the world of the poem, a world which is not new, but has been, one which "has no name to name it by". It marks the romantic's arrival at the other reality, the climactic moment of the dialogue between the poet's unconscious and that of the land.

This moment becomes also the culmination of the quest for her poetic identity. It brings her to an equation between the tribal and the poetic. The journey into the past of Australia has been for the poet a journey inwards, and a means to define her own subjectivity. Separation and objectivity, the Freudian markers of identity, are here replaced by relationship and connection. Any claim to the Enlightenment concept of absolute identity and autonomous subjectivity is relegated to the past. In an epistemology which is understood in relational and intersubjective terms, the self redescribes continuously its diffuse boundaries in terms of its encounters with others or the world outside. In seeking, rejecting and replacing, she arrives at the spiritual dimension within herself, within every man and within nature. She names it a 'love' and 'truth' common to the tribals and the poet.

Understanding of the impersonal (truth) through the personal (love) defines the poet's vocation. In her highly personal poem, "For My Daughter", we find an explicit explanation of this link between love and truth:

> While love is innocent
> the lion walks beside.
> But when the spell's undone
> and where the paths divide,
> he must be tamed, or slain,
> or else the heart's undone.
> The path I walk upon
> leads to his den again.
> . . .
> I pray to learn the way
> to tame him, not to kill.
> Then he may be my friend,
> as Una's once, in love,
> and I shall understand
> what gifts are mine to give. (*CP* 205)

Fruition results from the conjoining of love and truth, where truth is the end to which love is ordered, the end which determines the process, unconscious. But unerring, like the growth in the womb. In one of her essays Wright remarks:

> Poetry out not to be thought as a discipline, as a kind of praise. . . . Poetry is a means of regaining faith in man . . . a way of finding a difficult balance relating inner and outer.

Thus while her work transforms the contour and context of Australian experience, it leads also to a reaffirmation of her faith in herself and her work, based on the equation between the tribal and the poetic, reflected in what she says elsewhere about the poet:

> And though he is slain and many times over slain he is the one who dies to rise again. (*CP* 209)

WORKS CITED

Ken Goodwin, "Some Problems of National Identity," *Literary Criterion*, 30, 1-2 (1955).

Bruce King (ed.), *The Commonwealth Novel Since 1960* (London: Macmillan, 1991).

James McAuley, "Some Poems of Judith Wright," *Australian Literary* Studies, 3.3 (1968).

Judith Wright, *Collected Poems 1942-1970* (Melbourne: Angus and Robertson, 1971). Cited as CP.

______. *Preoccupations in Australian Poetry* (Melbourne: OUP, 1965).

Elizabeth Jolley's *Miss Peabody's Inheritance* and John Wain's *The Pardoner's Tale*: A Comparison in Theme and Technique

R. Kamala
S.D. College, Alappuzha
University of Kerala

Though the history of Australian literature is relatively short, its scope and magnitude is very great and its range and variety, very impressive. In the galaxy of Australian writers, especially women writers, Elizabeth Jolley's name is prominent. Jolley acquired international acclaim with the publication of her third and fourth novels *Mr. Scobie's Riddle* (1983) and *Miss Peabody's Inheritance* (1983).

This paper is an attempt to compare Jolley's *Miss Peabody's Inheritance* with the British writer John Wain's *The Pardoner's Tale*. Thematically and technically these two novels share many similarities. There is an interplay of two stories in each. Both novels depict the vulnerability of human life and the efforts of man to escape the destructive wheels of time through the medium of art and love. Jolley and Wain present characters who seek through art some sense of order in a chaotic world. Both writers explore the relationship between life and art or imagination and reality. In both novels there is a rite of passage to Australia. In Jolley's novel it is the reader Miss Peabody who finally reaches Australia; in Wain's novel it is Giles, the novelist, who in the end sets out for Australia.

Both Jolley and Wain deal with the theme of loneliness. Dorothy Peabody is a lonely English spinster whereas Helen Chichester Redfern is a deserted wife. They are embodiments of loneliness though Dorothy is living with her bedridden mother Mrs Peabody and Helen has her uncaring daughter Diana. Both Dorothy and Helen are fed up with their lives. Further Diana Hopewell, the novelist in *Miss Peabody's Inheritance*, is an invalid spinster living in a private nursing home and Giles Hermitage, the novelist in *The Pardoner's Tale*, is a deserted lover. The major characters in both novels seek a reconciliation with life through the medium of art—Diana and Giles through their writing, Dorothy and Helen by their reading and Diana, the daughter of Helen, through her music.

The very first page of Jolley's novel gives us a hint about the story-within-a-story structure of the novel. The opening line is "The nights belonged to the novelist" (MPI 1). Yet until page four we do not realise that this is part of a novel which Diana is writing. There are separate sections for both stories. Sometimes Diana's novel runs only to a single section but at times several sections are devoted to unravel the story. Jolley like Wain utilises the double narrative structure of her novel to explore the relationship between fiction and reality. Dorothy escapes from the monotony of her life by reading Diana's romantic tale. In the words of Joan Kirkby, Dorothy "takes up the mantle that Diana has offered her, the mantle of imagination, of creator" (Kirkby, n.d. 212).

Similarly we do not suspect that we are reading the fragment of a novel when we go through the first chapter of Wain's book. But the second chapter reveals to us the secondary plot of the novel. The first line takes us by surprise: "Giles Hermitage laid down his ball-point writing implement" (PT 57). This chapter also tells us about the author of the novel and what he considers about novel as an art-form. "Novel-writing was such a tedious subjective process . . . " (PT 57). We understand that Giles takes refuge in novel-writing to escape his disappointment in life.

Wain intertwines the two stories in such a way that we understand that the discontent of the novelist is mirrored in the novel he is writing. Thus Wain like Jolley shows how the novelist's imagination influences his view of reality. It should be said to his credit that Wain manages the two levels of fictional discourse with consummate skill. The 'real' and 'fictional' characters of the novels of Jolley and Wain equally attract the reader.

Through their fictional surrogates Diana and Giles, Jolley and

Wain present the dilemmas and aspirations of a writer, his mode of life and his method of writing. Both make explicit how the mind of a writer works. Diana's letters to Dorothy throw light on the life of an artist:

> Writers did not always use everything they wrote . . . (MPI 10)

> Perhaps it is in writing the novelist wrote that the writer re-makes himself and his world. (MPI 15)

> I do not always write everything in the order in which things appear in a finished book. There is a thin line between truth and fiction and there are moments in the writing of fantasy and imagination where truth is suddenly revealed. (MPI 15)

> The structure of my story . . . is so complicated that, in my notes, I have to use different colours. . . . I have even got some pieces of coloured paper to write on to help me when I am sorting out the different incidents. (MPI 33)

> Writers don't have any friends, the novelist wrote, and any friends the writer has don't read what that writer has written. (MPI 69)

> So much depends . . . in the writing of a novel on the impact of the imagination on someone else. A great deal depends too on the fiction which is mounted on truth. . . . The writer creates the imagined land from fragments of the real thing . . . (MPI 136-37)

Giles Hermitage faces similar predicaments. He finds that he can write only with a particular "stubby, metallic ball-point" (PT 57), his "word-pistol" (PT 108). He admits that he did not "feel confident of writing well with any other kind of pen" (PT 57). Giles also throws light on the life of a writer:

> . . . people like me just drift through life. Of course a good

> deal of my life is lived imaginatively . . . in a way it's my job to spend a lot of time day-dreaming, and when you do that you don't notice what is happening to you. (PT 172)

He comments on the process of writing:

> During the writing of a story, all life ceases except what goes on inside the skull. He would be out of life and yet observing it, moving restlessly among the scenes in which he had lived, recalling reality and re-shaping it. A ghost comes and goes as it pleases, has no experience of its own, feeds on that of others; it cannot act, but it can speak. (PT 64)

Technically speaking both novels share the novel-within-a-novel structure. Jolley and Wain dexterously intertwine the two stories. Critics have praised the double narrative structure of their novels:

> Mrs Jolley has written a wonderful duet of stories, so carefully balanced and alternated that she maintains an equal interest in both. Indeed, the novel is at its best at the moment it seesaws between novelist and reader Hopewell and Peabody . . . (Kirkby, 215)

Dale Salwak remarks: "Structuring a fiction (Hermitage's story) around a fiction (Howkin's story) provides Wain with a suggestive form of enormous resonance and flexibility." (Salwak, 1981: 104)

Diana Hopewell's novel in progress is about three Australian women, elderly lesbians who travel from Munich to Vienna. There are beautiful descriptions of the city of Vienna in this novel. On the other hand Giles Hermitage is writing a novel about a man named Gus Howkins who has run away from his home and from his tedious work. Both Wain and Jolley show how the novelists' imagination influences their view of reality.

In both novels there are many literary allusions. In Jolley's novel frequently there is a reference to the lines in *Othello*:

> But jealous souls will not be answered so;
> They are not ever jealous for the cause,

> But jealous for they are jealous: 'tis a monster
> Begot upon itself, born on itself (MPI 43).

She also alludes to Dickens' *Great Expectations* (23), to *Antony and Cleopatra* (88), to Bronte (150), to Psalm 84 (98), to Oscar Wilde (119), to Goethe (63, 168), to Wagner (97).

Wain in *The Pardoner's Tale* alludes to *The Myth of Sisyphus* (73), *Paradise Lost* (219), 'Lycidas' (220), *Antony and Cleopatra*, to Pope (294), to Bacchus (231). In both cases these allusions reinforce the novels' themes.

Jolley and Wain list the qualities of a writer. Diana is very curious to know about people and places. She is full of questions and comments which sometimes cause embarrassment to Dorothy.

> "Have you a small, straight brave back?" (MPI 12)
> "What sort of dresses do you wear" (MPI 2)
> "I am in love with your handwriting" (MPI 6)

Giles too is endowed with all the qualities of a writer. He is presented as a detached observer of those around him. He overhears conversations and watches people from a distance. His sensitivity marks him out from the rest of the people. He has a remarkable gift for symbolically condensing a series of incidents to analyse a person.

Diana Hopewell, a lonely spinster, is only too happy to receive a letter from her fan Dorothy Peabody. Giles Hermitage is likewise quite happy to get an admiring letter from his fan Helen Chichester Redfern. Dorothy is a typist in a London office leading a lonely life with a bed-ridden tyrannical mother whereas Helen is a cancer patient who lives with a daughter who has no affection for her. Jolley's novel divides its attention between the London typist and the Australian novelist and also focuses on the novel which Diana is writing. Wain's novel presents the lonely, discontented life of the writer Giles and also unravels the story which Giles is writing. Dorothy is thrilled when she receives the first draft and the working notes of a new novel which Diana has been writing along with a letter from the novelist. Likewise Helen is happy to see her favourite novelist Giles in her house.

Diana through her letters shares with Dorothy the experience of actually living in Australia. Dorothy the Londoner is greatly interested in knowing about the landscape of Australia, particularly about the novelist's whereabouts, especially her farm. For Dorothy, Australia is "a land of enchantment" (Kirkby, 216). Awakened by Diana's letters Dorothy imagines the land of Australia and pictures her dear novelist "dismounting from her horse at sunset to open the gates leading to her property" (MPI 5). Even in her first letter to Diana, Dorothy had written about her fascination for Australia. Dorothy is excited to read about the landscape of Australia, particularly the whereabouts of her favourite writer:

> I live on the gentle slope of a narrow valley, . . . I live in a ring of trees, very old trees and tall, taller, I suspect than your English trees. In between the bunched foliage of glittering narrow leaves there are spaces of sky. There is just such a clear space between the trees like a harbour in the sky directly above my house and my sheds. (MPI 8)

When Dorothy does not get Diana's letters she thinks "It was, after all, February, and though there was plenty of rain and slush from unsettled snow in England, Diana's farm was suffering from drought" (MPI 14). Dorothy's guess is right since Diana writes to her that she had been busy "burning off her paddocks and ploughing firebreaks. . . . The early rains had been welcome. . . . It was heavenly to smell more rain in the wind" (MPI 46).

Diana wants to know more about London and Dorothy finds that she had nothing exciting to write about except the descriptions of "crowded trains and of the men in the First class compartments seen from the corridor who always had their same seats and played cards during the repetitive journeys" (MPI 46).

It will not be an exaggeration to say that Dorothy's life becomes meaningful only after Diana responds to her letters. She dreamily reads the letters of the novelist and is transfigured by the experience. She forgets her real world and is transported to the imaginary world of art created by Diana. She is so much influenced by Diana's novel-in-progress that she even tries to imitate the actions of the main characters in the novel. Reading about the motel shower and the waterfight in Diana's novel, Dorothy takes a hot bath though it was not "her night for a bath" and in her new-found joy she even sings. "I'm a little prairie flower . . . / Growing wilder every hour" (MPI 20). Dorothy even tries to imitate the actions of Diana. In one of her letters Diana writes "When I see the sky harbour ahead, I know I am nearly at my place" (9). Reading this Dorothy adopts the same method. But Jolley humorously tells us "In the city, looking up made her neck ache, and she bumped into people. In no time her hat and spectacles were knocked crooked and several people had tripped, treading on her feet" (9).

There is another humorous scene in which she starts searching for Miss Thorne and her friends, fictional characters in Diana's novel who had gone to see Oscar Wilde's play *An Ideal Husband* in one of the theatres in London. In her frantic search for Miss Thorne, Dorothy forgets the fact that she is only a fictional character created by Diana. She stops everyone in the street just to ask where the play was being staged. But people misunderstand her question and their replies are very interesting.

> "I'm looking for *An Ideal Husband*" . . .
> "Aren't we all, ducks! Best of luck to you!" . . .
> "I've just walked out on mine. Good luck!" (MPI 125)

After her friendship with Diana, Dorothy tries to talk in a flowery language to her friends. "I like alcohol but alcohol doesn't like me" (MPI 85). All the events in the novel show that Dorothy has been intoxicated by reading Diana's letters. The letters fill her with doubts and Dorothy voices some of them to her colleagues: ". . . has anyone heard the curlew lately?" (MPI 65). Her questions make others consider her "mad" and she is advised to take leave from her secretarial job. She gladly does so as she is very eager to meet Diana in Australia. She is so excited that she asks foolish questions while she is flying to Australia. "It simply is not possible to get out, is it?" she said, with her brightest smile, to the passenger next to her in the plane. "I mean, I can't walk out there can I" (MPI 142).

Dorothy arrives in Australia only to find her dear novelist dead, leaving her an "inheritance". To her surprise she learns that Diana like her was also a spinster living alone in a private nursing home. Moreover, she was an invalid. She admires Diana for never even once complaining.

Because of letters Miss Peabody had known happiness. Dorothy who never felt lonely at the death of her mother, feels lost now that Diana has left her. "Miss Peabody could not stop crying. It was as if all the loneliness of years welled within her and spilled over in the tears" (MPI 147).

In Wain's *The Pardoner's Tale* Giles is presented as a successful novelist who is haunted by the loss of his girlfriend Harriet. To find relief from his sense of loss, he decides to meet Helen, his fan. He understands very soon that she intended to use the writer's insights to make some sense of her unhappy life. Her deathbed request to Giles is to write about a selfish person who comes to a mean end. It can be said that Giles fulfils her wish through his novel in progress. Giles forgets his personal loss while he is working on his novel. Finally the tide of events becomes favourable to him and he is reunited with his girlfriend in Australia.

Thus Dorothy Peabody and Giles Hermitage reach Australia to start afresh. Joan Kirkby rightly points out that Dorothy's inheritance, the manuscript of Diana's novel, is a "vision, energy and a rite of passage to Australia" (Kirkby 216). For Dorothy,

> Reading becomes an education in writing as she shares in the creative process, meanwhile creating her own imaginative version of the admired novelist and the Australian bush. The links, dualities and echoes between the novel in process and life in process suggest the power of the imagination and the ambiguous relationships between fiction and reality, mind and art, and subjectivity and life. (Wilde et al, 1994: 414)

Wain also teaches us "to think more clearly about books, their makers and the fascinating people who read them" (Salwak, 106).

WORKS CITED

Elizabeth Jolley, *Miss Peabody's Inheritance* (St. Lucia: University of Queensland Press, 1983). Cited as MPI.

Joan Kirkby, *Contemporary Literary Criticism*, Vol. 46, 212.

______, "The Nights Belong to Elizabeth Jolley: Modernism and the Sappho-Erotic Imagination of *Miss Peabody's Inheritance*", *Meanjin* 43.4, December 1984.

Dale Salwak, *John Wain* (Boston: Twayne, 1981).

John Wain, *The Pardoner's Tale* (London: Macmillan, 1978). Cited as PT.

William H. Wilde, Joy Hooton and Barry Andrews, *The Oxford Companion to Australian Literature*, 2nd ed. (Melbourne: OUP, 1994).

Reconciliation of Contraries: Douglas Stewart's *The Golden Lover*

Valsa Elizabeth Koshey
S.D. College, Alappuzha
University of Kerala

> Oh, you are woman indeed. You cannot have both.
> You ask the impossible.
>
> Douglas Stewart, *The Golden Lover*

The Golden Lover: A Comedy in Verse, gives expression to Douglas Stewart's belief that writers are seers, visionaries, sociologists but also traditionally entertainers. Stewart, one of Australia's leading playwrights, always sought to confine himself to heroic and mythological themes that had some bearing on lives in his part of the world:

> The playwright, I think creates the myths by which the people live: the heroic, gigantic, legendary figures, fathers of the race, ancestors spiritual or actual, to which the living man can point and say, "That is what I am made of; that is what makes us different from other people; that is what I believe in; those are my gods and my devils. (Sykes, 1977: 218)

Stewart wrote on a wide variety of subjects, from critical works to angling. For his verse plays he turned to the past. His interest in the complex workings of the human heart, his nostalgia regarding New Zealand, his desire to write about what was significant in the life he knew, led him to folklore, for "our countries are new in the world's literature and fresh to write about" (Sykes, xxii). He was fascinated by the mystery of the light-skinned red-haired strangers among the Maoris, the fairies, the people-of-the-mists who are portrayed in *The Golden Lover*. In James Cowan's book *Fairy Folk Tales of the Maori*, Stewart found the story of "Whanawhana of the Bush" or the "Legend of *The Golden Lover*". The play tells the story of Tawhai, the beautiful young Maori woman married to the fat, cowardly Ruarangi. All her life she has dreamed of a golden lover. She is carried away by the auburn-haired Whana, the chief of his tribe and she is not as indignant as she would want everyone to believe. Forced ultimately to make a choice between romance and security, she settles for a dull but secure life, proving Stewart's contention that the yearning for romance is subject to women's practical side.

Tawhai, married for two years to Ruarangi, who is obsessed with his roaring stomach and who "gurgled and whistled all night like a boiling spring" (*GL* 152), rebels against those constructs that relegate woman to an inferior, social position. She longs to escape the full repetitiveness of life.

> Meaningless, blind and endless in the Maori village
> Where the men are born for war and the women for childbirth.
> (*GL* 208)

She is all passion and romance and Ruarangi presents a pathetic contrast. He is afraid of the dark, of ghosts and refuses to work in the fields:

> I, a warrior
> The son of a warrior
> And the grandson of a warrior
> And the great-grandson of a warrior
> And the great-great-grandson of a warrior
> And the great-great-great-grandson of a great, great warrior.
> (*GL* 157)

The adventure of fishing in the dark, lonely waters of the river Waipa does not fascinate him. He prefers to sit in the sun, undo the knots of his fishing lines and boast while other Maori men venture forth to battle. He expects his wife to work in the fields and return home to cook the eel that "makes his belly sing like a bird" (*GL* 153). Ruarangi has very clear ideas regarding the male prerogative. It is the law of nature for man not to be questioned. Young wives should not scold or be lazy. From a woman he expects no more than from a bird or a female dog.

In the Maori village where women suffer for no crime except being born a woman, Tawhai is a refreshing contrast. She has individuality and assertiveness and finds the dark, mysterious and the unusual fascinating. She is enchanted by the men of patu paiarehe who are handsome, brave and fierce. She refuses to anoint herself with shark oil and ward off the fairy folk. She is openly contemptuous of her husband and voices the universal feminine protest: "I don't see why a wife should do all the work." His proud claim, "I the descendant/of generations of warriors, I who am I/Ruarangi" (*GL* 171) only earns her contempt. She responds with biting sarcasm:

> You little man
> You slug that creeps from one little leaf of life (*GL* 183)
>
> You have never been to battle in all your life
> The men are all women now. (*GL* 155)

Tawhai's innate desire for adventure and romance and Ruarangi's gross appetites and insensitivity aid her ravishment. Like the primordial ancestor Eve, Tawhai longs for the forbidden. She has had lovers and a husband, a husband and lovers and yet yearns for a golden lover. Wera, Tawhai's mother, knows that it is impossible to check her irrepressible spirit as it is to "hold the mountain stream/In her husband's cooking pot" (*GL* 169).

Whana, a chief among fairy folk, descends from the dark Pirongia mountain and carries Tawhai off. Her half-hearted protests are soon silenced. She becomes assertive once she is confident of his love. He raises her to the height of ecstasy for he is poetic, passionate, gentle, romantic, everything that Ruarangi is not. The walking joke, the roaring stomach, Ruarangi, is a terrible contrast to *The Golden Lover* who stood like a shadow on the fringe of the morning and was gone before you could ask his name (*GL* 175).

It is Whana who makes her aware of the pathetic life of the typical Maori woman;

> There where the women
> Grow shapeless with childbirth and gross with middle-age
> And bowed and bent and broken with toil in the fields;
> Where the smoke of the cooking fire stains and begrimes their faces
> And the stench of the cooking-fire fouls their skin and their hair;
> Where their fingers grow blunt and dirty with grubbing in the earth
> And their finger-nails are broken. (*GL* 178)

Whana invites her to share the freedom of the people of the mists. Tawhai is aware that she must pay a price, in communal loneliness. Tawhai is torn between earth and heaven, the nest and the adventure. Like the typical woman she wants both. The stench and corruption of a life devoid of adventure and passion crushes her spirit, but she is aware that the thoughts, songs and laughter of her people are a part of her being. She is woman incarnate and uses every ploy in the feminine bag of tricks to break the monotony of life. Keenly aware of the power of beauty she uses it to full advantage. Tawhai arrives at a typical feminine solution. She will keep both husband and lover. She is adept at handling all creatures, the earthly and the spiritual, Ruarangi and Whana. She convinces both of the vital need for her to play the dual role of wife and mistress.

Tawhai is filled with a longing for escape from inhibiting strictures to freedom. This longing incapable of fulfilment in a larger social context finds expression in a more limited and private sphere. She turns to one of the few avenues of self-expression open to her so that she can attain some measure of self-actualization within an inescapable, male-dominated social context. Tawhai's unusual arrangement helps her to reconcile the contraries, adventure and security, romance and communal bonding. She uses her new-found freedom and awareness of a powerful self to insult Ruarangi and claims that she is a woman bewitched.

The dual role does not last for long. Ruarangi is more easily deceived than Whana is, but even he suspects that the arrangement is ridiculous. Whana who is all spirit and intuitive knowledge, reads her thoughts. He demands a commitment, a total breaking away. He leaves her free to go but Tawhai insists, "My will is as water before you" (*GL* 176). She is able to make Whana let her return to her people, "bewitched as I am, but on my own terms". Tawhai's split consciousness is revealed in her efforts to attain a reconciliation of contraries:

> Hold me close, I am cold. Whana my dear one
> I cannot leave my people. (*GL* 178)

To Ruarangi she says:

> All day I am yours
> To admire and talk to
> But then at night, I am his.

Her arguments confuse Ruarangi to return to her people, "bewitched as I am, but on my own terms" and provoke Whana to cry out: "I should never have let you talk" (*GL* 180). He now understands why Nukuroa, Tawhai's father, prefers to think of fish.

Tawhai is forced to make a final choice. Whana and the tohunga leave her free. Tawhai realises that she cannot live life on her own terms and that the reconciliation of the contraries is impossible. Ruarangi will never enact the more productive aspects of the male sex role but a "husband is the fat round stone that holds the canoe at the moorings" (*GL* 197). She tells Whana, "You are all the world; but you cannot be my home" (*GL* 178).

Like Wera, Tawhai comes to realise that the yearning for one's own never leaves a woman. The best thing of all is sisterly bonding, for "children though pleasant are very much of a nuisance/And husbands though also pleasant are more of a nuisance" (*GL* 160).

The Golden Lover focuses on the two sides of a single consciousness—the desire to enjoy adventure and romance and yet preserve home, community and security. Even in the height of ecstasy Tawhai reiterates the love for her tribe. She realises that her search for selfhood must have a communal context and it is communal support that helps her to come to terms with life. The play presents the failed dream on a domestic scale. Stewart was obsessed with the portrayal of heroic dreamers like Scott (*Fire on the Snow*) and Ned Kelly (*Ned Kelly*). These plays envision man as a heroic dreamer who risks everything for a dream that is doomed to fail. The celebration of courage, the intrinsic worth of human endeavour fascinated Stewart. In her effort to bring together earth and heaven, Tawhai is in mythological terms aligned to Tahiri, the god of the elements who opposed the separation of his parents, Rangi, the Sky father and Papa, the Earth Mother.

The playwright employs a Maori myth to underscore the universality of the theme. Australia's ancestral heroes can be recognised in "The voyagers, explorers and pioneers who first broke through the wall of silence and sunlight beyond which the continent lay undiscovered (Stewart, 1995: 27). In one sense Tawhai is a pioneer, a voyager into unchartered territory, much in advance of her time and gives expression to the frustration of women in more advanced climes. But Tawhai is incapable of a total commitment and her dream of romance is doomed to fail. She chooses the mundane life of the earth and renounces the glorious life of the sky, that immortal splendour that we can recognise only in flashes here on earth. The wise man, the tohunga, echoes the voice of her heart and calls her back to earth, away from Whana who is all spirit.

> While *The Golden Lover* is by far the most erotic of Stewart's plays, it is in a sense the least romantic, primarily because Tawhai retains an unromantic grain of what is known as practical common sense. (Sykes, 1977: xxi)

Tawhai is not one of the great lovers of literature and is incapable of renunciation or even plain discomfort. She is filled with a wild longing

> A hunger for the apple on the bough
> Most out of reach. (*Yeats, Collected Poems*, 181)

In his Introduction to the play Douglas Stewart said, "It is a play about the acceptance of life" (Stewart, Introduction, 217):

> For this play is not merely a comedy of love, or an evocation of New Zealand, or the dramatisation of a Maori legend; it also seeks to express what I must call a view or a vision of life.

WORKS CITED

Alrene Sykes, ed. *Five Plays: Portable Australian Authors*, incl. Douglas Stewart, "The Playwright in Australia" and *The Golden Lover*. Cited as GL. (St. Lucia, Queensland: University of Queensland Press, 1977).

Douglas Stewart, "The Playwright in Australia", Australian Theatre Year 1 (1955-56).

W.B. Yeats, *The Collected Poems* (London: Macmillan, 1933; 1973).

Narrative with a Post-Modern Vision: A Reading of Peter Carey's *Oscar and Lucinda*

D. MAYA
University of Kerala

The resistance among writers in the '60s to the tyranny of social realism in Australian fiction sought expression in the ambiguity and obscurity of the modernist mode adopted by Patrick White and Randolph Stow, in the deradicalised realism of George Johnston and in the sexual imagery and commodity fiction of Thomas Keneally. Peter Carey's third novel, *Oscar and Lucinda,* assumes significance in this context as a voluminous experiment in fiction which embodies in itself the urge to break free from the bonds of realism and to represent the cultural plurality, the ethnic complexity and the socio-religious and politico-economic intricacies of the ever-expanding Australian experience. The work falls into line with classics like Sterne's *Tristram Shandy* and Furphy's *Such is Life*—which Furphy himself describes as "a loose federation of yarns" (Quoted in Narasimhaiah, 1980: 31).

This paper proposes that Peter Carey's *Oscar and Lucinda* (1988), which seemingly offers the satisfactions of a nineteenth-century realistic novel with its deceptively simple structuring, can be read as a post-modern narrative in which the seams of realism burst to include allegory and fantasy so as to convey experience the significance of which lies more in the telling than in the tale. Carey's novel is a product of the colonial experience with its attendant problematics of a multicultural schizophrenic existence. It disturbs old world certainties even as it conforms to the realistic mode of narration; it demythifies notions of history as truth and subverts realistic fictional concepts about the hero and the heroine; and it undermines assumptions about meaning and the intention of rationality, and the objectivity of the *bourgeois-rationalist-humanist tradition* (Shepherd, 1990: 34).

The use of 'I' as narrator sets the tone of the novel and dispels any expectations on the part of the reader about occupying a position of confidence in relation to the tale where an *objective, authoritative (authorial) voice*, knowing all, tells the meaning of events (Jackson, 1981: 28). The narrative voice of the confused/confusing I at the centre of the tale introduces us to this world of Quixotic characters, where the protagonist himself has an uncertain vision. The choice of the two eccentric characters—Oscar and Lucinda—to occupy the centrestage adds to the excitement provided by the fantastic. The narrator claims to be the great grandson of the protagonist whose marriage with his great grandmother, we realise at the end of the novel, had never been legally solemnised. The intruding voice of the narrator disturbs any illusion of realism, anticipates events, compares the image of Lucinda in the future with her mother's in the present. The choice of a narrator three generations removed in time sanctions the irreverence of tone characteristic of the post-modern narrative. The narrator's revisioning of the tale of Oscar and Lucinda has the qualities of a post-colonial rewriting of history that subverts the discourse of power and seeks a liberated medium.

The centrestage is occupied by Oscar Hopkins, a youth who travels from a Devonshire village to Sydney in the nineteenth century to become a clergyman, and Lucinda Leplastier, an orphaned young lady who journeyed from South Wales with the colonial burden of gains from occupied land, to Sydney to become the owner of a glass factory. Oscar Hopkins' story is introduced with a sentence that suggests the comic and absurd nature of his life as such: "There would have been no church at Gleniffer if it had not been for a Christmas pudding" (OL 7).

We have to wait for about 500 pages of energetic narration to reach the climactic event of the church-building. The first crisis in Oscar's life is triggered off by the Christmas pudding which he eats and delights in, despite his father's severe admonitions to the contrary. Oscar's theological dilemma engendered by the denial of something as delicious as the pudding results in his rejection of parental ties and his adoption of Stratton's church. Any expectations on the part of the reader regarding the sleepless hours of deliberation and agonising conflict that might precede such a crucial decision are dispelled when Oscar draws certain diagrams in the sand, throws a stone backward and adopts the Baptist church because the stone lands on the column marked alpha for the Anglican church. Similarly, the irreverence and scepticism in the depiction of the leaders of the different religious sects can hardly go unnoticed. Theophilus, Oscar's pious and austere parent who frowns upon the Catholic church as the creation of the anti-Christ, cannot claim his lost son because of the lack of conviction in his own voice; Hugh Stratton whom God told Oscar was his "chosen servant" is confused and uncertain when he realises Oscar's intentions; and Oscar himself is a full-fledged gambler by the time he becomes a priest. The climactic event of the novel—the conception and execution of the dream-church—is hardly motivated by religious ardour. It is more of an act of love indulged in with sentiments of chivalry close to that of medieval romances.

Both Oscar and Lucinda have a colonial past. Oscar is the offspring of a missionary appropriating the souls of the pagans; Lucinda is the beneficiary of imperialism which she resents. Her mother represents the typical coloniser with a nostalgic yearning for 'home' during the eleven years she was forced to spend with her husband in New South Wales. Characteristically enough, when she has the freedom to go home, she refuses to go because she doesn't want "to leave the country to the Irish (OL 88). The urge to rid herself of the burden of guilt is manifest in Lucinda when she says about the money got from selling her parents' land:

> This money did not belong to them, or to her either. The money was stolen from the land. The land was stolen from the blacks. She could not have it. It was thirty pieces of silver (OL 126).

She tries to give it to the church, but the church decides that as an orphan, she needed it. It is with this burden of colonial guilt that Lucinda sails to Sydney.

Among the multifarious strands of the story, the colonial enterprise with its proselytizing mission, appropriation of land and exploitation of economic resources, gets pushed to the peripheries. In the earlier parts of the novel, the trauma of displacement for the colonizer and dispossession for the colonized, is related in the dominant white discourse that submerges the voices of the bushmen and the blacks. The poverty and misery of the white Christian missionaries like Theophilus and Stratton, the nostalgia for 'home' that sustained Elizabeth Leplastier for eleven years, the loss of the labourers in the "hell Hole" of the glass factory, form parts of the pastiche of the imperial experience presented. Carey's technique is to juxtapose this with the allegorical presentation of the church-building in the last part of the novel.

The transporting of the glass church to Boat Harbour is a mission of love undertaken by Oscar to win the trust of Lucinda, but it soon transforms itself into an allegory of the colonial enterprise in its crudest and ugliest form. Jeffris with his ambition to map new and unexplored territories represents the typical colonizer, dehumanized by the desire for power and encroaching on tribal land cutting forest trees, killing the resisting bush natives and defiling whatever is sacred to them. The violence, brutal exercise of power, total indifference to the customs and traditions of the tribes and the appropriation of land and people by the use of the gun, re-enact the colonial drama. Oscar is scared by the transformation in Jeffris and remarks: "I feel I am not suited to this life. There is a cruel feel to it" (OL 451).

Through Oscar's reminiscences of the stories of the Kumbangiri tribe as told by his father we climb down the ladder of history to the coming of the first missionaries to the bush of Australia. The tribesfolk said: "Our people had not seen white men before. We thought they were spirits" (OL 468). Through Oscar's memories, Carey brings to visibility the untold story of the natives. About Kumbangiri Billy—commonly called come-and-get-it Billy—his father had said: He "had more brains in his nose than the whole shire council wrapped into one" (OL 466). The quiet, peace-loving and wise folk of the bushlands are overpowered by Jeffris, by the mere might of arms. The Narcoo tribesmen conscripted at Kempsey to guide the Europeans on the last leg of the journey are shot when they hesitate to violate age-old custom and show the way to Kumbangiri. The violence and brutality of Jeffris transforms even the timid Oscar into a red-eyed angry man. The rude exposure to what has been silenced, covered over and made 'absent' by the dominant culture, shakes Oscar. He feels crushed by the oppressive weight of evil and feels that retribution will follow. When Jeffris forcefully pushes him out of the tavern and kicks him, Smith attacks Jeffris and Hopkins brings the axe down on the head of Jeffris. Thus Oscar himself becomes the instrument of retribution, at the same time confirming his own participation in violence.

The disparity between imperial codes of recognition and values of the native—the other—are projected by giving voice to the silenced tribes. The callous destruction of trees that they loved and worshipped, provokes them to make songs about the spirits (as they call the whites) who chased off the bees, and denied firewood to men as a kind of punishment. The songs evolving from the new colonial experience tell of the rude appropriation and destruction of natural resources by the newly arrived 'spirits.' The natives discover that the glass brought by Oscar and his party is painfully destructive. It cuts. The oppressive nature of imperial machinery with its destructive weapons is suggested by the song about glass made by Odalberee. Their reactions to the situation show remarkable perception and extreme sensitivity. Odalberee, overwhelmed by his own role in the encroachment and destruction of land and men, confesses his crime to the Kumbangiri folk, and commits suicide by cutting himself with the white man's glass, as an act of penitence. The sensitivity and higher culture of the tribes, far removed from so-called civilisation, shine in contrast with the rampant materialism and power-culture of their rulers.

What had promised to be a journey of adventure and fulfilment—divine and personal—turns out to be a hoary tale of wickedness and violence. The romantic expectations of wish-fulfilment are rudely shattered as the innocent Oscar falls prey to the schemes of Miriam Chadwick—a lady doomed to a life of mourning—who tempts him into sin and extracts from him a promise of marriage. The mission of the glass church, conceived in a whimsical moment but carried out with conviction and ardour by Oscar Hopkins to win the trust of Lucinda, seems to undermine the very purpose behind it, once it is translated into reality. The vacuity and meaninglessness of all human endeavour is suggested by the anticlimax of Oscar sinning with Miriam and desiring to destroy the glass church. "All he could think was that the glass church was the devil's work, that it had been the agent of murder and fornication" (OL 500). Oscar's disappearance into the river and Miriam's claims to Lucinda's property as the widow of Oscar, mock the intentions behind the entire endeavour, and reduce the fiction to a work of no meaning.

The fictional nature of the story and its existence at a point of time which is just a speck in the continuum are driven home by references to Lucinda's future as a Labour activist and the beginning of her "real life after the loss of her factory," fortune and love. The attempts of realistic fiction to create the illusion of reality and of romance to conjure an ideal world of beauty and fulfilment, are subverted to accommodate the truth. The truth as spelt out by the novel seems to centre on the meaninglessness of existence and all human activity. The way it is presented shows the author had not intended to convey meaning—not even the meaninglessness of all meaning. The novel thus transcends the struggle of modernism for meaning and can be described as post-modern in vision and techniques.

The book can be read as an interrogation of 'the real' in its closeness to the fantastic. In the depiction of the eccentric Oscar Hopkins and Lucinda Leplastier, in their whimsical fantasies to fulfil the fanciful extravagance, there are elements so totally contrasting to the real that they can only be viewed as a subverting of the real and a questioning of it. The comic eccentricities of Oscar and Lucinda are exaggerated to the extent of reducing them to quixotic figures. Oscar, called 'Odd Bod' at Oriel, with his trousers three inches too short and a frock coat left over from the time of Newman, reads the Bible and discusses the doctrine of eternal damnation on the race track and places his bet listening to the voice of God. The 24-year-old Lucinda, on the other hand, is more fashionably dressed and much more worldly wise. Ironically enough, Lucinda first sees Oscar in a pathetic state, when he is being carried sick and moaning on a stretcher. Lucinda's confession to Oscar about her passion for gambling stirs the dormant fires in Oscar who justifies it as natural because we mortals are gambling our "mortal souls, every second of our temporal existence on the unprovable fact of His existence" (OL 261). The scandal provoked by the card game that continues till the early hours of the morning in the young lady's room and the unconscious condition of the clergyman as he is carried off by the stewards in the early hours of the morning, give rise to high comedy. Lucinda's eccentricities—her habit of turning up and remaining in Dennis Hatchet's room at all odd hours, causing his transfer to Boat Harbour, her "taking to cards like a duck to water" (OL 166), her confession to Oscar, her passion for glass and the foolhardy wager that makes her lose all that she held precious in life—are all narrated with a touch of the ludicrous. Oscar's triumphant moment of fulfilment when he sits in the middle of the glass church and prays to God at peace with himself, is presented through the perspective of the blacks who notice the flies inside the glass church rather than the priest. Dennis Hatchet, Lucinda's 'lover' who is to receive the glass church, is troubled by a leech in his shoes and is desperately trying to take it out when he first sees the glass church. The technique of juxtaposing the solemn and the ludicrous undermines the seriousness of the narrative. The climactic event of the erection of the church in Boat Harbour is narrated by a black whose niece became the first Christian. Oscar christened Kumbangiri Billy's niece Mary and told her: "You will live in Paradise" (OL 488). The solemnity of the achievement is shattered as Billy remarks: "It was a damn silly name for a Kumbangiri and if you want my opinion, Bob, it was ignorant to talk to us koories in that way" (OL 488).

The Oscar-Lucinda story reads like a fantasy in its violation of "what is generally accepted as possibility" (Jackson, 1981: 14) and subverts the dominant assumptions of realistic fiction. Past, present and future merge in the tale narrated by a great-grandson three generations removed from the protagonist. The pastiche of Australian experience presented includes theological controversy, the dialectic of the colonizer-colonized syndrome with all its attendant evils, the woes of the missionaries and the bushmen, gambling and its intricacies, the loneliness of the individual, the conditions of the labourers in the factories under the capitalist regime, and the rich landscape of the bushlands of Australia. The scepticism regarding absolutes, the absence of vision and the denial of the possibility of meaning denote the post-modern idiom.

Like Gabriel Garcia Marquez, what Carey attempts is the demythologizing of factual history and the creation of mythical realism. As in Kafka's fiction the traditional form of story-telling is adopted here without its truth content. We are forced to discard epistemological paranoia and enter a world devoid of meaning. The conflict of different theological dogmas and the failure of the glass church do not lead to any discussion of faith and doubt. Carey's fictional world is "a world of no issues, a diversion, a fabrication" as Michael Wilding remarks (Wilding, 1931: 31). The work itself is a fabrication, narrated in the contemporary idiom with brief chapters written in current vocabulary and moving with a sharp, quick pace. The author's preoccupation is with the fictionality of the work and the reader becomes a participant in the generation of the narrative. An intimate perception of the experience is made possible through the use of a narrator of contemporary times. If, as Michael Wilding claims, "the fabrication, the lie, the refusal of significance are the mark of the post-modern." Carey's work cannot be better described than by the term 'post modern.'

WORKS CITED

Peter Carey, *Oscar and Lucinda* (London: Faber and Faber, 1988). Cited as OL.

C.D. Narasimhaiah & C.N. Srinath (eds.), *The Literary Criterion*, The Flowering of Australian Literature, XV, Nos. 3-4, 1980.

Rosemary Jackson, *Fantasy: The Literature of Subversion* (London and New York: Methuen, 1981).

Karen Lamb, *Encyclopedia of Post-Colonial Literatures in English*, Vol. I, ed. Eugene Benson and L.V. Connolly.

Ron Shepherd, "*Midnight's Children* as Fantasy," *The Commonwealth Review*, Vol. I, No. 2, 1990.

Michael Wilding, *Australia*, in *The Commonwealth Novel Since 1960*, ed. Bruce King (London: Macmillan. 1991).

Singing the World the Barramatjara Way in Thomas Keneally's *Flying Hero Class*

Evangeline Shanti Roy
University of Kerala

Thomas Keneally is a writer who shapes his fiction from thought-provoking moral dilemmas. In *Flying Hero Class* he raises questions about the true nature of the relationship between the Australian Aborigines and the whites. The world tour undertaken by a group of Aborigine dancers belonging to the Barramatjara tribe provides the background against which the complicated question of who is the victim the world over is explored. The five member Barramatjara Dance Troupe consists of the leader Whitey Wappitji, the movie star, Bluey Kannata, the musician Paul Mungina, a maestro of the traditional didj, the tribal elder Philip Puduma and Cowboy Tom Gullagara. Their tour manager is a white Australian, Frank McCloud. They have embarked upon a tour to enlighten the world about their culture and tribal myths. This mission was revealed to Whitey in a dream by many important old men of the tribe. The authority that the dream conferred upon Whitey gave him the strength to paint and dance before the whites, despite the reservations of the present-day elders.

The troupe's performance consists of painting their own special designs on canvas right on stage, and then dancing out the myth before it: "The people re-enacted the earth-compounding journeys of their ancestors through dance and ceremonial . . . paintings. Their dance and their paintings were liturgy . . . a remaking of the eternal earth the ancestors had given them" (Keneally, 1991: 73). A white school teacher had suggested that they devise a one-day dance sequence to entertain the city-dwellers, but as Bluey tells McCloud, without Whitey's dream they would never have consented to display their private myths in public. Whitey's dream also revealed to him the origin of his tribe in the union between the marsupial rat Tutinjinga and the lizard-woman at Mount Dinkat. Their performance, therefore, included animal mimicry which frequently "transcended imitation and nudged at the edges of metamorphosis" (FHC 74).

McCloud is told by Bluey that by watching the performance, the white audience become relatives of the performers because "To see the designs which belonged to a particular person's dreaming or mystery, you needed to be a relative" (FHC 56). McCloud is shaken by the largeness of their gesture to the white world. Thus, at the very outset, Keneally upsets the usual equation of the white man as the giver, the doler of largesse and the colonised natives as the beneficiaries. Here it is the Barramatjara who are generous enough to share their most private and treasured possessions with the rest of the 'uncivilised' world. Twice the Christian missionaries from Europe had ventured into the remote Baruda country and tried to 'civilise' and convert the Barramatjara. Now "the Barramatjara were on their own mission to those who lay in that outer dark which went by the name of Europe and America" (FHC 12).

The action of the novel occurs aboard the aeroplane carrying the troupe from New York, where they had been received ecstatically by their audiences, to Frankfurt where they were going to give their next performance. Their plane is seized by five hijackers belonging to the Arab Youth Popular Socialist Front who start by informing the passengers that "those who had not been guilty of war crimes against the Palestine people" (FHC 36) would be very safe. They soon identify three 'guilty' people among the passengers—David Stone, a Jew who designed psychological profiling software which could predict the actions of enemies of the state like terrorists; and Cale, a journalist who wrote anti-Palestinian articles in the British right-wing press. McCloud, the central consciousness in the novel, is stunned to discover that he is the third guilty person, accused of being an accomplice of the CIA and the capitalist industry in their plot to deprive the Barramatjara of their ancestral land. The Arabs identify themselves with the Australian Aborigines as fellow victims, dispossessed of their land by the

Western world. McCloud is supposed to have embarked on this tour in order to keep the elders away from the tribe while crucial negotiations were being held, and also to soften them by being feted in America. McCloud's plea that he was totally ignorant of the motives of the CIA and the diamond drilling industry, and that as a friend of the Barramatjara he would never knowingly dupe them, is ignored.

In fact McCloud is a demoralised, ineffective personality, all too aware of his shortcomings. His wife Pauline, a highly successful, super-efficient tour manager, who is also on the plane, delights in pointing out his weaknesses, which she does with devastating accuracy. For the past three years he had been working on a novel which he had hoped to sell in New York, but the response of the publishers had been disappointing. He finds it hard to communicate with his wife though he loves her. He had just drifted along with the Troupe without really trying to understand them either. But basically he is not a man of evil intentions. He is typical of Keneally's "moral world inhabited and conditioned by guilt, suffering, sacrifice and atonement" (Goodwin, 1986: 235). The fact that he is bracketed with the other two so-called Zionists, stripped, humiliated and confined in the pit of the place, forces him into introspection about himself, his life, his relationship with the Barramatjara, as well as with the hijackers. He realises that "His temperamental tendency to blame himself as a means of forgiving himself needed to be combated now" (FHC 93).

At the same time the hijackers isolate another group whom they see as "exiles in their own land" (FHC 152), consisting of the Barramatjara dancers, and the exquisitely beautiful Daisy Nakamura, an American of Japanese origin. They are taken to the upper deck of the plane where Taliq, the leader of the hijackers, instructs them in his version of political history and then attempts to persuade one of them to be the judge who tries and sentences the three guilty men. When McCloud, along with the others, is brought to the upper deck, he is shocked to discover that Bluey Kannata is the judge who already condemns him.

Taliq then happens to injure his hand as he opens a tin of cashews, and Whitey rushes forward to wrap the wound with his bandanna. McCloud later sees him withdraw to the lavatory with the bloodstained bandanna. He sees him "reading Taliq's blood" (FHC 166) for a long time and then begin to sing or intone over the bandanna. McCloud had earlier been told by Bluey that Whitey was a 'featherfoot', a man who wore feather moccasins in spirit and could daze a wrongdoer with a song he couldn't even hear and then the man would die in a couple of days. Now McCloud was sure that Whitey "was persuading . . . some sort of inevitable event to enter Taliq's veins" (FHC 167), and this suspicion is confirmed when Whitey tells him that Taliq is "not a well man" (FHC 167). McCloud is strengthened and elated by "Whitey's infallible reading of the blood and with the curse of confusion and illness Whitey had sung into it" (FHC 167).

By now the plane has landed and the three are taken below to be tried before the assembled passengers. But as Bluey, the judge, is in the middle of his impressive, condemnatory speech, he falls down in a fit and has to be carried away. Then Taliq informs them that the expected exchange of prisoners for the hostages had not taken place and so they were to fly to another destination. Suddenly the urge overtakes McCloud to take control of his life at least now and not wait to be acted upon as he had always done. He decides, "I must not let anything more befall me. I have been a mere brute medium on which other forces have acted. I have sung the tunes proposed by other impulses than mine. Now I must become singer of my own songs. Now I must become an actor" (FHC 196). Whitey's message that there was no remote controlled explosive in the luggage compartment is the signal which triggers him into action. When Taliq collapses, gasping with pain from a duodenal ulcer, McCloud hesitates momentarily wondering if it was the right time to act. Then he reminds himself that "that was his failing, the limiting factor of his existence, to neglect the evident and wait for something more exalted to present itself" (FHC 201).

At that moment Paul Mungina begins playing on his didj and then Tom Gullagara's voice joins it and "McCloud became convinced that the song was meant to add muscle to Whitey's already uttered and sealed curse. . . . It struck him that, for no easily defined reason, they were singing him safe. . . . More astounding still they may even have been singing him brave" (FHC 202). McCloud overpowers Taliq and then leads the passengers in storming the hijackers. They are then joined by commandos who complete the job. Pauline hails him as the man who liberated the plane and McCloud has at last become a man and not a stooge.

The conclusion of the novel, which is as exciting as that of any thriller, points more importantly to the manner in which the Barramatjara dancers are able to instil courage, determination and purpose in the weak and vacillating McCloud. The white man is the recipient of their gift of strength. Perhaps Keneally is hinting that the vitality that is still to be found in those who live close to nature and their cultural heritage is what can revitalise jaded Western civilisation.

WORKS CITED

Ken Goodwin, *A History of Australian Literature* (London: MacMillan, 1986).

Thomas Keneally, *Flying Hero Class* (London: Hodder & Stoughton, 1991). Cited as FHC.

The Phenomenon of Contact: Mythical, Real and Discursive Antipodes

LIVIO DOBREZ
Australian National University

I should say at once that the three categories of my title do not represent three distinct alternatives. Obviously mythical antipodes are entirely restricted to the sphere of discourse and real antipodes, while they may or may not be actually experienced discursively (as the Structuralists maintained when they argued for the linguistic structure of the human brain), are at the very least, once experienced, immediately translated into discourse. Still, there are discursive antipodes whose operation differs from that of myth. So I have some reason for the distinctions in my title. This paper expands a few lines relating to the antipodes in a recent article. (Dobrez, 1996) More generally, it expands upon ideas put forward in a recent book entitled *Identifying Australia in Postmodern Times*, this being that cross-cultural contact remains the major underacknowledged event in historical accounts of the genesis of European modernity. (Dobrez, 1995)

Contact transforms the participants, and in specific ways. Its othering effect is experienced as traumatic. Readers of Defoe will recall that when Robinson Crusoe encounters the Caribs his first reaction is fear, his second, aggression. Contact participants in less drastic situations than Crusoe's react similarly, though trauma, the shock of the new, may express itself in pleasant as well as unpleasant ways. Moreover the othering process is not restricted to actual participants in the event of contact. It happens to people who remain at home too, once they feel the consequences of the event. I think that the crisis precipitated by contact has shaped the process of modernity in the last few hundred years as much as the industrial revolution or the dominance of science. Probably it helped to fuel economic and technological change itself. It goes without saying that contact, say in the colonial situation, involves *material* crisis. One thinks of the enslavement of Africans or Amerindians, the decimation of populations in the Americas and Australia, the introduction of diseases in the whole of the New World and the Pacific. The indigenous Eora population of the Sydney region was largely wiped out by exotic disease within a very few years of British settlement. Smallpox, for example, broke out in the first year of the landing. However, my concern here is with spiritual or intellectual crisis.

For Europeans, contact with what they chose to regard as primitive involved a double crisis, historical and psychological. In each case the crisis was also one of origins. To encounter the "savage" amounted to a proto-Darwinian contact with one's own supposed historical or pre-historical beginnings, now become Other due to the passing of time. Likewise to a proto-Freudian contact with one's supposed primitive instinctive or irrational depths, that's to say, the other-within as distinct from the other-before. Thus we are dealing with both temporal and psychic origin. Of course so-called primitives are never that. They are, as every anthropologist knows, in the strictest sense "modern". But we are now discussing European myth rather than fact. If you took the Hobbesian line of interpreting "primitives" as brutish, or the Christian one of interpreting them as degraded by sin (according to biblical exegesis relating to post-Flood or, specifically, post-Babel degeneracy), you were bound to tame the "savage" as you would subjugate either instinct or sin. (See Genesis 11.9 as source for ideas of post-Babel moral decline.) If, following Rousseau, early Rousseau especially, you interpreted primitives as free of social vices, you were likely to query the Christian ascetic, ultimately the puritan bourgeois, ethic of self-control.

As regards non-Europeans, contact equally transforms the mental landscape. The Mexicans coped, for an initial period, by recourse to the story of Quetzalcoatl. Thus a theological problem found a theological solution. In Australia, Europeans were often taken to be pale returning spirits of the dead, white pipeclay colour itself having some association with death, and pink pigmentation with skinned corpses, in the Murray mouth region of South Australia for example. A recent, admittedly highly polemical, book has sought to argue that much of Aboriginal ritual and religion may be interpreted as a response to a variety of historical contacts. (Swain, 1993) At any rate it is clear that Aboriginal practice, as in the case of the Macassans who visited the northern shores for some hundreds of years to fish for trepang, was to incorporate foreign material into existing Dreaming theology. Thus Yiritja moiety obsequies in the north of Australia reenact the departure of the Macassan *praus* for islands envisaged as the land of the dead. With Europeans too, contact precipitated reorganizations of philosophy and religion, along with military resistance, even practical attempts at exorcism. Aborigines generally smoke a place where someone has died, to encourage the spirit of the dead to move on. It appears such ceremonies were held to drive away Europeans. (Swain, 1993:123) But the Europeans lingered, like *poltergeists* or Aboriginal *mogwois*, and their presence produced disease, i.e. the ghosts generated death in others. We need to try to grasp the enormity of contact with the dead as a human experience. There are records of twentieth century events of this kind in new Guinea, where Europeans were also greeted as ghosts. The point is that the "ghost" one encounters in this way is not simply any ghost. One "recognizes" dead loved ones, one finds loved features in the alien face of the visitor, or in his or her behaviour. Thus "recognition" comes with a rush of emotion, perhaps with tears, or as an experience of the numinous. Films like *Close Encounters of the Third Kind* of course show that secular societies have their own versions of this hermeneutic. And the fact that one may quickly become disenchanted with the contact visitor does not alter the depth of the initial event. It merely reinforces it with further profoundly unsettling experiences. Just as Aboriginal contact with Europeans begins before the event of contact, prepared for by pre-existing discourses of death and the afterlife, so European contact with Australia begins long before the actual arrival of Europeans.

It appears the Greeks originally thought of the earth as a flat disc, those bits of it they knew being termed the *oikoumene* or inhabited world, that is, *terra cognita*. Pythagoras, credited in Diogenes Laertius with belief in a round earth, is also taken as a proponent of the existence of antipodes. Though some have attributed this view to Parmenides. In all probability the antipodes were invented, if not by Pythagoras, at least by a Pythagorean. By the time of Plato's *Phaedo* and *Timaeus* the notion of a spherical earth had wide acceptance. It finds a place in Aristotle's *Meteorology* which, however, argues that humans can only survive in temperate regions of the globe, thus providing ammunition for later, mediaeval, scholars wishing to discount southern inhabitants. The 220 B.C. Alexandrian world map of Eratosthenes excluded the antipodes, but the Greeks saw a need for southern land masses to balance those in the north (an argument maintained by Alexander Dalrymple in the eighteenth century and only finally settled by Cook's second voyage). So by the time of Ptolemy's celebrated second century map, a south land was included. As it was in Macrobius' c. 400 A.D. map. Thus Europeans may be said to have invented Australia before reaching it, as if its existence fulfilled a need.

Christian thinkers, however, debated the issue. In the third century Lactantius Firmianus thought nothing could be more foolish than the notion of upside-down humans. (Wallis, n.d.: 36) Augustine's *City of God*, one of the most influential books ever written, puts the case against the antipodes on biblical and on empirical grounds, even in the event of a round earth. (Britannica, 1952: 428) C. 540 A.D. the Egyptian monk Cosmas poured scorn on the idea of antipodes, as of a global world, on fundamentalist grounds. And scholars like Isidore of Seville and the Venerable Bede apparently also followed Augustine. Nonetheless the story of an upside-down Fourth Continent (after Africa, Asia and Europe) persisted throughout the Middle Ages and beyond. Some envisaged "sun-shaded footed men" or *skiapodes* existing outside the *oikoumene*. Others quoted scripture against Augustine, finding biblical support for inhabitants in unknown parts, as Jean Luis Arias did to Phillip III of Spain: "And other sheep I have, which are not of this fold". (Wallis: 36; Clark:2.3; John 10.16)

Certainly the antipodes could find little support in mediaeval, Jerusalem-centred, symbolic maps of the so-called T-O type, but the Renaissance reinstated Ptolemy and, with his map, the obsession with a great southern continent. The Nürnberg Chronicle of 1493 contains an illustration of a fabulous antipodean, not upside-down but, for some reason, feet facing backward. (Wallis; 36) Of course a year before that Columbus was testing the round-earth theory, in the event once and for all. As far as the south lands were concerned, the journal of another Italian contributed to the debate, one might say to this day. Marco Polo wrote of lands to the south of "Java", but it seems clear "Java" is a misprint or at any rate casual error for "Champa" in present-day Vietnam. (Latham, 1958: 251) This error generated an entire cartographic mythology of Australia as Java-la-Grande or Greater Java, illustrated in the sixteenth-century Dieppe maps which some believe to be based on stolen or copied Portuguese originals and consequently to provide evidence of Portuguese contact with Australia. The argument is unproven at best, though it may well be that the Portuguese did land in Australia. In any case amateur enthusiasts continue to search for the so-called "mahogany" ship supposedly wrecked on the coast of western Victoria. However, less fabulous maps of the time, like those of Mercator (1569), or Ortelius' 1570 atlas, *Theatrum Orbis Terrarum*, retain the original Ptolemaic southern land. After which we arrive at the already mentioned eighteenth century debate involving Dalrymple, eventually settled by Cook. The Great South Land progressively shrinks in size (in Ptolemy it provided a massive land bridge between Africa and Asia) and is transformed successively into New Holland, Terre Napolion (briefly), New South Wales and, finally, Australia.

But the myth of the antipodes, running parallel with the cartographic account I have sketched, continues to the present. *Terra Incognita*, like its counterpart, the European concept of the "savage", functions as a necessary doppelganger or mirror. Dante placed Mount Purgatory in the antipodes. Thomas More's *Utopia* is set in the region. Swift's Lilliput is sited north-west of Tasmania, and his land of the Houyhnhnms off the coast of New Holland, which Gulliver in any case visits briefly, an imaginary tourist shot by an imaginary arrow, since Aborigines do not use the bow and arrow. From the seventeenth to the early eighteenth centuries an entire series of utopias and dystopias found a ready setting in the antipodes, and it is revealing to note how frequently these depict inversions of European notions and customs, as if a mythical south might be the way to query, problematize, parody northern hemisphere institutions and beliefs. Thus, like More's *Utopia*, such texts serve to criticize, instruct or undermine, either morally or politically or both. Of special interest is the fact that they often make use of gender and/or sexual inversion, presenting the antipodes as a place of unisex hermaphrodites or masterful Amazons, in Latin "viragos".

The list of these texts is long and includes Joseph Hall's *Mundus Alter et Idem* (1605); the appropriately erotic *The Isle of Pines* (1668) by Henry Neville; Denis Vairasse's 1675 *History of the Sevarites* (Histoire des Sevarambes); Gabriel de Foigny's 1676 *The Southern Land, Known* (La Terre Australe Connue); and Hendrik Smeeks' 1708 *Description of the Mighty Kingdom of Krinke Kesmes*. All these fabulous texts are discussed in a book by David Fausett. (Fausett, 1993) The mythical uses of Australia continue well beyond actual historical contact. To see this one has only to turn to Mark Twain's account in which the place is seen as apt location for the most beautiful lies, true lies which actually happen. (Twain, 1973: 169) Or the development of the entire discourse of antipodean Inversion in Australia itself, post-1788, of which more in a moment. Or D.H. Lawrence's comments in the novel Kangaroo.

Indeed even the early accounts of historical contact by Europeans combine elements of myth and chronicle, fact and fiction. For Quirss, navigator in the service of Spain, the search for what he called *Austrialia del Espiritu Santo* was a religious pilgrimage. Once there he planned to found a New Jerusalem. Abel Tasman who unlike Quirss reached Australia, or at least Tasmania, gives a description of the experience of the place which is notable for its eeriness and the topos of gigantism which hovers over it. Writing in 1642 he records a misty region, inhabitants sensed rather than seen, signifiers divorced from their referents: distant smoke, notches cut in trees for the purpose of climbing, but *five feet apart*. (Clark: 15-17) In terms of European discourses of gigantism we have landed among the Nephilim, the fabled giants of *Genesis*. (Genesis 6.4) Or on Cyclops' isle as given in Homer. Or, scrambling chronology, we might say we have landed in Brobdingnag. After which why not add that, post-Gulliver, many imaginary Europeans travelled to a by then real Australia, people as diverse as

Abel Magwitch, the Micawbers, Mr. Peggotty, Mrs. Gummidge and little Em'ly, not to mention Arabella from *Jude the Obscure*?

Unfortunately we have little information regarding real or imagined non-European travellers. In addition to the Macassans and, it goes without saying, Papuans across the island stepping-stones of Torres Strait, we know the Chinese mounted a major, indeed an extravagantly-equipped and large naval expedition in the fifteenth century, led by the imperial eunuch Zheng He, but there is no evidence this reached Australia. (Rolls, 1992) As for the Arabs we have only Sinbad of the *Arabian Nights*, some of whose voyages are certainly in the right direction but appear to stop well short of Australia. I have no information regarding Indian contacts. To my knowledge the historical work in areas like these is yet to be done, only the Macassan journeys having been substantially studied by, for example, Campbell McKnight.

I do not have the time to go into the complex business of analysing contact situations involving the Dutch in Western Australia, as also Dampier in that region, or the British and the French in various parts of the continent, from the seventeenth to the early nineteenth centuries. To an increasing degree, when examining this material we are in the sphere of factual events. But this is not to say we are dealing with the real antipodes at last, at least not entirely. Banks and Cook on the first of Cook's voyages, the 1768-1771 voyage whose aim was to observe the transit of the planet Venus from Tahiti, generate a contact discourse which has as much to do with pre-existing European discourses as with the exigencies of actual contact. I mention in passing discourses of primitivism of the kind derived from European antiquity and outlined in a classical work of scholarship by Lovejoy and Boas. (Lovejoy and Boas, 1935; Boas, 1948) Banks and Cook encountered among others Fuegians, Tahitians and Australian Aborigines, but what they describe in their journals relates to such diverse discursive traditions as the biblical giants; Stoic primitives concocted by the Romans; Ovidian creatures of the Golden Age; Rousseauian Noble Savages. Not to mention the fundamental tropes of Eden and the Fall.

A word about Aboriginal discourses of contact. Aboriginal mythology is filled with accounts of arrivals, the best known being the Arnhem Land saga of Djanggawul and his two sisters, a trio who arrive by sea and, on landing, institute laws, name places and so on. (Berndt, 1952) The equally famous Wandjinas of the Kimberley region, who manage to get into Ezra Pound's *Cantos*, also suggest possible sea origins for Dreaming mythology, since they are associated with monsoonal clouds. If you visit a headland above Jibbon beach, in the national park just south of Sydney, you will come upon huge whales and other figures etched in sandstone and, so it's claimed, relating to a local Dharawal story of a sea voyage to the New South Wales coast in the time of the Dreaming, that once-upon-a-time time or, as the scholar Mircea Eliade terms it, *illud tempus*, Great time. (Mairet, 1968: 30)

Stories of this kind, supported by oral and visual evidence, but generally of a theological kind, are common in Australia. For example, rock depictions of Kaiara spirits in the Kimberley suggest they have pipes in their mouths and utilize rowing boats and sailing ships. (Crawford, 1968: 77) Some Kaiara may relate to the Timorese or, at a later date, the Dutch. But the critical point is that they have been incorporated into Aboriginal discourse. As I have already pointed out, the same happened with Macassan contact, and this is also the case with what are said to be earlier northern visitors to Arnhem Land, the Baiini. Moreover a few Aborigines seem to have sailed back to Indonesia with the Macassans and to have returned with further stories, some of which may be recorded in rock art. In each case the contact event is absorbed into Aboriginal religious mythology, translated and naturalized yet simultaneously transforming existing mythological systems. This seems to me a vital mechanism for coping with the critical challenge posed by the encounter with otherness and, *mutatis mutandis*, it is one utilized by Europeans too. It has the double advantage of part-neutralizing the threat of the new to existing intellectual structures while at the same time actively engaging the new situation. Aboriginal systems see little significance in linear time, unlike Europeans under the influence of the semitic religions and their subsequent secular versions, that's to say, modern philosophies of progress. Thus Aboriginal hermeneutics tackles important historical events by immediately situating them outside time, in *illo tempore*, the mythopoeic pre-time of the Dreaming. If something of significance happens, it has always happened, that's to say it happens in eternity, the eternal Now. Thus whereas we scrutinize European historical records for evidence of the crisis of cross-cultural contact, in the case of Australian Aborigines we need to examine myth, ritual, religion.

I now want to turn once more to European sources and to conclude my discussion with renewed focus on contact as a transforming, problematizing, traumatizing phenomenon. This in connection with two distinct but related areas, those of European science and European philosophical and theological concepts. Let's refer to these as empirical discourse on the one hand and moral and political discourse on the other. Australia presented Europeans with a fundamentally taxonomic dilemma. At the scientific level the question being how to categorize its flora and fauna, how to fit it into existing European schemata. In a world upside-down, everything showed evidence of inversion or of heterogeneity, i.e. of up-ending or confusing taxonomic categories. The convict artist Thomas Watling wrote of an "inversion of Nature" (Mackaness, 1945:31) and Barron Field, a colonial judge in Australia from 1817 to 1824, said "Australia is the land of contrarieties, where the laws of nature seem reversed". Thus "it is summer with us when it is winter in Europe . . . the north is the hot wind, and the south the cold . . . the swans are black . . . the kangaroo, an animal between the squirrel and the deer, has . . . claws . . . like a bird, & yet hops on its tail . . . the mole . . . lays eggs, & has a duck's bill . . . there is a fish, one-half belonging to the genus raia, & the other to that of squalus". (Geographical Memoirs on New South Wales; 461-2) That's to say, half ray, half shark. A similar point is made in the better-known context of Field's poem on the kangaroo, an uncategorizable creature for the colonial public servant and amateur naturalist, a living "contradiction", like the fabulous creatures of mythology; sphinxes, mermaids, centaurs etc. The poem concluding with a reference to Juvenal's *cygnus niger*, the "sooty swan" which is not exceptional but the norm in the antipodes, and to that other scientific impossibility, *ornithorhyncus paradoxus*, the platypus. (Eliot and Mitchell, 1970: 17-18)

In particular Australia breaks the mould because it gives the lie to Lucretius, who in *De Rerum Natura* had argued against the existence of mixed or hybrid creatures. (Latham. 1951: 198-9) This presented a more-than-literary difficulty for Europeans. Mammals were not supposed to lay eggs, but Australian monotremes such as the platypus do just that. Consequently when George Shaw examined the first platypus skin in the British Museum in 1798 he thought it a hoax. It was not until 1884 that the oviparous reproduction of the creature was properly established. We could say that Australia appeared in European scientific discourse at a crucial stage in its development. For a start it provided masses of new data. When Willem de Vlamingh displayed the first black swan in Batavia in 1674 he caused a stir. But late eighteenth and early nineteenth century travellers and collectors regularly overwhelmed the European scientific establishments with what they brought back, in part because their voyages were frequently informed by scientific aims, as well as economic and political ones. Cook's first voyage, with scientists like Banks and Solander on board, led to the formation of the celebrated herbarium at Banks' house in Soho Square. (Solander being a pupil of Linnaeus and Banks also following the lead of the Swedish taxonomist.) As Banks was president of the Royal Society for forty two years after 1778, his scientific influence was immense. It was Linnaeus himself who suggested Australia might be called Banksia.

Cook's second voyage, because it included on board the distinguished father-son team Johann and Georg Forster, fed directly into German scientific endeavours. Indeed Georg Forster's account of the trip to the young von Humboldt inspired the latter. The d'Entrecasteaux expedition, in Australia in 1792/3, fed into French science through the work of the botanist de la Billardihre. And the Baudin voyage of 1800, with Piron and other scientists on board and informed by the ideas of Joseph-Marie Degérando and the Société des Observateurs de l'Homme, the founders of European anthropology, returned with a staggering load of specimens and data. Piron, who underwent an intellectual crisis in Australia, rethinking the entire Rousseau discourse of the Noble Savage, had an impact on Lamarck. Matthew Flinders' 1801 circumnavigation of Australia with the famous botanist Robert Brown, who subsequently transferred the Banks collection to the British Museum, helped transform botanical classification away from the Linnaean model. In fact it has been argued that Australian data played a significant role in the collapse of the Great Chain of Being model (which envisaged a taxonomy of separate, unmixed species, from lowest to highest), and a not insignificant role, though in combination with many other factors, in the philosophic and scientific paradigm shift from the Great Chain of Being to the theory of evolution.

Banks held the eighteenth century view that nature formed a chain, each creature in its fixed place as imagined by Lucretius, from "Man, alone endowd with reason" all the way down to the humble oyster. (Beaglehole, 1963: 20) But Australia, as I have said, disrupted this decorous arrangement. John White, the first surgeon-general of the New South Wales colony, noted in his 1790 journal that a similitude ran through the flora and fauna of the country. (Chisholm, 1962: 148) Thomas Watling, whom White employed, made the same observation, (Watling, 1945: 32) and Governor Hunter put the issue in perspective: it was as if the fish, birds, trees of Australia had engaged in a "promiscuous" inter-species mixing or hybridization. (Hunter, 1968: 47) These comments evidently provide the model for Barron Field's anti-Lucretian statements both in prose and poetry and actually furnish him with some of his examples, such as the fish which is both ray and shark. What happened was that Hunter's views in his 1793 journal helped shape the theory of evolutionary development of species, as it were "promiscuously" one from another, envisaged by Erasmus Darwin, Charles' grandfather, in his 1794 *Zoonomia*.

The precise role of Australian data in Charles Darwin's later formulation of the theory of Natural Selection and its propagation is more difficult to establish. Though Darwin's visit to Australia preceded his elaboration of the evolutionary mechanism, fossils recovered from the Wellington caves of New South Wales, and interpreted by the noted palaeontologist Richard Owen, found their way into the argument of Lyell's 1833 *Principles of Geology* which Darwin read so avidly on the *Beagle*. T.H. Huxley, Darwin's great ally, spent a formative phase of his intellectual life in Australia. It was in Sydney that he began his major research on Medusas, met his future wife and failed to obtain the Chair of Natural History at the newly-established local university. Finally, the work of another ally, Joseph Hooker, on Tasmanian flora, greatly encouraged Darwin.*

But the real question is not to what extent Australian data contributed to evolutionary theory. Rather it is to what extent contact with radically different flora and fauna, in the antipodes and elsewhere, rendered the old static system of the Chain of Being untenable and so made new organic and evolutionary theory *possible*. Post-contact, Europeans simply had to move to a more complex, process-oriented view of things. Thus I would argue that while Australia's part in the Darwinian synthesis may be no more than one element among many, its influence, though more general, was of a fundamental kind nonetheless. Australia had a key role in subverting European scientific data and so in *necessitating*, if not the theories of Darwin, at least something like them. Contact forced Europeans to see that new data would not fit old paradigms. Its relativizing effect was precisely to generate relativist models such as Natural Selection, which for the first time placed humans on a par with the animal world, another and just as unsettling Copernican revolution, one that instals animal otherness at the heart of human "nature".

Of course scientific discourse and moral or metaphysical discourse are not separable. When Barron Field seeks to categorize the kangaroo he raises theological questions. His poem accordingly asks whether Australia might not have been created *after* the Fall, not along with the rest of nature *in principio*. Or, if fashioned *before* the Fall, whether its creatures do not proceed from divine error or levity:

> Join'd by some divine mistake,
> None but Nature's hand can make—
> Nature, in her wisdom's play,
> On Creation's holiday. (Eliot and Mitchell: 18)

It must have happened on the holiday sabbath, *after* the six days of creation. Of course these lines are themselves playful, as no doubt Darwin was in his view surely two Creators seems to have been at work. That is, one for Australia, another for the rest of the world. Still, the point is made. The antipodes simultaneously helped to demolish and reshape the empirical discourse of natural science *and* the discourses of European philosophy, theology and the social sciences. After all, the most radical shock of contact accompanies the encounter with other and different human beings. Here too it is not easy to separate the contact event of Australia from the larger cross-cultural event shaping modernity from the European Renaissance to the present.

At any rate the issue remains one of categories. Where do so-called primitives fit into the divine taxonomy, that is, morally, religio-historically and theologically? Again, how are they to be classified anthropologically, sociologically and politically? Even in non-religious contexts Europeans from the seventeenth to the nineteenth centuries returned to the trope of the Fall. Could some humans have remained in the state of Eden? Columbus was tempted to think so when he spoke of a "terrestrial paradise" in the west. (Fairchild, 1961: 6) The discourse of the Noble Savage which he initiated before Rousseau, though its roots are in Roman Stoicism and the elevation of plain-living Scythians and Germans, logically entertains the—to Christian Europe—subversive possibility that all humans might be born innocent of Original Sin. That attacks the heart of Augustinian orthodoxy. Either the savage is ignoble, that is, fallen or degenerate and so requiring Christian redemption, or the entire theological structure collapses. A development which leads directly to the secular Enlightenment, ultimately to Darwin. Where secularized, relativized Europe, in short post-anthropology Europe, could simply regard the savage as a morally neutral, if otherwise disturbing, Other, eighteenth and nineteenth century missionary pietism could not. Instead it withdrew into fundamentalist condemnation, and attempted redemption, of the *ignoble* savage, finding a not so unlikely ally in secular theories of evolution and subsequent doctrines of race superiority.

One way or another I want to argue that contact over several hundred years constituted a major, if not the only major, factor in bringing about a European crisis of faith and the emergence of secular society. In the discourse of the social sciences the question of the status of the supposed primitive raises basic questions regarding "nature", "society" and "civilization". It raises questions about the origins of civil society and political institutions, about historical teleologies, whether negative (tenacious avatars of the Golden Age from Ovid to the Rousseau of the treatise on inequality) or positive, as in teleologies of progress. If the European Other is revealed as, for example, an Australian Aborigine, will this prompt a theory of history as decline or as improvement? Of anthropological nostalgia for a hunter/gatherer, pre-industrial, even pre-agricultural existence? Or contempt for the past, acceleration of the scramble to transform the world by technology? This is the key question, taking innumerable diverse forms over the last few hundred years, which in its secular way recapitulates the problematics of the theology of Eden and the Fall.

In the event, the history of modernity demonstrates that Europeans and, after that, others throughout the world, have opted practically for the notion of history-as-progress. Still, we remain haunted and are perhaps becoming increasingly haunted by the other teleological idea, the option of history-as-decline or degeneracy. Of course indigenous peoples in general and Australian Aborigines in particular have no intrinsic connection with this problematic. The discourse of primitivism is a strictly European discourse which tells us nothing about real indigenous peoples and everything about imagined ones. That's to say which tells us everything about real Europeans. Nonetheless, the event of contact constitutes the real as distinct from the mythical antipodes, and that event remains momentous. The antipodes antipodize Europe. Even as post-Renaissance Europeans transform the world, the colonial experience transforms Europe. Europeans, it seems to me, are still slow to recognize this, though it is the explicit or implicit message of postcolonial and subaltern studies. Once it is generally recognized, we can rewrite the history of Europe and, since modernity now belongs to the rest of the world, world history too.

WORKS CITED

J.C. Beaglehole (ed.), *The Endeavour Journal of Joseph Banks* (Sydney: Angus & Robertson, 1963).

A.R. Chisholm (ed.), *Journal of a Voyage to New South Wales* (Sydney: Angus & Robertson, 1962).

R.M. Berndt (ed.), *Djanggawul: An Aboriginal Religious Cult of North-*

Eastern Arnhem Land (London: Routledge & Kegan Paul, 1952).
M. Clark (ed.), *Sources of Australian History* (London: OUP, 1957).
I.M. Crawford, *The Art of the Wandjina: Aboriginal Cave Paintings in Kimberley, Western Australia* (Melbourne: OUP, 1968).
Livio Dobrez, "Not European-Made: Civilization and its Discontents" in Maes-Jelinek, Collier and Davis (ed.), *A Talent(ed) Digger: Creations, Cameos and Essays in honour of Anna Rutherford* (Amsterdam/Atlanta: Rodopi, 1996).
______, "Being Australian: Identity, Identities and Traces of Identities" in Dobrez (ed.), *Identifying Australia in Postmodern Times* (Canberra: Bibliotech, ANU, 1994, reprint 1995).
B. Elliott and A. Mitchell (ed.), *Bards in the Wilderness: Australian Colonial Poetry to 1920* (Melbourne: Nelson, 1970).
H.N. Fairchild, *The Noble Savage: a Study in Romantic Naturalism* (New York: Russell & Russell, 1961).
David Fausett, *Writing the New World: Imaginary Voyages and Utopias of the Great Southern Land* (Syracuse: UP, 1993).
Geographical Memoirs on New South Wales (London: John Murray, 1825).
Captain John Hunter, *An Historical Journal of Events at Sydney and at Sea, 1787-1792*, ed. J. Bach (Sydney: A&R, 1968).
A.O. Lovejoy and G. Boas, *A Documentary History of Primitivism and Related Ideas in Antiquity* (Baltimore: Johns Hopkins, 1935); G. Boas, Essays on Primitivism and Related Ideas in the Middle Ages (Baltimore: Johns Hopkins, 1948).
G. Mackaness (ed.), *Letters from an Exile at Botany-Bay to his Aunt in Dumfries* (Sydney: Australian Historical Monographs, vol. XXXIV, New Series, 1945).
Myths, Dreams and Mysteries, trans. P. Mairet (London: Collins, 1968).
On the Nature of the Universe, trans. R. Latham (Harmondsworth: Penguin, 1951).
E. Rolls, *Sojourners: the Epic Story of China's Centuries-Old Relationship with Australia* (St. Lucia: QUP, 1992).
T. Swain, *A Place for Strangers: Towards a History of Australian Aboriginal Being* (Cambridge: CUP, 1993).
The City of God, XVI.9 in *The Confessions, The City of God, On Christian Doctrine* (Chicago: Encyclopaedia Britannica, 1952).
The Pythagorean Sourcebook and Library, compiled and trans. K.S. Guthrie, T. Taylor and A. Fairbanks Jr. (Grand Rapids: Phanes Press, 1987).
Mark Twain, *Following the Equator, Part I: Mark Twain in Australia and New Zealand* (Harmondsworth: Penguin, 1973), p. 169.

H. Wallis, "Visions of Terra Australis in the Middle Ages and Renaissance" in W. Eisler and B. Smith (ed.), *Terra Australis: The Furthest Shore* (Sydney: Art Gallery of NSW).

Thomas Watling, *Letters from an Exile* (Sydney: D.S. Ford, 1945).

The Travels of Marco Polo, trans. R. Latham (Harmondsworth: Penguin, 1958)

NOTE

Sections of the above account of science and Australia are particularly indebted to the following: B.W. Butcher, "'Adding Stones to the Great Pile'? Charles Darwin's Use of Australian Resources, 1837-1882"; *Historical Records of Australian Science*, 8 (1), December 1989, pp. 1-14; K.G. Dugan, "The Zoological Exploration of the Australian Region and its Impact on Biological Theory" in Reingold and Rothenberg (eds.), *Scientific Colonialism: A Cross-Cultural Comparison* (Washington: Smithsonian, 1987); A. Moyal, *Scientists in Nineteenth Century Australia: a Documentary History* (Melbourne: Cassell, 1976) and "a bright & savage land": Scientists in Colonial Australia (Sydney: Collins, 1986); A.M. Nisbet and M. Blackman (ed.), *The French-Australian Cultural Connection* (Sydney: School of French, U of NSW, 1984); B. Smith, *European Vision and the South Pacific, 1768-1850: A Study in the History of Art and Ideas* (London: OUP, 1960).

Figuring it out: The Australian-Spanish (Mis)Connection

ISABEL SANTAOLALLA
University of Zaragoza, Spain

"Allow yourself to be seduced by Australia: The Happy Continent The South also exists". Thus begins a Spanish tour operator's description of a proposal for a "magnificent" and "fascinating" trip to "Seductive Australia". I have singled out this quotation among the many other—equally inflated—phrases characteristic of our tour operators' jargon, because I think it encapsulates the spirit of what I have called the "Australian-Spanish (Mis)Connection". Most significant of all is the remark "The South also exists", which underlines the extent to which prospective Spanish tourists need reminding of even the mere *existence* of Australia. It is a place one simply doesn't *think of*.

As part of this project to research Spanish awareness of Australia, I approached at random ten travel agencies in Zargoza, Spain (700,000 population), and asked for Australian holiday brochures. After initial bewilderment ("Mmm. Australia. Surely we must have something somewhere". "Australia. Let's see. I don't think we have much. It's not a popular destination, you know?") thick brochures were eventually produced in which only about two or three pages would be dedicated to Australia, compared to the approximately fifteen or twenty devoted to destinations like India, the United States, South America or the Caribbean. Skimming through them, though, one could certainly learn a lot about Australia, and discover, for instance, that there are essentially three marketable Australias: there is, initially, a "seductive", "marvellous", "fantastic" Australia (whatever these hollow adjectives mean); there is also a "classic" or "colonial" Australia (Melbourne, Cairns and Sydney); and finally, there is a more "adventurous" Australia with trips which include the "Secrets of Australia" and the "Unknown Australia" experiences, as well as the "Crocodile Dundee" tour! Allowing for the understandable hyperbole of this kind of literature (all of it liberally sprinkled with adjectives such as "fascinating", "splendid", "impressive", "marvellous", "fantastic", and the like), I think one can still draw conclusions from the rest of the vocabulary which recurs in these descriptions: words like "happy", "charming", "exciting", "exuberant", "spectacular", "gigantic", or "natural wonder" try to project an image of a *big bright country*.

Since for Spaniards Australia has never been a favourite destination—and this despite their fondness for travel abroad—there is an amazing scarcity of images about the sixth largest country in the world. Lacking also the colonial link that has guaranteed, for instance, the availability of Australian cultural and commercial products in Britain (even if for some it may only have taken the form of TV teen-soaps like *Home and Away* or *Neighbours*, reputable white wines or T-shirts with aboriginal designs on them), Spain is almost barren of images of Australia.

A few points require clarification before further development of this argument, though. There is no question of undervaluing here the merits of those academics who are running programmes and carrying out valuable research on Australian literature and culture in a number of Spanish universities (the University of Barcelona, for instance, has played a leading role in promoting and fostering the European Association for the Study of Australia). It remains true, however, that even at university level, the study of Australian culture is extremely limited, as is demonstrated by the Spanish Australian Embassy's recent embarkation on a cultural policy including visits to every English Department in Spanish universities, offering small library grants to those which consider including Australian authors in their programmes. All this, however, falls outside the limits of this study. My intention here has been to engage with the wider context of popular culture in Spain. The specific aim, then, is to reflect on the shape that the 'idea' of Australia takes in the mind of the ordinary Spanish citizen, as well as to track the (limited) availability of Australian products in Spanish society, and, finally, to venture a few ideas on some of the possible ways in which those products may be modified—*translated*—in the process of being decoded by a community of consumers so different from the one which saw their conception.

Through a questionnaire which I distributed among colleagues, friends and family (see Appendix), I tried to investigate the number and nature of images which circulate among people not connected with English studies. The evidence confirmed my initial suspicion that not much is known about Australia. I must point out here that the range of people to whom I passed the questionnaire is not sufficiently varied for general conclusions to be drawn. And yet, the fact that most of them were university graduates suggests that even among reasonably well informed people in Spain, there is still a daunting lack of knowledge about Australia. Equally significant is the fact that, when asked whether they had ever thought of travelling to Australia, only four out of the 30 replied affirmatively. None of them had ever knowingly met an Australian person and only a few knew somebody who had been to Australia.

All sorts of anecdotes emerged as a result of the enquiries: some friends apologised and refused to fill in the questionnaire, claiming they did not know *anything* at all; some, at my insistence, did fill it in and returned it embarrassed at their failure to answer the majority of questions; and some even confessed to having resorted to an Encyclopaedia for "a bit of inspiration"! A provisional conclusion after reading the questionnaires is that, most obviously, the Australian experience and its cultural manifestation are remote from Spanish consciousness. Excluding "kangaroos", "koalas", "sheep", "desert", "Sydney Opera House", "2000 Olympic Games" and "Maoris" (interestingly confusing New Zealand and Australian aboriginal populations), few other names or images came to the mind of the majority of those questioned.

As for the items on Australian culture, hardly anybody could provide any information about TV programmes or Australian literature. Cinema, however, was a different matter, and for that reason offers suitable material for further discussion. Most managed to come up with names of actors or film titles. But even here an interesting division occurred: answers would either refer to films of the *Crocodile Dundee* (Peter Faiman, 1986) and *Mad Max* (George Miller, 1979) type—which interviewees loosely classified as action movies—or to films of a significantly different nature, namely, *The Piano* (Jane Campion, 1994), *Muriel's Wedding* (P.J. Hogan, 1994) and *The Adventures of Priscilla, Queen of the Desert* (Stephan Elliott, 1994).

Most relevantly here, given the importers' ignorance of the cultural specificities and production values of the texts concerned, these narratives appear to occupy a kind of vacuum-like space in their imagination. The question to be asked now is: how is the Australian experience figured (and most probably, dis-figured) in the process of assimilating the few Australian or Australian-related products that have reached the Spanish cultural circuits? Cross-cultural consumption is, of course, a key area of both intellectual and economic analysis in the modern world. Stephen Crofts, from Griffith University at Brisbane, carried out this type of cross-cultural analysis focusing on one single Australian film, *Crocodile Dundee*, arguing that readings are clearly affected by "the cultural knowledges which a given film-viewing community brings to the film". (Crofts, 1993:157) In fact, it could be maintained that more than simply affecting the way a text is read, the "cultural knowledges" of a given community of viewers or readers will also shape the way in which the country that has produced that text is 'figured' or 'imagined'.

With not many more points of reference at hand, present-day Spanish audiences have been fed a diet of outrageously kitsch and irreverent pseudo-comedies. Judging from their representation in films like *Strictly Ballroom* (Baz Luhrmann, 1992), *Muriel's Wedding and Priscilla, Queen of the Desert*, Australians are amazingly insolent, gaudy and definitely queer (in the wider sense of the term). Ignoring the historical and social conditions which have traditionally defined Australia as a white, predominantly "macho" country celebrating the bush worker as a colonial hero; ignoring also the literary tradition which has so often depicted—as Geraldine Stoneham puts it—"the theme of struggle, sacrifice and survival common to Australian nationalist literature" or "the anonymity of the victim and the sense of his (sic) vulnerability against the forces of nature," (Stoneham, 1996:724, 717) a Spanish viewer will hardly be aware that these three film texts are, in reality, quite removed from the native cultural tradition (not only as expressed in literature but also in the cinema itself), and that they are, actually, loudly contesting it.

Australian film criticism has, of course, acknowledged this fact. Articles published in Australian journals witness the critics' advocacy of a 'new wave' of Australian filmmaking. Turner's "Whatever Happened to National Identity?" or Quinn's "Dag, Drags and the Suburban Surreal" consider the revolutionary nature of this new style of 'trash aesthetics' which has been labelled "kitsch comedy" or "suburban surreal"—Jane Campion's *Sweetie* (1989) can also be included within this same group but, as it was never released in Spain, it lies beyond my field of analysis. (Turner, 1994:32-35; Quinn, 1994:23-26) In these articles, the authors attempt to explore both the *causes* of the emergence of these radical, innovative renderings of the Australian experience and, also, the effects on the way Australians perceive themselves and—given that these have been internationally acclaimed films—on the national image that is projected outside. After all—as Adrian Martin points out in his article "More than Muriel" published in the British film journal Sight and Sound—"currently, outside Australia, this national cinema is perceived mainly through the filter of its two most recent success stories: Stephan Elliott's *The Adventures of Priscilla, Queen of the Desert* and P.J.Hogan's *Muriel's Wedding*." (Martin, 1995:30)

For Martin, however, this panorama is starting to expand as a result of a number of film releases which in 1995 have brought about a "return to seriousness", or, as he also puts it, "a return home". (Martin:30) The films he reviews are *Hotel Sorrento* (Richard Franklin, 1995), *Vacant Possession* (Margot Nash, 1995), *Angel Baby* (Michael Rymer, 1995) and *Metal Skin* (Geoffrey Wrights, 1995). But these films have not hit the Spanish market. Neither, on their release, did films like *Picnic at Hanging Rock* (Peter Weir, 1975) or *My Brilliant Career* (Gillian Armstrong, 1979), which attempted to capture "the spirit of the land" in poetic, tasteful images and words—a stylistic tradition within which the internationally-acclaimed *The Piano* (Jane Campion, 1994) could probably be comfortably located (although produced in Australia, Campion is here inspired by memories of her native New Zealand). Unknown, too, was the first wave of the liberal, intellectual 'aesthetes' who were concerned with social, sexual and political mores, producing films like *Don's Party* (Bruce Beresford, 1976; Quinn, 1994:25) They simply never reached Spanish shores.

From a Spanish perspective, then, one is left with a rather limited and polarised representation of Australianness in film. It really is a question of "Max and Crocodile Dundee vs Muriel and Priscilla." Concerning this imaginary contest, it is to be noted that, whereas for an Australian audience the worlds of *Mad Max* and *Crocodile Dundee* clearly refer back to that national tradition of macho protagonists testing their strength in uncharted or hostile landscapes, the fact that these films clearly belong to the adventure and/or futuristic genres (depicting worlds which are, in the mind of the viewer, remote from real life) may well be said to turn their stories and characters—when viewed by an outsider—into mere archetypal expressions of unlocated, universal—and probably Americanised—film myths. Although admittedly the satiric vein in *Crocodile Dundee* is easily recognisable, I would argue that, for the Spanish viewer, it is much less obvious in *Mad Max*, a film whose screenings in Spain were basically attended by admirers of Hollywood-style 'action-movies'.

The characters and situations of *Priscilla* and *Muriel*, on the other hand, appear to be actually conveying some information about contemporary Australian society, about its geographical, cultural and economic contrasts. These films help create images of—admittedly unconventional but still believable—present-day Australian realities. The effect might well emerge from the clever combination, in both films of—as Wignall says—a "brash and brassy look" and "emotional complexity" (Wignall, 1994:31-34), which gives the characters a human dimension totally absent from *Mad Max* and *Crocodile Dundee*.

Critics have often pointed out the abundant stylistic and thematic similarities which link together *Strictly Ballroom*, *Muriel's Wedding*, and *Priscilla, Queen of the Desert*. Their "carnivalesque", "rambunctious" streak—celebrated by some, despised by others—is formally reflected in their disrespectful combination of styles and subjects, as well as in their disregard for, as Turner puts it, "the generic markers of 'art film.'" (Turner, 1994:32) A variety of commercial and popular motifs become an integral part of their narratives, in the process undergoing all sorts of—often comic—transformations and indigenisations. One of the major reasons for much of the films' success inside as well as outside Australia is their musical score and choreographed numbers. The three films resort to the nostalgic lure of 'oldies', tunes and all, though, appropriately imbued with large doses of irony. The Abba songs in *Muriel's Wedding* and in *Priscilla* (and here, also several other hits from the 70s), or the old-fashioned ballroom melodies in *Strictly Ballroom* are clearly meant to be taken irreverently. And yet they carry, above all, very positive meanings: their 'popular' connotations elevate their status and turn them into emblems of transgression. Muriel uses Abba songs to escape the tacky reality around her (as when she locks herself up in her room and listens to "Dancing Queen"), or seek attention and indirectly irritate her loathsome girl-friends (when she and her friend Rhonda gain their fellow revellers' applause as they perform an Abba routine in an island resort). The three drag queens who ride a silver bus nicknamed Priscilla through the Australian outback use their garish outfits and funky song-and- dance performances to assert their 'difference' and to abolish narrowly defined parameters of normality. And finally *Strictly Ballroom* adds a further dimension to this strategy and establishes a dichotomy between the popularised—but still strictly codified and highly artificial—routines of ballroom dancing, and the also popular—and, more positively ethnically authentic—flamenco rhythms with which the transgressive Scott Hastings finally wins his battle against tradition and corruption. It's worth noting that Paul Mercurio, the actor playing the leading role in the film, once explained the appeal of this film for him lay, firstly, in the fact that "ballroom crosses so many boundaries of class and culture." (Taylor, 1992:8-10)

This use of Hispanic 'ethnic' material caused me, when I first saw the film, great perplexity and amusement. It seemed so unlikely that an Australian story should involve a Spanish-speaking family, and that its visual dynamics should be to a large extent inspired by flamenco choreographies! My reaction is not uncommon. Firstly, it perhaps needs to be indicated that for a Spanish spectator, the setting itself of the film is almost surreal, as the whole flippant world of dancing contests familiar to Anglo-Saxon cultures (British TV often screens such contests, for instance) is practically absent from his/hers. This effect is increased by the fact that, precisely due to Spaniards' limited awareness of Australian realities, the idea of an Andalusian family in an Australian city slum may seem twice removed from reality. Only after discussing the film in Britain did I discover that flamenco is actually a highly popular form among Australians, long after I first saw the film and assumed, like many other compatriots, that its inclusion formed part of that surreal element apparently so dear to recent Australian filmmakers.

The above-noted anecdotal evidence illustrates one of the most common experiences of cross-cultural consumption: the impossibility of fairly judging the truth-value of elements forming part of a given cultural representation when the referent is unknown to the consumer. Obviously, this lack of awareness can manifest itself at any stage of the cultural exchange, i.e. not only in the decoding, but also, for example, in the coding. *Strictly Ballroom* can serve to illustrate this too, as, in fact, the audience's misreadings of elements within the film have their symmetric counterpart in the films' own inexact use of Hispanic materials, where Spanish and Latin American rhythms are conflated—as far as one can tell—unknowingly. Given that the film at no point explicitly acknowledges or narratively justifies the Spanish origins of Fran's family; given, also, that serious misrepresentations of Spanish musical lore are occasionally made, as when Fran's father's purely *flamencan* steps are incorrectly presented to Scott and the viewer as a *pasodoble*, there can be said to be a lack of cultural specificity which, as a result, promotes an incomplete and distorted version of Spanishness/Gypsiness. This, of course, does not invalidate the highly celebratory intentions which obviously inspired its inclusion in the film, something reinforced by the use of the lively *Rumba del burro* ('rumba of the donkey') as a musical epilogue to the happy ending. Thus the film's reciprocation in mis-figuring a foreign cultural manifestation somehow confirms the assumption that cross-cultural readings are often marked by distortion and transformation.

All this, however, need not necessarily be seen as entirely negative. The brief and provisional points made here have attempted to illustrate the contention that texts as well as nations can be subject to multiple *positioned* assessments. And there is probably much to be said in favour of this. One might want to argue, after all, that it is precisely this awareness of the inevitability of cross-cultural mis-configurations that gives the individual the freedom necessary to embark on risk-taking, creative readings of texts and cultures or, to put it differently, to revel in the pleasure of *figuring it all out*.

Films Cited

Angel Baby (Michael Rymer, 1995).
Crocodile Dundee (Peter Faiman, 1986).
Don's Party (Bruce Beresford, 1976).
Hotel Sorrento (Richard Franklin, 1995).
Mad Max (George Miller, 1979).
Metal Skin (Geoffrey Wrights, 1995).
Muriel's Wedding (Paul J. Hogan, 1994).
My Brilliant Career (Gillian Armstrong, 1979).
Picnic at Hanging Rock (Peter Weir, 1975).
Strictly Ballroom (Baz Luhrmann, 1992).
The Adventures of Priscilla, Queen of the Desert (Stephan Elliott, 1994).
The Piano (Jane Campion, 1994).
Vacant Possession (Margot Nash, 1995)

Works Cited

Stephen Crofts, "Cross-Cultural Reception Studies: Culturally Variant Readings of *Crocodile Dundee*", *Film/Literature Quarterly*, 2.2 (1993).

Jan Epstein, "Muriel's Wedding. Writer-director P.J. Hogan interviewed", *Cinema Papers*, 101 (October 1994).

Adrian Martin, "More than Muriel", *Sight and Sound*, 5.6 (June 1995).

Karl Quinn, "Dag, Drags and the Suburban Surreal", *Metro Magazine*, 100 (Summer 1994-5).

Geraldine Stoneham, "Australiasian Literature" in *Introducing Literary Studies*, ed. Richard Bradford (Hemel Hempstead, Hertfordshire: Prentice Hall, Harvester Wheatsheaf, 1996).

Ronnie Taylor, "Baz Luhrman's *Strictly Ballroom*", *Cinema Papers*, 88 (May/June 1992).

Graeme Turner, "Whatever Happened to National Identity?", *Metro Magazine*, 100 (Summer 1994-5).

Louise Wignall, "The Extraordinary in the Ordinary. P.J. Hogan talks about Muriel's Wedding", *Metro Magazine*, 99 (Summer 1994).

Appendix

Questionnaire on Australia

Name (optional)................................Profession/Studies:..................
Sex:..City/Town:..............................
Age:..

Name, ideas, concepts that first come to your mind when you think of Australia:

....
....
....

Say what you know/guess about the following aspects:

1. Geographical location:

....
....
....

2. Type of landscape:

....
....
....

3. Vegetation and fauna:

....
....
....

4. Climate:
....
....
....

5. History:
....
....
....

6. Society:
....
....
....

7. Race(s) and ethnic group(s):
....
....
....

8. Language(s) spoken:
....
....
....

9. Religion(s):
....
....
....

10. Economics:
....
....
....

11. Literature:.
....
....
....

12. Cinema:

....

....

....

13. Television:

....

....

....

14. Sports:

....

....

....

Other (further thoughts)

....

....

....

....

....

Have you ever been to Australia?

....

Have you ever met an Australian person?

....

Do you know anybody who has been to Australia?

....

Have you ever thought of going to Australia?

....

Indian Writers at Conference

K. Radha

PRINCESS ASWATI TIRUNAL GOURI LAKSHMI BAYI is the niece of the Maharajas, Sree Chithira Thirunal and Sree Uthradom Thirunal. Born to Maharani Karthika Thirunal Lakshmi Bayi and Col. Goda Varma Raja (Poonjar Palace), she is married to Sri R.R. Varma, Thiruvalla Palace, and has two sons Prince Marthanda Varma and Prince Aditya Varma.

She graduated in Economics from the Maharaja's College for Women, Thiruvananthapuram.

Has more than 150 poems in English to her credit. Her first two books were *Thirumulkazhcha* and *The Dawn* (published by Macmillan India Ltd). The third book *Sree Padmanabha Swamy Temple* is her first book of English prose. She is currently working on three books:

(a) *The Thulasi Garland* (English prose, on temples of Travancore)

(b) *The Lamp Eternal* (English prose, on Sree Chithira Thirunal Maharaja)

(c) *Hinduism for Children* (Malayalam prose)

Her articles and poems have appeared in leading publications in India: *Indian Literature* (Sahitya Akademi, Delhi), *Bhavan's Journal* (a Journal of Kerala Sahitya Akademi), *The Hindu, Indian Express, Malayala Manorama, Mathrubhoomi, Kerala Kaumudi*, etc. and in *The Delhi-London Poetry Quarterly* published from London and *Hinduism Today* from California.

Papers presented include: "Harmonisation of Diversities", under the auspices of the Indira Gandhi Foundation and "Temple Worship in Kerala" organised by INDIS and published by Sree Sankaracharya University of Sanskrit.

Chairman and Managing Director of R. Gac. Electronics, President, Guild of Service, Thiruvananthapuram (Orphanage), President, Bal Vikas Institute (for children in need of special care), Patron, Hindu Mahila Mandiram, Paul Harris Fellow of Rotary International, Past President of University Women's Association and Inner Wheel Club of Trivandrum, Past National Council Member of Indian Federation of University Women's Association, Past District Council Member of Inner Wheel District 321 and on the Board of Palace Charitable Trusts.

Address: Princess Aswati Thirunal Gouri Lakshmi Bayi
Kowdiar Palace, Thiruvananthapura 695 003
Kerala, S. India

KAMALA DAS

Born in 1932 at Punnayurkulam, Malabar, daughter of V.M. Nair and Balamani Amma, eminent Malayalam poet. Bilingual writer. Writes fiction in Malayalam and poetry in English.

Educated privately at home.

Prizes/Awards: The Asian Poetry Prize sponsored by the P.E.N. Centre, Manila in 1963; The Asan World Prize; The Chimanlal Award for Fearless Journalism; The Sahitya Akademi Award from New Delhi; The Lakshmi Award for Social Service; The Thirumalamba Award from Karnataka.

Nominated for the Nobel Prize in 1984.

She was Poetry Editor, *Youth Times, The Illustrated Weekly of India*, Poetry Editor, *Femina, a Times of India* publication, Bombay, President Kerala Children's Film Society, Vice President, State Council for Child Welfare, Trivandrum, Chairperson, Forestry Board, Kerala.

Founder President of the Bahutantrika Group, Bombay.

Founder President of the Sanghamitra, Cochin (an organization for the welfare of women).

Taught poetry at several Universities. Works translated into Serbocroat, Swedish, Italian, French, Russian, and German.

Poetry readings at Universities of Duisburg, Essen and Bonn, Concordia in Canada, Houston, Kingston, Singapore, Melbourne,

Monash, Flinders.

Publications include: *Summer in Calcutta, The Descendants, The Old Playhouse and Other Poems, Alphabet of Lust, A Doll for the Child Prostitute, My Story, Padmavathi the Harlot and Other Stories, Collected Poems of Kamala Das Vol. 1, Mathilukal, Pathu Kathakal, Naricheerukal Parakkumpol, Tharisunilam, Ente Snehita Aruna, Chuvanna Pavada, Pakshiyude Manam, Rajavinte Premabhajanam, Premathinte Vilapakavyam, Madhavikuttiyude Moonnu Novelukal, Madhavikuttiyude Kathakal, Ente Lokam, Irupathonnam Noottandilekku.* She has also published a large number of articles in English and in Malayalam in journals and magazines. A selection of her work and essays on her work were published in 1986 by the Centre for Research in Literatures in English, Flinders University, Adelaide.

Address: Kamala Das
c/o The Times of India
Chittoor Road, Cochin
Kerala, S. India

Dr. K.M. GEORGE, D.Litt.

Born in 1914, Aranmula. Was Professor at Madras Christian College, Visiting Professor, Chicago University; Visiting Professor, Kerala University; Visiting Fellow, Indian Institute of Advanced Studies, Shimla. Currently Chief Editor, *Masterpieces of Indian Literature*, National Book Trust. He is a writer in Malayalam and in English and a specialist in Dravidian linguistics. He has authored more than sixty books.

His publications include: *A Survey of Malayalam Literature, Western Influence on Malayalam Language and Literature, Place-names of Southern India, American Life through Indian Eyes, Kumaran Asan, A.R. Rajaraja Varma, Kesari Balakrishna Pillai, Modern Indian Literature: An Anthology and Masterpieces of Indian Literature, Facts of Indian Literature, Comparative Indian Literature.*

Dr. George has held numerous important positions including those of Chief Editor, *Malayalam Encyclopaedia*, Chief Editor,

Encyclopaedia of Indian Literature, Vice President, *Kerala Sahitya Academy*. He has been associated with several film award committees and panels.

He has visited Italy, Switzerland, France, Germany, England, the United States, Japan, Singapore and Russia on important assignments.

Honours and awards: Nehru Award, Padma Shri, Kerala Sahitya Akademi Fellowship, Sahitya Kalanidhi, Ezhuthachan Puraskaram.

Address: "Karimpumannil"
Kowdiar, Thiruvananthapuram 695 003
Kerala, S. India

M.T. VASUDEVAN NAIR

Born in 1934 at Kudallur, Palakkad. Son of Punnayurkulam T. Narayanan Nair and Madath Thekkepattu Ammalu Amma.

Editor of *Mathrubhoomi Weekly*. Celebrated novelist, short story writer, screen-play writer and film maker.

He has published numerous books including seventeen collections of short stories. His important works include: *Nalukettu, Raktham Puranda Manaltharikal, Olavum Theeravum, Iruttinte Athmavu, Bandhanam, Abhayamthedi Veendum, Pathiravum Pakalvelichavum, Vanaprastham, Manju, and Alkoottathil Thaniye.*

He is also the author of *Hemingway Oru Mukavura* and two collections of essays *Kathikante Kala* and *Kathikante Panippura*. He has also written plays and travelogues.

Numerous awards and honours have come his way. They include the Jnanapeeth Award, the Central Sahitya Akademi Award, the Kerala Sahitya Akademi Award, the Vayalar Award, the President's Gold Medal for film direction and the D.Litt. degree from two universities.

M.T., as he is popularly known, has given life to innumerable immortal characters, mostly rustics living in villages which are located like his own on the banks of the Bharathapuzha. He has become a cult figure among the people of Kerala.

Address: c/o The Mathrubhoomi
Kozhikode
Kerala, S. India

Dr. V.S. SHARMA, D.Litt.

Born in 1936, Haripad. Was Professor and Head, Department of Malayalam, University of Kerala, Dean, Oriental Faculty, University of Kerala, Dean of Fine Arts, M.G. University, Chairman, Kerala Kalamandalam.

He has won the National Akashvani Award for the best musical feature and the Senior Fellowship from the Government of India to work on theatrical arts.

Dr. Sharma has published about one hundred research papers, book reviews, short stories and essays. His publications include: *Kunchan nampiyarum Addehattinte Kritikalum, Ezhupathiyanchu Thullal Kathakal, Sangitika, Thullal Sahitya Charitram, Upasana, Sri Swathi Tirunal, Aarati,* and *Tiruvitamkur Rajavamsam.*

He has attended numerous international conferences and workshops including the International Conference of Anthropology and Ethnology, New Delhi and the Herman Gundert Conference, Stuttgart. He has delivered the Kunchan Memorial Lecture, the Swathi Tirunal Memorial Lecture and conducted several workshops including those on Natya Sastra and on Mohiniyattam. He is regarded as an authority in Indian aesthetics.

Address: "Nivedita"
Sasthamangalam
Thiruvananthapuram
Kerala, S. India

O.N.V. KURUP

Born in 1931 at Chavara, Kollam. Son of O.N. Krishna Kurup and Lekshmikuttyamma.

Retired as Professor of Malayalam. Distinguished Poet. His works include: *Ujjaini, Mayilpeeli, Neelakkannukal, Uppu, Choroonu, Marubhoomi, Mrigaya, Agnisalabhangal.*

He is also a very popular lyric-writer of film songs. Member of various cultural bodies.

At present, Chairman, Kerala Kalamandalam.

He won many prestigious awards for his poetry as well as for film songs, including those of Central Sahitya Akademi, Kerala Sahitya Akademi, Vayalar Award, Asan Prize, Ulloor Prize, Joshua Award, etc.

Address: "Indivaram"
Cotton Hill Square
Thiruvananthapuram
Kerala, S. India

KAVALAM NARAYANA PANIKER

Born in 1928 at Kavalam, Alappuzha. Son of Godavarma and Kunjulakshmiamma.

Graduated in Arts and Law. Associated with many cultural bodies.

Authored many plays and poems: *Avanavan Kadamba, Thiruvazhithan, Thiranottam, Sakshi*, etc.

Directed and produced many plays in Sanskrit and Malayalam.

Director of 'Spoanam', a popular drama troupe of Thiruvananthapuram.

Has won many awards of Sahitya Akademi, Sangeetha Nataka Akademi, etc.

Has visited many countries in connection with his theatrical activities.

Actively involved in literary ventures.

Address: "Sopanam"
Aramada, Thiruvananthapuram
Kerala, S. India

S. GUPTAN NAIR

Born at Kayamkulam in 1919. Essayist, Critic, Lexicographer and University Professor.

Has won the following awards: Kerala Sahitya Akademi Award

for Criticism, Central Sahitya Akademi Award, Mahakavi G. Sankara Kurup Award, Puthezhathu Rama Menon Award, Lalithambika Antharjanam Award, C.V. Raman Pillai Award, Sankara Narayanan Thampi Award, Fellow, Kerala Sahitya Akademi.

He was also President, Kerala Sahitya Akademi (1984-85), President, Writers Co-Op. Society (1984-85), Chairman, Govt. Cultural Publications (1991-96), President, Sri Chitra Thirunal Library, and Guruvayoorappan Trust, Ernakulam.

Has widely travelled in the West and in the Far East.

Address: "Viswabharathi"
Peroorkada
Thiruvananthapuram
Kerala, S. India

SUGATHAKUMARI S.

Born in 1934 at Thiruvananthapurm, daughter of the late Bodheswaran, noted poet and freedom fighter and Professor V.K. Karthiyayaniamma.

Celebrated Malayalam poet, has authored several books: *Rathrimazha, Kurinjippookkal, Muthuchippy, Ambalamanikal, Swapnabhoomi, Pavam Manavahridayam, Paathirappookkal, Irulchirakutal, Pranamam, Thulavarshappacha, Radha Evide.*

Has translated Judith Wright.

Editor of children's magazine *Thaliru.*

At present, Chairperson, State Women's Commission.

Established a well-known organization "Abhaya" to give shelter to poor women.

A staunch supporter and advocate of ecological preservation.

Address: "Abhaya"
Nandavanam
Thiruvananthapuram
Kerala, S. India

GEORGE ONAKKOOR

Born in 1941, Muvattupuzha. Ph.D. from the University of Kerala. Was Professor of Malayalam, Mar Ivanios College. At present, Director, The State Institute of Encyclopaedic Publications. Has served as Director/Member of various boards of literature and films.

Positions held: Director, The State Institute of Children's Literature for five years; Member of the Director Board and Executive Committee of Sahitya Pravarthaka Co-operative Society, Kottayam; Member of the Managing Committee, Kerala Sahitya Akademi; President, Kerala Film Critics Association; Has edited several books and was the sub-editor of *Deepika* (Malayalam Daily).

Literary critic and novelist. Author of twenty-five books. Some of them are: *Kerala Bhasha Ganga, Yuga Prathibha, Sahitya Sameepanam, Ithihasa Pushpangal, Akale Akasam, Oolkatal, Kalthamara, Ezhuthappurangal, Illam, Kamana (Malayalam Edition), Kamana (English Edition), Uzhavuchalukal, Nalu Poochakkuttikal, Nayakansankalpam Malayalam Novelil, Njan Kathirukkunnu, Njan Oru Kaioppu Maram, Rachanayude Rahasyam, Thapovanathile Sooran, Olivumarangalude Nattil, Marubhumiyude Hridayam Thedi, Maria Goretti, Mahatma Gandhi, M.P. Paul, Kalapathinte Thiruseshippukal, Nadu Neengunna Neram, Samathalangalkkappuram.*

Has written stories, screen plays and dialogues for several feature films in Malayalam and has acted in radio plays, and has participated in a number of other radio programmes, and in Doordarshan programmes.

Visited the State of Israel, Egypt, Italy, France, Bahrain, Oman and U.A.E.

Address: "Sudarsana"
Nalamchira
Thiruvananthapuram 695 015
Kerala, S. India.

Authors from Australia

Glen Phillips

More than a dozen authors attended the AASA's inaugural Australian Studies Conference at Kerala. Some of the writers also presented conference papers. Among the distinguished authors were Yasmine Gooneratne, Andrew Taylor, Beth Yahp, Nicholas Hasluck, Fotini Epanomitis, Adib Khan and Beverley Farmer, all of whom were supported by the generosity of the Literature Fund of the Australia Council. The Australia-India Council sponsored Chris Wallace-Crabbe, also a keynote speaker at the conference. Satendra Nandan was awarded an Australia-India Educational Fellowship. Other writers have relied on alternative funding sources and included Beate Josephi, Dennis Haskell, Annalisa Orselli-Dickson and Glen Phillips. Numbered among the delegates are also the noted authors Laurie Clancy, Carmel Kelly, Kirpal Singh (Singapore), Rajiva Wijesinghe (Sri Lanka), and more.

The inclusion of a significant group of authors amongst the academic delegates to the AASA Conference was a most welcome decision of the organisers. It provided university staff and students at the conference with an unique opportunity to meet "in person" many of the writers available for study in contemporary Australian Literature. It also enabled them to hear the definitive voices of these authors reading from their own created works. One of the conference highlights was the overseas writers meeting with writers from Kerala. These included the well-known Indian poet Kamala Das. The meeting was presided over by Her highness Princess Aswathy Thirunal, herself a distinguished writer.

FOTINI EPANOMITIS

Fotini Epanomitis was born in 1969 in Perth, Western Australia, the year her family migrated to Australia from Northern Greece. She completed her Bachelor of Arts with First Class Honours and her Master of Arts at Curtin University in Western Australia and has taught literature in various universities throughout Australia.

She has published short stories, essays and book reviews in various anthologies and journals. Her first novel *The Mule's Foal* was published by Allen & Unwin in 1993. It won the Australian/Vogel Award, the Victorian Premier's Award and was regional winner of the Commonwealth Writer's Prize. It was also short-listed for the Age Book of the Year Award and the NSW Premier's Prize. In 1995 it was translated and published in Greece. It has been optioned out for film in 1997.

Fotini has performed at festivals and conferences in Australia and overseas and has travelled in Greece, England, and Italy.

After completing a residency at Canberra University she has recently settled in Sydney where she is editing her second novel, and the fiction section of the National Library's literary magazine, *Voices*.

BEVERLEY FARMER

Beverley Farmer was born in Melbourne, Australia, in 1941. She graduated in Arts from the University of Melbourne to work as a secondary teacher and then in the restaurant trade. In 1965 she married a Greek migrant and they lived for some years with his family in a village near Pella in the north of Greece. While there she wrote her first book, *Alone* (1980). The collections *Milk* (1983) and *Home Time* (1985) contain stories which draw on the experience of self-exile, as does the novel *The House in the Light* (1995). A selection of her stories was published in the UK by Faber & Faber as *Place of Birth* (1990). Perceptions of estrangement and displacement underlie all her work.

She travels whenever possible and is otherwise to be found on the coast of Victoria, the setting for her novels *A Body of Water*

(1990) and *The Seal Woman* (1992). She has been writer-in-residence at the University of Tasmania and Deakin and Flinders in Australia, and Arhus in Denmark. Her most recent publication is *Collected Stories* (1996). She has a son aged 24.

YASMINE GOONERATNE

Yasmine Gooneratne, B.A. (Ceylon), Ph.D. (Cambridge), D.Litt. (MacQuarie) is Professor in English Literature at Macquarie University, New South Wales. Born in Sri Lanka, educated at the Universities of Ceylon and Cambridge, her sixteen published books include studies of British authors, Jane Austen, Alexander Pope and Ruth Prawer Jhabvala, literary essays and poems, a family memoir, and two novels, both of which have been shortlisted for the Commonwealth Writers Prize: *A Change of Skies* (1991), a satire on Asian and Australian attitudes to immigration, and *The Pleasures of Conquest* (1995) which studies imperial and contemporary manifestations of power. Her short stories have appeared in *Meanjin, Span* and *Short Story International*. In 1990 she received the Order of Australia (AO) for distinguished service to literature and education.

DENNIS HASKELL

Dennis Haskell is a poet and critic and Co-editor of Western Australia's leading literary magazine, *Westerly*. He has published eleven books of poetry or literary criticism, the most recent being *Abracadabra* (poems), *Tilting at Matilda* (criticism), *Aborigines, Women and the Church in Contemporary Australia* (criticism), *Collected Poems* (a scholarly edition of Kenneth Slessor) and *Australian Poetic Satire* (criticism). Until recently he was Director of the Centre for Studies in Australian Literature at the University of Western Australia. He heads the Creative Writing programme at the University, where he is Associate Professor in the Department of English and Associate Dean of the Faculty of Arts.

NICHOLAS HASLUCK

Nicholas Hasluck was born in Canberra in 1942. After outstanding success as a student of Law at the University of Western Australia and Oxford University he embarked on a distinguished career as barrister and solicitor. In recent years he was appointed Queen's Counsellor.

As an author his record is no less distinguished. His first novel, *Quarantine* (1979), was highly praised but he had already established his reputation in Australia as a poet and short story writer (*Anchor*, 1976 and *The Hat on the Letter O and Other Stories*, 1978). Six novels have followed, the most recent being *The Bellarmine Jug, The Country Without Music, The Blosseville File* and *A Grain of Truth*. All these were published by Penguin. His work has continued to win awards, including the Age Book of the Year (1984) and the WA Premier's Prize (1991) as well as short listing in the Miles Franklin Award (1988, 1991).

Additionally, Nicholas Hasluck has published *Resolutions and Images of the University of WA* (1987) and *Chinese Journey* (with Christopher Koch) (1985). His poetry and short stories appear regularly in anthologies and journals in Australia and overseas.

He has served on a number of literary boards and committees and lives in Claremont, a suburb of Perth, Western Australia.

BEATE JOSEPHI

Beate Josephi was born and educated in what was previously West Germany, and has a Ph.D. on contemporary Australian poetry. She has lived in Australia since 1974, first in Adelaide and now in Perth.

In Adelaide she worked mostly for radio, regularly writing and producing programmes in both German and English languages for both Hessische Rundfunk, in Frankfurt, Germany and the ABC in Australia. She also edited, produced and presented a weekly literary programme for Radio 5UV at the University of Adelaide which was broadcast nationwide. In 1986, and 1988 she was Chair of Writers' Week of the Adelaide Festival of Arts.

She has recently published a collection of her own poetry, *Pilgrim Routes* (Penguin Books, 1993) and earlier, *Miracles of Discontent* (Leros Press, 1985)—translations of poems by four women German-speaking poets. She is now a Lecturer in Media Studies and Journalism at Edith Cowan University in Perth.

ADIB KHAN

Adib Khan was born in Dhaka, Bangladesh, where he lived until 1973. In that same year he came to Australia to study for a Masters degree in English Literature at Monash University. Khan currently lives and works as a teacher and writer in Ballarat.

Seasonal Adjustments was Khan's first novel which won the Christina Stead Prize for Fiction and Book of the Year in the 1994 New South Wales Premier's 76 pa

He was shortlisted for the 1994 Age Book of the Year Award, and won the 1995 Commonwealth Writer's Prize for a First Book. His second novel, *Solitude of Illusions*, was launched at the Melbourne Writers' Festival in October 1996.

SATENDRA NANDAN

Satendra Nandan, born in Fiji, arrived in Canberra in December 1987. Before coming to Australia, he taught at the University of the South Pacific and was elected to the Fijian Parliament in 1982 and again in 1987.

He is currently Associate Professor of English and Commonwealth Studies and is a Regional Vice-President of the AASA.

He has published two volumes of poetry—*Faces in a Village* (1976, 1977) and *Voices in the River* (1985), and has edited *Language and Literature in Multicultural Contexts* (1983) for ACLALS. With Professor Stan Atherton of Canada, he has also compiled and edited *A Critical Anthology of Creative Writing from Fiji* (1985).

The Wounded Sea, a novel, was published by Simon-Schuster in 1991 to much critical acclaim. A volume of selected poems, old and new, titled *Lines Across Black Waters* was published in January 1997. His autobiographical book, *A Fijian Journey*, is due for publication in 1998.

Satendra has co-edited *Crossing Cultures: Essays on Literature and Culture of the Asia-Pacific* recently published by Skoob Books, London. In 1996 he was awarded an Australian International Fellowship to India.

Satendra Nandan is active in literary and academic spheres and is the recipient of numerous prizes, fellowships and honours. He lives in Canberra.

ANNALISA ORSELLI-DICKSON

Annalisa Orselli-Dickson is a lecturer in Romance Languages at Edith Cowan University, Perth, Western Australia. She has been teaching Italian language, cultures, and art in Australia for some ten years. Annalisa is a bilingual poet, writing in English as well as in her native Italian. She is interested in the multilingual possibilities of texts, multicultural writing and is engaged in experimental multimedia poetry, especially visual poetry. All her poetry is treated as a sort of mandala, or contemplation device, arising from a quest for meaning while being at the same time an exploration of the mystery of the creative process. Accordingly her major themes are poetry about poetry and poetry as a reflection of spirituality (especially Sufi or Islamic mysticism).

Professor Gabriel Mandel has invited her to publish her Sufi poems in Italy. This leading scholar, poet and artist has written the introduction for the book. Other books of experimental Sufi poetry, in English, are ready for publication. A number of poems have been, or are being published in various spiritual journals, including electronic web magazines, while some of her visual poetry (multimedia/ cross media) has been selected for exhibition in Australia and abroad.

GLEN PHILLIPS

Glen Phillips was born in Western Australia in 1936, at the remote gold-mining town of Southern Cross. After childhood in outback farming areas of the State he won a series of scholarships to study in Perth secondary schools and at the University of Western Australia.

His poetry has appeared in overseas anthologies, in USA, Italy, Singapore, China, Korea and Thailand. Four collections have been published, three in Australia, together with individual poems in many Australian literary magazines and in American journals. The most recent of his books was *Love Songs, Love Scenes*, in 1991. His *New and Selected Poems* will be published in 1997. He has co-authored a number of anthologies and textbooks and has collaborated with painters, composers, choreographers and photographers in a range of creative projects. The co-project *Landscape and You*, a series of twelve videos, received a national media award after screening on SBS in 1996.

He has read his work on radio and television in Australia and overseas and at literary seminars and festivals. As a founder-member and director of the performance poetry group *Poetry in Motion*, he appeared in many local and international programs at venues ranging from concert theatres to ferry boats, from pub parlours to outback wool-sheds.

Glen Phillips is a founder of the Katharine Susannah Prichard Writers' Centre and past State and Federal President and a Life Member of the Fellowship of Australian Writers. He lives in the Perth suburb of Mount Lawley and is an Associate Professor and chairperson of the English Department at Edith Cowan University.

ANDREW TAYLOR

Andrew Taylor was born in Victoria, Australia, in 1940 and educated at the University of Melbourne. After several years in Italy he returned to Melbourne to teach in the English Department of Melbourne University until shifting to the University of Adelaide in 1971. In 1992, he was appointed Foundation Professor of English at Edith Cowan University in Western Australia. He has travelled widely, especially in Europe and the USA, but this is his first visit to India.

He has been a member of the Literature Board of the Australia Council and of the Australia Council, and twice Chairperson of Writers' Week at the biennial Adelaide Festival of the Arts.

Andrew Taylor is the author of thirteen books of poetry and the critical study, *Reading Australian Poetry* (1987), as well as the libretti of two operas and numerous articles. His most recent books are *Selected Poems* (1988), *Folds in the Map* (1991) and *Sandstone* (1995).

CHRIS WALLACE-CRABBE

Chris Wallace-Crabbe was born in Richmond, Victoria in 1934. He was educated at Scotch College and the University of Melbourne and after ten years of city employment became Lockie Fellow in Australian Literature and Creative Writing at Melbourne University. In a distinguished academic and literary career he has been visiting fellow or professor at leading universities in USA, Britain and Italy. From 1989 to 1994 he was Director of the Australia Centre at the University of Melbourne and as well he holds a personal Chair in the Department of English.

His poems have been published in all significant literary journals in Australia and in many overseas poetry magazines. His work has also been widely anthologised. He was elected a Fellow of the Australian Academy of the Humanities in 1984 and was a recipient of the Grace Leven Prize for Poetry in 1986, the Dublin Prize in 1987, the FAW Christopher Brennan Award, the DJ O'Hearn Prize for Poetry and the Age Book of the Year (1995). He was general editor of the *Oxford Australian Writers, 1990-1996* and has edited many other anthologies. Chris Wallace-Crabbe has published numerous volumes of poetry and literary criticism as well as the novel *Splinters* (1981). His poetry collections include: *Selected Poems* (1973), *The Emotions Are Not Skilled Workers* (1980), *Falling Into Language* (1990) and *For Crying Out Loud* (1990). Chris Wallace-Crabbe lives in the state of Victoria near Melbourne and is married with four children.

BETH YAHP

Beth Yahp was born in Malaysia and came to Australia when she was twenty to study Communications at the University of Technology, Sydney. Since then, her fiction, essays and articles have appeared in a wide range of anthologies, magazines and newspapers, and she has edited or co-edited several collections of stories and essays, including *Family Pictures* (Angus & Robertson, 1994), *Picador New Writing 3* (Picador, 1995), *My Look's Caress: A Collection of Modern Romances* (Local Consumption Publications, 1990), and *Nothing Interesting About Cross Street* (Harper Collins,